Rex Grizell was born in Brighton and educated at grammar school and at Exeter College, Oxford. He had intended to teach languages, but while at Oxford was invited by a national magazine, to which he had contributed short stories, to join their staff as a feature writer. He thus became a journalist, remaining in Fleet Street as a feature writer and executive on newspapers and magazines for thirty years. Ten of those years were spent as Travel Editor of the London Evening News, during which time he visited all five continents and about a hundred different countries.

He and his French wife travelled both privately and on business in France for more than twenty years, but since 1983 have lived on a small fruit and cereal farm in the heart of Aquitaine.

Rex Grizell's interests include period furniture and nineteenth-century painting, rough carpentry, photography, and restoring old houses and gardens. He divides his time between writing, travelling, and helping round the farm. He has two sons, one daughter, and two grand-daughters.

Other Independent Travellers Guides include:

South-west France by Rex Grizell
Greek Islands by Victor Walker
Morocco by Christine Osborne
Portugal by Martha de la Cal
Provence, Languedoc & the Côte d'Azur by John Ardagh
Rome, Umbria & Tuscany by Derek Wilson
Southern Italy by Ian Thomson
Spain by Harry Debelius

MPC INDEPENDENT TRAVELLERS

Brittany and Normandy

Rex Grizell

MPC

Jacket photographs:
Front: Cap Sizun. (*International Photobank*)
Back/Spine: Near Nagent le Rotrou. (*Hedley Alcock*)

Published by: Moorland Publishing Co Ltd,
Moor Farm Road West, Ashbourne, Derbyshire DE6 1HD, England

ISBN 0 86190 531 8

British Library Cataloguing in Publication Data:
A catalogue record for this book is available from the British Library.

Typeset by Ace Filmsetting Ltd, Frome, Somerset.
Printed and bound in Great Britain by The Cromwell Press Ltd, Melksham,
Wiltshire.

Contents

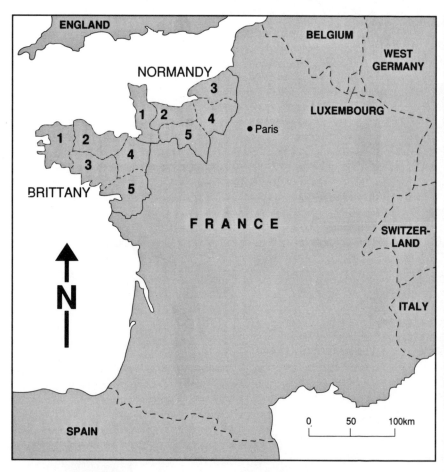

BRITTANY
1 FINISTÈRE
2 CÔTES D'ARMOR
3 MORBIHAN
4 ILLE-ET-VILAINE
5 LOIRE ATLANTIQUE

NORMANDY
1 MANCHE
2 CALVADOS
3 SEINE MARITIME
4 EURE
5 ORNE

Introduction

I live in the countryside of France. Within a few miles there is a small town and several attractive villages. All of them have the kind of restaurants which tourists from other countries dream of finding, with delicious food and wines at near give-away prices. We never eat in any of them: my wife finds them too close. 'It's not going anywhere to go there,' she says, 'it's not an evening out.' It is an understandable attitude, and is essentially the same feeling that has led to a decline in the number of British tourists taking holidays in the resorts of the French Channel coast.

Places such as Dieppe, Fécamp, Etretat, Dinard, Honfleur, Mont St Michel, Perros Guirec and many others were discovered towards the end of the nineteenth century by the British upper and middle classes, as they had earlier discovered the French Riviera, the Swiss Alps and winter sports, and, a little later, Majorca and the other Balearic Islands. Some went to the resorts of Normandy and Brittany for the casinos, some for golf, some for riding and horse-racing, some for the wine and food. Others took the children, and often Nanny as well, and went for the beautiful sandy beaches. That was in the 1920s and 1930s, and again in the 1950s, but with the arrival of cheap package holidays in the 1960s, ready to take people all over the Mediterranean at bargain prices, some holidaymakers began to feel that they were not really going anywhere if they just popped across the Channel to Normandy or Brittany.

But the advantages are all still there. The climate is better, the food is better, and inland and on the coast the scenery is beautiful. It is true that it is not far, and also true that it is not expensive – all factors which make these regions ideal for the independent traveller taking a holiday by car with family or friends. The resorts, still popular with the French themselves, who know value for money, have had to move with the times, and there are now more and better restaurants, and more leisure and sporting amenities than ever in the past.

The varied countryside of Normandy – rolling hills, green valleys watered by countless rivers and streams, great forests, rich dairy farms and apple orchards – seems immutable in its charm, and often when you look across the fields and see a steeple and a few roofs emerging from the trees, you can think yourself for a moment in some corner of Devon. In Brittany the 2,500 km of coast offer spectacular cliffs, coves, long sandy beaches, creeks and inlets, and picturesque fishing harbours, and again you will often come across an inlet with a few moored boats and some grey stone cottages, and can fancy yourself in some unfamiliar Cornish creek.

But the association between Britain and north-west France amounts to more than an occasional physical resemblance, and since Roman times they have been repeatedly involved in each other's history. The villages and towns, the splendid castles and manors in every corner of Brittany and Normandy are stuffed to the eaves with history. Few towns have a past as ever-present as that of Rouen, for example: in the Place du Vieux Marché a monument marks the spot where Joan of Arc was burned, while across the road is La Couronne, believed to be the oldest restaurant in France, founded in 1345.

For anyone with a healthy appetite, Norman cuisine based on superb farm produce, meat, chicken, game and what the French call *le poisson de la nuit* – fish caught the night before and prepared in an endless variety of recipes involving butter, cream, cider, and calvados (apple brandy) – is itself a holiday. Breton cuisine is equally good, some would say a little better because less rich, but with the bonus of all sorts of sweet and savoury pancakes.

Brittany and Normandy are next-door neighbours but, as is often the case with neighbours, they have very little in common. Both are completely individual, and also somewhat separate in spirit from the rest of France.

In terms of human habitation and history, Brittany is the lonely house across the moors, isolated, mysterious, at the end of the western world. There is none of this underlying feeling, akin to that of Ireland and the Western Isles, in Normandy, which by contrast is a gentler, cosier place, with a lush countryside, calmer coasts, and a down-to-earth, practical air, devoid of mystery.

Brittany in the past three or four decades has been obliged to become less itself. Fishing has declined steadily and is still declining, and this province of the sea is slowly turning its back on the ocean. Farming, too, is in crisis. While television recently reported the latest farming techniques from the annual Agricultural Show in Paris, it also showed pictures from Brittany of cows too weak to stand because farmers, ruined by the milk quotas imposed from Brussels, could no longer afford to feed them. However, considered as a whole Brittany has progressed and its economy has become more prosperous. Inter-departmental committees have worked together to find new industries and to help each other develop them; the old Breton tradition of every man, every village, every region for itself has been partly broken down, and the new ideas have been successful. Brittany can no longer be considered a poor relation of the rest of France.

But the progress has not been uniform. Side by side with modern-ised areas, now prosperous and active, are those which have clung to the old ways and are moving more slowly. In some places the population is 200 to the sq km, in others only twenty. Land in some places is £5,000 a hectare, in others only £50. The countryside is changing: hedges are being torn out and coppices cleared, to make larger fields which are more easily cultivated by tractor. Towns which had fallen asleep for a hundred years or more have woken up and become commercially active, others doze on. Steadily, a new and different Brittany is emerging.

Normandy, torn apart by total war less than fifty years ago, as perhaps no other region ever has been in the history of the world, has successfully recreated itself. But it is essentially the same Normandy that has risen from the rubble, solid, prosperous, realistic, going its own way.

Tourism is important to both these provinces, which have many communes depending very substantially on summer visitors for their livelihood. Both have done much to meet their needs, and both offer a great deal to the holiday-maker. All tastes are catered for, any and every form of recreation can be enjoyed in the ultra-smart resorts, or alternatively total relaxation can be found tucked away in a quiet cottage near a lovely beach or in the depths of unspoilt countryside.

This guide gives the essential facts about the resorts and country districts likely to appeal to tourists, and also describes briefly the history, character and way of life of the people of these fascinating regions.

A Brief History

The Romans

Two thousand years ago north-west France was inhabited by Gallic tribes who lived in rough-and-ready headquarter settlements and outlying hamlets. The names of the tribes are known and some of them survive in those of modern towns. Bayeux, for example, was once the headquarters of the Bayocasses tribe, and Evreux of the Eburovices.

These tribes were a savage lot, constantly fighting each other. Their lifestyle would have been appreciated by the more violent football fans of today; they were beer-drinkers, enjoyed a good rough-house and went into battle decked in all their finery, which included gold bracelets, necklaces and earrings. They were bloodthirsty and had some gruesome habits, enjoying nailing the heads of enemies to their doors and pointing them out to friends, no doubt with phrases like 'Look what I picked up in Bayeux last week'. But despite their ferocity they were no match in battle for the disciplined Roman legions, who defeated them on land in 58 BC and two years later beat the powerful Veneti tribe (whose capital is now called Vannes) in a sea battle in the Gulf of Morbihan. The Romans disliked the sea, avoiding it whenever they could, and this is believed to be their only naval victory outside the Mediterranean, but the Veneti were a sea-going tribe and Julius Caesar realised they had to be subdued at sea. He was there to watch the battle, though he took no part in it. The Romans called their new province, which included all Brittany and most of modern Normandy, Armorica, the 'province of the sea', and set about reorganising it at once.

Settlements They took the chief Gallic settlements and turned them into cities with all the usual Roman amenities: temples, theatres, public baths and so on. Settlements outside the main towns were called *villae*, which accounts for the number of modern towns which still have names ending in *ville*, such as Granville. The cities were linked by straight roads, and aqueducts were built to bring copious supplies of fresh water to them. In the country and along the coast richer merchants and officials built their villas.

Remains The Romans remained in Armorica for nearly 500 peaceful years, but despite their long occupation there are few Roman remains in the region today. The most important is the ruined amphitheatre at Lillebonne (near the River Seine, 30 km from Le Havre), a town which the Romans called Julia Bona in honour, some authorities say, of Julius Caesar's daughter. A fine Roman mosaic pavement was also discovered in Lillebonne and can now be seen in the Museum of Antiquities in Rouen.

A magnificent treasure of Roman vases, plates and figurines, all in solid silver, was discovered in a field near Brionne (between Pont Audemer and Evreux) in 1830, but apart from these few noteworthy things almost all evidence of the Roman occupation has been lost. The coastal villas, along with the cliffs on which they were built, have long since crumbled into the sea. A few roads can still be recognised as being of Roman origin, but that is all.

Christianity

The area which is now Normandy was partially Christianised from about the third century AD – the first bishop of Rouen, about AD 260, was a Welshman called Saint Mellon. Brittany was Christianised somewhat later, in the fifth and sixth centuries, by Welsh and Irish missionaries from Britain, who brought with them organised Christian groups. They called their new home Little Britain, then Bretagne, and part of it Cornouaille, after the place they had left, Cornwall. The Breton language developed from ancient Welsh, and even today the two peoples can understand each other in their own tongues. They adopted a diplomatic approach to the spread of their religion, at first judiciously incorporating the sites and symbols associated with older pagan beliefs into the Christian faith. They placed or cut crosses on the ancient menhirs and built churches near springs which had been associated with pagan rites.

Bishoprics had been established in Normandy at Evreux in the fifth century and at Coutances and then Lisieux in the sixth century. In Brittany the names of early Christian missionaries have survived in many place names, including St Malo and St Brieuc. These first teachers often wove the magical legends, witchcraft and superstition so much a part of early Breton beliefs into their own stories of Jesus, the Apostles or popular saints.

Although Christianisation started earlier in Normandy than in Brittany, it took longer to complete because the number of Christian immigrants into Brittany was much greater than it was in Normandy. In the seventh and eighth centuries important monasteries were founded in Normandy including those at Fécamp, St Wandrille and Jumièges, and later at Mont St Michel, but it was not until the time of Charlemagne, whose empire stretching from the Pyrenees to Poland had been built in the name of Christianity, that these abbeys could exert their power freely.

The Normans

From the time that the Roman Empire in the West collapsed at the beginning of the fifth century, the history of north-west France, particularly Normandy, became a long saga of battle and bloodshed. With the Romans gone, Clovis, the king of the Franks, who was based in Paris, captured Rouen and Evreux in AD 497 and named the area the Kingdom of the West.

Vikings

Vikings from Denmark and Norway did not care what it was called. They had been raiding the coastal villages since the third century, and continued to do so for hundreds of years. After Charlemagne died in AD 814, their raids became steadily more important. In 841 they sailed up the Seine and ransacked Rouen and burned the abbey of Jumièges. They raided Rouen again in 856 and 876, and in 895 they sailed up as far as Paris and laid siege to the city, then just an island in the Seine.

Unable to stop the raids, the king of the Franks, Charles the Simple, a nickname which meant straightforward rather than foolish, signed a treaty with Rollo, the leader of the Viking pirates, in AD 911. By this treaty Rollo became the first Duke of Normandy, and his people were allowed to settle throughout the region from Rouen west to Avranches. Thirty years later Louis IV stabilised the position created by his father by making a gift to William Longsword, the second Duke of Normandy, of all those lands which had been occupied by the Normans. Rollo and his descendants showed themselves to be energetic and efficient rulers; they established law and order throughout their territory and built castles to maintain it, and they encouraged Christianity by restoring the abbeys and churches which their ancestors had repeatedly destroyed.

William the Conqueror

A man directly descended from these Normans, and who was destined to change the history of England and all western Europe, was born in 1028 in Falaise, Normandy. He was the illegitimate son of Duke Robert the Magnificent by a tanner's daughter named Arlette. In France he was known as William the Bastard and later in England as William the Conqueror. Robert the Magnificent died on a Crusade when William was a child, but had persuaded his nobles to accept the boy as his heir. In theory they did so, but in practice they were soon fighting among themselves to gain power at the expense of the seven-year-old boy. It was not until 1060, when he was more than thirty years old, that William finally subdued his enemies.

William was an intimidating man, nearly seven feet tall, powerful and hot-tempered, but he was also a man of great administrative ability and a diplomat. He married Matilda, daughter of the King of Flanders, thus making himself a powerful ally. Matilda, who also happened to be William's cousin, had refused him at first, saying she would rather enter a convent than marry a bastard. It was not the best way to tackle him: he was not put off, and is said to have used some physical persuasion, beginning by dragging her round the room by her hair. Nevertheless, the marriage apparently worked out quite well, since Matilda gave William five sons and four daughters, and acted as regent for him in Normandy while he was away in England.

On his deathbed the king of England, Edward the Confessor, had made his nephew, Harold, his heir. But William felt that he had a valid claim to the throne of England, as Edward, in recognition of military aid he had received from William, had previously named him his successor, and Harold had recognised this on oath. So William called his barons together at the castle of Lillebonne and persuaded them to join him in attacking England. Harold, who had been obliged to take his army to the north to fight off an attempted invasion by the king of Norway, returned to the south with a depleted and exhausted army, which was defeated at the Battle of Hastings on 14 October 1066.

William was crowned as the lawful heir to Edward the Confessor at Westminster on Christmas Day 1066. The absolute authority which William and his barons exercised is demonstrated by the Domesday Book, which registered the ownership of every acre of land and every ox, cow and pig on England's farms.

During William's absence in England, Normandy was ruled by Matilda and their son, Robert, who soon sought the aid of the French king in rebelling against his father. William died in 1087, the year after the Domesday survey, in an expedition against the French king and was succeeded in England by his second son, William Rufus, and in Normandy by Robert. When William Rufus died in 1100, he was succeeded by his younger brother, who became Henry I of England. Within six years he had taken Normandy from his brother Robert, and successfully resisted all attempts to take it back.

Norman conquests

The people of Normandy today are the direct descendants of these early Normans, who were men to be reckoned with. The spirit of adventure and conquest was bred in their bones, and England was by no means their only acquisition. Many Norman barons had left Normandy during the harsh reign of William's father, Robert – sometimes called the Magnificent, but also called Robert the Devil. They set out ostensibly on a Crusade, but some of them stopped off on the way to conquer Sicily and set up a kingdom there which lasted from 1042 to 1194 and brought prosperity to the island. A Norman baron, William de Hauteville, established another kingdom, in Apulia in southern Italy, in the late eleventh century, and during the first Crusade, which started in 1096, Bohemond Guiscard, another Norman, set up a principality around Antioch in Syria, which his successors held until 1287.

Brittany

While the Normans were developing their strength and creating a duchy, Brittany was struggling for an identity and independence. In AD 831 Charlemagne's son, Louis the Pious, appointed a Breton nobleman, Nominoë, as king of Brittany. He beat off a strong Danish force which landed at Tréguier and in 845 he defeated the Frankish army of Charles the Bald, which had occupied the region of Ille-et-Vilaine. Nominoë stabilised the boundaries of Brittany, which are the same today as they were then.

During the next 200 years, while the Normans were strengthening their hold on Normandy, Brittany was divided by rival factions and declined into a condition of feudal anarchy.

The Plantagenets

In 1154 Henry Plantagenet became king of England. He was the son of the granddaughter of William the Conqueror and her second husband, Geoffrey of Anjou. He was already Duke of Normandy, and in 1152 had married Eleanor, Duchess of Aquitaine and former queen of France. Together they ruled the whole of western and southern France from the Channel coast to the Pyrénées, so that in 1154 Brittany and Normandy were at the centre of Plantagenet domains which stretched from the Spanish frontier to the Scottish border.

The Hundred Years' War

Under the 'English' Plantagenets the income from their French territories considerably exceeded that of the whole of England. This Plantagenet wealth and splendour was the subject of the bitter envy of a succession of French kings. In 1324 the French king, Charles IV, sent an army into Aquitaine, which succeeded in capturing most of the Plantagenet territories in the south-west, and so began the hostilities between England and France known as the Hundred Years' War, although it continued intermittently for almost 130 years.

Edward III pursued the war with vigour. In 1355 he appointed his son, the Black Prince, Lieutenant General of Aquitaine, and at the Battle of Poitiers in 1356 an English army led by him defeated a much larger French force, led by King Jean II. In the course of the battle the French king was captured, and later taken to England and held to ransom. Under the Treaty of Brétigny in 1360 the French king regained his freedom, and in return almost all the Plantagenet domains of 200 years earlier, with the exception of Normandy, were restored to England and Edward III renounced his claim to the French throne.

Bertrand du Guesclin

Brittany was not much concerned in the Hundred Years' War except in the person of Bertrand du Guesclin, one of the great soldiers of the late Middle Ages. Du Guesclin was born in 1321 in a village south of Dinan and was so ugly as a child that his father refused to acknowledge him. At meal times he was placed alone in the corner of the great hall of the family castle while the rest of the family ate at the main table. He put up with this treatment until he was about eight years old. Then one day a roast capon was brought in and his mother began to serve the others. Bertrand got up. 'Is it for you to eat first? I am the eldest. Give me my proper place.' He sat down at the head of the table and began to help himself, and when his mother made to strike him he overturned the table, sending all the food and drink on to the floor. It was the end of family injustice for Bertrand. Beneath his displeasing exterior Du Guesclin had the qualities which would have made him a great soldier in any age: courage, audacity, ingenuity, judgment and leadership. He was also cruel and ruthless. Once, English soldiers who had discovered from his chambermaids that he was away from his castle, made an attempt to capture it. His sister roused the guards and the attack was beaten off. When Du Guesclin returned he ordered the chambermaids who had betrayed him to be sewn up in sacks and thrown in the river.

Henry V

It was Du Guesclin who, five years after the Treaty of Brétigny, defeated the English at Cocherel and drove them out of Normandy. A relatively peaceful period followed, and it was not until the accession of Henry V to the throne of England that hostilities were renewed and Normandy again became involved. Henry V wanted to show that the house of Lancaster could deal with the French as successfully as the Plantagenets had done more than fifty years earlier at Crécy and Poitiers. In 1415 he defeated the French at Agincourt, just outside Normandy in Picardy, and then began the subjugation of Normandy itself. Caen, Evreux and Alençon surrendered without a fight, and he captured Rouen and the Pays de Caux.

Henry's next step was in line with recognised royal tactics of the day: if you can't beat them, marry them, and if you can beat them, marry them anyway to strengthen your position. By the Treaty of Troyes Henry was to marry Catherine, one of the daughters of Charles VI of France, and any heir would rule over both countries, leaving each with its own institutions. But when Henry died in 1422, leaving a son only nine months old, and then the mad Charles VI also died, the nineteen-year-old Dauphin of France proclaimed himself King Charles VII.

Joan of Arc

The French general Dunois had succeeded Du Guesclin and though capable, was far from his equal, but Fate brought him a remarkable ally, Joan of Arc. She inspired French resistance and with her lieutenants succeeded in raising the siege of Orléans in 1429. From this time on English fortunes began to decline. Joan was sold to the English and burned as a witch in the Norman city of Rouen, but this savage action only served to strengthen French resolve. In 1452 Henry VI sent John Talbot, Earl of Shrewsbury, to Aquitaine with an army of 6,000 men, but in July 1453 at the Battle of Castillon he and his son were killed and the English army routed. It was the last battle of the Hundred Years' War. In 1486 Normandy became a province of France and was then governed as such.

The Dukes of Brittany

While the French were fighting the English in the early part of the Hundred Years' War, the Bretons were split among themselves and fighting a war of succession for the ducal crown. The war was between Jean de Montfort, the half-brother of Duke Jean III of Brittany, and Jeanne de Penthièvre, wife of Charles de Blois. De Montfort was an ally of the English and de Blois of the French. The war went on for twenty years and ended with the victory of Jean de Montfort at Auray, and he became Duke Jean IV of Brittany. He reigned from 1365 to 1399, and his son Jean V from 1399 to 1442.

These two long reigns saw the development of a strong, independent and increasingly rich Brittany. Jean V was a great ruler, who centralised the government of Brittany, minted his own money, developed a properly organised army and sent his ambassador to the Pope. It was a period of prosperity, which continued through the short reigns of several succeeding dukes until 1488 but, having got rid of the English, the kings of France became increasingly covetous of this last independent and rich duchy, and in 1488 the army of Charles VIII completely defeated the Bretons at St Aubin du Cormier, near Rennes.

Anne of Brittany

A treaty was made between the ailing Duke François II of Brittany and Charles VIII, the most important condition of which was that the duke could not marry his daughter, Anne, who was also his heiress, to anyone without the permission of the French king. But when her father died within a few weeks and Anne became duchess she favoured an independent Brittany and, hoping to make a strong ally against the French, she arranged to marry Maximilian of Austria. But Charles VIII demanded adherence to the treaty of 1488, and made his position clear by sending his troops to capture Nantes and then proposing to Anne. Everyone expected trouble from the strong-minded duchess, but with the unpredictability of youth – Anne was fourteen, quite old enough to be a queen in those days, and Charles was twenty-one – the couple fell in love and were married in 1491.

Charles died suddenly seven years later from a violent bang on the head when he ran full tilt into a low doorway in the Château of Amboise. Anne had borne him three children but they had all died young, and in the absence of a direct male heir the throne passed to another branch of the Valois-Orléans family and Louis XII became king. Anne went back to Brittany to live in Nantes but did not stay there long. It had been part of her marriage contract with Charles that in the event of his death without an heir she would have to marry the new king, if he so wished and, of course, Louis XII did wish it. The whole point of royal policy over the previous decade had been to make Brittany part of France, and Anne knew it as well as he did, but her common sense told her that she could do more for Brittany as a reigning queen than as a defeated duchess. Louis was already married but did not care for his wife, Jeanne, daughter of Louis XI. Jeanne was a brave and capable woman and but for the Salic Law would have been queen of France. She was also ugly and a hunchback, and did not own Brittany. Louis managed to get the marriage annulled on the grounds of too close a blood relationship, which was not true, and on the further grounds of non-consummation, which was almost certainly not true. Jeanne did not believe that Louis, a most Christian king, would swear to it on the Bible, but he did.

So, on 4 January 1499, Anne of Brittany became queen of France for the second time. Louis was thirty-seven and said to be prematurely old. Anne was still only twenty-two, but she obtained a marriage contract which was very favourable to Brittany. Louis undertook to respect 'the liberties, voting rights, and customs of the Duchy'. Taxes were not to be imposed without previously having been approved and voted by the Breton government. Bretons were not to be tried except by their own judges, and were not obliged to fight outside their own territory, unless in cases of extreme necessity. The Bretons kept their separate administration and these privileges until the French Revolution in 1789.

As queen, Anne took advantage of her position to protect and advance her countrymen. Anne was not a beautiful woman. She was thin in build, though she had a chubby face and also a slight limp. On the other hand, she was both highly intelligent and well educated, and her strong character was enlivened by charming manners and fair-mindedness. She was considered in Brittany, and is still remembered there, as the 'good Duchess Anne'. By Louis XII she had a daughter, Claude, who married the Duke of Angoulême, who became François I of France. Claude was apparently a compliant wife whose chief interest was gardening – the delicious greengage, the Reine Claude, is named after her. By her marriage treaty Claude ceded Brittany to France in perpetuity, but it was not until 1532 that the province was officially incorporated into the realm of France.

The Religious Wars

When Protestantism was spread through France in the sixteenth century by Calvin and his followers, many Normans adopted the new faith. During their occupation of Caen (1417–50), the English had founded a university there, and in the sixteenth century this became a central point for the dissemination of Protestantism. When the Religious Wars broke out Normandy was badly affected, and battles between Catholics and Protestants took place all over the region and for many years.

Rouen was seized by the Protestants in 1562 and later recaptured by the Catholics; Avranches, St Lô and Carentan also changed hands more than once. In Lisieux the Catholics burned several Protestants alive, then Honfleur and Falaise were captured by the Protestants, who also ransacked the cathedrals of Bayeux and Lisieux. Many other towns were attacked, including Evreux, Alençon, Argentan and Mortagne.

One reason for the savagery of these wars was that it was not a one-sided conflict. Many of the most influential and noble families of France – generals, admirals, intellectuals and even members of the royal family – were Huguenots (French Protestants), and had the resources in men and money to fight against persecution. This was the case in Brittany where, although the impact of the conflict was less bloody than in Normandy, there was an important Huguenot presence led by distinguished families including the Montforts, the former Dukes of Brittany, the Lavals, the de Colignys, the Rieux and the Rohans. The number of ordinary people who remained faithful to Catholicism was much greater than in Normandy, but though many towns on both sides were attacked the actions were less bloody and there were no massacres.

In 1582 the Catholic Duc de Mercoeur was appointed governor of Brittany. He was brother-in-law to Henri III, king of France, but was himself married to a member of the Breton ducal family of Penthièvre, the same family who had lost the war of succession against the Montforts for the ducal throne of Brittany nearly 200 years earlier. Mercoeur used the cover of the religious wars in an attempt to revive the ambitions of his wife's family and take over Brittany for himself.

When the effeminate Henri III was assassinated in 1588 he left no children, and the clear heir to the throne was Henri of Navarre, a Protestant. Mercoeur at once stepped up his efforts and led the Catholics in Brittany against the new king, at the same time strengthening his own position. The province became split between those who were for the king and those who were for Mercoeur, and at one time each party had its own capital and its own government in Brittany. In this confused situation, several barons took up brigandry and pillaged large stretches of country around their castles, and much of Brittany was given up to anarchy.

The Edict of Nantes

The situation became so bad that the Bretons appealed to Henri IV for help. Henri, who had already destroyed the opposition to his right to the Crown by becoming a Catholic, now put an end to the Religious Wars in 1598 by signing the Edict of Nantes, which allowed the Protestants considerable freedom of worship. Unfortunately, in 1610 Henri IV was assassinated. His son, Louis, was only nine years old and the queen, Marie de Medici, Henri's second wife, was a vain and silly woman unable to govern effectively. The situation again deteriorated and religious strife soon broke out once more. When he came of age,

Louis XIII, brought up as a Catholic, sometimes took part in the fighting himself, and there was intermittent violence throughout the seventeenth century. Under Louis XIV the Protestants were persecuted and often expelled, and relationships between France and Brittany remained tense for many years. The guarantees given by France to Anne of Brittany were little respected and the excessive taxes imposed to pay for Louis XIV's wars led to a widespread Breton revolt in 1675, which had to be put down by the French army.

When Louis XIV revoked the Edict of Nantes in 1685 half a million Huguenots, many of them from Normandy and Brittany, left France to find a home in England or other countries where they could practise their faith freely. The Huguenots were hardworking and capable people, skilful in commerce and dominant in many industries including weaving, silk manufacture and glass-making. The economy of Normandy, where they had been particularly active, suffered badly following their exodus.

The French Revolution

When the Revolution against royal autocracy broke out in 1789 it was at first welcomed throughout the French countryside, at least in theory. The general attitude in the devout and largely Catholic Brittany became anti-Revolutionary, however, when laws were introduced against the Church and its priests and churches were attacked and converted to secular use, and this opposition was strengthened by the heavy taxes imposed by the Revolutionary government.

Jean Paul Marat

In Normandy, the Revolution had more drastic effects than in Brittany – in the town of Bayeux alone, for example, ten churches were destroyed. The Normans had also recognised the need for reforms and were not opposed to the Revolution as such, but strongly resented the interruptions in daily life and trade which it caused. In the early part of the Revolution, Caen became a headquarters of the right-wing Girondin party who were bitterly opposed to the left-wing extremist, Jean Paul Marat. The Girondins sought to raise a large part of France, including Normandy, Brittany and the South West, against the central government and to separate from it. Charlotte Corday, a twenty-five-year-old Norman girl living in Caen, was inspired by the Girondin cause and felt that Marat was bringing nothing but death and disaster to the country she loved. She decided to act on her own.

On 11th July 1793 Charlotte Corday arrived in Paris, and took a room in a small hotel. On the twelfth she wrote an 'address to Frenchmen who are friends of the laws and of peace', an inspired appeal to her compatriots to re-establish national unity and save France. In it she announced that she was going to kill Marat and said,

'My wish is that my head, borne through Paris, may be a rallying signal to all friends of the laws.' The following morning she bought a cheap table knife with an ebony handle, and took a coach to Marat's house. She was refused admittance twice during the day, but at half-past seven in the evening was allowed in to see him.

Marat, who was in poor health, was resting in his bath, where he spent a lot of time in the belief that it was good for his eczema. After a short discussion, Charlotte Corday rose from her chair and killed him with a single blow. She made no attempt to escape, told no lies, and made no excuses.

Her trial took place on 17 July 1793 at eight in the morning. The previous night she had written a last letter to her father. 'Farewell, my dear Papa, I pray you to forget me, or rather to rejoice in my fate. It is in a fine cause.' She was guillotined on 30 July 1793. She had succeeded in her single-minded objective, but to no avail – the Girondin revolt was crushed and many of them were guillotined.

By 1794 a royalist party in Brittany was in revolt and was supported by many Catholics and royalists from the Vendée region who objected to being called up to serve in the army. Four brothers called Cottereau, smugglers by trade, helped to organise the revolt. Their leader, Jean Cottereau, was known as Jean Chouan, a local name for an owl, as he used the bird's call as a recognition signal. From this, the revolt was known as the *Chouannerie*. It lingered on until 1804 without success, and an attempt by the madcap Duchesse de Berry to revive it in 1832 failed.

Although the Bretons continued to resent the French throughout the nineteenth century, both Brittany and Normandy were a good deal more at ease under Napoleon I than they had been during the Revolution. Within four years from 1799 Napoleon had settled the internal affairs of France, drawn up the Code Napoleon, restored religious worship and launched constructive projects all over France. Normandy benefited from the building of a full-scale port and military base at Cherbourg, ordered by the emperor, and although this work was not completed until 1859, during the time of Napoleon III, it contributed much to the nineteenth-century prosperity of Normandy.

Seafarers

Throughout their long history both Bretons and Normans have remained true to the seafaring and adventurous spirit of their ancestors, and have produced a long succession of explorers, privateers and great sailors.

As early as 1402 Jean de Béthencourt, a Norman from the Pays de Caux, made an expedition to the Canary Islands. He conquered

Lanzarote, intending to set himself up as king, but stayed only three years in the islands before returning to France. His son, Maciot, stayed many more years. Béthencourt, spelt in a variety of ways, remains one of the commonest family names in the Canary Islands.

Even before de Béthencourt, in the 1360s, sailors from Dieppe had sailed down the west coast of Africa as far south as what is now Sierra Leone, and set up a trading post which they called Petit Dieppe.

Jean Cousin

In the fifteenth century Jean Cousin, also of Dieppe, set out on an Atlantic exploration trip and reached the coast of Brazil. It is said that he landed at the mouth of a great river which he called Maragnon, now better known as the Amazon, and from there sailed back across the Atlantic and touched at what is now the Cape of Good Hope, and from there back to Europe. Different authorities give different dates for this voyage, but none later than 1488. The story of Cousin seems to be well documented; when the fame of Christopher Columbus and Vasco da Gama reached Dieppe some years later, Dieppe asserted its claim that Cousin had made these discoveries earlier, but it went unnoticed because at the time all France's attention was directed on King François I's ill-advised and disastrous expedition against Italy, where he had been captured at the Battle of Pavia.

Another Norman sailor, Paulmier de Gonneville, also reached Brazil in the early years of the sixteenth century, and a few years later Jean Denis, sailing from the same port, Honfleur, reached the mouth of the St Lawrence river.

Jean Ango

The Portuguese regarded all other ships sailing in West African waters as pirates, and attacked them. The French king, François I, authorised the construction of a fleet of privateers (ships whose captains had 'Letters of Mark' from the king authorising them to attack hostile vessels) to combat the Portuguese. The fleet was built by Jean Ango, a mariner, merchant and shipbuilder of Dieppe, and within a few years had captured more than 300 Portuguese ships, forcing the king of Portugal to change his maritime policy.

Ango had also organised expeditions to America, including one in 1524 which was led by Verrazano, François I's chief sea captain. It was the first to reach Manhattan Island and the future site of New York. Ango, whose ships brought furs from Canada, ivory from Africa, and silks and spices from the Orient, on top of the booty taken by his privateers, became enormously rich and a sort of king of the seas. He built himself a palace in Dieppe – as a shipbuilder, he built it in wood, much of it elaborately carved. He also had a manor, in stone, at Varengeville, five miles outside Dieppe. This splendid house, in which he regally entertained François I and Diane de Poitiers, decayed over the years and less than a hundred years ago was just a dilapidated farmhouse, but it has since been very well restored and is open to the public. Ango died in 1551 and his palace in Dieppe was destroyed in 1694 when English warships bombarded the town.

Jacques Cartier

Contemporary with Ango was the Breton Jacques Cartier, from St Malo. François I, jealous of the riches brought back from Central and South America by Spanish and Portuguese sailors, commissioned Cartier to cross the Atlantic to the northern lands, said to be rich in gold. Jean Denis had visited the mouth of the St Lawrence more than a decade earlier, and for some years Breton fishermen had been fishing for cod off Newfoundland. In 1534 Cartier landed there with his crew of sixty Breton sailors. The following year he sailed far up the estuary of the St Lawrence, and gave the Indian name, Canada, to the newly discovered territory, claiming it in the name of the king of France. He made four voyages to the St Lawrence. One of his ships, *La Petite Hermine*, left there on the second voyage, was discovered 300 years later under five feet of mud.

Quebec

There were other Norman expeditions, to Florida and to Africa, but the most significant of all was that of Samuel de Champlain, who sailed from Honfleur and founded a Norman colony in Quebec in 1608, and was followed there by both Norman and Breton settlers. It was Norman sailors who, in the name of the king of France, took possession of Martinique and Guadeloupe in 1635, islands which to this day are part of 'Metropolitan' France, sending members to the French Parliament. In 1682, de la Salle, from Rouen, made his way down the Mississippi and annexed Louisiana.

René Duguay-Trouhin

The Breton port of St Malo, known as the city of corsairs, has produced some of France's greatest sailors. One of the most famous was René Duguay-Trouhin, born in 1673, the son of a local shipowner. At the age of sixteen he joined a frigate privateer owned by his father; at eighteen he was master of a ship of his own, and captured seven other ships as prizes and brought them safely into St Malo; at twenty-one he was captured by the English and held in Plymouth, but with the help of a local girl he escaped and sailed a small boat to Brittany in forty-six hours; and by his mid-twenties he had made such a reputation as a privateer that he was invited to join the French navy with the rank of commander, an offer which he accepted.

During his career Duguay-Trouhin defeated twenty-five armed vessels, and captured more than 150 merchant ships. His greatest exploit was in 1712, a time when the Portuguese were allies of the English against the French. He raised a fleet of seventeen large ships, embarked several thousand soldiers and sailed for the Portuguese colony of Brazil. There he succeeded in capturing the Brazilian capital, Rio de Janeiro, and held the city to ransom for an enormous sum. Though he lost some of his ships and some of the booty in a storm on the return journey, he arrived back in France with great riches. Duguay-Trouhin rose to become lieutenant general – that is, commander-in-chief – of Louis XIV's navy. After his stormy youth, his last years were peaceful and he died in 1736.

**Robert
Surcouf**

A hundred years later St Malo produced another remarkable corsair, Robert Surcouf, who was related through his mother to the Duguay-Trouhin family. He was born in 1763 and like Duguay-Trouhin went to sea at sixteen. At seventeen he was already second in command of a privateer, and in his mid-twenties, during the French Revolution, he was the terror of the Indian Ocean, capturing ships off Mozambique, Madagascar and Réunion. His exploits against the rich merchant ships of the British East India Company put a price of 250,000 francs on his head, and the English insurance companies refused to insure ships and cargoes crossing the Indian Ocean. During the Napoleonic Wars the Emperor offered Surcouf the command of two frigates and the rank of captain, but unlike Duguay-Trouhin he preferred to carry on his career independently. So successful was he that he was made a Chevalier of the Legion of Honour and a Baron of the Empire.

Surcouf was a man of great bravery and a ferocious fighter. One of his officers once said of him, 'When he addressed a boarding party before sending us into action, you would have thought he was breathing fire.' A story of Surcouf well illustrates his character. One morning in the autumn of 1816, a time when there were still a good many English and German soldiers in France, he was in the Café Joseph in the Place Duguay-Trouhin, smoking a pipe and having a drink with friends, when a dozen Prussian officers from the garrison at Dinan burst in clanking their spurs and clashing their sabres, and treating the café as conquered territory. One of them barged into Surcouf, who lost his temper. A row broke out and Surcouf challenged each of them to a duel. The fights took place on the sands opposite the Ile du Bé at low tide, with his friends Mainville and Brisebarre as his seconds. Surcouf sliced off the sword hand of his first adversary, wounded the second and third in the thigh, and the fourth in the stomach, and so on to the eleventh, all slightly or seriously wounded. When there was only the twelfth man left, Surcouf turned to him and said, 'If you do not mind, monsieur, let us leave it at that. I would prefer you to return home to your country able to tell them how one of Napoleon's old sailors defended his honour.'

Surcouf's exploits made him a very rich man. He died in 1827 on his estate near St Servan, now a suburb of St Malo. He had asked to be buried in St Malo and for his body to be taken there on the sea he loved – it was placed in a frigate with black flags, and accompanied by fifty smaller boats carrying priests, soldiers and guests. An escort of honour was provided by privateers who had sailed with him, described by one French author as 'a hundred wounded heroes, with scarred faces, and fiery eyes, who for that day had put on their old battle uniforms, ragged, patched, burned by gunpowder, to mount guard for the last time around the chief who had so often led them to victory'.

Surcouf was the last of the great corsairs. By international agreement, privateering was stopped in 1856.

The Nineteenth Century

In 1843 the railway, the nineteenth century's clanking herald of change, reached Rouen from Paris and made a great difference to the daily life of Normandy. Because goods could be taken to Paris by rail from Rouen much more quickly than by the winding and uncertain Seine, Rouen steadily became much more important as a port, and by the end of the century there was a comprehensive rail network, much of it designed by British engineers and built by British workmen, over the whole of Normandy and Brittany.

Industriali-
sation
In Normandy the nineteenth century also saw a certain amount of industrialisation. Making use of the local supplies of wool, linen and hemp, textile industries developed, at first in the river valleys where use could be made of natural water power, though with the coming of steam the industries moved to the towns. Cotton was imported through Le Havre and was turned into cotton goods in Rouen, which became a sort of Manchester of France; there were also major spinning centres at Louviers, Evreux and Elbeuf. Lace was produced in Caen, Honfleur and Falaise. Easy access to the coast by rail, and the fashion set by the imperial court and French society, also led to the gradual development of Normandy's coastal resorts.

Brittany did not enjoy the same boost to its economy in the nineteenth century as Normandy. Its rail and road communications were less good than those of its competitors, and it was further from the big centres of population. Transport costs were higher, and producers were obliged to sell their goods at non-competitive prices. As in all other parts of rural France, the peasant population was not slow to realise that one of the advantages of the railway was that it made it easier to get away. The story of Brittany in the nineteenth century is one of depopulation, of a steady drift to other parts of France and to the big cities, and of emigration abroad.

In 1870–71, during the Franco-Prussian War, German troops occupied some towns and villages in Upper Normandy, but the farmers kept them supplied with copious quantities of calvados, the local apple brandy with a kick like an angry mule, and this kept them relatively docile.

The World
Wars
Both Brittany and Normandy escaped the devastation that was the lot of much of north-eastern France during the four years of the First World War from 1914–18, but they both sent many soldiers to fight in the trenches, and Brittany is said to have had a higher proportion of

men killed than any other region which sent men to the war, on either side.

Normandy battleground

Twenty years later the Second World War broke out. Five years later, as this war drew to an end, the whole of Normandy became a battleground. On 6 June 1944, D-Day, the Allied armies landed on the beaches of Normandy, intent on liberating Europe. For nearly three months the most Titanic battles in the history of the world raged across the region. Well over two million men were involved and more than 200,000 buildings were destroyed. Major towns, including Caen, St Lô and Cherbourg were completely demolished. In Rouen the whole of the industrial zone was destroyed, as well as much of the historic old quarter. And when the fighting had finished elsewhere, the Germans held on in Le Havre until mid-September. The town suffered 146 bombing raids, nearly 5,000 civilians were killed, and most of the town was flattened.

Reconstruction

In Brittany, the towns of Brest and Lorient, used by the Germans as submarine bases from which to attack the Atlantic convoys, were repeatedly bombarded, and had to be totally rebuilt from their ruins after the war.

In Normandy the amount of reconstruction which had to be undertaken when the war ended was awe-inspiring. Whole towns had to be given new street plans, new drainage systems, new hospitals, schools and parks. New industrial zones were laid out, residential areas completely rebuilt; cathedrals, churches and other historic buildings had to be restored or replaced. In the countryside, new villages and farmhouses rose from the rubble of the old. In the ports, the docks and warehouses were renewed and expanded.

It was all a tremendous undertaking but with their practical, let's-get-on-with-it attitude the Normans set about it, and now after nearly half a century of maturity, the new towns no longer seem new, just solid and prosperous, and the devastation is just a memory.

Normandy and Brittany Today

The political system

According to the 1989 census, France has a population in excess of 57 million. The country is divided into ninety-five departments, including the island of Corsica, and the departments, usually in groups of four or five, make up twenty-two administrative regions.

Normandy is divided into two administrative regions: Upper Normandy, consisting of the departments of Seine Maritime and Eure, and Lower Normandy, made up of Calvados, Manche and Orne. Brittany is one administrative region with four departments: Côtes d'Armor, Finisterre, Morbihan and Ille-et-Vilaine. The department of Loire-Atlantique, which historically is part of Brittany, is also included in this book, though it is now part of the region of Pays de Loire. Each department is divided into cantons, and the cantons into communes.

Suffrage France is a democracy with a freely elected government, headed by a President who holds office for seven years, though there is a move to reduce the term to five years to coincide with the normal life of a government. There are two kinds of suffrage in France. The first is universal direct suffrage, by which the people as a whole elect the President, the members of Parliament, the regional councillors, the general (departmental) councillors and the municipal councillors. Those elected in this way then become a privileged group of electors who themselves elect the members of the Senate, the upper House equivalent to the House of Lords. This system is known as indirect universal suffrage.

Government France is a large country by European standards, more than four times the size of England and twice that of Great Britain, and much of the work of government is of necessity decentralised. The affairs of the regions are directed by regional councillors, those of the departments by general councillors, one of whom is elected from each canton, and those of the communes by municipal councillors. Much of the authority in each commune is invested in the *Maire*, who is elected by and from the municipal councillors. There is thus a freely elected network of authority from the *Maire* and the councillors in the communes, right up through the departments and the regions, to the central government and the President.

The Fifth Republic

There has been a succession of republics in France; in times of crisis the constitution has been changed and a new republic formed. The present one is the Fifth Republic and was created in 1958 by General de Gaulle, following the failure of the Fourth Republic and the demission of its government during the Algerian War, at a time when France itself was in economic difficulty.

The Fifth Republic differs from all previous ones, the changes in its constitution having been put forward by General de Gaulle to enable him, he said, to govern effectively. They were agreed by a referendum of the people, who showed themselves more than two-thirds in favour. The changes in the constitution gave a great deal more power to the President in person, and at the same time reduced the power of Parliament. The system now lies somewhere between a dictatorship and a true parliamentary government, rather closer to the latter than the former. One of the most important differences is that under the Fifth Republic there is no Council of State. In all previous republics the Council of State, which was a kind of successor to the old monarchical council, was requested by the President to form a cabinet, which had to be confirmed in office by a vote of the members of Parliament. The President of the Council of State and all government ministers were obliged to be members of Parliament.

Under the Fifth Republic the process is less democratic. The President names his Prime Minister, and the Prime Minister proposes his ministers to the President, who may accept or refuse them. The Prime Minister and ministers do not have to be members of Parliament, but in practice they almost always are. There were thinking Frenchmen who considered De Gaulle a dictator, and in theory the constitution of the Fifth Republic would allow the President himself to form the entire government and to control it. In theory there need be no member of Parliament in it, though it is certain that in practice such a situation would not be tolerated by Parliament nor by the people as a whole. However, with the rise in popularity of the Fascist National Front and its leader, Jean Marie le Pen, there are those who find the possibility disturbing.

So this hybrid form of government has moved some way from complete parliamentary democracy, though Parliament retains some power and the people have a free vote in elections at every level. However it may be classified, the Fifth Republic has already lasted nearly forty years. Its governments have been stable, remaining in power for several years with relatively few ministerial changes, and it seems to be popular with the nation as a whole, although there remains a nucleus of influential businessmen and academics both right and left of centre inclined to resist any further moves away from true democratic government.

Political parties
There are two parties of the Left – the Communists, who have lost favour steadily in recent years and who now have little more than 5 per cent of the vote, and the Socialists, who until the 1993 general election were the largest single party. The right is divided between the RPR (*Rassemblement Pour la République*), the UDF (*Union Démocratique Française*), which is nearer the centre, and the extreme right National Front, which now has between 10 and 15 per cent of the vote nationally and considerably more in the Marseilles region. The election was a catastrophic defeat for the Left. Of 657 parliamentary seats the Socialists won only 53, the Communists 20, and the combined right-wing parties 571.

Parliament
Parliament sits for about five-and-a-half months of the year. Television coverage of important debates reveals rows upon rows of empty seats, with just a few martyred members looking like a village bowls club, who by mistake have booked the Albert Hall for their annual general meeting.

Regionalism
The most significant aspect of French political life is its regionalism. Regardless of which party is in power, or who its dominant personalities are, the outlook of the average man is focused on his region. In the South West, where I live, I have heard local men, even teachers, say, 'France begins south of the Loire.' In Brittany, the common attitude is even more parochial. Many Bretons think of themselves as belonging to Roscoff, or Quimper, or Brest, rather than as Bretons. Outside Brittany they become Bretons, but wherever they are the interests of France come a long way behind those of Brittany, and those a long way behind those of their own town.

In Normandy the regional feeling is hardly less intense, though its identity as a duchy or a province is historical only, but to the Normans it is as separate as Cornwall is to the Cornish. In the French provinces the central government seems remote, and would seem more so were it not for the ritual appearances on television of its key members. The same feeling is reflected in the daily press. The 'national' newspapers of Paris have a small sale in the provinces, where every region has its own daily paper devoted almost exclusively to local problems and events.

Bureaucracy

The French bureaucratic system is highly developed. It can be very long-winded and pernickety, but for those who conform it can also be easy-going.

Identity cards
The French find it difficult to believe that the British are not required to carry any identification, for in France your 'papers' are of paramount importance. Anyone stopped, for example, for a motoring

offence or during a routine check is at once asked for the documents relating to the car, a driving licence and their identity card. For foreigners, a driving licence and a passport (it can save bother always to carry it in France) are sufficient, but whatever else he can show, a French citizen who cannot produce his identity card is at once suspect to the police and will be questioned closely. On the other hand, a motorist who happened to have horns and a forked tail might well be perfectly acceptable to the police, if his papers were in order and no offence had been committed. The French are brought up always to have their identity cards with them and to expect to have to produce them. If they cannot, there may well be a serious reason.

Livret de Famille

In addition to identity cards, every family is expected to have a family booklet, the *Livret de Famille*, which is given to every couple at the time of their marriage and to every unmarried mother. It contains spaces in which to record the birth date and name of each child and any deaths which occur in the family, as well as other events such as divorce, remarriage, adoption and so forth. It must be presented at the *Mairie* on each such occasion to be officially stamped and signed.

The Mayor

For the average inhabitant bureaucracy begins and ends with the Mayor (*Monsieur le Maire*). He it is who registers the births and deaths of the citizens of his commune. He can marry a couple if at least one of them lives in the commune, and if they live together outside marriage he can provide a certificate of *concubinage*, which allows them certain tax and other advantages. If crops are damaged by hail, or if there is a domestic or hunting accident, or a quarrel between neighbours, and in countless other events of daily life, the *Maire* is the man on the spot to establish the facts. On the face of it he does all this for limited expenses, fixed at national level in proportion to the number of inhabitants in his commune. In practice he is likely to be no more disinterested than the councillors in any average small town in Britain whose businesses, in some mysterious way, thrive so well. It is also a fact that the route to the top in French politics very often begins in a *Mairie*. Almost without exception every important political figure is also the Mayor of a large town and carries the major part of its vote with him into Parliament.

Efficiency

All systems are most fairly judged by results and by this rule the French system is sound. The towns are clean and well lit, the rubbish is collected and disposed of efficiently, the postal service is reliable, the trains are clean and run on time, the telephone system is reasonably efficient, no aspect of the superb road network is neglected, and the hospitals are modern, efficient and comfortable.

Law and education

The big disaster area in France is the legal system, which is cumbersome, dubious both in efficiency and in the justice meted out, and intolerably long-winded. French television frequently gives news of important trials taking place which refer to crimes which occurred four or five years previously. A man may be arrested and accused of a crime and held for years before being brought to trial. He may be found innocent but has still served four years in prison, and has a prison record for life. He is entitled to compensation, but it would be very little and could take years to obtain. 'The French legal system,' says one jurist, 'is archaic in its concept, medieval in its methods, often far removed from justice, and utterly unsuited to the needs of modern society.' It is at present being heavily criticised from all sides.

Policing In the towns, law and order is maintained by the police, who are civil servants. In the country the *gendarmes*, who are attached to the army, have this responsibility. Policing the roads is shared between them, though motorcycle police are usually not *gendarmes*. The uniforms of both police and *gendarmes* are blue, but police wear military-style caps and *gendarmes* wear *kepis*. In the country there is also an officer called a *garde champêtre* who is a kind of maid-of-all-work village policeman.

Demonstrations French politics often tends to become physical, with frequent banner-waving marches, demonstrations and clashes with the police or the security forces (CRS). Two subjects which arouse particularly intense emotions are education and agriculture.

Education Like the legal system, the educational system is under severe stress in France. Parents criticise its effectiveness, and students complain of overcrowding and badly maintained buildings with broken equipment and dirty toilets. In the past the system was effective, producing a population with a high average level of culture, though little individuality. Discipline in French schools was strict, but this has been relaxed in the past few years, causing over-reaction among pupils, with widespread smoking and, to a lesser extent, drug problems among the young.

1968 The events of 1968 – when a student revolt against proposed university reforms was quickly joined by the trade unions in violent protest against the cost of living, leading to clashes with the police and three deaths – are still fresh in the minds of politicians and public alike. It is not uncommon to hear public figures – writers, singers, media professionals – saying, 'I was there in '68, on the streets . . .' or words to that effect. Most of the students who fought the police in May 1968 are now themselves parents, but public and political memory is still hypersensitive.

Universities Attempts to make university education – which in theory at least is now open to everyone – more closely related to genuine ability have all failed. The problem has not gone away: it has become much worse, and thousands of students gain the right to university places which simply do not exist. The universities are already more crowded than the prisons, which commonly contain three times the number of prisoners for which they were designed.

Agriculture

Political activity is a term which farmers all over France have tended to take literally in recent years. If for one reason or another they find their markets shrinking, as was the case during the run-up to Spain's entry into the EC and again when Brussels cut down the milk quotas, then the farmers take to physical demonstrations, overturning lorryloads of imported produce and dumping their own unsaleable surpluses of tomatoes, peaches, potatoes, apples and so on, on the streets of the town centres.

Peasant farmers

The French peasant has always felt himself to be oppressed and taken advantage of, and throughout history has rebelled against his situation. The feeling is very strong in Brittany, where over the past twenty years peasants have greatly increased their productivity. Where many of them were content with subsistence farming, they now produce three or four times as much and sell the surplus on the open market, constantly seeking to increase their standard of living. The change has come about from the desire to catch up with the earnings of industrial workers, coupled with the government's policy of giving big loans to farmers at low rates of interest, as well as subsidies to modernise. Farmers who had only ten cows forty years ago are passing on herds three or four times as large to their sons. But though the peasant produces more from the same land, he cannot sell it, or increased production brings a fall in price. He slides back a step for every one he takes forward. This apparently everlasting situation makes the peasant hypersensitive to whatever he feels to be injustice.

Population

Though they differ in so many respects, Brittany and Normandy have one thing in common, which is that, compared with the rest of France, they still have a relatively high percentage of the population employed in agriculture. The only large towns in Normandy are Rouen and Le Havre, which together have about one-fifth of the population of the two Normandys. In Brittany, Rennes and Brest are the largest towns, though Nantes, now in Pays de Loire, is somewhat larger. The only one of these towns which, with its suburbs, can claim a population of more than half a million, is Rouen. The rest of the inhabitants are scattered through the countryside, in villages, and in towns which rarely have more than 30,000 people. In Brittany the population is much denser in the coastal belt than in the interior, with the exception of Rennes.

The working day

Business and commercial life in Brittany and Normandy, as in the rest of France, starts about an hour earlier than it does in Britain. With few exceptions the working day starts at 8 a.m. in most offices, shops and even banks. Lunchtime is still sacred and runs to two hours, not one, starting at 12 noon. Almost all shops close, particularly in small towns and rural areas, except food shops which stay open until 12.30, so that people can buy something for lunch. Hypermarkets which have their own restaurant stay open during the lunch hour. Those which do not have a restaurant close until 3 p.m. or later, and food shops, butchers, fishmongers etc, open again at about 4 p.m. and remain open until 7 p.m.

Farmers start work even earlier. Most of them are out and about soon after 6 a.m., and return to the farmhouse for a light breakfast at about 8 a.m. Like almost everyone else, they stop at 12 noon sharp for lunch – much the most important meal of the day. They rest after the meal, and start again at 1.30 or 2 p.m., according to the season, and continue working until 6 p.m., though at certain times – ploughing and harvesting – they often continue as long as daylight allows. Some harvesting is done by headlights in the dark.

Costs

The high cost of farm machinery, as well as artificial fertilisers and sprays, means that most farmers have to borrow at high rates of interest and are heavily in debt. They have been able to keep going because they have lower expenses than 'townies'. Almost all farmers live in an inherited farmhouse, and have no rent or mortgage to pay. They supply a surprisingly high percentage of their own food, and so have low household bills, and they enjoy favourable insurance and social security costs. Even so, their economy has been fragile for several years, and the recent combination of droughts for several years running and the imposition of milk quotas by the EC has been the last straw.

Changes

The general result of the changes and difficulties in agriculture in Brittany and Normandy in recent years is that farms have become fewer and larger as the more efficient have absorbed those that were less viable. In many places land prices have fallen sharply, but even so there are still many farms for sale. Where land has been sold, unwanted farmhouses are being sold off as holiday homes.

Discontent is rife. A successful farmer who recently imported seventy British lambs for breeding purposes because there are simply not enough available in France, got up one morning to find that they had all been poisoned by neighbouring farmers. My neighbour, a fruit farmer, cultivates his orchards year round, pruning, fertilising, spraying. When harvest comes he is ordered from Brussels to pick the crop and plough it into the ground. The compensation is meagre, the anguish soul-destroying. The whole agricultural system in France is in chaos. Crops rot where they stand, and more and more land is left uncultivated, because the farmers are paid more to leave it fallow than they can earn by growing a crop.

Social security

France is a highly developed welfare state whose social security benefits are generous by the standards of many other countries. Its health service, though at present under stress, offers a very wide range of medical benefits at low cost, including many medicines. Even visits to masseurs, physiotherapists, or treatment in spas to take the waters are paid for, provided they have been authorised by a doctor. Some treatments are reimbursable at 100 per cent and others at 70 per cent, while private medical insurance is available which covers the other 30 per cent.

Unemployment

There has been a steady increase in unemployment in France over recent years, with no sign of improvement in the situation. Unemployment benefits and generous family allowances encourage large families among the poor and unemployed, who are sometimes able to live almost entirely from these benefits.

Crippling costs

The high cost of social security is gradually bringing the internal economy to its knees, with a heavy deficit every year. The system has significant self-destructive elements. Small employers, for example, are closing down by the thousand because they cannot afford the social security charges they are obliged to pay for each worker. Some of their men are able to find other work, but others swell the ranks of those collecting unemployment benefit, ultimately increasing the charges on the remaining employers, so that yet more of them give up. The question of pensions is also causing trouble and demonstrations. Recent estimates suggest that within the next twenty years workers will have to contribute up to 40 per cent of their pay towards their pension, if it is to retain the same sort of purchasing power as today. It is not likely that this will be possible, and so French society in the near future will include many impoverished old people.

In the meantime the government desperately scratches around, hoping to unearth a solution that will not cost votes.

The future

So what is the future of this curious Fifth Republic, with its powerful President and its separation of the executive from the legislative power, so that ministers do not have to sit in Parliament and do not even have to be members of it? French politicians of all parties consider the unification of Europe with deadly earnestness, tinged with a slight but positive sense of panic. Until recently they were all busy selling the future to the electorate as a Europe which would be led by France. They may not seriously have believed this themselves, but they certainly saw France as a near-equal partner of West Germany at the head of Europe. But a united Germany presents a different picture of the future, one at present illustrated by the difference in physical stature between Helmut Kohl and François Mitterand, and French politicians are at present, to quote one French financial expert, 'putting on a brave front but running scared'.

The President and the Prime Minister repeatedly assure the nation on television that the economy is in a healthy condition. Perhaps it is, but a look round the shopping sections and industrial zones of most towns reveals numerous empty shops and closed factories. Part of the trouble is that the French have paid themselves too much for too long, not only in their social security services, which are heavily in debt, but also to workers in key industries which now find it hard to compete in world export markets. These problems are not diminishing.

Religion

Brittany and Normandy differ strongly from each other in their religious attitudes and traditions. Under de Gaulle, France as a whole was strongly Catholic, but in recent decades the place of religion has weakened considerably, and the decline has been so marked in some areas, especially Mediterranean France, that the term 'dechristianisation' has often been used. In the 1950s 30 per cent of Catholics throughout France attended mass regularly, but by the 1970s this figure had fallen to 7 per cent attending not regularly but once or twice a month. Since then the figures have fallen further in most of the country.

Among the reasons put forward for the falling off of religious worship are the steady increase in alternative weekend occupations, especially the development of leisure and sporting activities which has been very marked in France; the increasing ownership of private transport enabling family visits to be made; and the greater emphasis on scientific and technical instruction.

Catholicism   In France in general Catholicism has suffered more than Protestantism. The liberation of women, the use of the Pill, and more relaxed attitudes towards contraception and abortion have all brought modern couples into conflict with the parish priest, whose interference in their lives is tolerated less and less – modern wives do not want to be told when and under what conditions they should sleep with their husbands. The decline of Catholicism is most positively shown by the disappearance of the priests. There are now only 36,000 in all France, and fewer than 200 are ordained each year. It is estimated that there will be less than 12,000 by the end of the century, and it is now rare to see a priest in clerical dress even in the country villages. Many priests are already responsible for more than one church, and services will become more and more rare.

Brittany

But Brittany is not representative of France as a whole, and it remains strongly Catholic. The proportion of people attending Mass in Nantes is more than double that in Marseilles, and in the smaller towns and villages of Brittany the proportion would be a great deal higher.

Though the arrival of Protestantism in the sixteenth century did not make much impact on Brittany and the duchy did not suffer greatly in the Religious Wars which followed, it is interesting to note that some of the most positive expressions of the deep Catholic faith of the Bretons – the parish enclosures and calvaries – date from this period. The *enclos paroissial*, or parish enclosure, around the church consisted of a small cemetry, a calvary and a charnel-house or ossuary, and the whole was approached through a triumphal arch. The charnel-house, often beautifully decorated, was used to house the bones which had to be taken from the graves in the very small cemetries to make room for new burials. They are still sometimes used for funeral services. The triumphal arch symbolised the gateway to Heaven, and the triumph celebrated was that of the soul passing into Heaven and immortality.

The pardon

Another aspect of Breton Catholicism which has survived to the present day is the *pardons*. These are combined pilgrimages and feasts in honour of the patron saints of particular churches, and are very old-established, some dating back to as early as AD 500. They are meant to be, and for the most part still are, strongly religious occasions, of which the most impressive aspect is the procession of the faithful, in their most splendid traditional costumes and carrying banners, on the way to the church where they will ask forgiveness of their sins and make an offering to their patron saint. Some of these *pardons* have acquired a commercial and touristic side, and some have become little more than local fairs. Others, particularly those which occur on saints' days outside the main tourist season, remain fervently religious.

In the past some of the *pardons* were extremely violent affairs. One held at St Servais in the Arrée Hills in central Brittany every 13 May in honour of the saint who protected the growing corn from frost and ensured a good harvest, was always attended by thousands of people both from the Cornouaille and the Morbihan region, who were sworn enemies. On one occasion the men on both sides arrived armed with cudgels. A banner was placed at the end of the nave, with its staff attached to the altar rail. According to one old account, this is what followed: 'After the Magnificat, the cudgels were raised, and the people from Cornouaille shouted at their saint "Give us wheat in Cornouaille", and the people from Vannes (Morbihan) shouted "Wheat, oats, and buckwheat for the Vannetais". The banner was carried out of the church, the clergy ran for the safety of the sacristy. The cry of "Down with the frost" rose from thousands of voices, and the conflict began in earnest. Each side fought for the banner and the small statue of the saint (a new one was needed every year) which would bring them an abundant harvest. Women fought alongside their men for the favour of the saint. Arms were broken, heads cut open, and men sat on the graves with blood streaming from their mouths. . . .' This violent *pardon* more than once led to deaths on both sides, and it was eventually banned by joint action of the religious and secular authorities.

Ancient religions   No tourist should leave Brittany without having seen some of these aspects of Breton Catholicism, but the roots of religious feeling in Brittany lie much further in the past than the Christian era. The megaliths, the alignments of great stones at Carnac, and the many dolmens, which were burial chambers, are often much older than the pyramids of Egypt, sometimes pre-dating them by as much as 1,000 years. Of these curious arrangements of stones, not clearly understood by modern thinkers, two things can be asserted. First, they were the work of a people sufficiently advanced to have the technical and mathematical skill to handle with precision blocks of stone weighing up to 350 tons each. Secondly, all this was the work of a religious people. Wherever burial chambers have been found, it has been shown that they indicate a belief in an afterlife.

No one knows now what purposes, what ancient rites and ceremonies, were associated with these great, eternal stones, so carefully arranged. The first Christian missionaries put their cross on top of some of the most important stones, and held their services by them, recognising their religious importance. This ancient thread of mystery still courses in the blood of the Bretons, intermingled with their profound Christianity. Some authorities go so far as to say Catholicism has survived in Brittany because it espoused the old pagan rites, creating a unique kind of Catholicism which has lasted because it is deeply rooted in immemorial customs and local activities. It is also relevant that, though Brittany has made great economic advances in the past forty years, the duchy was poor for centuries and, as in other poor parts of France such as Auvergne, the peasants in their misery turned to their God for help and comfort. And not only to God – the Breton peasant was riddled with belief in charms, superstitions, phantoms and in 'ghoulies and ghosties and things that go bump in the night'. Every Breton has a tale of the supernatural at the tip of his tongue, every old house is haunted.

Normandy   The situation in Normandy is much more representative of that of France as a whole. There are no parish enclosures, no *pardons*, in Normandy. There were no mysterious inhabitants in the far distant past who arranged great stones in geometric patterns, no traditions linked to ancient pagan rites, less superstition, and none of the sense of waiting death, so common in Brittany. The Normans were much more ready to take up Protestantism than the Bretons. In Brittany, it was mainly the influential and aristocratic families who became Protestants, whereas in Normandy many of the ordinary people were also converted.

Love and Marriage

There seems, to the British mind, to be something different about the French idea of marriage. Although numerous marriages fail in Britain, they usually begin in an atmosphere of mutual commitment. In France, however, there is a certain reservation on both sides. An obvious aspect of this is the marriage contract, which establishes at once the strong material element in French marriage. Legally there has to be a contract, either creating common ownership of property between husband and wife, or separating the property of the one from the other.

There is also a kind of reserve at official level. When Françoise Dubois marries Pierre Le Bec, she becomes Madame Le Bec as far as neighbours, tradesmen and business colleagues are concerned, but to the state she is Françoise Dubois first, *épouse* Le Bec second, and remains Françoise Dubois, *épouse* Le Bec as long as she is married to him. If M Le Bec dies first, she remains Françoise Dubois, but widow Le Bec.

Perhaps the lack of commitment from the outset is the reason for the high rate of divorce in France as a whole: one marriage in two in Paris ends in divorce, one in three in the provinces, but fewer in Catholic Brittany.

There are also many homes in France in which people live together without the formality of marriage. This situation is known as *concubinage* and in most areas it raises no eyebrows whatsoever, though the Bretons do not approve.

Homes and houses

The typical Breton house and the typical Norman house, particularly in the countryside, are utterly unlike each other. The Breton house is solidly built of granite with a slate roof, and is often rather squat and sturdy looking, and not often elaborated with turrets or towers, though in some areas there may be dormer windows. These houses, which in the villages sometimes give the impression of being huddled together to protect each other against Atlantic storms, are reminiscent of many to be seen in Cornish and Welsh villages.

Normandy The classic picture which Normandy calls to mind is of an apple orchard in flower with a few brown-and-white cows browsing in the lush grass, with in the background a half-timbered farmhouse with rose-red brick between the exposed beams, and often with a thatched roof. These half-timbered houses are typical of a wide swathe of the Norman countryside. They differ in other respects from the Breton style, especially when of manorial dimensions, in often having turrets and a high-pitched roof with dormer windows. The roofs are frequently tiled, rather than slated or thatched.

As in all areas which have been inhabited for centuries, there is a variety in the domestic architecture from one locality to another, depending on the raw materials which were available on the spot for building. In the valley of the Seine there are many buildings in the chalky stone quarried from the riverside cliffs. In the heart of Calvados, around Caen, there are many stone buildings, both public and private. Caen stone was well known in the Middle Ages and was used for many famous buildings; some was even shipped to England for use in the building of Westminster Abbey. When Caen was rebuilt after being almost totally destroyed during the Allied invasion in 1944, much of it was reconstructed in its own stone, and in the same style as before.

A surprising number of Normandy's finest old buildings did survive the bombardments of D-Day and succeeding weeks, and in the towns there are still many lovely stone mansions of the flamboyant Gothic and early Renaissance periods to be seen. In those towns, both in Brittany and Normandy, where old quarters survive there are still many half-timbered houses, often dating from the sixteenth century.

Dovecotes

Another distinctive feature of the Norman landscape is the attractive dovecote to be seen on many Norman farms. The right to erect these buildings, called *pigeonniers* further south but *colombiers* in Normandy, was granted by feudal lords to their vassals, and was one of the benefits the vassal received, along with accommodation and land and the right to harvest the crops for his own use, in return for his loyalty to his lord and the obligation to fight for him when required. No one else could have a *colombier*, and the right was defended by a law which was not abrogated until the French Revolution. It was in a sense a status symbol, and because of this many of them in Normandy are little masterpieces of the builder's art. Many are circular with a conical roof, and some are rectangular and half-timbered. They all have numerous openings for the pigeons, and many have a projecting course of brick or stone about half-way up to prevent predatory animals climbing the walls.

In recent years there has been a lot of new building, particularly in the coastal strip all round Brittany. Some of the houses are still built in stone, and others in cheaper materials, but many of them look alike because they are painted white and have slate roofs. In Normandy there has always been more variety, because of the wider range of available materials. New houses are often in the traditional Norman style, though mainly now in brick and tile.

Sanitation

The peasant farmer's house is often quite spacious by British standards, and that was their chief comfort. Until quite recently the plumbing was rudimentary, and even quite impressive houses had no bathrooms. All that is changing, and the new houses now have all the latest features. There is no main drainage in the countryside of France and, because of the large distances between houses, there is never likely to be.

Home ownership

One of the important changes in French society in recent years has been the general introduction, half a century later than in Britain, of the mortgage system of house purchase. Fifteen years ago it was almost unheard of, but it is now quite common.

With the spread of house ownership other changes have come about. In the past the ordinary Frenchman was not a gardener, but in the past few years one of the boom areas in the economy has been the development of nurseries and garden centres. Every year new ones open and the competition is fierce. This has been paralleled by the great surge in DIY centres, and *bricolage*, as the French call do-it-yourself, has become a national pastime. They believe it saves them money and, as the average Frenchman is good with his hands, it probably does.

Furniture

The traditional furniture of both Breton and Norman houses is remarkable for its combination of solidity and elegance, and in Brittany particularly for the constant repetition of the same designs. The most characteristic piece of Breton furniture is the *lit-clos*, the closed or box bed. In many of the ordinary Breton houses there was one large living-room, and the *lit-clos* gave both privacy and protection from the cold. The bed would occupy a recess in a corner of the room and would be typically closed off by sliding doors, often ornately carved, or by one large door in northern Brittany, or sometimes by heavy curtains. Some of them had two levels, like modern bunk beds. The *lit-clos* always had a coffer-bench against it, serving as a seat and a place to store the bedclothes, and also as a step up to make it easier to get into the bed. The traditional *armoire*, a large cupboard with double doors, was often placed next to the *lit-clos*.

In Norman houses the key pieces of furniture are the grandfather clock, the buffet or sideboard, and the *armoire*. All of them are imposing, solid, well-proportioned and often beautifully carved with a wealth of detail, garlands of flowers, fruits, birds and geometric patterns. The *armoire* often played a symbolic part in marriage. Norman girls collected their trousseau together in such an *armoire*, and when she moved from her parent's house the *armoire*, complete with trousseau, would be borne in state to the bride's new home, with suitable celebrations.

Family life

The rural areas of Normandy and Brittany are considerably more conservative than the towns, and for most farmers family life is still of great importance. In the countryside the family is a workforce as well as a blood relationship. Even the farmer's wife, in addition to running the household, cooking for the family and other workers on the farm, and looking after the farmyard with its chickens, ducks and pigeons, is expected to help with the harvest, pick fruit, cultivate her vegetable garden, and drive a tractor if necessary.

Older members

In the country it is usual for the family to take care of its older members. The'*mémé*' and the '*pépé*', the grandmother and grandfather, continue to do whatever they can around the farm as long as they are able. The *mémé* prepares the vegetables for cooking, the fruit for jam-making, and plucks the chickens. The *pépé*, although officially retired and enjoying his pension, may still do work around the farm, such as looking after the vineyard, according to his physical strength.

French families are traditionally headed by the oldest member, man or woman, without whose approval important decisions are not normally taken. They can be dictatorial. One young farmer told me that his grandfather had refused to allow them to spend money on an indoor toilet and a bathroom. 'I have lived all my life without either, and I'm eighty,' he said. 'You don't need them. It's a waste of money.' This attitude is dying out, though every expense is still considered with great caution.

Sundays

Sunday in the country is a day for visiting friends and relatives. It is the usual custom to take with you, not a bunch of flowers or a bottle of wine, but a cake from the *pâtissier*. On Sunday mornings in every town and village these shops are crowded and a succession of customers can be seen leaving with beribboned and carefully wrapped boxes of delicious *gâteaux*. It is one of France's many pleasant customs that every shop will offer to gift-wrap a purchase for you, free of charge, and they do it beautifully.

People who do not eat in each other's houses on Sunday often form a family group, small children included, and book a large table in a restaurant for Sunday lunch. For this reason it is advisable for visitors travelling on Sunday in the high season to reserve in advance at restaurants.

Feeding the family

Food is very important to the French. In the past the peasants often went hungry. Today a usual greeting is, 'Are you well?', but an older one still sometimes heard in the country is '*Tu mange à ta faim?*' or 'Are you getting enough to eat?'.

Hypermarkets
The French spend a lot of money on food, and with all the temptation put before them, now that there are no shortages, they would have to be superhuman not to. Hypermarkets with parking for hundreds of cars are to be found on the edge of even small towns throughout Normandy and Brittany, as everywhere in France. The selection of food in them is remarkable. Fifty kinds of cheese, twenty kinds of bread, a hundred different wines, fresh meat, fish and shellfish, locally grown fruit and vegetables – the choice of food is inexhaustible. But every other household need is also catered for: cleaning materials, clothes, washing machines and televisions, books, gardening needs, bicycles, fishing rods, furniture – it's all there under one roof.

Traditional markets
You might think that with all this so easily available there would be no place for a traditional market, but you would be wrong. Markets thrive all over Brittany and Normandy, every day in the large towns, twice a week in the small towns, once a week in the villages. They are all fascinating. When you walk through them you are sharing in one of the timeless activities of society. Everywhere you will find knots of three or four men and women, discussing the price of something they themselves grow, or the health of a friend or relative (almost invariably not what it was), or the marriage recently past or forthcoming (and none too soon) of someone they all know, or the recent birth of a girl, or better, a boy.

In addition to food of every kind on sale in these markets, there are chickens and quail roasting on spits, vans selling freshly made pizza to take away, and in our local market a huge paella is prepared in a pan four feet across. By lunchtime every portion is sold. There are also regular ecological markets selling untreated fruit and vegetables and, in the small villages, there are Sunday morning markets for home-made produce. This is where you can buy farmhouse cheeses, jams, local honey, feather-light tarts and sponges, home-cured hams and other rare delights.

The impact of tourism

The steady increase of tourism, both from within France and from abroad, has been of considerable benefit to the economy of Brittany. It has helped to combat the effects of the inexorable decline in the fishing industry, and to a lesser extent is now helping farmers in difficulty. They can often get grants from local authorities to help them convert cottages and outbuildings into holiday *gîtes* for letting.

Resorts
Every beach resort in Brittany, large or small, has expanded in

recent years. New houses have been built in and around all of them. Most of these new houses are holiday homes for people from Paris or other northern cities, and many are available for letting to holiday visitors from abroad. There are also many new hotels, and older ones have been refurbished and have had extra accommodation added.

Sailing

A specialised aspect of tourism which is very important to Brittany is private sailing. Over the past two decades the French have shown themselves to be a nation of seamen, and they have produced some great sailors, both men and women, from Eric Tabarly to Florence Arthaut. Every single-handed transatlantic or round-the-world race has a predominance of French entrants, all willingly backed by an important French commercial enterprise, and as every active school-boy footballer thinks he is another Pele, every other Frenchman secretly fancies himself as a world-beating yachtsman. More importantly, very large numbers of them buy yachts. As most of the 'personality' sailors are either Bretons, or based in Brittany, this is where the sailing people are, and the yacht harbours are crammed to capacity everywhere round the coast.

Normandy

Unlike Brittany, where tourism in the past was confined to painters, writers and intellectuals, in other words rather small groups, Normandy has had established resorts for the past hundred years or more. They, too, have developed in recent years and have added to their resources and amenities, and continue to attract increasing numbers of visitors. But the increase is less noticeable than in Brittany, partly because the Norman economy has been less vulnerable, and partly because the growth in tourism in Normandy has been less marked.

Regional characteristics

The Bretons and the Normans are basically two separate races, as different as the Welsh and the English. They are unlike each other both physically and in character.

The Bretons are the descendants of the Ancient Britons who were driven into Wales and back across the sea to Brittany, from which they had originally come, by the Anglo-Saxon invaders of Britain. The Normans are the descendants of the Vikings from Scandinavia who conquered Normandy in the tenth century, and then crossed the Channel under William the Conqueror and defeated the Anglo-Saxons and remaining Britons in 1066 to become the rulers of England.

Physical characteristics

Physically the typical Breton, man or woman, is of medium height, lean, with black eyes and hair, drawn features, and an expression which is often sad or wild-eyed. By nature the Breton is very conservative, disliking change, even more chauvinist than the French. For centuries the men kept to the same style of dress as their ancestors, and wore their hair to their shoulders, and it is only in recent times that they have become more like the rest of France. Though few women now wear their regional dress – there were more than a hundred different local styles of their famous Breton lace headdress – it is still seen at the religious festivals called *pardons*, and sometimes as a tourist attraction.

The typical Norman is noticeably bigger and more strongly built than the Breton or the average Frenchman from further south, often bull-necked, hook-nosed, and eagle-eyed. His hair may be black but is often a particular shade of light brown or dark blonde with a reddish tint, and he is clean shaven, whereas in Brittany beards are common-place. Like their men, Norman women are often robust, have good, though not sylph-like, figures, and pleasant features.

Character traits

In the past the Bretons were sharply divided between the well-to-do and educated classes, and the peasants, who were ignorant, devout and superstitious. Even fifty years ago there were many children in Brittany who were kept at home to work around the farm, rather than being sent to school, and illiteracy was common. The peasants and workers in Brittany were extremely poor and, like all people leading a very hard life, were obliged to be very careful with their money. They were reckoned to be even meaner than the Normans who, as any reader of de Maupassant or Flaubert knows, were renowned for their love of every *petit sou*.

Though this tightness with money is perhaps less obvious now than it once was in Brittany, it was certainly visible only thirty years ago. One traveller who toured Brittany then stayed in fifteen different hotels. The staircases in every one of them were bare boards, a carpet being considered a foolish expense on what was a purely functional, non-decorative part of the building. Lamp bulbs were often naked, on the grounds that a shade merely cut down the light being paid for, and in one hotel the used paper tablecloths reappeared, torn to a convenient size, in the toilets. The development of tourism has forcibly changed things for the better.

The modern Norman has channelled his adventurous and aggressive instincts into trade and business. He is fierce in defending his interests, energetic in the pursuit of profit, acquisitive, and keeps a tight hold on what he gains. On the other hand, he sometimes gambles. In one hotel in which I stayed the landlord was playing dominoes at the bar with two customers. On this occasion they were playing just for the round of drinks, but dominoes is a favourite game with the Normans, as it is in the north of England, and they sometimes bet heavily on the outcome. Peasants have been known to lose a cow, or even one of their farm fields, playing dominoes.

Both Bretons and Normans are colder and more northern in nature than the people of the southern half of France. The Bretons are noticeably more reserved than the French as a whole. They are less loquacious, more direct, and quicker to come to the point. Unlike the French in most parts outside the large cities, they rarely shake hands with each other, and do not kiss anyone outside the family, certainly not in greeting, as is widely done throughout the south, often twice on each cheek.

Like the Welsh, the Bretons are fond of singing, and traditionally are skilled and energetic dancers. One Breton writer has said, 'If God were to organise a poll asking Bretons what occupation they would like to find in Paradise to help them pass eternity, ninety-nine per cent would say "dancing".' When Catherine de Medici organised an international dance competition, the Bretons beat the Basques in the final. Exhausted by a hard day's work in the fields, the Bretons can still dance half the night, and find that it relaxes tired muscles and refreshes the spirit. The dances, and there are many of them, are both graceful and formal. The Normans, on the other hand, do not sing much, and hardly dance at all.

In the Breton language there is no *tu*, and even in French they address everyone as 'you', as we do in English, so there is no problem of whether to say *vous* or *tu*. There are still more than half a million pure Breton speakers, and the language is once again being taught in schools, having been banned for a long time.

Breton religion and beliefs

The Breton is imaginative, with a melancholy streak, frequently turning to thoughts of death. The suicide rate in Brittany is the highest in France. Though religion probably holds a less dominant place in their lives than formerly, the Bretons remain strongly Catholic.

In pre-Christian times they worshipped different gods and holy places, and with the coming of Christianity their allegiance was transferred to saints whom they associated with particular localities. The *pardons*, which are now Christian processions and festivals linked with particular saints, nevertheless often have an underlying paganism, suggesting a propitiation of the gods in return for a blessing on the harvest or their farm animals. The sacrifices once made to pagan deities became offerings of fowls, lambs, butter, honey and corn, which were presented to the shrine and then sold by auction at the foot of the cross in the cemetery.

According to one old writer, 'The idea of Death is present everywhere to the native (Breton) imagination, and seems to have haunted it through long centuries . . . Nowhere does one see more numerous and more beautiful memorials of the dead – ossuaries, reliquaries, exvotos and Calvaries. . . . Under one form or another we have a Christianised cult of the dead which has its roots in the (prehistoric) necropolis, turning the soil of Brittany into one vast charnel house.'

A famous Breton writer, Anatole le Braz, in *La Légende de la Mort* shows how the Divinity of Death, which the Bretons call *l'Ankou*, has inspired a host of creepy legends and traditions. According to the preface of the book, the dead mix with the living: 'Souls do not remain enclosed in tombs, but wander at night on highways and lonely lanes. They haunt the fields and the moors . . . They revisit their old homes in the silence of the night, and, from the shelter of the *lit-clos*, they can be seen crouching about the expiring brands of the hearth.'

An old woman said to Le Braz, who was writing at the turn of the century, 'The saying used to be "You will be wiser dead than living", and we then had a continual solicitude for the departed, so that when we, in turn, became ancestors, we should not be forgotten. It is better to have the goodwill of the dead than their hostility; their resentments are terrible, and their revenges inevitable.'

There were few, says Le Braz, who had not heard the coach of death rolling over the roads and picking up souls on its way. In seaside parishes the last-drowned sailor was said to haunt the beach until a successor came to take his place.

One of the most ancient of all mankind's beliefs is that birth is associated with the incoming tide, and death with the ebb-tide. According to Fraser in *The Golden Bough*, this belief is said to persist along the east coast of England from Northumberland to Kent, and to have been known to Shakespeare, who makes Falstaff die 'even just between twelve and one, e'en at the turning o' the tide'. And much later it is mentioned in Dickens: 'People can't die along the coast,' said Mr Peggoty, 'except when the tide's pretty nigh out. They can't be born, unless it is pretty nigh in – not properly born till the flood.' In Brittany, a land of the sea, superstitions concerning the tide are strong. 'The Breton peasant,' says Fraser, 'fancies that clover sewn when the tide is coming in will grow well, but . . . sown at low water or when the tide is going out, it will never reach maturity. . . . His wife believes that the best butter is made when the tide has turned and is beginning to flow . . .' Fraser also says that the Breton peasants attributed magical qualities to mistletoe (the 'golden bough' itself) and hung great bunches of it outside their barns and stables to protect their animals against witchcraft.

It is to the fanciful Breton mind that we owe many of the best-known legends, such as that of King Arthur and the Knights of the Round Table. The magician, Merlin, was said to have been born on the Ile du Sein, off the Point du Raz, and Arthur and his knights are said to have searched for the Holy Grail in the forest of Broceliande.

Norman attitudes

By contrast, the Norman character is more practical, much more concerned with the day-to-day realities of life. The Norman is always aware of what it going on around him, and is very observant. Walk through a Norman market and watch both sellers and buyers: their eyes are everywhere. But if the Norman is wary, he is also fair-minded. It was the Normans who brought the notion of trial by jury to England, and respect for the courts. Norman integrity, and Norman justice, based on an absolute belief in individual rights, together formed the basis of the British legal tradition.

The Normans, whether as adventurers or farmers, have always been stolid, hardworking and resolute. They were described by a court official reporting to Louis XIV as 'Headstrong but calculating, bold but prudent'. A Norman saying, *Peut être bien que oui, peut être bien que non* (perhaps it is, perhaps it isn't) does not show indecision, but a concern to see all sides of a question before making a decision. Unlike the Breton, the Norman is not in the least fanciful. He is down-to-earth, and as the work of local writers such as Flaubert, Maupassant, Barbey d'Aurevilly and André Maurois shows, is often given to irony and cynicism. The modern Norman is inclined to think that religion is all right, so long as it is kept in its place and does not interfere with everyday life.

But their self-assurance makes them relaxed and amiable towards strangers unless they sense some animosity. They may not go out of their way to help others, but do not refuse a kindness when approached. In the end, perhaps, they are a people who in their strength and self-sufficiency inspire respect rather than affection.

When and How to Go

Climate

Brittany

Brittany has a temperate oceanic climate which, in a strip 30–40 km wide all around the coast, is extremely mild. Its average winter temperatures are the same as those on the Mediterranean coast of France. In this oceanic Brittany, where frost is almost unknown, exotic plants grow in profusion – not only fuchsias, hydrangeas, camellias and rhododendrons, but also many plants which one would expect on far more southerly shores. Mimosa, palms, pomegranates, eucalyptus, myrtle, oleanders, figs and aloes all thrive, and add colour in the tourist resorts.

Inland Brittany is a shade cooler in winter and a little warmer in summer. Rainfall is spread throughout the year, but is often quickly followed by sunshine. There are many 'soft' days when the coastal areas are enveloped in salt-laden sea mist or drizzle, but the total rainfall is very little higher than the average for France as a whole. A week's holiday in northern Brittany in autumn might be marred by rain, but rainy spells rarely last more than two or three days.

Brittany is sunnier than Cornwall, and its sunniest part is its southern coast from Quimper to the mouth of the Loire. The best months for holiday-makers are June and July, and there are often long sunny periods on the southern coast in March and April. The temperature of the sea for bathing is the same along the northern coasts as it is in English south coast resorts, but along the south coast of Brittany it is noticeably warmer, and this with the many beautiful, safe beaches is an important attraction.

Surrounded and invaded as it is by the sea – some of its fjords, called *abers*, thrust inland for up to 30 km – Brittany is also subject to Atlantic gales, more common in winter than in the summer months. The sight of the Atlantic breakers whipped to a frenzy by these gales, and bursting in huge towers of spume and spray against the granite rocks and cliffs of the Pointe du Raz and other beauty spots, imprints itself unforgettably on the mind.

Normandy

Like Brittany, Normandy has a mild coastal strip, where the summers are warm rather than hot and the winters are free of frost. Cherbourg and the Cotentin peninsula have a climate similar to that of much of Brittany, but in inland Normandy it is a different story. Here the winters can be very cold, and it is not unknown for the landscape to be snow-covered even in March. Summer temperatures in inland towns such as Evreux and Alençon can be several degrees higher than those on the coast.

Both Brittany and Normandy enjoy a more positive summer than is usual in Britain, and tourists who prefer pleasant and comfortable weather to extremes, and like to be able to sunbathe without being roasted, would be happy in any resort in these areas.

Seasonal sights

Brittany, with its magnificent coastline and inland moors, is scenically beautiful at all times. The autumn colours of the woods and moorland are splendid, and after what the Bretons call the 'black months' of November and December, spring transforms the countryside with great drifts of daffodils, gorse and broom, roadside ditches carpeted with millions of wild violets, and primroses beside the woodland streams.

Normandy, too, can be delightful in spring and autumn: no crowds, thousands upon thousands of apple and pear trees in bloom in spring, and the great forests offering a palette of flaming colours in autumn. The smaller resorts may well have closed up out of season but the towns, both big and small, will have hotels open to cater for their year round business trade.

So, for typical summer holidays in resorts keep to June, July and August. But for visitors who want to see the sights, enjoy the superb food and see the countryside at its very best, there is a lot to be said for spring or autumn breaks in towns such as Quimper, Vannes, St Malo, Rouen, Caen or Dieppe.

How to go

By car

Tourists taking their cars to Normandy or Brittany now have the choice of crossing by the Channel Tunnel or one of the short sea crossings, together with a cross-country drive in France which, depending on the resort, may be relatively short or 650 km or more. Alternatively, there is a choice of six other ports: Roscoff and St Malo in Brittany, and Cherbourg, Le Havre, Caen and Dieppe in Normandy. One of these ports is likely to be within reasonable reach of the holiday destination.

By plane and/or train

Information on air services (some seasonal) to Nantes, Deauville, Rouen, Cherbourg, Dinard, Caen, Le Havre, Quimper and Rennes can be obtained from Air France, Colet House, Hammersmith,

London W6 7JP. In conjunction with the French Railways (SNCF), Air France also offers a good value system by which you can fly from any one of sixteen British airports direct to Paris, and continue from there to your destination by train.

It is also possible to do the whole journey by train, buying a ticket at any British Rail station to the station of your choice in Normandy or Brittany.

Travelling Around

Some package holidays, almost all of them in self-catering accommodation – either camp sites or holiday cottages (*gîtes*) – are available and they normally include the return ferry crossing in the price, as well as the accommodation. But whether you go with a tour operator or independently, a car is likely to be essential, if only for shopping, and even more so if you want to explore and see some of the sights.

By road

France is a large country and the distances between places can be considerable. It is impossible to manage in the countryside of France without your own personal transport, and so virtually every family has a car of some sort.

France has the best and most diverse road system in Europe, and in Brittany and Normandy it is as good as anywhere else in the country. French motorists almost invariably keep to the main roads, and many secondary roads are free of all but local traffic. Throughout Brittany and Normandy they often offer splendid views, charming picnic spots, and sometimes a gem of an old church or a forgotten castle.

Documents Whenever you are driving in France, you should have your current driving licence and your passport with you, plus the car's registration documents and an insurance certificate, and a letter of authorisation from the owner, if the car is not yours. If you are stopped by the police for any reason, even a routine tyre check, they will expect you to produce all of them.

Conventions Remember to drive on the right, particularly when entering roundabouts, after stopping to take petrol or a meal, after using a one-way street, and at T-junctions. Note that if a driver flashes his headlights at you in France it means that he has priority and you should give way, the opposite of British usage. In daylight, headlight flashing by oncoming cars is a warning that there are police down the road, so keep within the speed limit.

Offences Recently the French police have become much stricter about speeding and drink-driving offences (the limits are the same as in the UK). If you are stopped for speeding the minimum fine is 1,300 francs (£15). You will almost certainly be breathalysed and if you are over the limit, you can be fined from 2,000 to 30,000 francs (£23–350). Fines are payable on the spot, though this is not always insisted on.

50

The normal speed limit in built-up areas is now 50 km/h, but it may be less. On other roads it is 90 km/h, on dual carriageways 110 km/h, and on motorways 130 km/h. At this speed you will be overtaken by almost every other car, and you are unlikely to be in trouble if you keep at around 140 km/h, but keep your eyes open for motorcycle traffic police.

Signposting

Roads are usually well signposted, although the system is not consistent. Some signs point slightly or frankly down the road to the destination they name while others, admittedly easier to read, lie at right angles to the correct road, which is behind the sign, not to the left where it seems to point.

Priority

Be sure to respect the law of *priorité à droite*, which means that you must give way to any vehicle coming from your right. If you infringe this law, you will be held responsible for any consequent accident. The only exceptions to this rule are on main roads where a sign with a broad arrow crossing a thin line, or an alternative sign of a yellow diamond, indicate that you are on a main road with priority over a side road beyond the sign. A yellow diamond cancelled with a black line shows that you do *not* have priority.

Remember that great stretches of Brittany and Normandy are farming country, and on those picturesque minor roads there may be a slowly moving tractor or a lorry loaded with fruit or vegetables just round a blind bend. Place yourself carefully, and anticipate the worst.

Parking

The police are now quite strict about parking offences but are rather more lenient towards tourists in resort towns. In towns with a mainline station it is worth trying the station car park, normally free, and often with space available between major train arrivals, sometimes hours apart.

Park your car carefully overnight, and take everything of value out of it. Car break-ins are so commonplace, particularly in the Channel ports, that the police merely shrug their shoulders. It is wise to choose a hotel with private lock-up parking – in the modern chains this is often free. Otherwise leave nothing of value visible and park in the best-lit place available.

Garages

If you find your car needs attention, do not hesitate to take it to a local garage. Workmanship is first-class and labour costs about half those in Britain. If you have a French car, it is not a bad idea to have it serviced by the local dealer for that make. It will be much better done at a far cheaper rate than in the average British garage. You can normally have it back on the day you put it in.

Petrol

There is no standard price for petrol in France, it is always more expensive than in Britain, and most expensive on autoroutes. The cheapest petrol is usually found in the stations attached to large hypermarkets, and unleaded petrol is always the cheapest kind. If you intend to drive off the beaten track on a Sunday, make sure you have enough in the tank when you start, for many petrol stations are closed on Sunday even in summer, and finding one open in country districts is a matter of luck.

Autoroutes

Autoroutes are best avoided altogether on the Fridays, Saturdays and Sundays closest to 2, 15 and 31 August, when most of the French population is either going on holiday or is on the way back, and the tailbacks at key points are up to 20 km long.

Car hire

As an alternative to taking your own car, a number of fly–drive arrangements are available through airlines or tour operators, or you can hire a car on arrival in France. Costs vary considerably according to the car hire agency, the type of car and the length of time it will be needed. Weekly rates with unlimited mileage are the best bargain. There are exceptions, but in general you have to be between twenty-three and sixty-five to hire a car.

Road signs

Chaussée déformée – uneven road surface and/or edges for the distance shown

Travaux – road works

Fin de chantier – end of road works

Nids de poules – potholes

Déviation – diversion

Cycling

Both Normandy and Brittany offer great tracts of good cycling country, with fine scenery and few steep hills. As cycling is the national sport, motorists are considerate towards cyclists. If you take a British-made bike to France, it is a good idea to have spare tyres with you, because readily available French sizes may be different. Cyclists are welcomed as customers in hotels and restaurants, where the management will be happy to find a safe place for your machine. Cycle touring holidays with holiday accommodation (and baggage transport) can be booked in Britain.

By bus

Apart from services taking children to and from school, and in the larger towns services used by workers travelling to and from their place of work, bus services are very limited in France. Long distance services are so infrequent as to make organising a bus tour almost impossible. On the whole it is better for tourists to forget about buses.

By taxi

Taxis can only be had at a taxi rank, and they are not allowed to pick up passengers anywhere else. At the time of writing the pick-up charge is 11 francs and then from 3.50 francs per km according to region. In all except the largest cities the kilometre rate is in fact double the basic charge, because there is often only one taxi rank and the driver cannot get another fare until he returns to it, so you have to pay for both directions. Check that the taxi does have a meter, and for long journeys discuss the charge with the driver before starting.

By train

The high speed TGV network serves Brittany. With trains running up to 300 km/h, Rennes is reached from Paris in only two hours. Although France has a fast, clean and punctual rail service between major towns, there are many smaller towns which no longer have any rail service at all. If you do wish to travel between towns by rail, check whether you qualify for a discount – there are many special tickets for the young and old, and for families. All tickets must be stamped in the orange machine marked *Compostez votre billet* beside the entrance to the platform. It is an offence not to do this.

Full details of the range of tickets available can be obtained at any mainline SNCF station, or from the SNCF office at 179 Piccadilly, London, W1V 0AL.

Where to Stay

Hotels

There is no country in the world that can offer a better range of hotels than France. They vary from those delightful family-run establishments where Papa is the chef and Mama watches over everything else with an eagle eye, to what the French still love to call the 'palace' hotel, incredibly luxurious and impossibly expensive.

Traditional hotels and *aubergos*

Though there have been great changes in the French hotel scene, and there are now ever-expanding groups of modern hotels all over France, there are still a great many of the traditional family-run hotels throughout the countryside of Brittany and Normandy. Many of them these days, though by no means all, are members of the *Logis de France* organisation (see p. 57). The great advantage for the holiday-maker of the traditional French inn is that it represents the 'real' France, rather than the functional but anonymous standards of the 'modern' chain hotel, characteristic of no particular country and to be found almost everywhere. In contrast, the typical *auberge* remains individual, though they often have certain things in common: a flowery terrace with tables shaded by coloured parasols, a dining room on the sombre side, with a beamed ceiling, a range of copper pots and some old farm implements as décor; and a grandfather clock which may or may not tell the time. The bedrooms have roomy double beds, the riotously flowered wallpaper found only in French farmhouses and hotel bedrooms, and wooden shutters to the windows. The bedrooms are often smaller than they once were, because one corner has been partitioned off to make a bath or shower room. But at its best, in a well-run hotel with friendly proprietors, the overall effect is charming.

Chain hotels

The chain hotels, and there are now many of them including Sofitel, Novotel, Mercure, Ibis, Climat, Campanile, Fimotel and others, are quite different. They have their advantages, but one thing they almost never are is charming. Their décor has been carried out by a professional team, the beams (when there are any) are plastic, and the restaurants often have more to do in appearance with those of California or Florida than France. At the lower end of the scale, the tight-budget versions of such hotels make little more than a gesture towards comfort. There is an *en suite* bathroom, but certainly not one in which cats could be swung. Children or small women can get into the bath, sitting up with knees bent, but six-foot men give up at a glance, only to find that the shower is at shoulder level.

The majority of the chain hotels outside the largest cities are meant for one-night or short-stay clients, businessmen or tourists on their way to another destination, and for visitors of this kind they are practical. The rooms are large enough, the beds are almost invariably comfortable, and the *en suite* bathroom, though rarely spacious, is usually satisfactory. The fact that when you have seen a hotel in one of these chains you have seen them all, is not necessarily a disadvantage, especially for the *en route* traveller. You know exactly what to expect, and at the end of a long day's motoring, many people do not want to take the gamble of looking for something which may be marvellous or may be a disaster.

On the other hand, these functional modern hotels add very little to the pleasure of a holiday, whereas a stop in a good traditional hotel, carefully chosen and booked in advance, on the way to a final holiday destination, can add interest and pleasure to a holiday and make it seem longer.

Star rating   Hotels in France are placed in official categories from one star to four star luxe, but this classification should be taken into consideration only in the most general way. It is sensible to expect a four-star hotel to be better, as well as a lot more expensive, than a one-star hotel. On the other hand, it does not necessarily follow that for any particular client a two-star hotel is better than a one-star, or a three-star better than a two-star. This is because the official classification is based on the physical nature of the hotel and its amenities, and has nothing to do with its 'atmosphere' or the efficiency with which it is run, or whether it has a lovely view of the countryside, or overlooks a railway goods yard. Star rating is concerned with things like the number of bedrooms and their size, whether or not there are telephones in all bedrooms, the size of the reception area, what percentage of rooms have private bathrooms, numbers of lifts in relation to the number of floors, and so on. Even in one-star hotels more than thirty requirements are listed, more in higher grades. Some of the distinctions are of little interest to the holiday traveller, though they may matter to businessmen. No hotel, for example, can have two stars or more unless it has a telephone in every bedroom.

For a one-night stay, it is important to bear in mind that the best rooms in a one-star hotel will be better than some of the rooms in a two-star, and so on up the scale. The official classification does not help you with this, nor does it take good management into account, so a well-run two-star hotel may be noticeably better than an indifferently managed three-star. This is an important point in the modern chain hotels, which are all franchised, so that much depends on the couple in charge. Guides that specialise in hotels and restaurants can be useful because they do consider these points.

Choosing a hotel

In France, you have the right to look at any room offered to you and to ask to see another one if it does not suit you. It is a good idea to exercise this right, because it is part of the French way of life that everyone is expected to look after his own interests. To the French mind, not looking at something you are going to pay for is as good as saying that you don't care, and so you are more likely to be given a room next to a lift or a public bathroom, or just above the back entrance where the rubbish is collected at five in the morning, or facing an all night garage across the street – the other side of the corridor may have rooms overlooking a peaceful garden and with a view across the countryside. It is, perhaps, not so necessary to inspect rooms in the modern chains, as in any particular hotel most rooms are identical, but the question of noise still arises, so ask for a quiet room when booking in. If for some reason you do not like it, you can always go back to reception and ask to change.

Do not expect too much of a hotel which has a tatty reception area. The style, character and standards of a hotel are always focused there. In a large hotel the smartness of the doormen, lift boys, receptionists, furnishing and décor, the degree of tidiness, state of the carpets and ashtrays, missing light bulbs – a dozen different things combine to produce an effect. What you see there is likely to be repeated elsewhere in the hotel.

In the traditional family-run hotel, similar things apply on a smaller scale, and the welcome you receive counts for much. In the chain hotels you are anonymous, a room number, a credit card number. In the smaller hotels, after a night or two you are greeted by name and with a smile.

In many of the country hotels a double room will have a double bed, and if you prefer twin beds it is important to say so at the time of booking (ask for *une chambre à deux lits* or *des lits jumeaux*). In the chain hotels there are rather more twin-bedded rooms, and in some rooms there may be a double and a single bed, or a convertible sofa which can be made up into an additional bed. Some of the big chains (eg Novotel, Climat, Campanile) do not charge extra for children under eleven years old in their parents' room.

Prices

Until a few years ago hotel prices in France were controlled by the government, and a small percentage increase was authorised each year, but this restriction has now been lifted and competition is the only control. Repeat business is important to all hotels, especially those outside large cities, and for this reason, in resorts or country towns where there are several hotels, you can expect prices to be similar for comparable accommodation.

In the gazetteer section of this guide a representative cross section of hotels is suggested for each area. There are good reasons for each selection, but the choice is not intended to be comprehensive (many people do not realise that there are a good many hotels which are not in the red Michelin guide, or even that many towns and villages with acceptable hotels are not listed in it).

Hotels in modern chains such as those already mentioned, and those in marketing chains such as Mapotel, Inter Hotel, Best Western and *Logis de France* can normally be relied upon to be satisfactory and price-competitive, though a lot still depends on individual managers. Some are a good deal more efficient all round than others.

Logis de France

What exactly is a *Logis de France*? It is a small, privately owned hotel or inn situated in a village, small town, or in the countryside itself, which belongs to the *Logis de France* association, which is itself a marketing organisation. There are more than 4,000 hotels and 500 *auberges* (inns too small to be classified with hotels) throughout France affiliated to the organisation. Membership has often enabled proprietors to borrow money at favourable rates of interest to upgrade their hotels, particularly in providing better bathroom and sanitation facilities. In return for marketing services which include listing in an annual guide, *Logis de France* members pay an annual subscription and undertake to adhere to a quality charter which guarantees a warm personal welcome to guests, comfortable accommodation in accordance with their tourist star rating, cooking which features regional dishes and the chef's own specialities, and prices which include service.

Most *Logis de France* hotels are fairly modest one- or two-star establishments, and they are normally required to be in a tranquil situation, but this is not always the case. The annual handbook, which can be obtained from the French Government Tourist Office, Maison de France, 178 Piccadilly, London W1V 0AL, includes some hotels on main roads and on the edge of large towns, so check when you reserve if you want somewhere peaceful.

Booking hotel rooms

There was no need a few years ago to book hotels in advance when travelling through France; it was usually quite safe to start looking for that night's hotel early the same evening. This is no longer the case during the June to September holiday season. The problem is aggravated in high summer because some French motorists reserve in two or three hotels spaced out along their route, uncertain of which one they will reach. In order to cover themselves against those who do not turn up, the hoteliers are obliged to overbook and indulge in guesswork, which sometimes leads to difficulties all round. Wherever possible, the hotel suggestions in this guide include at least one hotel with a fair number of rooms, on the grounds that it will be more likely to have one available. Other criteria which have been taken into account include the existence of a good restaurant in or near the hotel, pleasant grounds, swimming pools, shady terraces and attractive views, all of which can add enjoyment even to a brief stay.

The best procedure is to book in advance, if possible at least a day ahead. French hoteliers normally ask when you expect to arrive. The answer to this does not matter much if you are booking into one of the chain hotels, but in the smaller, more traditional hotels, if you arrive much later than the time you have given you may find the room has been disposed of. So, if you are going to be late, confirm the booking while you are *en route* and give a new arrival time. Private hotels with their own restaurant will also ask whether you intend to have dinner. It is better to answer yes to this question. If you say no, you may well find that the hotel is fully booked. Someone who rings five minutes after you saying that they do want dinner may well get a room.

On Saturdays and Sundays it is often possible to find a room, even in the height of the season, if you book ahead to one of the chain hotels. This is because many of them are situated in the *zones industrielles* on the edge of larger towns, and most of their clients are businessmen, who do not use them at weekends. Some of the smaller traditional hotels whose restaurant is used by businessmen during the week may close it on Sunday evenings, especially outside the summer holiday season.

If a hotel has private parking it is sensible to use it, even if there is a small charge. If you are obliged to leave your car parked in the street near your hotel, take your luggage and valuables with you into the hotel, and leave the car in the best-lit spot you can find (see also Travelling Around, p. 51).

Hotel breakfasts can be surprisingly expensive, particularly continental breakfast taken in your room, which is expensive for what you get and has room service added. The enticing help-yourself-to-everything buffet breakfast which is now the rule in the modern hotels has everything from ham and cheese for the German tourists, to cornflakes and boiled eggs for the British, plus fruit and yoghourt and a great deal besides – excellent for those who like a hearty breakfast, but do not expect to pay less than about 35 francs per head. It is more economical not to take it, but to stop *en route* for coffee and croissants at the first likely-looking café.

Booking in English
Almost fifty hotel groups with hotels in France have representatives or offices in Britain through which room reservations can be made in English. They include such large chains as Ibis/Arcade, Campanile, Climat de France, Interhotel and Novotel. Most of the tourist-orientated departments of France have set up officially backed booking services, called *Loisirs Accueil*, who will reserve hotel rooms and, in some cases, *gîtes* or camp sites, and usually charge no fee for the booking. Some of these services will not book more than five days in advance. A list of *Loisirs Accueil* services, and of hotel groups with offices in Britain, can be obtained on request (sae) from the French Government Tourist Office, Maison de France, 178 Piccadilly, London W1V 0AL.

Apartment hotels

There are some apartment hotels – blocks of self-catering flats with some hotel facilities such as reception and cleaning – in the main tourist areas of Brittany and Normandy. They are often called *Résidences de Tourisme*, and the flats can be booked by the day, the week or the month. In some cases they consist of cottages rather than flats. There are a number of them on the southern coast of Brittany. Full information of what is available can be obtained from the *Syndicat d'Initiative* in the main town of the area which interests you.

Camping

The whole region is a camper's paradise, with hundreds of official camp sites by beaches, on riversides and in the deep country. They are classfied from one to four stars. The one-star sites have road access and all the essentials, though comfort is basic. The three- and four-star camps have numbered places and facilities such as security guards, snack bars or restaurants, and sometimes a laundry room.

In addition to the classified camp sites there are also facilities for the true camper who uses a tent. These are either camping areas called *Aire naturelle de camping* and often indicated by a wigwam sign, set aside for the purpose in open country, limited to twenty-five installations per hectare, and with piped water, showers and basic sanitation, or camping on farms, sign *Camping à la Ferme*, approved by the National Federation of *Gîtes de France*. On these sites there are six places each of 300 sq m for not more than twenty campers, and a sanitary block. There are also some *Camping Rural* sites, for not more than twenty campers, only 100 sq m per place, and arbitrary sanitation.

If you see a farm field or other spot where you would like to camp, it is inadvisable to do so without first asking permission from the owner. Farmers' dogs can be extremely aggressive with strangers, and so can some farmers. Almost all French farmers have guns, and some open their conversation with them. As most people who have been shot at leave rather quickly, it saves wasted time and words.

Camping season

Many of the official camp sites, especially those in resort areas, have an extremely short season, in some cases only from the end of the first week in July to the end of August. Some open earlier but almost all close as soon as the children return to school at the beginning of September. Most of those which stay open outside these dates, and there are some which are open all the year, are the *Camping Municipals* belonging to and usually on the outskirts of a town or village. Some of these are very well sited, and most of them are of the two-star level. Outside the holiday season you can drive into these camps and pick your own spot, and often nobody bothers to collect a fee.

Booking

If you plan a camping holiday in July or August, you should either book ahead or, better still, take a camping package from one of the numerous British companies which specialise in such holidays. There are some cowboys in this business, so try to pick a company with a good reputation and years of experience. One of the best is Canvas Holidays of Bull Plain, Hertford, Hertfordshire, who have a choice of hand-picked camps throughout the area. Operators of this kind look after your ferry crossing and any *en route* hotel bookings, and provide a spacious, well fitted-out tent at the site and a resident courier to iron out any problems. Purists who like to do things on their own and take off into the wild blue yonder may find that it is a bit more yonder than they thought if they have not booked somewhere. Better to take a camping guide and use it to book from one stop to the next.

Villas, flats and country cottages

The great advantage of a holiday in a rented country cottage, or a flat or villa by the sea is the freedom to do what you want when you want, without being tied to hotel routines. Another aspect which makes the holiday more of an adventure is that you are really living in France, doing your own shopping, going to market, eating out in your own choice of restaurants, or trying your hand at local specialities at home.

Gîtes ruraux

Brittany and Normandy have a great deal of holiday accommodation of all kinds for rent. Country cottages are known as *gîtes ruraux* (*gîte* alone means a lodging of any kind), and a number of British tour operators specialise in package holidays in these country cottages. As well as the accommodation, the holiday price includes the Channel crossing, insurance and documentation giving advice on routes and driving times, as well as recommending overnight hotels which have been vetted by the tour operator. Most important of all, because this is now a highly competitive business, the operators are able to impose their standards on the *gîte* owners in the contracts they sign with them. Regular inspections are carried out to see that the proprietors do maintain standards, and unsatisfactory *gîtes* are dropped.

Most of the *gîtes ruraux* have been converted from farm cottages or farm outbuildings. The average French peasant farmer is rather closer to his money than a coat of paint to a wall. Generations of experience have taught them that they cannot expect a good crop if they do not spend money on seed and fertiliser, and it looks as if it will take generations before they learn the same lesson in respect of tourism. Left to themselves they would spend nothing on improving existing properties, except in the most basic fashion. I have seen alleged *gîtes* with huge patches of mildew on the walls and furniture with corners propped up on old books.

The French government, well aware of this state of affairs, took the initiative some years ago by offering loans at advantageous rates to farmers ready to create holiday homes in the countryside. *Gîtes de France* is an association of such properties, and hundreds of them are listed in an annual handbook which can be obtained from the French Government Tourist Office in London (see p. 57 for address). Owners who have taken advantage of the loan scheme have to undertake to let their properties through *Gîtes de France* for a number of years, so there is always a large number of such *gîtes*. Despite the improvements, however, there is still a big difference in the levels of amenities provided. The earlier you book, the better the choice.

The best *gîtes* in most areas are taken by British tour operators. This is because they can guarantee a longer letting season than the owners would get with French holiday-makers. The pioneers in this field were *Vacances Franco-Brittaniques* of Cheltenham, and they are still the specialists, with over a hundred selected *gîtes* in Normandy and Brittany alone.

There are people who do not like to organise holidays too much in advance. France is one of the few countries where you can, with luck, enjoy an off-the-cuff holiday, just taking the car across the Channel and looking for accommodation once you have disembarked. Local Tourist Offices or *Syndicat d'Initiatives* usually have a list of *gîtes* in their area, may have their own system of classification indicating the level of comfort, and may know which are free. But it is very much a question of pot luck, and in the high season you will be getting the leavings, if any. Either side of the season is much safer.

Resort flats and villas

There are also tour operators who offer villas or flats in seaside resorts. Villas and flats can also be rented directly from estate agents (*agents immobiliers*) in resort towns. A politely worded letter to a local Tourist Office or *Chambre de Commerce* saying that you want to rent a flat or villa should bring a helpful reply. It is as well to write well in advance as there is keen competition in the summer season, and to indicate your readiness to pay the usual deposit in advance in French francs. It is necessary to go to some trouble for high-season bookings, and it helps if you have a friend resident in France who is willing to help, but the arrangement has the advantage that all you pay is the rent of the villa, irrespective of the numbers in your party, and this is likely to be less than the cost of buying a package holiday each. In any sizeable resort, outside July/August it is probably sufficient just to walk into an *agent immobilier*'s office and ask. He will almost certainly have a choice to offer you.

Eating and Drinking

Traditional French cuisine is the finest in the western world and, if the overall impact has been somewhat diluted in recent years by the spread of American-style fast-food restaurants, snack bars, and by restaurateurs who have become cynical as a result of the increase in numbers of undemanding tourists, there remain thousands of the old-style, serious restaurants throughout France.

When I say 'old style', I do not mean that old. In the nineteenth century the food available in French hotels was universally considered to be poor, when it was not awful, and it is really only in the past fifty years that this has changed. A traveller who made a tour of Normandy early this century wrote, 'There is something unsatisfying about the dinner menu at a French hotel. The monotonous soup, always thin; the dull variety of nameless white fish, which seems to be kept in stock as a staple; the little tasteless pieces of veal, all the same size and shape ready cut on a dish; the leathery and half-raw mutton, cut in the same way; the very small variety of vegetables, and the utter absence of an attempt at sweets is not an appetising menu.' He was writing in 1905 and quoted a traveller of eighty years previously who said almost exactly the same thing, with the added comment that the dinner was the same in each hotel he stopped in and that breakfast was always exactly the same as dinner. Happily things have changed very much for the better, but it is interesting that it is only very recently that guide books have made any reference to French food, or restaurants. Authors writing only twenty or thirty years ago, apart from the occasional adverse comment, never mentioned the subject.

Prices Although there have been changes in French restaurants in recent times, one thing has not changed. It is still possible, even usual, to eat very well but inexpensively. Prices have gone up certainly, but not at the same rate as in Britain, and it is roughly true to say that for a good meal in a traditional restaurant you pay half what you would in Britain, less if you include a reasonable wine. There are still country restaurants where you can have a three-course meal, with the patron's choice of wine included, for 60 francs per head. They are becoming less common, but 65 francs is not unusual at the time of writing. Some of the very best restaurants have menus at about 100 francs on weekdays. Many restaurants, though not all, drop their cheapest menu on Sundays.

Local cuisine

With the exception of the region around Lyon, the cuisine of Normandy and Brittany probably contributes more to the high reputation of modern French cuisine than that of any other part of France. They both offer the best of all kinds, superb fish from their own coastal waters, top quality beef from their own farms, lamb from the salt meadows in the south of the Cotentin and Morbihan, game birds and venison from the forests of Normandy, and hares, partridges and other game from the moors of Brittany. To go with all this are apples, pears and cherries from the vast orchards, and all the desserts made from them, and the fresh spring vegetables from the market gardens of Brittany.

Norman cooking is rich and delicious, with sauces based on milk, fresh cream, butter, cheese and cider. Like all cuisines which feature rich and complicated sauces, that of Normandy runs the risk of allowing good sauces to disguise second-rate materials, and the further risk that, because many of the typical dishes are, from the restaurateur's point of view, complicated and expensive to produce, corners will be cut. There is often a shortfall, for example, between the *sole Dieppoise* which you get in an average restaurant and the real thing, which is elaborate and expensive both for the restaurateur and the customer.

But the raw materials are themselves so good – the sole, turbot, sea trout, mussels, beef, lamb and chicken of Normandy, and the same again in Brittany plus the whole gamut of shellfish from lobsters down, and the famous Nantais ducks – that it is a poor chef who cannot please his customers in this region. The cuisine of Brittany is similar to that of Normandy, though less rich and emphatic, and it is a great mistake to think that the only thing worth eating in Brittany is fish. The Bretons themselves are sharply divided between the inland farmers, who rarely eat fish, and the coastal communities where many people do eat fish, but only on Fridays, or special occasions.

Crêperies

Holiday-makers do not always want three- or four-course meals, and very few areas of France are better equipped than Brittany with cafés, snack bars, pizzerias and, above all, *crêperies*. Brittany is the home of the *crêpe*, where it exists in endless variety. Basically, there are two kinds, those made from buckwheat flour which are given all kinds of savoury fillings, such as cheese, prawns, mussels, crab etc, and those made from ordinary white flour given sweet fillings such as chocolate sauce, honey and syrup, and offered as desserts. Some *crêperies* are as well furnished as restaurants, but they are not substitutes for them, and despite their often delicious flavour *crêpes* are not satisfying, and are disappointing for hungry people. Those mothers who still make jam or lemon pancakes on Shrove Tuesday will know how many two or three hungry children can get through before they have had enough – it's the same with *crêpes*, and those bought in a real *crêperie* can become poor value for money. Those bought from market stalls are often just as good and much cheaper. Visitors on self-catering holidays should try some of the excellent cakes and biscuits, made with plenty of the local butter, for which Brittany is known all over France.

Hotel restaurants

As there are many holiday resorts in Normandy and Brittany, and many resort hotels, it may be useful to point out that resort hotel restaurants differ from all other restaurants in that they have a captive 'audience', that is, consumers with no choice. Many resort hotels in France, especially the smaller ones, require their guests to take at least half-board. They may well be open to the public, but at any time, particularly in the summer season, a high percentage of diners are residents of the hotel. A consequence of this is that the chef may have become used to aiming rather less high than he would have to do in a competitive restaurant which has to attract new customers every day. There are, of course, some resort hotels, usually the best and most expensive, which have good restaurants.

On the other hand, hotels in country towns and villages often have excellent restaurants because they have a passing, not a captive trade, and a good restaurant attracts clients all year round to stay in the hotel. These hotels, which depend on French businessmen as much as on tourists, are among the best places to eat, particularly when there are two or three in competition in the town centre.

Restaurants

There are also restaurants, often good or very good, which offer rooms as well. Although the rooms may be comfortable, or even in some cases luxurious, such establishments do not call themselves hotels, because they lack some of the recognised amenities of a hotel. The most usual reason is that there is an inadequate reception area, or no public lounges, or limited bathroom arrangements. Some of the finest restaurants in France fall into this category, and include among their customers serious gourmets who like to eat and drink their fill, and have no wish to go anywhere after dinner except to bed.

Most French restaurants away from big cities aim to offer sound cuisine to regular customers, local inhabitants and businessmen, and tourists who may come back another day. They have no pretensions to *haute cuisine*, though they may offer very good cooking based on the products and traditions of their region. There are many restaurants of this kind throughout Normandy and Brittany.

Haute cuisine

Then there is a minority of restaurants which go in for *haute cuisine* and which are picked out by stars, rosettes, chef's hats etc in the popular guides specialising in restaurants. Some of the ambitious chefs in these restaurants are satisfied with their classification, and to maintain that standard. There are others who are constantly trying to add another symbol to prove their excellence and, of course, to enable them to put up their prices. It is in these restaurants, while they are on their way up, that you eat best of all. In cooking, as in mountain climbing, when you reach the top there is nowhere to go but down, but at the right moment and sometimes for years on end these restaurants offer you the choice of eating and drinking marvellously well at reasonable prices – they are never cheap – or of spending a great deal of money on a meal which may include some of the chef's specialities, rarities, and superb vintage wines. There are not many such restaurants in the region covered by this book, but they do exist. What you will find in both Brittany and Normandy is a large number of establishments where the cooking is well above average, and many more where you will get good food at moderate prices.

Relais Routiers

No chapter on eating out in France should omit a mention of the *Relais Routiers*, those restaurants originally meant for and still very largely used by the long distance lorry drivers (*routiers*). They normally offer exceptional value for money, in a rather noisy and jovial atmosphere. They do have menus, but the great attraction is the *plat du jour*, and any lorry driver who regularly follows the same routes knows what will be on offer each day of the week in each *Relais Routier* on his road. Like all other workmen in France, he stops for lunch at 12 noon, and he will arrive at his chosen *Relais Routier* within a few minutes of that time, to make sure he gets that *plat du jour*. Those who arrive late, including tourists, will be likely to find there is none left. There will be a choice of other dishes, but the one the chef really worked on will be finished. A corollary of this is that if you are thinking of lunch and see a *Relais Routier* at 12.15 with only two lorries outside it, don't bother to stop. It is not likely to be good.

Menus gastro-nomique

In Normandy and Brittany, as in all other regions of France, many restaurants offer a *menu gastronomique*. The majority of such menus are nothing of the kind. Gastronomy means the 'art or science of good eating', and a gastronomic meal should be one in which rare quality is allied to simplicity with a touch of originality – quantity has nothing to do with it. It should be built around one superb dish, accompanied by a good wine. Some gourmets would put it the other way round, and say a superb bottle of wine with a couple of good courses matched to it. I have heard great chefs say that they would like to dictate to their clients what wine they should drink with their specialities, but as they are in business they cannot afford to, and they suffer as some clients get it hopelessly wrong.

'Gastronomic' menus have nothing to do with these concepts. They concern quantity rather than quality, and simply have five or six courses instead of three. The average chef in an average restaurant does not become a culinary genius because he is preparing a *poulet Vallée d'Auge* for a 'gastronomic' menu. He does it as he always does it. The fondness of country restaurateurs for 'gastronomic' menus comes from two things: first, that it is part of peasant philosophy that the good life consists in eating and drinking a lot, and that is what they expect to do when they bring the family to a restaurant for a rare festive occasion; and secondly, they are more expensive. The customer gets more, but he also pays a lot more, and often the only thing to wonder at in a 'gastronomic' menu is the size of the bill.

In truth, all dishes produced by a good, conscientious chef are 'gastronomic', while those cooked by an indifferent chef never are, however copious. It is because there are still large numbers of discriminating clients in France, able to distinguish between the two, that it remains possible to eat so well in so many places.

Choosing a restaurant

The proof of the pudding is in the eating, and the only way to judge a restaurant is by what you get on your plate and how much you pay for it. So deciding where to eat in an unfamiliar place can be a problem, but as with hotels there are some pointers which may help. For instance, it is useful to know the car registration number of the department you are in (the last two figures): if you see a restaurant where the cars parked outside include several with this number, it shows that the locals think well of it.

Menus

By law, menus and prices, including supplements for special dishes, must be displayed outside restaurants. It is a good idea to look at the menus, not only to see what is listed but also to see how it is written and presented. I am put off by menus where the ink is so faded that the menu has evidently not been changed for months. It shows a certain amount of indifference and lack of enterprise, and a complete disregard for what may have been fresh in the market that day.

There is a lot to be said for a limited selection of menus, especially when it is neatly presented. As a rule they indicate prudent budgeting, and are to be preferred to those which seem to list every known variety of meat, fish, or fowl. Long menus mean large refrigerators, rather than plenty of fresh raw materials. Large restaurants can afford to have more varied menus, because of the more rapid turnover, but the principle remains the same – no chef does everything well. If in a strange place you find yourself with no choice but a restaurant which appears to be attempting too much, remember the refrigerators and take the *plat du jour*, or something popular and not too expensive.

Cutting costs

There are several ways of keeping down the cost of a meal. There are still many country restaurants where a carafe of wine is included in the price of the cheapest menu. Coffee is always an extra and can add 20 francs or more to a bill for two. It is never cheaper to eat the same dishes à la carte as you could have on the menu, but if you do not want a complete three- or four-course menu, it can be cheaper to eat just a main dish à la carte, or even one dish accompanied by a starter or a dessert. You are not obliged to take more than one dish, and desserts are often overpriced.

If you are going to drink wine with a meal, it is better, unless you are celebrating, to take the reasonably priced house wine than to pay three times or more (I have seen six times) the retail price for an ordinary wine. Restaurants which have a good local business trade would never get it without a reliable house wine.

Variations

French restaurateurs are flexible and reasonable, so it is always worth asking for a variation from what is offered. If, for example, there is one course in a menu which you do not like, you can always ask to take something from the à la carte instead. If it is more expensive you will be charged the appropriate supplement; if they are the same price, it will just be changed.

A lot of people prefer fish or meat plain grilled rather than with a rich sauce. If you are one of them, ask for it to be served *nature*. This is the usual term for something without sauce or dressing. All good restaurants will be happy to make minor adjustments of this sort to suit the customer. In many restaurants flexibility extends to other arrangements. French couples will often share one menu between them, or share a *plateau de fruits de mer* for one person as a starter for two, or one will order a three-course menu and the other just one dish à la carte, and the one who has the menu gives either a starter or a dessert to his partner, so that both have two courses. There is no reason why tourists should not do the same, just order two covers and tell the waiter what you want to do. In the great majority of restaurants there will be no objection.

All meat in French restaurants, including game and even duck, will be undercooked and bloody, unless you specify otherwise. When the order for roast or grilled meat is taken, you will be asked how you want it cooked. The recognised grades are: *bleu* – lightly cooked on the outside but practically raw inside; *saignant* – rare or bloody; *à point* – medium; *bien cuit* – well done.

A final word which can help things to go smoothly. French waiters do not like to be addressed as *'Garçon!'*. What they do answer to is *'S'il vous plaît'*, or better still, *'S'il vous plaît, monsieur'*. Whistles and snapped fingers just brand the tourist as ignorant.

Menu vocabulary

Here are some of the less familiar terms which you may wonder about as you read restaurant menus.

À la Normande – with a sauce based on fresh cream.

Fish	*Bar* – sea bass. Usually very good.

Bar – sea bass. Usually very good.

Barbue – brill, a flat fish like turbot, but smaller.

Bigorneaux – winkles.

Brandade – a kind of fish pie made from dried cod (*morue*), potatoes and some garlic.

Bulots – whelks.

Cabillaud – fresh cod.

Coques – cockles.

Coquilles St Jacques – scallop.

Crevettes grises – shrimps. *Crevettes roses* – prawns.

Dorade – sea bream. The *royale* and *rosé* (red sea bream) are better than the grey.

Écrevisses – freshwater crayfish. A small relative of the lobster, good but needs patience.

Homard – lobster.

Huîtres – oysters.

Langouste – spiny, or rock, lobster.

Langoustine – scampi or Dublin Bay prawn.

Lieu – coley. Rather more esteemed in France than in Britain.

Lotte – monkfish. So is this.

Moules – mussels.

Palourdes – clams (also called *praires*).

Rouget – red mullet. Really a Mediterranean fish, rare in the north.

Truite – trout. *Truite au bleu* is not undercooked, but cooked in a *court-bouillon* based on white wine and herbs, after being rolled in vinegar, which turns it blue.

Sandre – zander (pike-perch). A good freshwater fish.

Poultry and game

Bécasse – woodcock.

Caille – quail.

Chevreuil – young roe deer. Served roast or stewed. Less gamey than true venison (*venaison*).

Civet – a stew of rabbit (*lapin*), hare (*lièvre*), or young wild boar (*marcassin*). Always prepared with red wine and some blood in the sauce, like jugged hare. Stewed rabbit in white wine sauce is called *gibelotte de lapin*.

Confit – joints of goose, duck, chicken or pork, cooked in their own fat and then bottled in it. Served reheated with sliced potatoes, which absorb the fat and should leave the *confit* crisp. A speciality of the South West but also found in Normandy.

Offal

Andouille – a large sausage made from finely chopped chitterlings. Usually sliced and served cold as a starter. *Andouillette* is a smaller version, normally served hot as a main course. Those made in the Vire and Caen regions of Normandy are considered the best.

Boudin noir – black pudding, a speciality of the Perche region of southern Normandy.

Cervelles – brains (usually *cervelles d'agneau*, lamb's brains).

Foie – liver. *Foie de veau* – calf's liver.

Foie gras – the liver of force-fed geese (*oies*) or ducks (*canards*), cooked and served without sauce. *Foie gras rosé* is very lightly cooked, not far from raw. Although a speciality of the South West and Strasbourg regions, it is becoming more common in Normandy, where it is usually duck's liver, which is prepared by being marinated for six hours with sliced apple and *pommeau* (a mixture of apple juice and calvados) before being pressed into the terrine and cooked.

Ris d'agneau – lamb's sweetbreads. Note that *ris* with an 's' means sweetbreads and should not be confused with *riz* with a 'z', which means rice.

Rognons – kidneys.

Meat	*Agneau* – lamb. Usually the best bet in French meat.

Jambon – ham. *Jambon blanc* or *jambon de Paris* is like York ham. *Jambon de pays* or *jambon de campagne* is salt-cured, country-made ham. It varies: some is excellent, and some is more suited to shoe-mending than eating.

Sanglier – boar. Not always wild, some is raised on farms.

Vegetables	*Asperges* – asparagus.

Champignons – mushrooms. Several kinds are served in restaurants, *cèpes* and *morilles* are the most usual, both excellent.

Choufleur – cauliflower. Both this and asparagus are very common in Brittany.

Oseille – sorrel. A popular soup is made from this in Normandy.

Cheese	Poems have been written about the cheeses of Normandy and

encyclopaedias could be compiled about their variety. France is the world's third-largest producer of milk, and an awful lot of it is made into cheese, a good deal of it in this part of northern France.

The four great cheeses of Normandy are Pont l'Éveque, Livarot, Neufchâtel and, of course, Camembert. The first two date back to the thirteenth century, and Neufchâtel has also been made for hundreds of years. Camembert is a village in the Pays d'Auge, near Vimoutiers, and the now famous cheese was perfected there in the farm of Beaumoncel, which still exists today, by the farmer's wife, Marie Harel. She is said to have received the recipe from a priest whom she sheltered during the French Revolution. But Camembert owes its universal fame to a sawmill employee named Georges Leroy who, in 1890, invented the light, round wooden boxes which enabled it to be sent anywhere. Until very recently Camembert was the only one of these great cheeses not to have an *Appellation d'Origine Controlée*. It was imitated in factories all over France, but the real thing comes from Normandy, from the Pays d'Auge in the department of Calvados.

Pont l'Éveque, which is usually factory made these days, and Neufchâtel, a similar cheese, really should be made from fresh milk still warm from the cow, and there is a variety of Pont l'Éveque called Trouville which is still made on farms in this way. Other cheeses which belong in the Pont l'Éveque/Neufchâtel family, are Carré de Bray, Mignot and Pavé d'Auge.

Livarot is a cheese with a flavour rather more delicate than its ripe and aggressive smell – it is matured in a cave for at least a month. So popular in the nineteenth century that it was known as the working man's meat, Livarot is now much appreciated by gourmets.

Other well-known Normandy cheeses include Bricquebec, a yellow, fairly strong cheese developed by the Trappist monks of Bricquebec Abbey who have a famous dairy herd managed by the most up-to-date methods, including computerised feeding. Brillat-Savarin is a delicious, mild triple-cream cheese invented in the 1930s by a member of the Androuet family, who still have a famous cheese shop and cheese restaurant in the Rue Amsterdam in Paris. Excelsior and Lucullus are similarly creamy and very fatty (75 per cent) – cheeses of the same kind as that named after Brillat-Savarin, the great gastronome, whose book *The Physiology of Taste* really started the movement towards better cooking in France.

Two well-known soft cheeses which originated in Normandy and are still made there, as well as all over France, are *demi-sel*, a mild, uncured cheese with a little salt, and Petit-Suisse, a fresh, unsalted cheese, delicious with brown sugar or honey. These are just a few of the many cheeses made in Normandy. Any village market will have others, made and brought in for sale by the farmers' wives themselves.

A good cheese board is one of the most difficult things for a restaurateur to maintain and any restaurant which consistently serves a fair selection of cheeses in good condition is being well run. Except for those diners addicted to ammonia, it is a mistake to eat cheese which is over-ripe and runny, as the fine distinctions of flavour between one cheese and another are completely lost. Cheese in this condition is called *bien fait* or *trop fait*, a cheese which is just right is called *à point*, and one which is on the young side is *pas trop fait*.

Desserts

One thing you will never go short of in Normandy is apple tart, served, of course, with fresh cream. It comes in all sizes and several different recipes, including apple turnovers, and is the chief stand-by for desserts. *Crêpes* with sweet fillings, and a rather special rice pudding flavoured with cinnamon called *tergoule*, are other favourites.

Drinks with a difference
Cider

The people of Normandy and Brittany do drink wine, at least some of them do, sometimes, but cider is the champagne of this part of France. The ordinary, everyday drink is dry cider, made with water added to the juice of the pressing. In the bottle it is still, but is very gently sparkling in the glass. On anniversaries, feast days and any other time when it seems a good idea, a somewhat more robust version is brought out.

According to the best Norman chefs, cider is the equal of champagne for use in cooking and it features, dry and sometimes sweet, in numerous recipes throughout the North West. The merits of this or that cider (or these or those apples) are topics for endless discussion, but in general in Normandy that from the Pays d'Auge is reckoned the best, and in Brittany those from Fouesnant, Beg-Meil and Pleudihen-sur-Rance are worthy of note.

Perry

A lot of pears are also grown in Normandy, particularly around Domfront in the south, and a lot of pear cider, or perry, is made from them. It is sweet and delicious and goes very well with desserts such as fruit tarts, but should be treated with caution as it goes to the head very quickly.

Calvados

No wine is produced in Normandy, but that does not mean that there is no brandy. Calvados, a brandy distilled from fermented apple juice, is still made on Norman farms, illegally. The more reliable stuff is produced commercially but even this, like any brandy in any country, can vary drastically. At its best, after four or five years in the cask, it can be very good, but it needs to be ten years old to have developed its full flavour and perfume. As with all brandies, the age is reckoned between when it was made and when it was bottled, in other words how long it spent in the cask. Unlike wine, it does not improve with bottle age. There are ten regions with a right to an *Appellation Reglementée* for their calvados, and the best is reckoned to be that from the Pays d'Auge.

The famous *trou normand* is a glass of calvados, taken half-way through a heavy meal, usually after the main course, to wake up the digestion and make room for the cheeses and rich desserts. Some restaurants now serve the *trou normand* as a few drops of calvados poured over an apple sorbet, an economy for the restaurateur but a pointless elaboration from the diner's point of view, since anything cold inhibits the flow of digestive juices. Calvados is also served as a *digestif* at the end of a meal, and there are those who say that it prevents the increase of cholesterol levels in the blood. Like the Spaniards, many Normans enjoy a dash of brandy in their coffee, and a *café-calva* is popular as a breakfast or mid-morning drink.

Normandy is also the home of one of the world's great liqueurs, Bénédictine, made in Fécamp (see pp. 102–3) and bottled nearby in Tourville-les-Ifs. The Norman apéritif is *pommeau*, a drink made from a mixture of apple juice and calvados. The proportions vary from place to place but a quarter calvados is usual.

Wine

Cider is as popular in Brittany as in Normandy, but Brittany also makes wine. Muscadet, which has been an AoC wine for more than fifty years, is produced only in the Nantes region, but is drunk throughout Brittany. At its best it is a dry, fruity wine which goes well with fish and shellfish. Another old-established Breton wine – it has been cultivated in the Nantes region since the sixteenth century – is the Gros Plant du Pays Nantais. A VDQS wine, it is made from a different grape from that used to produce Muscadet. It gives a light, dry wine, with less body than Muscadet, but it also goes with shellfish and is ideal for a *plateau de fruits de mer.*

Some wine is still produced in the Morbihan, in the Rhuys peninsula, but according to a popular Breton saying you need four people and a wall when it is being drunk: one to pour it, one to drink it, two to hold him, and the wall to stop him falling backwards. But it makes a good brandy when distilled. They also drink mead in Brittany, which is as good as saying they will drink anything, and they make a good strawberry liqueur. I have heard rumours that there is even a Breton whisky, but I have not come across it yet.

Leisure and the Arts

Cinemas

There is no shortage of distractions anywhere in these regions. Even small country towns have their cinemas, discos and dancing clubs. Cinemas often have a choice of three or four films in different viewing rooms. Most are in French, but some films, usually American, are shown in English with French subtitles, and some are dubbed in French. Admission is about 40 francs.

Theatres

Some towns also have a theatre. Where they exist they are surprisingly active, with one-man shows by French comedians, singers and theatre or cinema stars, alternating with plays or, occasionally, concerts. Repertory theatres as such are rare but not unknown, and they reach a high standard.

Dancing and clubs

Apart from an annual music festival in July/August at Mont St Michel, and another at Rennes, also in the high season, there are fewer music festivals in the North West than in the tourist regions further south. Dancing of all kinds is popular in France, and the clubs and discos tend to go for their own special clientele. There are clubs for the traditional Bal Musette dancing, with accordion music, others where Latin American music is the strong point, and there are discos for youngsters, others with general appeal and others for homosexuals. It can be useful to have a local opinion before making a choice. The police keep an eye on discos and most of them are well run. Any over-exuberant behaviour is dealt with by bouncers, called *videurs*, and those that don't look that tough are all judo experts. The average admission charge to discos is 60 francs, which includes a drink.

Firework displays

Firework displays are very popular in France, and there are some superb displays during the summer, notably on 14 July and 15 August, when even villages put on their own displays, and those in the resort towns are really impressive.

Sport

Sailing

Sailing is the great leisure activity, particularly in Brittany, and there are numerous ports and marinas all round the many hundreds of miles of the north-west coast which are important centres. They do not exist only for tourists. Brittany, with its centuries-old tradition of seafaring, has thousands of sailing *aficionados* among its resident population. Tourists who do not have their own boat have a big choice of short and long sea trips in all the resorts.

Normandy, though with a shorter coastline and fewer marinas, has no less a tradition of the sea and in the St Malo and Le Havre areas, as well as Dieppe, there are extensive sailing facilities.

Water sports

Windsurfing, water-skiing, canoe-kayak, scuba diving and sea fishing are among other water sports practised all round the coast. Land yachting on three-wheeled frames with a large sail is also common, and high speeds are reached on the bigger beaches. Wind-skating, using a large skate-board with a sail attached which is manoeuvred like a windsurfer, is also popular. Protective clothing should be worn, as falling off is more dangerous than in the water.

Freshwater fishing

There is good freshwater fishing in the rivers, but it is strictly controlled and usually a permit to cover the season is required, though this may not be much more than the cost of a couple of organised sea-fishing trips. First inquiries should be made at your local tourist office or *Syndicat d'Initiative.*

Walking

Wherever you are inland in Normandy and Brittany, you will be close to ideal walking country. Several of the national footpaths (*Grandes Randonnées*) criss-cross the area, linking the great forests and following the coast or the river valleys. The GR22/223 follows the western and northern coast of the Cotentin from Mont St Michel to Barfleur; the GR21 follows the Lézarde valley to the coast and then along the cliff tops of the Seine Maritime to St Valéry-en-Caux; the GR2 wanders along the Seine valley, and the GR221 through the Suisse Normande. Among those which explore Brittany are GR37, 38 and 380. The special maps for walkers published by the French National Rambling Association are best obtained at good map shops in Britain, as they are always in very short supply on the spot in France.

Cycling and pony trekking

The countryside is also ideal for cycle tours and pony trekking and there are numerous centres for both.

Tennis

There are a great many tennis courts. La Baule is a famous centre and holds international competitions, but tennis throughout France is organised into clubs and the courts are not usually open to non-members. Rather than pay a full season's membership, the best thing to do, unless you are in a hotel with its own court, is to approach a nearby village club – even quite small villages in France now have good modern hard courts, some with floodlighting – and offer to pay for limited use. Many of them are glad of extra funds, and will allow you to play, particularly if you say you will not want to play in the evenings or at weekends, which is when their members have time to play. It is something which depends on the amiability of the club secretary. You may be lucky.

Golf

There are twenty-five 18-hole golf courses in Normandy and many more 9-hole courses, and as many again in Brittany.

Art

The clear light, the ever-changing skies, the shifting moods and colours of the sea, have for nearly 200 years attracted artists to the coasts of Normandy and Brittany.

Impressionism

On the outskirts of Honfleur, on the road to Trouville and on a hill overlooking the estuary of the Seine, there is today a rather grand hotel, the Ferme St Siméon et son Manoir. It has its covered swimming pool, its tennis courts and gardens overlooking the sea, and a superb restaurant. It was rather different more than a hundred years ago. It was the farm St Siméon even then, but in those days it was a simple *auberge* run by the Mère Toutain, who liked to welcome there a group of rather disreputable painters with names like Boudin, Jongkind, Corot, Sisley, Pisarro, Monet, Seurat, Marquet, Van Dongen and others. They talked about their art, and under the influence of Mère Toutain's cider became more and more relaxed and expansive. They went back to their studios and, abandoning the traditional French classical and historical approach to painting, began to paint in a more relaxed manner, which became known as Impressionism. Among their earliest efforts were views of the cliffs, beaches, estuaries and ports of the Normandy coast, and one of Courbet's paintings is called *Le Jardin de Mère Toutain*.

Richard Parkes Bonington

But they were not the first painters to have worked by the coasts and rivers of Normandy. Probably the first and certainly the most influential was the young Englishman, Richard Parkes Bonington, whose father, also a painter, had set up a lace-making factory in Calais and hoped that his young son would do the designing. But Bonington was one of the great natural geniuses in the history of painting. He turned his back on the factory and in less than ten years, between 1818–28 – he died of consumption at the age of twenty-five – produced a series of lovely oils and watercolours, magical combinations of strength, grace and charm, which so influenced French artists that painting in France took a new course. Monet, Corot and Delacroix were among French painters whose early style and development owed much to Bonington. Two well-known paintings by him, of Lillebonne and of Le Havre, have since disappeared, and may well still be hanging somewhere in Norman farmhouses.

Poussin, Géricault, Millet, who was from Cherbourg, and more recently Raoul Dufy, who was born in Le Havre, and Fernand Léger, were other great painters of Norman origin, though most of them made their way to Paris where it was easier to find buyers.

Galleries

Normandy is therefore a sort of promised land to those visitors interested in painting. The Musée des Beaux Arts in Rouen has one of the finest collections in Europe of works from the sixteenth century onwards. There are other splendid collections at the Musée André

Malraux in Le Havre, which includes many famous Impressionist works including Monet's *Towers of Westminster*. Among the paintings in the Musée des Beaux Arts in Caen, and the Musée Eugène Boudin in Honfleur, there are more than sixty works by Boudin. At Giverny, near Vernon, not far from the south-eastern limits of Normandy, the house where Claude Monet lived from 1883–1926 has been restored to its condition as he knew it, and the gardens are maintained exactly as they were when he made his famous studies of water lilies. The whole is open to the public as the Musée Claude Monet.

Pont Aven
Painting in Brittany is mainly associated with the attractive village of Pont Aven, situated where the river Aven becomes a tidal estuary. In the latter half of the nineteenth century it attracted numerous artists; in 1886 Paul Gauguin, already thirty-eight years old but at the beginning of his career as a professional painter, was one of a group of about twenty artists working in Pont Aven. He was unknown at the time, and stayed only a few months before leaving for the South Seas – the village has certainly capitalised on his later fame. The group of artists became known in retrospect as the School of Pont Aven, and today there are many picture galleries and frequent exhibitions; but the community does not possess a single Gauguin.

Literature

Normandy
From Pierre Corneille onwards the area has produced a succession of major writers. The great French dramatist was born in Rouen in 1606 and was educated at the Jesuit College there which has since become, as the Lycée Corneille, one of the best-known schools in France, whose students have included Flaubert, Maupassant, the painter Corot and André Maurois.

Flaubert, born in Rouen, where his father was chief surgeon at the Hôtel Dieu hospital, was one of a group of painters and writers, including Alexandre Dumas, who made Trouville fashionable. Maupassant lived in Etretat, a town much liked by Victor Hugo, and later often visited by André Gide. Alphonse Karr, a novelist and editor of the newspaper *Figaro*, himself a Norman, helped to make Etretat fashionable with Paris society and English visitors throughout the middle of the nineteenth century, until Deauville became the more stylish resort towards the end of the century.

de Tocqueville
Another Norman writer but of a different kind was Alexis de Tocqueville, one of the most influential political thinkers of the mid-nineteenth century. His *Democracy in America* is still remarkable for its clarity and almost prophetic quality. 'There are today two great peoples on the Earth who . . . seem to be advancing towards the same end: they are the Russians and the Anglo-Americans . . . Their point

of departure is different, and their routes separate; nevertheless, each of them seems to be called, by some secret design of Providence, to hold one day in their hands, the destinies of half the world.' He was writing in the 1850s. De Tocqueville lived and worked in the majestic château (privately owned) in the village of the same name 22 km west of Cherbourg.

Brittany

Brittany has its own literature in the Breton language, but is also associated with two great names in French literature. François René de Chateaubriand, whose combination of brilliant style, rich imagination and impassioned eloquence had a widespread influence on other French writers, was born in St Malo, where his father was a shipowner, in 1768. He spent his childhood there, roaming the quays and the beaches, and his youth a few miles away in the gloomy château of Combourg, once the property of the du Guesclin family, then bought by his father towards the end of the eighteenth century.

Though not a Breton herself, Madame de Sévigné, another of France's great literary figures, lived in Brittany at the Château des Rochers-Sévigné, near Vitre. Most of the letters which made her literary reputation were written from her home in Brittany to her daughter at Grignan in Provence. It was her granddaughter Pauline who first collected her letters for publication. The first edition appeared in 1734, nearly forty years after her death, and they have been in print ever since.

Pierre Loti

Pierre Loti came from Rochefort, further south on the west coast, but in *Iceland Fisherman* and *My Brother Yves* produced some of the most telling descriptions of Breton life and scenery and the endless struggle with the sea that exist in French literature. As a naval officer, he knew Brittany well. Loti was a hypersensitive and entirely subjective writer who had read very little himself and knew almost nothing of literature. He simply reacted to what he saw, and much of his work has an exotic flavour based on the intense feelings which certain places aroused in him during his many voyages. He wrote books set in Senegal, India, Persia, French Indo-China, Japan, Constantinople and Tahiti. The fact that he placed Brittany among all these, not once but twice, is indicative of Brittany's special and individual character.

General Basics

Consulates

● Normandy: **British Consulate**, c/o P & O Ferries, Gare Maritime, Cherbourg, tel. 33 44 20 13.
● Brittany: **British Consulate**, 6 Rue Lafayette, Nantes, tel. 40 63 16 02.
   These consulates will also handle important matters for Irish, New Zealand, and Australian nationals.
● The nearest consulate for **American citizens** is at 2 Ave Gabriel, Paris 8, tel: 42 96 12 02.

Conversions

● 1 kg is equal to 2.2 lb. 0.5 kg is 500 g, and is often called *une livre* in shops and markets, which means a pound and is equal to just over one Imperial lb.
● A mile is equal to 1.6 km, and a km to 0.62 of a mile. 10 km is approximately 6 miles, and 50 km about 30 miles.
● If you subtract 2 from a Centigrade temperature, then multiply by 2 and add 30, the answer will give you the approximate Fahrenheit temperature.
● A UK gallon is equal to 4.54 litres. 50 litres of petrol is equivalent to 11 gallons.
● Most clothes and shoe shops know the European equivalent of British and American sizes.

Documents

British nationals and citizens of Eire need only a valid passport, either a full ten-year British passport, or a British visitor's passport valid for one year, or a British excursion document for travel to France, available from a post office, and valid for one month for trips of up to sixty hours each. Visitors from the USA need a valid passport but not a visa.

Visitors from some other countries who are not EC, Swiss, Monaco, Andorra or Liechtenstein citizens, may require a visa. Check with your nearest French consulate.

If you travel to France by car (see also Travelling Around p. 50) you will need a full driving licence (but not an International one), the car's logbook, third party insurance and, if the car is not yours, a letter from the owner authorising you to use it. A green card is not necessary, but can save time and trouble. A GB, EIRE or other international distinguishing label should be clearly visible on the car.

Make a habit of carrying your passport with you in France. If you are stopped merely as part of a routine check, the police will ask to see it, and the car's documents. They may be satisfied with your driving licence, but not usually.

Electrical current

The electrical current in France is 220 volts (including on graded camp sites), so transformers are not required for British appliances. However, plugs have to be changed to the round-prong French type, and often two-pin instead of three-pin. Adaptors can be bought in Britain, or the correct plugs can be obtained in any French electrical shop or hypermarket.

Health

No vaccinations are needed. Do not hesitate to use French medical services, if necessary – they are first class. Even in the country villages there are excellent general practitioners, combining up-to-date knowledge with a family doctor approach. They are quite prepared to visit outside surgery hours, but charge more. Normal surgery consultation is now 100 francs, a visit 125 francs, on Sunday 225 francs.

If you need medicine on Sunday and the nearest chemist's shop is closed, it should have a notice in the window giving the address of one which is open. One in each locality has by law to open on Sunday. First aid, medical advice and night service rota are all available from pharmacies.

Payment Hospitals in major French towns are very well equipped and nursing standards are high. Under a reciprocal EC agreement, British visitors can obtain approximately the same benefits from the French health service as they can get at home, provided they produce form E111, which can be obtained from your local DSS office. The French health service is not entirely free, some things are reimbursed at 100 per cent and others at 70 per cent. The patient has to pay his bills and then claim the benefit back from the local sickness office (*Caisse Primaire d'Assurance Maladie*) – the address will be in the local telephone directory. If you have to visit a doctor, he will give you a sickness form (*feuille de soins*) to take to the pharmacy, where they will stick on labels to show what medicines were prescribed and supplied. It is the *feuille de soins* with its labels, plus the original prescriptions, which you take to the *Caisse Primaire d'Assurance Maladie*.

Insurance

If you travel with a tour operator, an insurance policy covering most contingencies is likely to have been included in the price of the holiday. If you travel independently, take one of the standard travel policies offered by insurance brokers.

Money and banks

Banks issue money in notes of 20, 50, 100, 200 or 500 francs. There is a 100 franc coin, but there are not many about. The normal coins are 50 centimes, 1 franc, 2 francs, and 5 francs (all silvery), 10 francs (brassy with a silvery centre), a larger 20 franc coin, also brass with a silvery centre, showing Mont St Michel, and 5, 10 and 20 centimes, all brassy. Five centimes is sometimes ignored either way, in giving change or paying.

Holiday money is best divided into some cash, some traveller's cheques and some Eurocheques, all kept separately. The Visa/Barclaycard (called the *Carte Bleue* in France) is widely accepted in hotels, shops and restaurants, and can be used for drawing cash in a bank. Some garages do not accept British Visa cards.

Opening hours Bank opening hours vary slightly from place to place, but are generally from about 9 a.m. to 12 noon and from 2 p.m. to 4.45 p.m. Some banks are closed on Saturday and Sunday, and some on Sunday and Monday. There are thus always some banks open on Saturdays and Mondays, though the first one you go to may be closed. Be ready to show your passport.

Motoring

(see Travelling Around)

Shopping hours

In provincial France most shops are closed during the normal lunch hour, which is from 12 noon until 2 p.m. This does not apply to food shops, which stay open until about 12.30 to enable people who have stopped work at 12 to buy something for lunch. They then close until about 4 p.m. All shops remain open until about 7 p.m.

Many shops, including ironmongers, clothes shops, opticians etc are closed all day on Monday. Newsagents are open all day and on Sunday morning. Some food shops are closed on Mondays. Hypermarkets are open on Mondays, and those with their own cafeteria do not close for lunch on any weekday – this is often the easiest time to shop. They normally have one night a week, often Friday, for late-night shopping, up to 10 p.m. In villages and smaller towns some bakers and food shops are open on Sunday morning until about 12.30.

Other opening times

Museums
There are no fixed opening times for museums, but the majority of State-owned museums are closed on Tuesdays and public holidays. Municipal museums close on Monday and admission is free on Sundays. The majority of museums close for the two-hour lunch break, but a few remain open all day during the summer high season. Privately owned museums may close one day a week, but many remain open in the high season.

Châteaux
Some châteaux are owned by municipalities or departments and some are in private hands, and the general rules for opening times are as for museums. Be careful not to get locked in at lunchtime. Many châteaux, both private and public, are closed for long periods outside the summer season, so check locally.

Cathedrals
Cathedrals and churches are normally closed during the two-hour lunch break. There are no guided visits during services, and services must be respected. There may be a charge to visit certain chapels or the sacristy. Many villages have interesting old churches but only a visiting priest, so many churches are closed, but inquiries will usually turn up someone who has a key and some knowledge of the church.

Caves and Grottoes
There are no fixed opening hours but they are normally open every day from spring to autumn, and closed in winter. A few may be unexpectedly closed after heavy rain, when the level of underground rivers may rise dangerously.

Palm Sunday to All Saints Day are the most common limits of the open season for châteaux, grottoes and other sights.

Post Offices

The larger post offices are open all day from 8 a.m. to 6 p.m. Smaller branches either close for lunch or stay open through lunch and close at 4.30 p.m. Post offices are closed on Saturday afternoon. In the larger post offices you can buy stamps at any window, but apart from that work is divided, so make sure you are in the right queue. It is usually quicker to buy stamps in shops with the *Tabac* sign outside.

Public Telephones

Most post offices have booths (*cabines*) from which you can telephone. You ask for a line at the counter and will be allocated a booth. The call is registered electronically at the counter, where you pay afterwards. There are also public call boxes in the streets. They are usually aluminium and glass, and in small towns and villages may well be in working order, but there are no directories. A few accept coins, but most require phone cards. If you are likely to make many phone calls, the phone card (48 or 96 francs) can be convenient. It can be obtained in PTT boutiques or at a post office.

There are supposed to be complete sets of telephone directories (*annuaires*) for all France in main post offices, but there are usually some missing. The Yellow Pages are included in each directory and can be useful in finding particular services.

Telephoning

● **England to France** Dial 01033 followed by the regional code and subscriber's number.

● **France to England** Dial 19, wait for the continuous tone, then dial 44 followed by the STD code (without the first 0).

Public Holidays

The following are public holidays, when most shops, and museums, châteaux and other sights not privately owned are closed. But in small towns and villages some food shops treat public holidays like Sundays, and are open in the mornings. Hypermarkets are closed.

● **1 January**, New Year's Day.
● **March/April**, Easter Monday.
● **1 May**, Labour Day.
● **8 May**, Victory in Europe Day.
● **May** (movable), Ascension Day, forty days after Easter.
● **May** (movable), Whit Sunday and Monday.
● **14 July**, Bastille Day.
● **15 August**, Assumption of the Virgin Mary.
● **1 November**, All Saints Day.
● **11 November**, Remembrance Day.
● **25 December**, Christmas Day (not Boxing Day).

Talking to the French

French manners are a good deal more formal at all levels than British or American. If you want a polite answer, you must ask a polite question. When you address a stranger in France, it is important to begin with *s'il vous plaît, monsieur*, or *madame*, or *mademoiselle*, as the case may be. Note that *merci* means 'thank you' except when you are offered a drink, a cigarette, or a second helping of food, when *merçi* is the accepted way of saying 'No, thank you'. If you do want whatever it is, say *s'il vous plaît* first, and *merçi* after you get it.

Useful phrases

Where is...?	*Où se trouve...?*
When...?	*Quand...?*
How much...?	*Combien...?*
Do you speak English?	*Parlez-vous anglais?*
Is there anyone here who speaks English?	*Est-ce qu'il y a quelqu'un ici qui parle anglais?*
I don't understand...	*Je ne comprends pas..*
I understand...	*Je comprends..*
Please write it down...	*Notez-le s'il vous plaît*
I'm lost...	*Je me suis perdu...*
Can you direct me to...	*S'il vous plaît, pouvez-vous m'indiquer la direction de...?*
I'm looking for...	*Je cherche..*
I'd like...	*Je voudrais...*
That's enough...	*C'est assez..*
Do you have anything cheaper?	*Avez-vous quelque chose de moins cher?*
Do you have anything bigger/smaller?	*Avez vous quelque chose de plus grand/petit?*
That's too expensive...	*C'est trop cher...*
The light does not work...	*La lumière ne fonctionne pas..*
The toilet does not work...	*Les toilettes ne fonctionnent pas..*
Where is the main shopping centre?	*Où se trouve le centre commercial?*
How far from here?	*À combien de distance d'ici?*
I want to buy...	*Je voudrais acheter...*
Can you recommend a good restaurant near here?	*Pouvez-vous me recommander un bon restaurant près d'ici, s'il vous plaît?*

Can I have the bill, please?	*Donnez-moi l'addition, s'il vous plaît..* (a signing motion in the air is universally understood)

Some useful words

Chemists

Chemists' shops are indicated by a large green cross

Aspirin   *de l'aspirine*

Insect repellent   *de la crême contre les insectes* (a proprietary brand called Mousticologne, available as a cream or a spray, is very effective against mosquitoes)

Pill   *comprimé*

Sanitary towels   *des serviettes hygiéniques*

Sleeping tablets   *des somnifères*

Stomach pills   *des comprimés digestifs*

Garage

Brakes   *les freins*

Clutch   *l'embrayage*

Engine   *moteur*

Exhaust pipe   *tuyau d'échappement*

Oil   *huile*

Petrol   *essence*

Starter   *démarreur*

Steering   *la direction*

Tyre pressure   *pression des pneus*

There is something wrong with...   *Il y a quelque chose qui ne va pas avec...*

Health

Doctor   *médecin*

Medicine   *médicament*

Pain   *douleur, mal*

I need a doctor   *J'ai besoin d'un médecin*

I have a fever   *J'ai de la fièvre*

I have a pain here   *J'ai mal ici*

It's urgent   *C'est urgent*

Hotels

A double room with bath/shower   *une chambre pour deux personnes avec salle de bains/douche*

A double bed   *un lit double* or *un grand lit*

Twin beds   *des lits jumeaux*

Can I see it?   *Je peux la voir?*

We don't want breakfast   *Nous ne voulons pas le petit déjeuner*

A quiet room, please   *Une chambre tranquille, s'il vous plait*

It's too noisy   *C'est trop bruyant*

What time do you start serving dinner?   *Vous servez le dîner à partir de quelle heure?*

Household	Battery *une pile*
	Electrical plug *une fiche*
	Light bulb *une ampoule*
	Matches *des allumettes*
	Washing-up liquid *liquide vaisselle*
Shops	Baker *la boulangerie*
	Bookshop *librairie* (newspapers are sold here or at kiosks; library – *bibliothèque*)
	Butcher *la boucherie*
	Chemist *la pharmacie*
	Delicatessen *la charcuterie*
	Fishmonger *la poissonerie*
	General food shop *alimentation*
	Hairdresser *coiffeur*
	Hypermarket *hypermarché*
	Supermarket *supermarché*

Other useful words
Bank   *banque*
Cash   *liquide*
Change   *monnaie* (NB *monnaie* never means 'money' – it always means change in coins)
Money   *argent*
Money exchange   *Change, Bureau de Change*
Stamps   *timbres*

To book or reserve   *réserver*
Today   *aujourd'hui*
Toilets   *toilettes*
Tomorrow   *demain*

entrée   entrance
fermeture annuelle   closed for annual holidays
gare routière   bus station
gare SNCF   railway station
mairie   town hall or village equivalent
marché   market
place   square
plage   beach
rez de chaussée   ground floor
zone bleue   controlled parking area
zone piétonne   pedestrian zone

In Brittany
aber   estuary

85

argoat   wooded country inland
armor   coast, country of the sea
bassin   harbour, basin
beg   headland, point
brao   beautiful
crêperie   pancake restaurant
dolmen   prehistoric stone structure
enclos paroissial   group of parish church buildings
menhir   single huge stone
presqu'île   peninsula
ti   house

Gazetteer

Introduction

The great majority of holiday visitors to Brittany or Normandy are based in one locality, either in a rented cottage or villa, a camp site or a hotel, and almost all of them are likely to be either on the coast or within easy reach of it. This gazetteer is therefore mostly concerned with coastal resorts, but many tourists, while enjoying a seaside holiday, like to do some sightseeing within easy reach of their base, so the most important historical sites and places of interest, such as Mont St Michel, old Rouen, the D-Day beaches, Brittany's unique parish enclosures, and many others are included.

With the exception of Rouen, not much attention has been given to large towns which are not also holiday resorts. An idea of their history and importance in their province is given, but they are treated more as possibly useful overnight stops than as holiday destinations, though any interesting sights which could be seen during a short stop or an excursion are included. Where a town is essentially boring or trouble-some, I have said so, irrespective of its importance.

Brittany and Normandy together cover a large area, almost half as big as England. Normandy consists of two administrative regions, Upper and Lower Normandy. Upper Normandy is made up of the departments (counties) of Seine Maritime and Eure, and Lower Normandy of Calvados, Manche and Orne. The whole of Brittany is one administrative region made up of the departments of Ille et Vilaine, Côtes d'Armor, Finistère and Morbihan. Loire Atlantique, which historically was always part of the duchy of Brittany, is also included, although it is now part of the administrative region of Pays de Loire.

How the gazetteer is organised

In this wide area there is a great deal of variety and interest, and the gazetteer is of necessity selective. Brittany alone has 2,500 km of coastline with beaches of every kind, from those with a few cottages and a café to resorts with every conceivable modern amenity, and many with nothing but the rocks, sand and salt sea spray. Because the interest is by no means evenly distributed between them, this gazetteer is not broken down into the different departments, but into areas of interest which in some cases may straddle parts of two departments.

The gazetteer treats Brittany and Normandy separately. A tourist in eastern Normandy is not likely to have much to do with western

Brittany, and vice versa. Even by the shortest route, Dieppe is nearly 640 km from Brest. But there is a considerable area of overlap, with plenty of interest, between the two regions.

Normandy has been covered from east to west, with diversions from north to south. It begins with Dieppe and the Alabaster Coast, then Rouen and the valley of the Seine, followed by Calvados with the Côte Fleurie and the D-Day beaches, then Suisse Normande and the Bocage, and finally the Cotentin Peninsula from Cherbourg to Mont St Michel. The system followed is designed for the convenience of the motorist or other independent traveller. Places which are in fact near or next to each other will in general be found near each other in the guide.

Brittany has been treated in an anti-clockwise direction, beginning with St Malo and the Emerald coast, then the north coast from St Brieuc to Perros Guirec and the Corniche Bretonne, into Finisterre and down to Quimper and La Cornouaille, then to Morbihan, with Vannes and Carnac, and finishing with La Baule and the resorts near the estuary of the Loire.

The main purpose is to enable a tourist spending a holiday in a particular resort or a country cottage in any one of these areas to be aware of all the main points of interest within easy reach, say a comfortable day's drive at the most, including a break for lunch.

In each area a range of hotels suitable for overnight stops or more extended stays is suggested, as well as some of the better restaurants at each price level.

Prices
Restaurants

As most restaurants have a range of menus at different prices, they are classified according to the price of their cheapest menu. You can always take something more expensive if you want it. Note that a high proportion of restaurants do not serve their cheapest menu at weekends. (See also Eating and Drinking.)

Hotels

Hotels have been placed in the following categories, based on the average cost of a double room with bath: *expensive*, which means that except to oil sheikhs they are really expensive; *medium plus*, which means that they are noticeably above the average without being really expensive; *medium*; and *low*, which means that they are a bit cheaper than average. Sometimes a combination of two terms has been used to give a more precise idea. Really cheap hotels have not usually been recommended, since many of them tend to detract from rather than contribute to the pleasures of a holiday. (See also Where to Stay.) Note that LdF means *Logis de France*.

Opening and closing times

When specific dates are given they are approximate, and may change from year to year, according to days of the week, school or public holidays, and so on. When they are general, eg 'closed November to March', they are inclusive, ie closed from the beginning of November to the end of March.

NORMANDY

Dieppe and the Alabaster Coast

With several trains every hour at peak times and a 35-minute crossing, the Channel Tunnel service is the quickest way to reach French soil, but the practical advantages are largely commercial. Some holiday-makers heading south or east may find it useful, but the advantages are limited in eastern and non-existent for western Normandy and the whole of Brittany. For those travellers who feel that a dive into a tunnel is a good deal less romantic an introduction to a holiday than a sea crossing, there is a choice of Dieppe, Le Havre, Caen or Cherbourg as points of arrival by sea in Normandy, and St Malo or Roscoff in Brittany.

Dieppe

Newhaven–Dieppe has never been the fastest or most popular of the Channel crossings, but it is to be hoped that it will survive the competition of the Tunnel because it is one of the quickest ways to the real France. After the relative torpor of Newhaven, the vitality and interest of Dieppe is a surprising and pleasant contrast. Almost as soon as you get off the ferry, you are in the heart of it. It has been said before that Dieppe is 'instant France', but it bears repeating. As soon as you set foot there, you seem to smell the wine, the *plateaux de fruits de mers*, the Gauloises and the coffee.

Apart from being the fifth most important fishing port in France, Dieppe is also a genuine holiday resort. Its beach, which stretches for 2 km west from the river mouth, is pebbly at high tide, but has wide, flat sands as the tide goes out. There are good hotels, restaurants of all

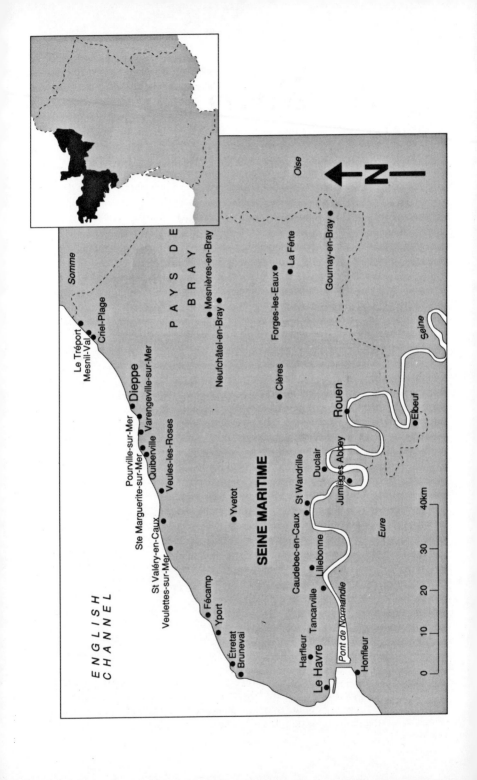

kinds, bars, a good casino, places to dance, public tennis courts, a good golf course close by and good sea fishing. There is an interesting and unusual museum in the castle, and there is the permanent entertainment of the port activity.

History

Dieppe has a long and lively history associated with the sea (see History, p. 21). Towards the end of the nineteenth century Dieppe began to attract French painters and writers. Alexander Dumas *fils* had a villa at Puys, just outside Dieppe, where his father, the famous historical novelist died in December 1870. A few days before his death he is said to have looked at a 20 franc piece in his hand, which made up his worldly wealth. 'People ought not to call me a spendthrift,' he said. 'I started in life with 20 francs, and there they are.' In between he had earned, and spent, more than £300,000, the equivalent of more than £3 million today.

A little later, around 1900, Dieppe became fashionable with British society, led by Lord and Lady Cecil who had a villa at Puys. Another member of the English smart set was Lady Blanche Hozier, so addicted to gambling that she would sometimes queue outside the casino waiting for it to open. She was the mother of Clementine Hozier, who became the wife of Winston Churchill. The casino, which had two towers with onion domes, like a Russian church, was used by the Germans as their headquarters in Dieppe during the Second World War. It was destroyed during the ill-fated Dieppe raid on 19 August 1942, and there was severe damage in other parts of the town. The British force of 5,000 troops, largely Canadians, suffered great losses. Almost one-fifth of the soldiers were killed, including 697 Canadians, and more than another two-fifths were wounded or taken prisoner. Ninety aircraft and twenty-eight tanks were lost. The lessons learned at Dieppe are considered to have saved tens of thousands of lives in the 1944 invasion.

Dieppe today

After the war there was a good deal of reconstruction in the town, which, apart from the Dieppe raid, had been bombarded forty-eight times. The new casino, architecturally a much less interesting building than the previous one, was built in the same area but further back from the beach. Today, between the seafront buildings and the beach itself, there is a wide and grassy esplanade, impressive to look at and dear to dogs and joggers.

The port itself is divided into four different basins, the *avant port*, nearest the sea, which is used by the cross-Channel boats; the *arrière port* where the boats bringing bananas and other exotic fruits from West Africa and the West Indies are unloaded; the Bassin du Canada, where timber from Scandinavia and other commercial products arrive; and the Bassin Duquesne, the fishing port. Every morning on this quay fishermen sell their catch direct from their boats, and then have a drink and a chat in one of the waterside cafés, with barrels of mussels and shrimps here and there, and they and other workmen in blue overalls tuck into great plates of *fruits de mer* at all hours.

But there is more than fish to Dieppe. Its hinterland is rich farming country, and on Saturdays the Grande Rue, pedestrianised, becomes a market which is an entertainment worth anybody's time. The farmers and their wives bring their produce in and sit beside their baskets or trestle tables of eggs, home-made cheeses and pâtés, rich dairy cream, live chickens and ducks, fresh vegetables and flowers. There are stalls heaped with fish and Cancale oysters. Behind them there is a wonderful variety of shops, fashion boutiques, delicatessens, silversmiths, *pâtisseries*, a shop selling every kind of kitchen utensil that chefs ever dreamt of, shoe shops, cafés, and *bar tabacs*. In side streets in this old quarter around the great, cathedral-like church of St Jacques there are more superb food and wine shops.

What to see
Musée du Château

The fifteenth-century castle on a hillside at the western end of the town has been restored several times, most recently after being damaged in the Second World War. It now houses the town's museum, well worth a visit for its unusual collection of ship models, prints by the artist Braque, who lived nearby, and carved ivories. In the seventeenth century, when Dieppe had an active trade both with Africa and the Far East and much ivory was imported, there were more than 300 ivory carvers working in Dieppe. The museum includes a reconstruction of a typical studio, with the tools which were used. The small tablet dials, compasses, and navigational instruments produced by these craftsmen are today collectors' items.

As well as the Braque engravings there are also some good Dutch and French paintings, and a collection of pre-Colombian pottery from Peru. Altogether an interesting and original museum.

Where to stay

Hôtel de la Présidence, Blvd de Verdun, Dieppe 76200, tel. 35 84 31 31. Modern style with sixty of its eighty-nine rooms overlooking the sea. Its restaurant, Le Panoramic, also has a view of the sea. Both rooms and meals at medium plus prices.

Hôtel de l'Univers, 10 Blvd de Verdun, tel. 35 84 12 55. The Blvd Verdun directly overlooks the esplanade (with its lawns and parking places) and the sea. Thirty rooms at medium rates. The restaurant offers good traditional Norman cuisine at a little above medium prices.

Hôtel Ibis, Le Val Druel, tel. 35 82 65 30. On the inland side of the town, this is one of the well-known modern chain, recently completely renovated. Forty-five rooms at low medium rates. Functional restaurant also at low medium prices.

Where to eat

Marmite Dieppoise, 8 Rue St Jean (parking in the Place Nationale), tel. 35 84 24 26. Speciality is the fish stew, Normandy style, after which the restaurant is named. Also very good is the shellfish platter (*plateau de fruits de mer*), and the *tarte au calvados*. Closed Thursday evening except July/August, Sunday evening, and Monday.

La Mélie, 2 Grande Rue du Pollet, tel. 35 84 21 19. Just across the port in the old fishermen's quarter, Le Pollet. Plain décor, but above-average and original cuisine. Closed Monday, and Sunday evening. High medium.

Le Sully, 97 Quai Henri IV, tel. 35 84 23 13. Pleasant restaurant, serious cuisine, menus from low price upwards. Closed Tuesday evening, and Wednesday.

Du Port, 99 Quai Henri IV. Harbourside bistro, with a wide choice of dishes and several menus from cheap to moderately expensive, but all very good value.

Around Dieppe

The countryside behind Dieppe is pleasant, with the charming river valleys of the Béthune, the Eaulne, the Varenne and the Scie leading into the Pays de Bray, with its rich pastures and wooded hillsides. There are also some fine forests.

Arques la Bataille and Miromesnil

What to see

Only 6 km from Dieppe by the road from the Le Pollet quarter, Arques La Bataille stands at the confluence of the Varenne, the Béthune and the Eaulne. It has a fine church in the Flamboyant Gothic style, and the ruins of a feudal castle on a low, rocky hill above the town.

The **castle** is interesting because the Normans were the first builders of stone castles, and this was one of the earliest. It was built by William of Arques, the uncle of William the Conqueror, in 1040, and rebuilt by Henry I of England, also Duke of Normandy, in 1123. In all its long history the castle was never taken by force of arms, only as a result of treachery, or by siege and starvation.

The castle was abandoned over the centuries and allowed to become an overgrown ruin. The Office of Historic Monuments has done some work on it in recent years to make it safer and more accessible, and although it is a ruin, its towers and battlements and the massive keep, 20 m square, are still to be seen. There are panoramic views from the hill.

Château de Miromesnil, a few km west of Arques (turn left off the D54), is claimed by some to be the birthplace of the writer Guy de Maupassant; he is known to have spent some of his early childhood there. Apart from its de Maupassant associations, the château is a splendid building well worth visiting. It was built after the Battle of Arques, about the year 1600, in rose brick and lines of light-coloured stone, with an impressive Louis XIII façade (1640) on the courtyard. The south front is in the simpler, classical style of fifty years earlier.

The reception rooms contain some fine Empire furniture and the collection of books which belonged to the Marquis de Miromesnil who lived here in the late eighteenth century. There is a pleasant garden and a lovely beech wood, on the other side of which is a sixteenth-century chapel, which has some sixteenth-century wood carving, beautifully sculpted stone statues from the same period, and a mixture of modern and sixteenth-century stained glass.

Where to stay and eat

Auberge du Clos Normand, Martin Église, 76370 Seine Maritime, tel. 35 04 40 34. About 7 km from Dieppe by the Abbeville road, and about 2 km before Arques la Bataille, this is a fifteenth-century Norman inn, on the edge of the Arques forest. There are seven comfortable bedrooms in a garden annexe, available only to those who take dinner, which is first-class traditional Norman cuisine, à la carte only. Rooms are medium prices, meals somewhat more expensive. Closed Monday evening and Tuesday.

Le Tréport

Dieppe and Le Tréport, to the north-east at the boundary of Normandy, are the closest seaside resorts to Paris, one of the results of which is that on fine autumn weekends, particularly after a spell of poor weather, it is impossible to find a hotel room in either of them unless you have booked in advance.

What to see

The great chalk cliffs which give the name the Alabaster Coast to the shore at the mouth of the Seine, begin here. There is a chairlift to the top, where there are good views over the town and the coast. The long beach is shingle but there is sand at low tide and safe bathing.

Eu

Five km inland from Le Tréport, and on the edge of the huge Forest of Eu, this is a quiet, orderly town, stirred to life for a few weeks of the year by the summer rush to Le Tréport. It is another place with a long history. It was here that William the Conqueror – then just Duke of Normandy – married his cousin, Matilda, in 1053. It was here also that Joan of Arc was taken prisoner, a capture that led to her trial and death at the stake in Rouen.

What to see

Queen Victoria and her consort visited Louis Phillippe at the **Château of Eu** in 1843 and 1845, and struck up the friendship which meant that Louis Phillippe was welcomed to Claremont in Surrey in 1848 when he was obliged to go into exile. It was originally built in 1578 by the Duc de Guise, head of the Catholic League, who directed the notorious St Bartholomew's Day massacre in August 1572, when nearly 4,000 Protestants were slain. His ambitions frightened King Henri III, who thought he might seize the throne, so he had him assassinated.

The château has been often restored, but it was never an attractive building, and it still is not, though its size is impressive. The last private owners were the Counts of Paris, heirs to the French monarchy. It became the property of the town in 1954, and doubles as town hall and museum. The interior is worth a visit for the quality of the décor and furniture, which shows the nineteenth century at its most impressive. Open a.m./p.m. April to October. Accompanied visits every half-hour. Closed Tuesday.

The church of **Notre Dame and St Laurent** in the centre of Eu is interesting as a very fine example of early Norman Gothic. It was built between 1186 and 1280, and was added to in the fifteenth century, when the apse was rebuilt with the addition of radiating chapels around the deambulatory. The church was restored in the nineteenth century by the ubiquitous Viollet-le-Duc, who would rebuild anything as soon as look at it. The St Laurent in the name of the church was Laurence O'Toole, Archbishop of Dublin, who died in the monastery at Eu in 1281.

Between the rivers Bresle and the Yères, to the west, lies the **Forest of Eu**, which covers more than a hundred square km. It has stately glades of beech as well as conifers introduced from abroad and is full of game, including deer and wild boar. There are signposted footpaths, and many lovely picnic spots.

Five km and seven km south of Le Tréport are the charming little resorts of **Mesnil-Val** and **Criel-Plage**, where the Yères flows into the sea. Each of them is set in a cove between high chalk cliffs, and has a shingle beach with sand at low tide.

Where to stay **Hôtel Picardie**, Place de la Gare, Le Tréport 76470, tel. 35 86 02 22. Thirty-two rooms at low medium rates. Meals slightly above medium prices.

Hôtel le Petit Trianon, 44 Blvd du Calvaire, Le Tréport, tel. 35 86 27 01. Only seven bedrooms, but a pleasant little hotel with inexpensive full board.

Hostellerie de la Vieille Ferme (LdF), 23 rue de la Mer, Mesnil-Val 76910, tel. 35 86 72 18. Based on a delightful eighteenth-century farmhouse in an attractive setting, with thirty-four quiet rooms and a reliable and serious restaurant. Both rooms and meals from low medium prices upwards.

Le Pavillon Joinville, Route du Tréport, Eu 76260, tel. 35 50 27 37. Former hunting lodge of Louis Philippe, with twenty-one spacious, nicely furnished rooms at medium plus rates. Swimming pool and tennis court. Restaurant at high medium prices and half-board obligatory in season. Closed Sunday evening and Monday out of season, and January to March.

Pays De Bray

Between the Forest of Eu and the Forest of Eawy (pronounced Ay-ah-vee), which occupies the triangle of land between the rivers Varenne and Béthune, from just south of Arques for more than 20 km, is a stretch of delightful countryside with a mixture of wooded hillsides, rich pastures and small river valleys.

Almost the whole of the area is devoted to dairy farming and supplies the French market with inexhaustible amounts of butter, cream, *demi-sel* and cream cheeses, of which the best known are from Neufchâtel-en-Bray, which produces both a *carré de Bray* (square) and cylinder-shaped cheeses called *bondons*, and Gournay-en-Bray, chief production centre for the soft Gervais and Petit-Suisse cheeses. You can buy farmhouse cheeses in the markets: Tuesday and Saturday in Neufchâtel, Tuesday, Friday and Sunday in Gournay.

St Germer de Fly

Six km to the south of Gournay, there is an early Gothic church with an impressive nave and a particularly beautiful choir. The church was damaged during the Hundred Years' War and has been partially rebuilt. The thirteenth-century stained glass in the apse has been restored.

Forges-les-Eaux

Until the local deposits of iron ran out in the sixteenth century, Forges, as its name suggests, lived and had lived for many hundreds of years on the forging of iron tools and weapons. But at about the same time as this activity died, the virtues of its **mineral water springs** were discovered. It is said that his happened when a local nobleman, unable to bring himself to kill a favourite horse crippled with old age and rheumatism, turned it loose instead. The horse did not die: it drank the waters of Forges-les-Eaux and was revitalised. So the story goes, but this is what might be called an evergreen spa myth. The same story is told of the discovery of the rejuvenating qualities of the waters of Vichy, but there it concerns a shepherd and his old dog.

The three main springs are named La Royale, La Reinette and Le Cardinal, commemorating a visit made there in 1632 by King Louis XIII, his queen, the beautiful Anne of Austria, and Cardinal Richelieu. It was not that they thought there was anything special about Forges-les-Eaux, but after sixteen years of marriage Anne had failed to produce a child – or it might be fairer to say that Louis, whose sexual inclinations were few and far between, had failed to father one. As a result, Anne spent years touring spas in the hope that taking the waters might help. In fact it was another six years before a son was born, though he made up for the delay by reigning as Louis XIV, the Sun King, for seventy-two years.

In fact, Forges-les-Eaux is reputed to be good for anaemia, rather than sterility. Today it is a rather smart little place, set in greenery with pleasant boating lakes, a little river, the Andelle, and three leafy and well cared for parks. Since 1919 when it was made illegal for casinos to be closer than 100 km to Paris, Forges-les-Eaux, which is 119 km from Paris and has a casino, has been a popular weekend destination for Parisians.

Aumale

In the extreme east of the Pays de Bray, at the limit of Normandy, Aumale is another charming little dairy town, with cobbled streets, but most of its old houses were destroyed during the war.

Where to stay

Hôtel du Grand Cerf (LdF), 9 Grande Rue Fausse Porte, Neufchâtel-en-Bray 76270, tel. 35 93 00 02. Twelve rooms at low rates. Good restaurant at medium prices. Closed Monday.

Relais du Bois des Fontaines, Route de Dieppe, Forges-les-Eaux 76440, tel. 35 09 85 09. Nineteenth-century brick manor house in its own grounds with ten comfortable bedrooms at low/medium rates. Restaurant at high medium prices and half-board obligatory in season.

Hôtel du Dauphin, 27 Rue St Lazare, Aumale 76390, tel. 35 93 41 92. A well-established *auberge*, with a very good restaurant. Popular lunch stop for Parisians on their way to the coast. Meals at medium prices and very good value. Thirteen rooms at low/medium rates, not all with bathrooms.

Where to eat

There are several restaurants on the Quai Francois I, Le Tréport, with little to choose between them in price or quality. The **Homard Bleu** has good menus at medium prices.

La Gare, 20 Place de la Gare, Eu, tel. 35 86 16 64. A good regional restaurant with menus at medium prices. Closed Sunday evening and Monday lunch. (Also a LdF hotel with ten rooms at low/medium rates.)

La Paix, 17 Rue de Neufchâtel, Forges-les-Eaux 76440, tel. 35 90 51 22. Sound cuisine and good value. Range of menus from cheap to slightly above medium. Closed Monday lunch. (Not a hotel as such, but it does have five cheap rooms.)

Auberge du Beau Lieu, au Fosse, Route de Paris, Forges-les-Eaux, tel. 35 90 50 36. 1.5 km south east by D915. A fine restaurant in an attractive, well-restored farm property. Menus at medium prices up which offer superb value. Excellent wine list. (Three pleasant rooms at low medium rates in an adjoining house.)

Le Mouton Gras, 2 Rue du Verdun, Aumale 76390, tel. 35 93 41 32. Old-style *auberge* with traditional restaurant, and good value at medium prices. Also nine rooms at low rates.

For Lyons la Forêt and its region, which has good inns and restaurants, and is not far from Gournay, see The Valley of the Seine, p. 125.

The Alabaster Coast: west of Dieppe

The main D925 runs direct from Dieppe to Le Havre, parallel to the coast and turning inland at Fécamp, but a smaller road nearer the sea also follows the coast and serves a whole string of resorts. Its number changes from time to time, but it begins from Dieppe as the D75.

All the resorts on this coast have some things in common, whether towns or villages. Each of them is set in a gap between high chalk cliffs, they all have a beach which, at least at high tide, is pebbly or shingly, and the tide comes in quickly at all of them. There are differences in that some include small fishing ports and yacht marinas and some do not, some are more wooded than others, and some are more stylish than others. Most people exploring this coast will find a place they like a lot, but for different people it will be a different place.

Pourville-sur-Mer

The first resort outside Dieppe in this direction is Pourville-sur-Mer, which was fashionable with artists and writers at the same time as Dieppe, at the turn of the century. It is now a fairly ordinary resort, less smart than it once was, but it has a good little restaurant, the **Trou Normand**, an old favourite with those who know Dieppe.

Varengeville-sur-Mer

The road climbs up from Pourville to Varengeville-sur-Mer. Most of this commune is not, in fact, down by the sea but scattered on the wooded plateau above it, where a labyrinth of leafy lanes hides groups of attractive houses, many of them behind their own screen of trees. The descent to the beach is easy enough but it is a stiff climb back up.

What to see

There are several things worth visiting in and around Varengeville. The church and the cemetry stand by themselves in a beautiful setting near the edge of the cliff overlooking the sea. The **church** is mostly thirteenth-century, with a sixteenth-century porch, and was restored recently. The interior has two naves, side by side. In the southern nave there is a stained-glass window representing the Tree of Jesse, by the famous artist Georges Braque who, in his old age spent a lot of time at Varengeville, where he had a studio. He was buried in the cemetry here in 1963, and his grave is on the left near the entrance. There are more of his stained glass windows in the **Chapelle St Dominique** in Varengeville, on the Dieppe road.

Parc des Moustiers is a beautiful small estate off the road which leads to the church and in a valley opening towards the sea. The house was designed at the end of the nineteenth century by Edwin Lutyens for the musician Guillaume Mallet. It was one of the first commissions of the famous architect who, twenty years later, was responsible for the building of New Delhi. The gardens around the house were laid out by the best-known landscape gardener of the time, Gertrude Jekyll, with whom Lutyens worked on several English country houses.

The delightful gardens are at their finest in May and June, but there are masses of flowers from April to October, and even in early November the autumn colours of the trees are worth seeing. Open mid-March to mid-November, a.m./p.m. except Sunday morning. The house is open in July and August, except Tuesdays, and is also closed Wednesday and Sunday mornings, and public holidays.

The **Manoir d'Ango** is the Renaissance country house of the famous seventeenth-century shipowner, Jean d'Ango (see History, p. 21). In the huge courtyard there is a magnificent round *colombier* (dovecote) in polychrome bricks with a domed roof, and room for 1,600 doves.

The house was neglected for many years and became in the end a dilapidated farmhouse. It is still a farm but was well restored some years ago in the interests of tourism. As it is a working farm the property is not always open to the public, so it is advisable to check with the Tourist Office in Dieppe (Blvd Général de Gaulle) before making a special trip.

The nearby resorts of St Marguerite, Quiberville and St Aubin are quiet, do-as-you-like places. **St Marguerite** has a Roman villa, and an interesting little church with a nave which has a twelfth-century left-hand side, and a sixteenth-century right-hand side. The stone main altar also dates from the twelfth century, the fonts are Renaissance, and the stained-glass windows date from 1956.

Beaches

Quiberville is a prettily situated village with a sandy beach and salmon-trout fishing in the mouth of the 3aane river. Rather 'trippery' in the high season. At **St Aubin-sur-Mer** there is a gap of more than 1 km between the cliffs, and the sandy beach is flatter and safer for children.

Where to stay

Hôtel de la Terrasse (LdF), Vasterival, 76119 Varengeville, tel. 35 85 12 54. Situated near the Cap d'Ailly lighthouse at Vasterival (which also has a pretty botanical garden worth seeing), this is an old-established, family-run hotel with good home cooking. Menus from low medium prices, twenty-two rooms at low medium rates. Lovely views. Closed October to mid-March.

Hôtel Les Falaises Quiberville 76860, tel. 35 83 04 03, and **Hôtel L'Huîtrière**, tel. 35 83 02 96. Two hotels with the same proprietor, both LdF and both with good restaurants (strong on oysters and mussels). Thirty rooms between them at low/medium rates. Menu prices medium.

Veules-les-Roses

Hôtel le Clos Normand (LdF), Promenade de Guynemer, St Aubin-sur-Mer 14750, tel. 31 97 30 47. Twenty-nine rooms at low to medium rates. Sound regional restaurant at medium prices. Closed October to April.

This is a summer resort in miniature, a charming place situated between high wooded cliffs. A trout stream trickles through the town, and in summer the gardens really are full of roses. There is a shingle beach with a children's beach club with the usual climbing frames and equipment and friendly 'trainers' to look after them. There are swimming pools, restaurants beside the beach, and a neat little casino. It is a lively little town in summer, but strictly seasonal.

Where to eat

Les Galets, Veules-les-Roses, on the sea front, tel. 35 97 61 33. It is a surprise to find this fine restaurant in so small a resort. Chef Gilbert Plaisance is a *Maître Cuisinier de France* who brings a creative touch to traditional Norman recipes. Prices are high. Closed Tuesday evening and Wednesday, except July/August and December/January.

St Valéry-en-Caux
History

Situated in a wooded valley and with a sheltered harbour, St Valéry-en-Caux has a long history. The town is named after a monk who founded a monastery here in the seventh century. St Valéry's reputation was based on his ability to perform miracles, one of which was to bring back to life a man who had been hanged.

During the Second World War the town was almost completely destroyed, not following the D-Day invasion but in 1940 when the 51st Highland Division and a French Cavalry Division fought a delaying action to protect the British armies retreating to Dunkerque. German troops forced the two divisions down to the beach, where they were obliged to surrender. The German officer who accepted the surrender was Erwin Rommel, who later led the German forces against the 8th Army in the North African desert.

St Valéry was rebuilt after the war and is today an attractive place, combining its activities as a resort and a sailing centre, and even a few fishing boats put out from the picture-postcard harbour. St Valéry has a pebbly beach with sand at low tide, a promenade, hard tennis courts, a small casino, several hotels and quayside cafés and restaurants.

Les Veulettes From St Valéry-en-Caux the main road turns inland, but the secondary, cliff road, now the D79, leads past an atomic power station to another little resort, Les Veulettes (10 km). Beautifully situated in the gap formed by the little river Durdent, which has the loveliest valley in this part of Nomandy, Les Veulettes is a less sophisticated resort than Veules-les-Roses or St Valéry-en-Caux, but it is an easy-going, friendly place, popular with young people and families. There is more than 1 km of pebbly beach, with shingle and sand at low tide. The village has been rebuilt since being damaged in 1940, but it has a fine old Romanesque church about 1 km from the beach.

What to see **Notre Dame du Bon Port** in St Valéry is a modern church, built in 1963 to an unusual and attractive design. A beamed wooden construction with a soaring slate roof, with the side walls and those of the choir of coloured glass, it was designed by André-Louis Pierre. There is a sixteenth-century parish church about 1 km from the town centre, and near it is the military cemetery where the 500 British and French soldiers who were killed here in 1940 are buried.

There are some pleasant walks from St Valéry. Keen walkers may like to know that the national footpath GR21 follows the coast, with some interruptions, from Dieppe to Etretat, and offers splendid cliff views as well as descents into the picturesque valleys.

On the way down the Durdent valley (D10 from Les Veulettes to Cany-Barville and then D268) the moated seventeenth-century **Château de Cany**, designed by François Mansart, is worth a visit. The panelled rooms still contain most of their original furniture, and there is a collection of Chinese porcelain. About 3 km south of Cany, in the village of **Grainville la Teinturière** there is an eighteenth-century church which contains the tomb of Jean de Béthencourt, who discovered the Canary Islands in 1404 and reigned there as king for a year.

Where to stay **La Marine**, 113 Rue St Leger, St Valéry en Caux 76460, tel. 35 97 05 09. This little hotel, with only seven bedrooms, is an *Auberge de*

France. Adequate rooms and good traditional cooking, both at low prices. Restaurant closed Friday.

Hôtel Les Terrasses (LdF), Rue Le Perrey, tel. 35 97 11 22. Good situation near the beach. Twelve bedrooms, some with sea views, at medium rates. Good cuisine at medium plus prices.

Hôtel Altea, 14 Ave Clemenceau (overlooking the yacht marina), tel. 35 97 35 48. Modern functional hotel with 153 rooms at medium prices. Restaurant medium plus prices.

Hôtel Les Frégates (LdF), Rue de la Plage, Les Veulettes 76450 Cany-Barville, tel. 35 97 51 22. On the promenade facing the sea, with sixteen rooms at low rates. Sound cuisine, medium prices.

For those who want to explore the valley of the Durdent there is a delightful little hotel just outside the village of Héricourt-en-Caux. The **Auberge de la Durdent** (LdF) has fifteen rooms at low rates and a good value restaurant.

Where to eat   **Le Port**, 18 Quai d'Amont, St Valéry-en-Caux, tel. 35 97 08 93. Good restaurant, specialising in fish dishes, menus at medium prices. Closed Sunday evening and Monday.

Pigeon Blanc, near the old church, tel. 35 97 03 55. Pleasant restaurant with good range of menus at less-than-usual prices. Closed Sunday evening and Monday.

Fécamp

History   About 15 km of winding coast road from Veulettes, Fécamp is a curious place with a long and chequered history. It gets its name, apparently, from the Latin *fici campus*, the field of the fig tree, though some say it is derived from *fiscanum*, fish haven. According to legend, at some time during the first century AD a hollowed-out fig tree was cast up on the shore. In it there was a lead container holding some of the blood of Christ, taken by Joseph of Aramithea when he buried Him. It had been bequeathed by him to his nephew, who kept it all his life until a dream voice warned him of the approach of the Roman legions and to cut down the fig tree. This he did and threw it into the sea at Sidon, where he lived, praying to God to lead it to some honest place.

It landed at Fécamp. The legend does not say how anyone then at Fécamp knew this story, or why some say it was Nicodemus who took the blood, but the relic soon attracted pilgrims and an abbey was set up there.

The Vikings   The early Vikings were not Christians and had no respect whatever for Christian legends, but they liked Fécamp because of its safe harbour and it was one of their favourite landing places on that coast. In AD 846 they destroyed the abbey, but two hundred years later as

Dukes of Normandy they rebuilt it as part of their effort to bring civilisation and prosperity to their duchy.

Nothing now remains of the great abbey of Fécamp, apart from the twelfth-century abbey church, now called **Église de la Trinité**. The abbey was suppressed like so many others during the French Revolution, and the monks dispersed.

Fishing   Fécamp has been a fishing port from its earliest days, and until 1973 it was still the fourth most important fishing port in France, but the cod fishing has been abandoned, though there is still a deep-sea and a coastal fleet, and Fécamp still has fish canning, freezing and allied industries, and also smokes salmon imported from Iceland and Norway. The port has five small harbour basins and is in some ways reminiscent of Dieppe, but with no cross-Channel traffic.

Tourism   In addition to fishing there is also some small commercial activity, but as its fishing has declined in recent years Fécamp has gone in for tourism. The town is strikingly situated between high cliffs – that to the east is the highest on the coast at 127 m – but its steep, pebbly beach is not very exciting, though bathing at low tide is possible. Windsurfing is popular and the yacht marinas have berths for more than 500 pleasure boats. There is a modern casino with a panoramic bar. There are tennis courts and a swimming pool, and an excellent choice of restaurants. Altogether, although it is not the normal sort of resort, Fécamp appeals to those people who prefer a place of character with a life of its own to those artificial resorts which live for two months of the year only and then shut down.

What to see   The church is a fine example of very early Gothic. Its cathedral size
Gothic church   and proportions make it impressive – the nave is 123 m long and 23 m high, and the transept has a lantern tower 64 m high. The choir, with eleven chapels, some of them Renaissance, is also impressively spacious, but although the church is light inside, the décor is very simple and there is not much colour, and the overall effect is austere. The church still houses the relic of the Precious Blood in a white marble tabernacle by the Italian sculptor, Girolamo Viscardo (sixteenth century), and it still attracts pilgrims on the Tuesday and Thursday following Trinity Sunday.

Benedictine   It seems that for a liqueur to be taken seriously the recipe has to have
museum and   been originated by a monk, then lost, preferably during the French
distillery   Revolution, before being perfected, then later rediscovered and improved before being marketed. Benedictine is no exception. It is said to have been originated in 1510 by a monk called Vincelli at Fécamp Abbey. The recipe was discovered 350 years later by a man called Alexandre le Grand, a merchant of Fécamp, in an old scrapbook in the family attic. He used it as a base for a liqueur which he called Bénédictine and commercialised with great success. As a setting for his liqueur he commissioned an extraordinary building, now known as the **Palais Bénédictine**. With all its arches, towers, spires, turrets,

statues, balustrades, patterns of polychrome brick, wrought-iron railings and twiddly bits, it is a sort of encyclopaedia of architectural ostentation. The interior is no less surprising, with Gothic beamed halls, a distillery and a museum which has some fine exhibits, including a seventeenth-century Christ delicately carved in ivory; handwritten and illustrated Books of Hours of the fifteenth century, earlier than the first printed books; Limoges enamels; and a collection of 700 fake bottles of Bénédictine from all over the world. The visit takes an hour and if you retain your ticket, you are entitled to a free tasting to finish off. Open a.m./p.m. April to mid-November.

Château de Bailleul   This very attractive Renaissance château, built in stone in 1553, faces green lawns in the centre of a beautiful park about 10 km south-east of Fécamp. It is best reached via Ganzeville, Bec de Mortagne, Daubeuf Serville, and then the D10. Its harmonious design is closer to the châteaux of the Loire than to a usual Norman château, and it has many original features, including the statues in lead of Justice, Strength, Prudence and Temperance which crown the steeply pitched roof. The interior is full of fine furniture, and tapestries, paintings and works of art of the seventeenth and eighteenth centuries. In the grounds there is a sixteenth-century chapel and an eighteenth-century dovecote. Guided visits a.m./p.m. mid-June to mid-September. Outside this period, open Saturday, Sunday and public holidays. Closed Monday. At the time of writing a maze is in the making.

Yport   Yport is a former little fishing port, like a cove transplanted from Cornwall, now converted to a charming family resort with a beach which has the important advantage on this coast of being sheltered from the west wind. Only a few km from Fécamp and a good alternative for those who like to have a town handy but prefer to stay outside it.

Where to stay   **Hôtel Angleterre**, 91–96 Rue de la Plage, Fécamp 76400, tel. 36 28 01 60. Well-run hotel with thirty-two bedrooms at low/medium rates. Restaurant also very reasonable.

Auberge de la Rouge, Hameau Le Chesnay, 76400 Fécamp; near St Leonard 2 km south of Fécamp by the D925. Eight comfortable rooms opening on to a garden, at low medium rates. The restaurant – menus at medium prices – is very good value. Chef-proprietor Claude Guyot can prepare you a fresh lobster – *langouste* – from his own tanks at any time. Closed Sunday evening and Monday.

Hôtel Normand (LdF), 2 Place Jean-Paul Laurens, Yport 76111, tel. 35 27 30 76. Simple hotel with thirteen rooms and meals at low prices.

Where to eat   **Le Viking**, 63 Blvd Albert 1er, Fécamp, tel. 35 29 22 92. A comfortable restaurant on the seafront, mostly seafood, very well prepared and at medium prices. Closed Monday. Same owner as the slightly less expensive **Le Maritime**, tel. 35 28 21 71, facing the yacht harbour.

Etretat

Situation

Of all the resorts on the Alabaster Coast, Etretat is the most splendidly situated. It lies in a valley on a small, gently curving bay enclosed by the most dramatic and grandiose cliffs anywhere on this coast. These precipitous cliffs, which include huge hollowed-out arches bridged to the main cliff and isolated chalk needles just offshore, one of which is 70 m high, are truly spectacular and appear on posters and publicity everywhere. They are also reminders that the whole of this coast is being eaten away by the sea at what is, geologically, a very fast rate, and that the cliffside churches and houses will eventually tumble into the sea, just as the summer villas of wealthy Romans have done.

Etretat is reached from Fécamp by the main road, which curves inland and then back again, 17 km, or by the twisty coast road which takes longer and is more picturesque. The site is what might be called a 'natural' for a summer resort. It was a well-known Parisian journalist, Alphonse Karr, editor of *Le Figaro*, who in the middle of the nineteenth-century sowed the seeds of its popularity. He said, 'If I had to show the sea to a friend for the first time, it would be Etretat that I would choose.' Karr, who knew the great writers and painters of his day, intrigued Paris society with this statement and Etretat, which until that time had been just a small fishing village, soon became fashionable. It remained so until the turn of the century, when Deauville with its horse-racing, grand casino and the villas of the rich became the 'in' place with the *beau monde*, which was what the jet set were called in the days before aeroplanes.

Golf

There has long been a wonderfully sited 18-hole clifftop golf course with an adjacent hotel at Etretat, and before the Second World War many English holiday-makers came here for the golf. They still come, but in fewer numbers, and today it is popular with Parisians, some of whom have summer flats or villas here. The beach is pebbly with some sand at low tide, but there are pleasant beachside bars converted from old fishing boats.

What to see

Etretat is a place with things to do rather than to see. There are some good walks along the clifftops on either side. Behind the chapel on the **Falaise d'Amont** there is a monument to two French aviators, Nungesser and Coli, who were the first to attempt to fly the Atlantic non-stop. They took off from Paris on 8 May 1927, but disappeared somewhere over the sea and were never seen again. The last sighting of the plane as it headed west was from this point on the cliff at Fécamp. The clifftop here is reached by steps (180) with a handrail from the end of the promenade, and a footpath. It can also be reached by car.

Though Etretat was badly knocked about by the Germans during the war, as they fortified it and made room for gun emplacements, it still has some of its former character. The **covered market place,** with its wooden pillars and beamed roof, has been reconstructed in the Place Maréchal Foch.

Where to stay

Hôtel Dormy House, 40 Route du Havre, Etretat 76790, tel. 35 27 07 88. On the Falaise d'Aval cliff by the golf course, and popular with golfers. Fifty-one rooms at high medium rates, pleasant garden, restaurant rather expensive. Closed mid-November to March 1.

Hôtel Welcome, 10 Ave de Verdun, tel. 35 27 00 89. Cheerful, friendly hotel, right in the centre. Twenty-two rooms at low medium rates. Restaurant with menus at medium prices, closed Wednesday.

Where to eat

Le Cabestan, Place Général de Gaulle, tel. 35 27 02 82. Pleasant dining room with view of the cliffs and seafood specialities well prepared by chef Bernard Boucher. Prices from medium up. Closed Tuesday evening and Wednesday.

Le Galion, Blvd R-Coty, tel. 35 29 48 74. Sound restaurant with menus at medium prices up. Closed Wednesday, except July/Aug.

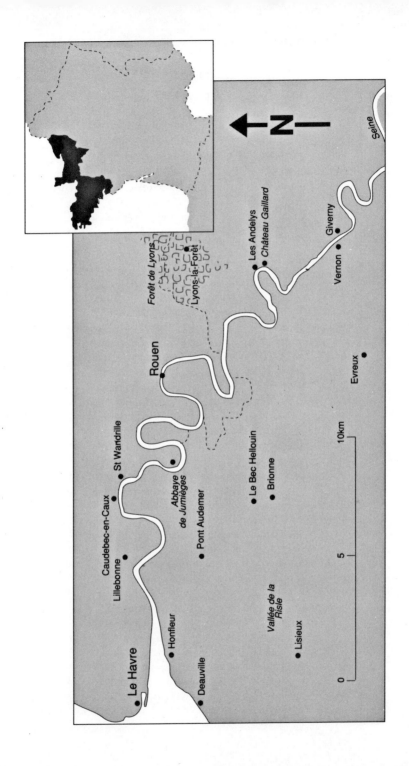

The Valley of the Seine

Le Havre

The best approach to Le Havre is by the D940, close to the coast, and which offers good views of the town and the estuary as you come down to Le Havre through the attractive suburb of St Adresse. A great many tourists have been to Le Havre, but not many have seen it. They land from the cross-Channel boats and drive out of it without so much as a backward glance. It would perhaps surprise them to know that Le Havre is itself a good holiday centre. It has 2 km of sandy beach, overlapping St Adresse and Le Havre itself, a lively casino, five discotheques, four cinemas, an 18-hole golf course, interesting museums, a first-class fine arts gallery, and the best selection of good hotels and restaurants in this part of France.

If buildings are worth seeing simply because they are old and belong to a different architectural style, it seems logical to say that a town is worth seeing when it represents nothing but the present. In this respect Le Havre is one of the most under-estimated towns in France.

History   Le Havre was originally built in 1517 by order of King François I to replace the port of Harfleur, where the harbour was silting up. At first more of a naval base than a conventional port, Le Havre gradually expanded its commercial activities, and became an important port during the American War of Independence, when supplies to aid the rebel armies were sent from Le Havre. The link with the United States was retained, and between the two World Wars some of the finest liners ever built, including the *Normandie* and the *France*, sailed between Le Havre and New York.

During the Second World War Le Havre was repeatedly bombed, and was already heavily damaged at the time of the D-Day invasion. The success of the Allied armies isolated Le Havre and the battle swept past it, and when the Battle of Normandy was virtually over, in mid-August, there remained strong German forces in Le Havre who refused to surrender. The Allied commanders decided that it would have to be taken and Le Havre was bombarded for nine days, with the

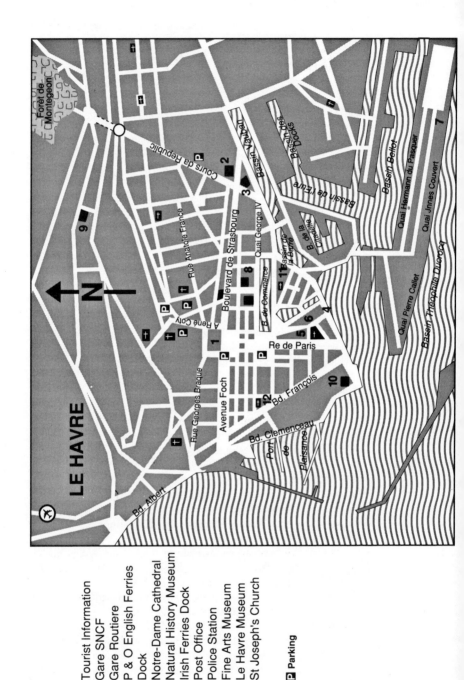

LE HAVRE

1 Tourist Information
2 Gare SNCF
3 Gare Routiere
4 P & O English Ferries
   Dock
5 Notre-Dame Cathedral
6 Natural History Museum
7 Irish Ferries Dock
8 Post Office
9 Police Station
10 Fine Arts Museum
11 Le Havre Museum
12 St Joseph's Church

🅿 Parking

result that the city was flattened and 90 per cent destroyed, beyond any hope of restoration.

Le Havre today

The Le Havre which emerged from the rebuilding is, whether you like it or not, extremely interesting. It is a concrete town with some remarkable buildings. The new Le Havre was planned with fine open spaces and splendid avenues – the Avenue Foch was intended to rival the Champs Élysées, and does. Le Havre is now the second port of France, after Marseilles, and in the planning some of the docks and basins are integrated in the town itself. From the windows of the Hôtel Bordeaux in the heart of the city, for example, you look out on the glassy surface of a basin, reflecting buildings, bridges and ocean-going boats with startling clarity.

It is an exaggeration to say that Le Havre is beautiful, but it has its attractions, is certainly not ugly, and is, equally certainly, impressive. Its heart is the square called Espace Oscar Niemeyer, designed by the famous architect who built the extraordinary capital of Brazil. This square contains two strange, mushroom-shaped buildings, one a cultural centre with a 1,200-seat theatre, and the other a conference centre.

Le Havre is an excellent base for excursions, within easy reach of the resorts of the Alabaster Coast and, via the Pont de Tancarville, those of the Côte Fleurie. It is handy for the Parc Régional de Brotonne, with its magnificent forest, and the abbeys of St Wandrille and Jumièges, and it is only a fast 80 km by autoroute from Rouen, and its antiquities.

What to see
Place de l'Hôtel de Ville

This impressive square is one of the largest in Europe, and has a public garden in the centre with a monument to the Resistance. Around the square the buildings vary between three-storey blocks with terraces and ten-storey towers. The whole of one side of the square is occupied by the town hall, which has a 72 m tower. The square, and most of modern Le Havre, was designed by Auguste Perret, who died in 1954, and was known in France as the 'genius of reinforced concrete'.

Avenue Foch

As you face the town hall, the main road from the square on your left is the Avenue Foch. This magnificent avenue, lined with trees and lawns on both sides and more than 1 km long, is and was meant to be a modern rival to the Champs Élysées, and is certainly one of the most impressive streets in Europe.

Église St Joseph

This remarkable concrete edifice, forbidding from the outside but with a kind of stark but transcendent beauty in the interior, was also designed by Perret. The body of the church is a square with sides of 40 m, with the altar in the centre. The great octagonal tower of the church, 109 m high, the top 84 m forming a lantern tower, is carried by four groups of four square pillars, one group in each corner of the body of the church. Each of the side walls, and each of the eight sides of the tower, is pierced by scores of uniform windows divided into scores of panes of different-coloured stained glass, producing unceasing changes of light from dawn to dusk.

Espace Oscar Niemeyer

A walk from the Town Hall square down the Avenue Foch and then down a side road to the left to the Église St Joseph, and then back down the Rue Louis Brindeau to the Espace Oscar Niemeyer, enables you to see the essence of Le Havre.

Museums

Musée des Beaux Arts

The original Museum of Fine Arts, established in 1845, was destroyed in 1944, and was replaced after the war. Opened in 1961, the Musée des Beaux Arts is a building in glass and metal, in an impressive situation at the entry to the port. The side of the museum facing the sea is almost entirely glass, with fine views of shipping movements. The different floors of the museums are connected by gangways, a maritime note.

The collections include nearly 300 pictures by Eugène Boudin, as well as works by Fragonard, Delacroix, Corot, Millet and Courbet, and a good collection of Impressionists including Monet, Sisley, Renoir and Manet. There are also many paintings by Dufy, Braque and Friesz, who were natives of Le Havre, as well as Art Deco works and paintings of the post-war Paris school. The Musée des Beaux Arts is open from 10 a.m. to 12 noon, and 2 p.m. to 6 p.m. Closed Tuesday.

Musée de l'Ancien Havre

This museum is situated at 1 Rue Jerome Bellarmato, in the St François quarter, near the Bassin du Commerce. In the 1930s the writer Jean-Paul Sartre taught philosophy in Le Havre for several years and there wrote his first novel, *La Nausée* (1938). Very little of the town that he knew survived the war, but some souvenirs have been gathered together in this old Norman house of the seventeenth and eighteenth centuries, itself damaged by the bombardments in 1944 and restored in the 1950s. It contains plans, drawings and documents relating to Le Havre from its earliest days, plus photographs, and a section on the history of street music in Le Havre.

Where to stay

Hôtel Bordeaux, 147 Rue Louis Brindeau, Place Gambetta, Le Havre 76600, tel. 35 22 69 44. Well-run hotel in the centre of town, with thirty-one sound-proofed rooms, some of which have a view of the Bassin de Commerce and the Espace Niemeyer. No restaurant. Room rates on the high side of medium.

Hôtel Mercure, Chaussée d'Angoulême, near the Centre International de Commerce, tel. 35 21 23 45. Well-equipped modern hotel with ninety-six rooms at high medium rates. Restaurant menus at medium prices.

Hôtel Astoria, 13 Cours de la République, opposite the railway station, tel. 35 25 00 03. Comfortable, thirty-seven rooms at below medium cost, and restaurant cheaper than usual prices. Small private parking, restaurant closed Sunday.

Hôtel Le Marly, 121 Rue Paris, tel. 35 41 72 48. Close to the Ferry terminal, thirty-seven comfortable rooms at medium rates. There is no restaurant.

Where to eat

Le Petit Bedon, 39 Rue Louis Brindeau, short stroll from Espace Niemeyer, tel. 35 41 36 81. Pleasant restaurant, serious cuisine, a little above medium prices. Closed Saturday lunch and Sunday.

La Petite Auberge, 32 Rue St Adresse, tel. 35 46 27 32. Good value little restaurant with a range of menus at medium prices. Closed August, and Sunday evening and Monday.

Excursions from Le Havre

Apart from places already mentioned within easy reach of Le Havre, such as Etretat and Fécamp, there are easy drives into the Seine valley from Le Havre.

Caudebec-en-Caux

This little town, very pleasantly situated beside the river in some of the loveliest countryside of the lower Seine valley, was the capital of the Pays de Caux and an important port until overtaken by Le Havre.

The River Seine here used to experience a tidal wave, or bore, every equinox, caused by the meeting of the incoming tide and the current of the Seine. It was always severe and in some years very bad, flooding the town and causing damage and deaths. Between 1830 and 1852, 105 ships were wrecked by the bore and many people were drowned including, in 1843, the daughter and son-in-law of Victor Hugo. They are buried in the churchyard of the neighbouring village, **Villequier**. Work on the Seine estuary has greatly reduced the importance of the bore which, although it can still be observed at certain times, is no longer dangerous.

Until the Second World War Caudebec was itself an extremely picturesque town, with narrow streets lined by scores of ancient houses. In medieval times Caudebec was famous for its tanneries, and it is said that the kid gloves made there were so fine and soft that a pair could be put in a walnut shell. The medieval houses were made very largely of wood, and when the Germans set fire to the town in 1940 it was almost completely destroyed.

What to see

The **Church of Notre Dame**, a superb example of the Flamboyant Gothic style, was started in 1426 when Caudebec was under English occupation, and was finished between 1490 and 1515. It has been damaged and restored several times during its history. Some of the carving in the delicately worked triple porch is restoration of war damage, and was carried out by contemporary Norman sculptors. The belfry, with a square tower rising in three stages and crowned by an octagonal spire (rebuilt in 1886), is one of the finest in Normandy.

The interior has several points of interest, including fifteenth- and sixteenth-century stained glass. The choir stalls, and the finely carved Louis XIII reredos in the first chapel on the left, came from the Abbey of St Wandrille. On the right side, the second chapel of the deambulatory has a fine seventeenth-century entombment which came from the Abbey of Jumièges. The church has a remarkable sixteenth-century organ with more than 3,000 pipes, known to musicians all over the world for its reverberant tones.

The **Maison des Templiers** was badly damaged by the 1940 fire, but its thirteenth-century façade survived and is one of the rare examples of domestic architecture from this early period. The interior has been altered and restored and now houses the **town museum**. Open a.m./p.m. June to September, and Saturday and Sunday p.m. in April/May.

Those interested in boats and water-borne transport will like the **Musée Maritime de la Seine** which covers the history of navigation on the Seine, its ports, shipbuilding yards, import and export via the river, types of boats used, ferries and so on. Open a.m./p.m. every day July/August, and at various other times during the year (ask at the *Syndicat d'Initiative*).

St Wandrille

The **Abbey of St Wandrille**, in a wooded hollow which is an outlying part of the Forêt de Brotonne, is not the most fascinating of abbeys, though the ruins of the old abbey church of St Pierre, surrounded by greenery, have a certain romantic appeal. In the abbey itself the southern gallery of the cloisters dates from the early fourteenth century – it is open for guided visits every afternoon at 3 p.m.; the other galleries are from about 200 years later. Gregorian chant can be heard there on weekdays at 9.25 a.m. and on Sundays at 10 a.m.

The abbey was founded by Count Wandrille in AD 649 . In the tenth century it was destroyed by Norman invaders, but the monks rebuilt it and made it one of the chief centres of the Benedictines in Normandy in the eleventh century.

The abbey was closed and the monks dispersed during the French Revolution, and it began into fall into ruin. In the nineteenth century it became a textile mill, and was then bought by the Marquis of Stacpoole, who added the monumental gateway and restored some of the stonework. Then it was for several years the home of the writer Maurice Maeterlinck, author of *The Blue Bird* and other plays of 'enchantment'. The Benedictines returned in 1931.

Forêt de Brotonne

Between Caudebec and St Wandrille the Seine is crossed by the Pont de Brotonne. This great bridge, opened in 1977, is 1,280 m long, has pylons 125 m high, and the road it carries is 50 m above the river, so that large ships on their way to Rouen can pass beneath it. The road leads directly into the Brotonne Forest, 7,400 hectares of beech, oak and pine forest, with more than 350 km of signposted footpaths. The area around the forest and the neighbouring marshlands of the Marais Vernier, 40,000 hectares in all, forms the **Parc Naturel Régional de Brotonne**. Regional parks differ from national parks in that they are created in inhabited areas with the object of preserving the traditions and stimulating the economy of the area, often through tourism, as well as protecting the natural features and wildlife. The forest, which still has many deer, wild boar and all kinds of small game, was once a favourite hunting ground of the French kings.

What to see   As well as the footpaths, the forest is criss-crossed by roads and forest tracks, and by 80 km of signposted bridlepaths. With its low hills and little valleys, the forest offers scores of picnic spots. A tourist circuit exists around the edge of the forest, linking villages and sites illustrating the way of life and traditional crafts of the region. At St Opportune-la-Mare, on a hillside overlooking the Marais Vernier, there is an apple museum, **La Maison de la Pomme**, with everything relating to apples and the making of cider and calvados.

Although across the river from the main part of the Brotonne forest, the ruined **Abbaye de Jumièges** lies within the Parc Naturel Régional de Brotonne and is its most important attraction. Set on a wooded height within a loop of the Seine, these old ruins, partly overgrown with creepers and rock plants and with ash trees growing among them, are extremely picturesque. The twin towers of the west front soar to 52 m, high above the trees, the roofless nave still has two rows of pillars and arches, and part of the apse and the lantern tower remain. The building was originally more than 100 m long and 50 m wide, and the whole complex, including chapter house, cloisters, store-rooms and the chapel of St Pierre, can be explored for hours.

The abbey was originally founded by St Philibert in AD 654, but was destroyed by the Vikings in AD 851. It was rebuilt by William Longsword, the son of Rollo, first Duke of Normandy, and was consecrated in 1067 in the presence of William the Conqueror during his triumphal tour of Normandy after his conquest of England. The Benedictines made it a centre of learning and the abbey stood, with restorations at intervals, until the Revolution, when it was closed down. The hundreds of monks were dispersed and the buildings were sold to a timber merchant, who started to pull them down and sell off the stones.

Jumièges has strong associations with Charles VII and his lovely mistress, Agnès Sorel. When Charles came to Normandy in 1448 to campaign against the English, she accompanied him. She was his favourite mistress – he called her *La Belle des Belles* and paid a great compliment to her beauty. He gave her the estate of Beauté-sur-Marne, so that she was known everywhere as *La Dame de Beauté* (The Lady of Beauty). According to old records 'she was admired by all and loved by many'. During their visit to Jumièges he stayed in the abbey, and she in her own house, called Mesnil-le-Bel, close by. She died there, aged twenty-eight, on 9 February 1449, after giving birth to her fourth daughter. She bequeathed her heart to the abbey and it is buried beneath a black marble slab inscribed in her memory.

Where to stay   **Hôtel de Normandie** (LdF), 19 Quai Gilbaud, Caudebec-en-

Caux, tel. 35 96 25 11. Facing the Seine, fifteen rooms at low to medium rates. Good value restaurant with regional menus, medium prices. Closed Sunday.

Hôtel Normotel, 18 Quai Gilbaud, tel. 35 96 20 11. Modern hotel with twenty-nine bedrooms, at low to medium rates. Nice dining room, cuisine without frills but generous, medium-priced menus.

Hôtel de la Poste (LdF), 286 Quai de la Libération, 76480 Duclair. Duclair is a pleasant riverside village about 15 km from Caudebec by the D982 towards Rouen. An old mansion in a lovely situation facing a great loop of the Seine, with twenty-three modernised bedrooms at low rates. Good restaurant. Closed Sunday evening and last two weeks of July.

Where to eat

Manoir de Retival, Rte St Clair, Caudebec-en-Caux 76490, Seine Maritime, tel. 35 96 11 22. On the side of a hill with views of the Seine and the Brotonne forest. A serious restaurant offering excellent cuisine (Michelin star) in comfortable surroundings but at fairly high prices.

Auberge Deux Couronnes, at St Wandrille, near the abbey. Good value restaurant in an old Norman house. Medium prices.

Le Grand Sapin, Rue Louis Le Gaffric, Villequier, 4 km from Caudebec. Large restaurant with terrace beside the Seine. Classic cuisine, good range of menus at low medium prices. Closed Tuesday evening and Wednesday, except July/August.

Rouen

Eighty km from Le Havre by autoroute, and 61 km from Dieppe by direct main road, Rouen is a fascinating, Jekyll-and-Hyde sort of place. As a sprawling, industrial complex and port, it is ugly, dirty, swamped with traffic, evil-smelling, badly signposted, easy to get lost in. On the other hand, despite the fact that it was burned in 1940, and bombed and shelled almost out of existence in 1944, Rouen is one of the great tourist attractions of France, a good place for a weekend or off-season break, and certainly worth an overnight stop from any part of Normandy. It is a place which, in the centre, is full of fine things, a place to walk in and take your time over. It is not advisable to drive into Rouen in the hope of 'doing' the town in a day. You will end up exhausted and bad-tempered, having spent most of your time trying to park or find your way, and not having seen half of its many attractions.

History

Rouen, now the *préfecture* of Seine Maritime, was made the capital of Normandy by Rollo, the first Duke of Normandy, and remained for hundreds of years the capital of the duchy. After the conquest of England in 1066, Rouen became closely associated with the affairs and

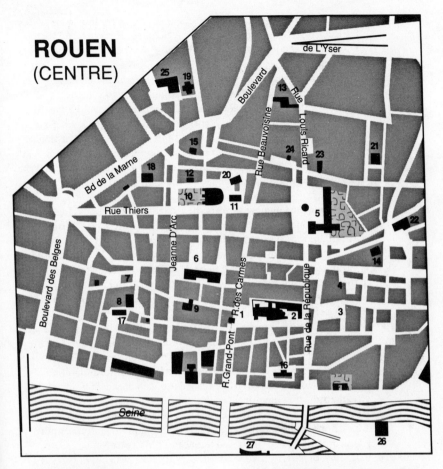

ROUEN
(CENTRE)

1 Tourist Office
2 Cathedral and Archbishop's
  Residence
3 Saint Maclou Church
4 Aître Saint Maclou
5 Saint Ouen and Town Hall
6 Palace of Justice
7 Old Market
8 Hôtel de Bourgtheroulde
9 Big Clock
10 Art Museum and Municipal Library
11 Wrought-iron Works Museum
12 Ceramics Museum
13 Museum of Antiquities and
   Natural History

14 National Museum of Education
15 Jeanne d'Arc Tower
16 Feretory Saint Romain
17 Protestant church Saint Eloi
18 Saint Patrice
19 Saint Romain
20 Saint Godard
21 Saint Nicaise
22 Saint Vivien
23 Chapel of Corneille College
24 Saint Louis' Chapel
25 Railway Station
26 Mooring for Boats
27 Préfecture

history of England during the Conqueror's reign and those of his successors, William Rufus, Henry I, Stephen, Henry II, Richard the Lionheart and John, all of them Dukes of Normandy as well as Kings of England.

The hapless and incompetent John, who had his nephew Prince Arthur murdered in the castle at Rouen, lost the duchy to King Phillippe Auguste of France in 1204. During the Hundred Years' War the town was captured by Henry V in 1419, after a siege of seven months, and remained English until 1449. While it was under English occupation, Joan of Arc, who had inspired the French armies in several victories over the English, was captured and sold to the English by the Duke of Burgundy, and was condemned and burned at the stake in Rouen.

During the Religious Wars of the sixteenth century both Huguenots and Catholics attacked and pillaged the city. In 1651, Charles II, escaping from England and on his way from Fécamp to Paris, stayed a night in Rouen. He and his companion, Wilmot, had difficulty in getting into an inn in the fish market, as, from the state of their clothes they were taken for vagrants.

The town was occupied by the Germans for eight months during the Franco-Prussian war of 1870–71.

Industry   The industrial strength of Rouen was built up in the nineteenth century, largely on the manufacture of cotton cloths and thread – at the turn of the century the cotton mills had a million spindles. There are also numerous dye works, chemical factories, foundries and shipbuilding yards: Rouen has often been called the Manchester of France. The textile industries have declined, but the town has diversified into other industries and is still, although it is 170 km by water from the sea, the fourth most important port in France. In common with most other large ports, this activity is also in decline.

What to see   Much of what is now called Vieux Rouen has been heavily restored
Vieux Rouen   – in some parts recreated is a more accurate word for what has been done. But the work has been tastefully carried out and the overall effect of the narrow streets of the old quarter with something like 1,000 'old' half-timbered houses, its magnificent churches and other superb buildings, is so overwhelming that for most visitors it ceases to matter what is really old, restored, or hygienically recreated.

There are about 3 km of pedestrian streets in old Rouen, and it is an important part of the charm of this quarter that there is almost as much pleasure to be had in just wandering about as there is in visiting the particular buildings.

Cathédrale de   This is probably the best place to begin a walking tour, because the
Notre Dame   *Office de Tourisme*, where you can get information and a map of the old quarter, is just across the square from the front of the cathedral.

The cathedral itself is considered by many to be one of the finest examples of French Gothic architecture. It was started in the twelfth century, burned down in 1200, and rebuilt during the thirteenth century. It was altered and embellished in the fifteenth century, and again in the sixteenth, and in the nineteenth century a new spire, made of cast iron and at 150 m from the ground to the top the tallest in France, was added. There are enthusiasts who say that it is the variety and detail which give the cathedral its attraction, and purists who say that the exuberance of the different architects, each going his own way and with no regard for the work of his predecessors, has resulted in a building without unity.

The great west front is framed by two towers of different periods. On the left the Tour St Romain is mostly twelfth century, only the top part is fifteenth century, and on the right the Tour de Beurre, 75 m tall, was started by one architect in the fifteenth century and finished by another in the sixteenth. (It is called the Butter Tower because it was partly financed by rich people who were, in return, given a dispensation allowing them to eat butter during Lent.) The central doorway of the three between the towers is sixteenth century, those on either side twelfth century with thirteenth-century tympani. The fenestration above the triple porch is fourteenth- and fifteenth-century Flamboyant Gothic. It was this intricate west front , with all its pinnacles and delicate carving, its niches and saints, which so fascinated Claude Monet that he spent two years (1892–94) on a series of Impressionist paintings of it in every state of light from dawn to dusk, grey days and sunny.

The north portal, which opens into the Booksellers Court, where there were shops until the end of the seventeenth century, includes some masterly carving. The tympanum has a fine Last Judgment, with the Raising of the Dead in the lower part, and the separation into the Good and the Bad in the upper section.

The interior is grand and austere, but curiously uninspiring. The transept is dominated by a lantern tower 51 m high, carried on four huge pillars with twenty-seven columns in each. The thirteenth-century choir is lighter and nobler in style than the nave, and has stained-glass windows showing the story of St Peter and St Paul, the Passion, and the story of the Good Samaritan.

In the ambulatory there are the effigies of Richard the Lionheart (died 1199) and his elder brother Henry (died 1183), and of Rollo, first Duke of Normandy (died 932) and William Longsword, the second Duke (died 943). The effigy of Rollo is a copy of the original, too badly damaged in 1944 to be restored, but the others are all thirteenth century.

The Lady Chapel has some fine fourteenth- and fifteenth-century glass, and the splendid, intricately sculpted Renaissance tomb of the two cardinals d'Amboise, Georges I and his nephew, Georges II (on the right), shown kneeling one behind the other.

St Maclou
Church

The Rue St Romain which leads from the cathedral to St Maclou is lined with half-timbered houses of the fourteenth to nineteenth centuries, some of them now antique shops.

Unlike the cathedral, St Maclou is remarkable for its unity of style, and is a masterpiece of Flamboyant Gothic. It is the work of Pierre Robin, who was one of the royal architects of Charles VII, and was paid forty-three French pounds of the time, 1437, for the job. Work on the church continued until 1517. It is named after a monk from Wales who arrived in Brittany in the sixth century, became a bishop, and died near Saintes in 561. Though not as large as either the cathedral or St Ouen, it excels them both in its overall harmony and beauty; it really is a lovely church.

The façade is dominated by a superb convex porch with five arches with traceried gables. Three of the arches have finely sculpted and pinnacled doorways. The beautifully carved wooden doors themselves are thought to be the work of a famous sculptor, Jean Goujon, who was killed during the St Bartholomew's Massacre. In the interior the organ loft (1521) is supported on two black marble columns, and is approached by a sculptured stone spiral staircase with open tracery. It strongly resembles an exterior staircase of the François I wing at the Château de Blois, and may have been a model for it.

Aître St
Maclou

Not far from the apse of St Maclou, down the Rue Martainville which has many half-timbered houses, is the entrance to the Aître St Maclou. This is one of the last surviving examples of a medieval charnel house and burial ground. It was first used as such in 1348 when the Black Death was at its worst and 100,000 people died in Rouen, but the present half-timbered buildings on the west, north, and east sides of the courtyard were built between 1526 and 1533. Those on the south side date from 1651. The galleries were open between the wooden pillars, and the bones were piled on the floor. There was originally no upper storey – it was added in the eighteenth century. Then, and in the nineteenth century, the buildings were used by artisans as workshops, and later as a convent school for orphans. They are now used by the École des Beaux Arts.

If you walk back from the Aître St Maclou, past the church itself, you can turn right into the Rue Damiette, a narrow street lined by many well-restored half-timbered houses, which is described in tourist publicity as having preserved its 'charm of ancient times'. I think it is worth quoting what Theodore Andrea Cook, a late nineteenth-century scholar who wrote several books on medieval towns, including one of more than 400 pages on Rouen, had to say about the streets of medieval Rouen:

'Above the mire and stench of the street rise houses which seem to topple forward into the morass beneath; each storey overhangs the last, until the frowsy gables almost rub against each other at the top, and nearly shut out every breath of air or glimpse of sky. Close above the pavement, and swinging in the rain, a multitude of signs and strange carvings blot out the little light remaining; Tritons, and syrens, are cheek by jowl with dragons . . . Vast gilded barrels, huge bunches of grapes, images of the Three Kings of the East, six pointed stars, enormous *fleur de lys*, great pillars painted blue or red, cockatrices and popinjays and bears and elephants; a whole menagerie of fabulous creatures hang over the lintels of the houses. . . .' (In those days, when streets were not numbered, private houses as well as taverns, inns and shops were distinguished by signs.) Cook continues: '. . . Higher up still the long thin gargoyles peer into the clouded air. . . every one in actual service, spouting showers of rain and refuse from the roof into the crowded road . . .'.

It seems likely that the 'hygienic restoration' mentioned earlier has a good deal more charm than the medieval original.

St Ouen   This great abbey church, slightly larger and higher than the cathedral, is one of the jewels of the Flamboyant Gothic style. Started in 1318, its building was delayed by the Hundred Years' War and it was not finished until more than a century later. With the exception of the west front, which was spoiled by rebuilding in the nineteenth century, the whole church is a symphony of lightness and balance, and the huge, lofty interior with its unobstructed vista of soaring, slender columns, all flooded in shafts of jewelled light from the great stained-glass windows, is spellbinding in its simple beauty. In summer the effect of the sunlight through the windows – there is said to be 4,000 sq m of glass, some of it original fourteenth century – is best in the late afternoon.

The church suffered badly during the Religious Wars when the Huguenots sacked it and made bonfires of the stalls, the pulpit and the priests' robes. During the French Revolution it became a museum, then a blacksmith's forge, and then an arms factory. It was at this time that the screen was destroyed, unintentionally creating the impressive vista down the nave to the ambulatory.

Adjacent to the church are the abbey buildings, now used as the town hall, dating from the early eighteenth century, except for the façade which was altered about 100 years later. A passage between the church and the town hall leads to a pleasant public garden from which there are good views of the exterior of St Ouen.

Palais de   This fine example of a civil building in the Flamboyant Gothic style
Justice   was originally built at the turn of the fifteenth and sixteenth centuries and a right wing was added in the middle of the nineteenth century. The major part of the building, though not the right wing, was badly damaged in August 1944 and was left a shell behind the splendid façade, but it has been very well restored.

Place du Vieux   If you turn right from the front of the Palais de Justice you come to
Marché   the Place du Vieux Marché, the square where Joan of Arc was burned at the stake. A modern church, the **Église Jeanne d'Arc** stands in the

square, surrounded by sixteenth- to eighteenth-century houses. It was completed in 1979 to a design which invites adjectives such as bizarre, or curious, and it has been suggested that the grey slate and bright copper used in the construction and the lines of the roof are meant to evoke the ashes and the flames of the burning. The building is not at ease in its setting – it needs more space around it – but the interior, partly lit by 500 sq m of sixteenth-century stained glass saved from the ruins of St Vincent's Church, destroyed by bombs in 1944, is entirely successful.

A monumental steel and concrete cross, 20 m high, marks the spot where Joan of Arc was burned, and is meant to commemorate her rehabilitation. It seems completely out of keeping with the event.

Hôtel de Bourgtheroulde

Just off the Place du Vieux Marché, in the Place de la Pucelle, is the Hôtel de Bourgtheroulde (pronounced 'Bootrood'). This once splendid private house was built in that period at the beginning of the sixteenth century in which so many fine buildings, including the Palais de Justice and the Bureau des Finances (Treasury) were put up. Drawings made in 1525 show the entrance façade to have been in the Flamboyant Gothic and early Renaissance style, splendidly ornate, but that has gone and it is sober now. However, the courtyard still has some fine work of the period. On the left is the **Galerie d'Aumale**, built between 1520 and 1532. The frieze beneath the arches is interesting because it is a contemporary representation of the meeting between Henry VIII and François I on the Field of the Cloth of Gold, near Ardres, which took place from 7–24 June 1520. The frieze above the arches illustrates the Triumphs of Petrarch. Both these interesting carvings are very much worn by time.

Rue du Gros Horloge

Turn back towards the Place du Vieux Marché and then immediately right into the Rue du Gros Horloge, an attractive pedestrianised street lined with half-timbered houses and shops at ground-floor level. Half-way along the street, above a low arch, is the great golden-faced clock which has become a symbol of Rouen. Once housed in the fourteenth-century belfry beside it, the clock was put in its present position in 1527. The Renaissance arch which carries and frames it was built for the purpose. It was given its ornate, gilded decoration at the end of the nineteenth century, and was very carefully renovated in 1969.

The fourteenth-century belfry has some rooms with an exhibition of ancient clocks and bells, and for those with the energy to climb the 163 steps to the top there is a panoramic view of the city.

If you carry on beyond the clock arch along the Rue du Gros Horloge, you arrive back in the Place de la Cathédrale, from which you started.

Museums

Rouen has a number of very good museums. Three of the most interesting of them are close to each other and within walking distance of the Palais de Justice described above.

Musée Le Secq des Tournelles

This is one of the world's finest collections of wrought-iron and metal work of all kinds. It is made up of 15,000 pieces made in non-precious metals, mostly wrought-iron, bronze and copper, from the third to the nineteenth century. The collection is housed in the disaffected church of St Laurent, with the larger pieces effectively displayed in the nave and transept. On the right of the nave are the splendid thirteenth-century wrought-iron gates from the abbey of Ourscamp. There is also a wonderful collection of ancient keys and complicated, beautifully worked locks. In the aisle on the south side of the nave there are all kinds of domestic tools and utensils, flat irons, spinning wheels, coffee mills, corkscrews, nutcrackers and incense burners, covering hundreds of years.

In the gallery above the north aisle there are old surgical and dental instruments, and those formerly used by barbers and wigmakers, bakers, gardeners, cabinet makers, blacksmiths and armourers – more than enough to show that some aspects of civilisation have become a great deal more refined than they once were. Altogether, this is a very unusual and interesting museum. Same opening times as for the Musée des Beaux Arts – see below.

Musée de Céramiques

These collections are housed in the de Hocqueville mansion, a fine late Renaissance building. In the seventeenth and eighteenth centuries Rouen became a centre for the manufacture of the glazed and brightly coloured earthenware called *faience*. The pieces made in Rouen were of good quality and this museum contains a selection showing the development of styles over the years and the introduction of different colours. There are also collections from other parts of France and other countries. The effects of the Revolution, competition from Wedgwood, and the rise in popularity of the more delicate porcelain, led to the gradual closure of the *faience* works in Rouen at the end of the eighteenth century.

Musée des Beaux Arts

Facing the Musée Le Secq des Tournelles, the Museum of Fine Arts contains one of the best collections of paintings of all periods in France. In addition to the great French painters, including Georges de la Tour, Corot, Delacroix, Fragonard, Ingres and the Norman painters Géricault, Poussin and Dufy, there are works of the Flemish, Italian and Spanish masters, among them David, Perugino, Caravaggio, Rubens, Veronese and Velasquez. An Impressionist room has pictures by Renoir, Sisley and one of Monet's of the cathedral, among others. Another room given over to the local artist Jacques-Émile Blanche (1861–1942) has portraits by him of famous writers, musicians and intellectuals, including Bergson, Valery, André Gide, Cocteau, André Maurois, Francois Mauriac and Stravinsky.

This only gives a suggestion of the importance of this museum, whose collections are spread through more than forty rooms. It is open from 10 a.m. to 12 noon and from 2 to 6 p.m. Closed Tuesday, and Wednesday morning.

Musée
Départemental
des Antiquités

Not far from the above group of museums, but a little further away from the centre in the Rue Beauvoisine in the buildings of a seventeenth-century convent, this museum concentrates on antiquities from Seine Maritime, though there are some from Egypt and Mesopotamia. It is particularly strong in ivories, enamels, tapestries, ancient sculptures and wood carvings, and also houses the beautiful third-century Roman mosaic showing Apollo pursuing Daphne, which was found at Lillebonne. Open a.m./p.m. Closed Thursday and public holidays.

Where to stay

Hôtel de la Cathédrale, 12 Rue St Romain, Rouen 7600, tel. 35 71 57 95. Pleasant old-style hotel in the pedestrian quarter near St Maclou church, with twenty-four rooms at low medium rates. No restaurant (very few of Rouen's numerous hotels have a restaurant).

Hôtel de Dieppe, Place B. Tissot, tel. 35 71 96 00. Good provincial hotel, run by the same family for 100 years. Near the railway station, but rooms (forty-one) modernised and soundproofed, at medium plus rates. One of Rouen's best. Good restaurant, **Les Quatre Saisons** (see below).

Hôtel Mercure, Rouen Centre, Rue Croix de Fer, tel. 35 52 69 52. Well-equipped modern hotel near the cathedral in the pedestrianised old quarter, with 125 rooms at medium plus rates. No restaurant.

Hôtel Versan, 3 Rue Thiers, tel. 36 70 63 33. Centrally situated, near the church of St Ouen. Modern, with thirty-four rooms well soundproofed. Practical, low on charm, medium rates.

Hôtel Arcade, 20 Place de l'Église St Sever, tel. 35 62 81 82. Large modern hotel on the other side of the river from the old quarter, but with restaurant, parking and garage for fifty cars. Air-conditioned rooms (144) at low medium rates. Restaurant at medium prices.

Where to eat

Rouen counts its good restaurants in dozens. What follows is just a short selection.

Gill, 9 Quai Bourse, tel. 35 71 16 14. Generally reckoned to be the best in Rouen (two Michelin stars). First class in every way, from the welcome to the coffee. Superb cuisine with original touches. Expensive but not excessively so. Closed Monday.

Les Quatre Saisons, Place B. Tissot, tel. 35 71 96 00. The restaurant of the Hôtel de Dieppe (above). Brasserie style, animated, and cuisine strictly in the best Norman tradition at medium plus prices.

L'Auberge du Vieux Carré, 34 Rue Ganterie (pedestrian area), tel. 35 71 67 70. Charming restaurant with terrace in a flowery courtyard in the heart of the old town. First-class cuisine from medium prices. Closed Sunday evening and Monday in season.

La Couronne, 31 Place du Vieux Marché, tel. 35 71 40 90. Said to be the oldest restaurant in France, founded in 1345. After all that practice they reach a high standard and are rather expensive, but there is a menu at 150 fr.

Les Maraichers, 37 Place du Vieux Marché, tel. 35 71 57 73. One of a number of bistros and restaurants in and around Place du Vieux Marché. On the whole the bistros offer better value than the more pretentious restaurants, some of which are priced for gullible tourists. Les Maraichers is one of the better bistros. Low/medium prices.

Brasserie de la Grande Poste, 43 Rue Jeanne d'Arc, opposite the Palais de Justice. Typical French brasserie, lively atmosphere, open all year. Medium prices.

Les Andelys

The view of the Seine at Les Andelys, with its great white cliffs crowned by the majestic ruins of Château Gaillard, is a classic of geographical textbooks and tourist brochures, and deserves to be. As with many striking places, the actual sight is a great deal more impressive than any picture.

Les Andelys itself, 40 km by road from Rouen and much further by the great loops of the river, is a town which would scarcely rate a mention in guidebooks were it not for its association with Château Gaillard. In fact, it was the building of the fortress which was the origin of Petit Andely, beside the Seine, where a whole community of labourers and craftsmen settled as they worked on the castle. Grand Andely, further away from the river, developed later, and is the more important part of modern Les Andelys.

What to see
Château
Gaillard

Château Gaillard was built by Richard the Lionheart. At the time Normandy was an English possession, or, rather more accurately, England was a Norman possession. Richard, as King of England and Duke of Normandy, had signed a treaty with Philippe Auguste, King of France, not to fortify the frontier between France and Normandy. The construction of Château Gaillard was a cynical breach of the treaty, and Philippe Auguste was enraged by the action. 'I would take it,' he ranted at Richard, 'if the walls were made of iron.' To which Richard replied, 'And I would hold it, if they were made of butter.'

From its clifftop site, Château Gaillard had extensive views over the countryside and the river, and was strategically placed to block the route from Paris to Rouen, the heart of Normandy. Building started in 1195, and according to legend was finished in one year, but despite the fact that the energetic Richard was his own architect and supervisor, most modern scholars say that legend is one thing and the facts are that it took three years, and even that was considered quick for a fortress. Richard's choice of site has sometimes been criticised, because it is dominated by a higher hill (now the site of a car park) behind it on the landward side. But Richard was a skilled soldier and did not make that sort of mistake. He was concerned with the weapons of his time, and knew that nothing existed which could bridge the gap between the higher hill and the fortress.

Château Gaillard served its purpose as long as Richard was alive. Philippe Auguste dared not attack it. But in 1199 Richard died of wounds suffered during the siege of Chalus, and was succeeded by his brother, John, not a man who inspired apprehension in Philippe Auguste. In 1203 the French king laid siege to Château Gaillard, and eventually starved out the English garrison. The castle fell in 1204, Rouen surrendered three months later, and France then annexed Normandy.

A hundred years later Château Gaillard became the prison of Marguerite de Bourgogne (the duchy), Queen of France, and Blanche de Bourgogne (the *Comté*), wife of the future Charles IV, who were condemned for their adultery with the brothers d'Aunay. The brothers were executed at Pontoise in 1314. Marguerite was assassinated at Château Gaillard in 1315 – some accounts say that she was strangled with her own hair – so that the king, Louis X, could be free to marry again. He died less than a year after his marriage to Princess Clemence of Hungary, poisoned it was thought by Mahaut d'Artois, the mother of Blanche, so that her son-in-law, Philippe, who was married to Blanche's sister, Jeanne, could become king, which he did. Blanche survived seven years of imprisonment, was divorced from Charles IV and became a nun. (The whole story is wonderfully told in Maurice Druon's *The Cursed Kings*.)

The great fortress is a ruin today, but a lot remains to be seen. The château can be reached by footpaths from Petit Andely, a stiff climb. By car, the approach is from Grand Andely, well signposted. The first car park you come to is the higher one, and a climb to the castle. There is a second car park, a good deal closer, with less walking to do. The château is open a.m./p.m. from mid-March to mid-November. Closed Tuesday and Wednesday a.m.

Excursion from Les Andelys

Half-an-hour's easy drive from Les Andelys along the D1 and D2 via Écouis brings you to Lyons la Forêt, a charming village in the heart of one of the most splendid beech forests in France. The **Forêt de Lyons** is impressive not only for its area, about 200 sq km, but for the great size and quality of its trees and the splendid vistas among its gentle slopes. There are signposted footpaths and bridlepaths, and it is criss-crossed by a network of narrow but pretty roads.

Lyons la Forêt, on the banks of the little River Lieurre, is what the French call a *bourg*, a very useful word describing a community which is too big to be a village, and too small to be called a town. It has about 800 inhabitants. Its best feature is its eighteenth-century covered market with its massive oak pillars and beams. There are many old half-timbered houses, some colour-washed, and an old church, heavily restored in the fifteenth century, which has a wooden belfry, a wood-panelled nave, and large wooden statues.

Lovers of art and those with a historical turn of mind may like to stop at **Ecouis** on the way to Lyons la Forêt and have a look at the collegiate church. It is a large Gothic building, unexceptional from the outside, but it contains some remarkable works of art and is associated with one of those terrible stories that throw a searchlight on medieval times. Enguerrand de Marigny was born in Lyons la Forêt in 1260, of a good though undistinguished family. But he rose to become chief adviser and Superintendent of Finance to Philippe IV, who was king from 1285–1314. In this position de Marigny wielded immense political power and became one of the richest men in France. He was a benefactor of his home district, and had this church built between 1310 and 1313. But his wealth and power had made him many enemies, and when Philippe IV died they turned against him, led by Charles de Valois.

A year before his death Philippe IV, afraid of the power of the Knights Templars and covetous of their great wealth, had put 15,000 of them on trial, burned their leaders at the stake, and imprisoned the rest. Their riches fell into the hands of the brother of Enguerrand, Jean de Marigny, Archbishop of Sens, who pledged the gold and jewels on behalf of the king but kept enormous wealth for himself. De Valois knew this and threatened to expose the archbishop unless he testified against his brother. At the trial de Valois accused Enguerrand de Marigny of sorcery and this, together with his brother's testimony, led to his condemnation to death. His victorious enemies left his body hanging on the scaffold for two years. *Sic transit gloria mundi.*

When Enguerrand built the church, he ordered fifty-two statues for the interior. Twelve of these superb early fourteenth-century sculptures remain, including one, variously said to represent Mary Magdalene or St Agnès, of a woman clothed from head to foot in nothing but her own hair.

Where to stay and eat

Hôtel de la Chaine d'Or, 27 Rue Grande, Petit Andely 27700, tel. 32 54 00 31. Overlooking the Seine. Not much to look at outside, but genuine old Norman interior. Ten rooms at medium plus rates. Pleasant, comfortable restaurant offering classic Norman menus at medium plus prices. Restaurant closed Sunday evening, Monday and January.

Hôtel Normandie, 1 Grande Rue, Petit Andely, tel. 32 54 10 52. Another old inn overlooking the Seine. Modest standards but good value. Ten rooms from low to medium rates, restaurant medium prices up. Closed Wednesday evening and Thursday.

Hôtel de la Licorne, Place Benserade, Lyons la Forêt, 27480, tel. 32 49 62 02. Good, comfortable rooms around an attractive courtyard. First-class cooking. Prices for rooms and meals medium plus.

Hôtel du Grand Cerf, Place de la Halle, Lyons la Forêt tel. 32 49 60 44. Old half-timbered inn in the market place. Ten rooms at low medium rates. Restaurant, medium plus prices, closed Tuesday and Wednesday.

Vernon and Giverny

Vernon is a pleasant residential town situated on an attractive reach of the Seine, with islands in the river and wooded slopes on either side. It owes its riverside promenade with swimming pool and flower gardens to the reconstruction which took place after heavy war damage in 1944.

Henry I of England built a wooden bridge across the Seine here, using the island near the modern bridge as a 'stepping stone'. Some of the piles of his ancient bridge can still be seen between the island and the bank, and beyond them amongst the greenery the vestiges of the Château de Tourelles, which he built to protect the bridge. In Vernon itself, on the opposite bank, the keep, now called the Tour des Archives, is all that remains of the twelfth-century castle built by Philippe Auguste.

Only 80 km from Paris, Vernon, with its riverside promenades and tree-lined avenues, and several good restaurants, is a popular weekend destination with Parisians. There are two good short excursions from Vernon.

Château de Bizy Only about 1 km from Vernon, this château was originally built about 1740 for the Duc de Belle-Isle, Marshal of France, who was the grandson of the notorious Fouquet, Minister of Finance to Louis XIV, who at state expense built himself one of the world's loveliest palaces, Vaux-le-Vicomte. Invited to the opening banquet, the young Louis XIV was so jealous and enraged at the display of wealth that he put Fouquet in prison for the rest of his life. He then built Versailles to show that he could outdo Fouquet, but by comparison it is a failure.

Anyway, the eighteenth-century Fouquet, Duc de Belle-Isle, shared his grandfather's taste for beautiful châteaux, and Bizy, though it has been much altered, remains attractive. Its owners have included King Louis XV and King Louis Philippe, who had the beautiful park replanted.

The interior of the château has some early nineteenth-century wood-panelled salons with eighteenth-century tapestries, original furniture from Napoleonic times, and a fine carved oak staircase. There are souvenirs of three of Napoleon's great marshals: Massena, Davout and Suchet, Duc d'Albufera, ancestor of the present owner, also Duc d'Albufera. There is a collection of vintage cars in the eighteenth-century stables. The château is open for guided visits a.m./p.m. every day (except Tuesday in September), April to September.

Open Saturday and Sunday, October to 24 December, and 5 January to end March.

Giverny This is the village, only 4 km from Vernon, where the great Impressionist painter, Claude Monet, lived from 1883–1926. His house, his studios and the gardens with the famous water-lily pond, are open to the public. The gardens are said to have been recreated as they were in Monet's time, using old photographs and the records of the nurseries which provided Monet with plants.

Claude Monet died in 1926, and the property was taken over by his illegitimate son. He, too, was an artist and looked just like his father, but was not a great painter. He was an alcoholic and met his death in 1966 when he staggered drunkenly into the path of an oncoming car. He had made no attempt to maintain the property, the house had become dilapidated and invaded with damp and dirt, and the gardens were wild and overgrown.

It was restored by the Academy of Fine Arts with the help of generous donations from wealthy art lovers in Europe and America, and opened to the public. There are about 1,500 visitors a day, every day that they are open from April to the end of October, with about 2,000 per day in May and June, when the gardens are at their best. The water garden, with its water lilies and Japanese bridges which Monet painted in every kind of light, is different from what it was in his time. Then it consisted of just the large pond and the bridges, surrounded by grass and trees. It has since been embellished by planting water-loving plants all round the edge of the pond.

Monet, who was one of the few artists to earn a good income from his paintings during his lifetime, and who also won a lot of money in a lottery, employed five gardeners to maintain the garden, and as it is now it requires seven full-time gardeners to keep it up.

In addition to the house and gardens, Monet's old studios are open to the public and contain copies of his paintings. At present there are no original Monet paintings on view. A shop sells postcards, books etc connected with the artist. The **American Museum** in the same complex is dedicated to 'the understanding and appreciation' of American art. It may help in this respect, but the spacious modern building with its formal terrace and gardens seems out of place in Giverny. The museum is open April to October. Closed Monday.

Where to stay **Hôtel d'Evreux Le Relais Normand**, 11 Place d'Evreux, Vernon 27200, tel. 32 21 16 12. An old building full of beams and old fireplaces, once the home of the Counts of Evreux. Twenty rooms at low to medium rates. Restaurant sound, but medium prices not quite justified.

Château de Brécourt, Douains, 27120 Pacy-sur-Eure, tel. 32 52 40 50. For those who want to see Giverny from a luxury base, this hotel half-way between Pacy and Vernon may appeal. In a Louis XIII mansion with moats still intact, it has fifty acres of grounds, an indoor swimming pool and tennis. Twenty-nine spacious and attractive rooms at top rates. Superb meals served in the majestic dining room, moderately expensive.

Where to eat

Les Fleurs, 71 Rue Carnot, tel. 32 51 16 80. Pleasant restaurant with meals à la carte, house wine included, at medium prices. Closed Sunday evening and Monday.

Les Jardins de Giverny, Chemin Roy, Giverny, tel. 32 21 60 80. Close to Monet's house, a serious restaurant with a very good wine list, and menus at medium plus prices upwards but good value for money. Closed Sunday evening and Monday, and February.

Evreux

At the centre of a flourishing agricultural region, Evreux is an important market town with some industry, but apart from its interesting cathedral there is not much to attract the visitor. It is an alternative base to Vernon for touring the valley of the Seine, the Eure and the Risle.

What to see
Notre Dame Cathedral

This cathedral in itself illustrates the long and stormy history of Evreux. First built in the tenth century, it was burned down and destroyed by Henry I of England in 1119, and rebuilt by 1193. But disaster struck again the following year. King Philippe Auguste was at war with the English, trying to make Normandy part of France. King John, feigning conciliation, invited 300 French guests to a banquet in Evreux and then treacherously slaughtered them all. Philippe Auguste was so enraged that he burned the town and destroyed the cathedral. The people patiently rebuilt it. The cathedral was burned again in 1356 by King John of France because the Count of Evreux, who took the English side in the Hundred Years' War, had murdered the Constable of France. It was not repaired until 100 years later. At the beginning of the sixteenth century the fine façade and portal of the north arm of the transept were added.

Some restoration was carried out in the nineteenth century by that ubiquitous renovator Viollet-le-Duc, who managed to spoil the roof of the nave. The upper parts of the cathedral were badly damaged by fire in 1940, when a German air raid set fire to the town, which burned for nearly a week. As if all this were not enough, some of the beautiful stained glass, which had been removed for safety in 1939, and was replaced after the war, was damaged by a summer storm in 1983. It has since been restored.

The variety of styles over so long a period is surprisingly harmonious, and the overall effect is austere but beautiful, yet it is full of rich and remarkable detail. The stained glass, progressing from before 1400 – those examples in the apse are considered to be some of the finest in existence – to the seventeenth century, is a reference library of that art. There is a nobility about this cathedral which makes it one not to be missed. It is a monument to man's irresistible patience, determination and faith, as well as his superb craftsmanship.

The former archbishop's palace, adjoining the cathedral, is a fine example of domestic Flamboyant Gothic architecture. It now houses the **Municipal Museum**, not without interest on a wet afternoon.

St Taurin

The ancient Benedictine abbey of St Taurin no longer exists, but its church still remains. This fourteenth- to fifteenth-century building is worth a visit, if only to see the superb thirteenth-century reliquary of St Taurin, originally given to the abbey by Saint Louis (Louis IX). It is made in silver and gilded copper, decorated with enamel and studded with gems, and is said to be the finest thing of its kind in France. The reliquary, about 1 m long and 60 cm high, represents a chapel in miniature, and the figures include that of St Taurin with his cross and mitre. It is in fairly good condition, despite the fact that the original gems have been stolen, and that during the Revolution it was thrown into a barn, damaging some of the smaller figures and decorative pine cones, which were restored in the 1830s.

Where to stay

Hôtel de l'Orme, 13 Rue des Lombards, Evreux 27000, tel. 32 39 34 12. Good modern two-star hotel with sixty-two rooms at medium rates. No restaurant.

Hôtel Ibis, Ave Winston Churchill, tel. 32 38 16 36. One of the popular chain, modern and functional. Sixty rooms at low medium rates. Private parking. Restaurant (low/medium prices) closed Sunday lunch.

Hôtel de France, 29 Rue St Thomas, tel. 32 39 09 25. A terrace overlooking the garden and the river, and fifteen attractive bedrooms at low medium rates. Unpretentious, but a very good hotel, complemented by a first-class gourmet restaurant, with a fine wine list. Prices medium plus but fair. Restaurant closed Sunday evening and Monday.

Where to eat

Le Français, Place Clemenceau (the market place), Evreux 27000, tel. 32 33 53 60. Brasserie/*crêperie* on the ground floor; restaurant on the first floor with menus based on fresh market produce at medium prices, house wine included. Closed Sunday.

Auberge de Parville, Rte Nationale 13, Parville, 27930 Evreux, tel. 32 39 36 63. West of Evreux 3 km by the N13. Dining room with exposed beams and large chimney, well-equipped and comfortable. First-class cuisine (Michelin star), so menu prices medium plus, but fair. Closed Sunday evening and Monday.

Towards the Côte Fleurie

With the possible exception of the Pays de Caux, which is monotonous in parts though it has some wooded valleys and a coast with pleasant resorts, the Norman countryside is attractive, combining the picturesque and the tranquil, and will appeal to those who like a country holiday. It is also full of interest, scattered with historical towns and villages, châteaux, old churches and lovely gardens.

Conches-en-Ouche

What to see

The 18 km from Evreux to this little town, attractively sited on a narrow hill within a loop of the River Rouloir, is a detour worth making to see the late fifteenth-century **church of St Foy**, famous for its Renaissance stained glass. The seven windows of the chancel, each 10.5 m high and installed between 1520 and 1534, are considered to be among the finest in Europe. The lower half shows episodes in the life of St Foy, and the upper half pictures scenes from the life of Christ. There are more magnificent windows, of an earlier date and by different craftsmen, in the aisles, including the Mystic Wine Press (south aisle) which, according to some experts, is a visual metaphor of the Eucharist.

There are several fifteenth- and sixteenth-century half-timbered houses in the main street opposite the church, as well as the studios and workshops of different craftsmen.

Where to stay

Hôtel Le Cygne (LdF), 36 Rue du Val, Conches-en-Ouche 27190, tel. 32 30 20 60. A delightful old building with fifteen simple rooms at low to medium rates, and a good traditional restaurant with menus at medium prices. Closed Monday.

Where to eat

Hôtel le Grand Mare, 13 Ave Croix de Fer, tel. 32 30 23 30. Good and ambitious restaurant with menus from medium prices up. Closed Sunday evening. Also eight simple rooms at low rates.

La Toque Blanche, 18 Place Carnot, near the church, tel. 32 30 01 54. The good, traditional Norman restaurant *par excellence*. Cellar has local ciders, perry from Domfront, and calvados up to 100 years old. Good range of menus from medium upward. Closed Monday evening, and Tuesday.

Harcourt

Travel from Conches via the D840, or direct from Evreux by the N13 and D840, in either case to Le Neubourg, a not very exciting drive through fertile but ordinary farming country. From Le Neubourg take the D137 west to Harcourt.

What to see

Originally a feudal castle in the English sense, the **Château d'Harcourt** was transformed into a livable château, in the French sense, at the beginning of the eighteenth century by the Comtesse d'Harcourt, but later became dilapidated. It lies in the centre of a forested park of 100 hectares, which includes a five-hectare arboretum with trees introduced from all over the world. This was started in the early nineteenth century by M Delamarre, and some of the trees he planted are now magnificent specimens. He left the property to the French Academy of Agriculture in 1828, and they have maintained and expanded the arboretum, and gradually restored the château.

The interior of the château, where some of the apartments have been restored, contains souvenirs of the Harcourt family, one of the oldest and most aristocratic in France. The château is open from 2.30 p.m. to 6 p.m. March to 15 November. Closed Tuesdays.

Until recently the **Château du Champ de Bataille**, about 7 km from Harcourt via St Opportune, was also owned by the Duc d'Harcourt. It is now a privately owned leisure and cultural centre, with an 18-hole golf course and a programme of musical concerts on summer evenings in season. The park has fine trees, wild rhododendrons, and a herd of deer. The château is an elegant late seventeenth-century building, very large but of fine proportions. The interior has some panelled rooms, huge fireplaces, a superb staircase, Gobelin tapestries and other works of art. The château is open a.m./p.m. from mid-March to mid-November, all day from July 1 to the end of September. Concerts begin at 9.30 p.m. Closed Tuesdays.

The Valley of the Risle

From Harcourt it is only 7 km to the pleasant little town of Brionne, which is a good base for exploring the valley of the River Risle, lovely at any time of year but especially beautiful in autumn, when the many trees are burnished with every shade of orange, brown and gold.

What to see

The village of **Le Bec Hellouin**, one of the most attractive in all Normandy, would be well worth a visit even if it did not have its interesting Benedictine abbey. There are several half-timbered houses, shady trees and flowers everywhere, and a classic example of the Norman country inn.

The abbey was founded in 1034 by the knight Herluin, who gave up his sword for the cross. In 1042 he and his few companions were joined by a monk called Lanfranc, of Italian origin, who had been teaching at Avranches. Lanfranc was learned, energetic, and far-sighted. In 1045 he founded a school at Le Bec Hellouin and under his influence and that of his successor, Anselm, also an Italian, it became the greatest European centre of learning of the eleventh century. (See also Caen: Abbaye aux Hommes, p. 150.)

The monks were expelled at the start of the French Revolution, and the buildings were used as a cavalry barracks, and then gradually sacked and destroyed over the years. In 1809 the abbey church was pulled down and sold for scrap.

It was not until September 1948 that the monks, a group from Mount Olivet near Siena, came back to the abbey. They have steadily restored it, and have made their church in the restored refectory of the old building. Of the original building little remains but the fifteenth-century tower of St Nicholas which, though it has lost its spire, still rises above the surrounding woods.

Like most abbeys these days, Le Bec Hellouin has a significant commercial side. There is a large shop which sells some rather good pottery made by the monks in the abbey, as well as paintings, engravings, religious books and other souvenirs. A **museum** adjacent to the abbey contains a collection of fifty vintage cars, including six

Bugattis, all in working order. The abbey is open for accompanied visits morning and afternoon, except Tuesday, and in the afternoons only on Sunday and public holidays. The car museum is open morning and afternoon, closed Wednesday and Thursday in winter.

Where to stay **Auberge de l'Abbaye**, Le Bec Hellouin 27800, tel. 32 44 86 02. An attractive eighteenth-century building, though one is tempted to describe both exterior and interior as 'overdone' Norman. Really more a restaurant than a hotel, but it has ten modest rooms at medium prices. Cuisine with tasty Norman dishes well prepared at medium prices upwards.

Pont Audemer It is a very pleasant drive from Le Bec Hellouin to Pont Audemer by the D130, which follows the right bank of the Risle with views over the river and the valley. But Pont Audemer is a confused little industrial town which does not look much from the main road that skirts around it. All the same, like the curate's egg, it is good in parts, and a practical place for a coffee or lunch break, with a walk around, or even an overnight stop. The Risle here divides into two arms which are linked by several smaller waterways, and around the St Ouen church there are old streets with a number of medieval half-timbered houses, some leaning over the water, some arching across blind alleys. James II of England spent a night in one such house during his flight to Paris, after his defeat at the Battle of the Boyne.

What to see Founded in the eleventh century, **St Ouen's** is one of those French churches which has drifted through history being fiddled with every few hundred years, but the interior is well worth visiting for the wonderful series of Renaissance stained-glass windows in the side chapels. There is also some impressive modern (1949) stained glass by Max Ingrand, one of this century's best craftsmen in this field.

France owes a lot to one man who was born in Pont Audemer, Taillevent, who was cook to Charles V in the fourteenth century, and who wrote the first French cookery book, *La Viande Royale*. This book was handed round in manuscript for well over 100 years, before being printed in 1515. It remained in print for another 100 years, but is not much use to chefs today, except to show what progress has been made in the culinary arts and how much better almost anyone can eat today than did the medieval kings.

Where to stay **Auberge du Vieux Puits**, 6 Rue Notre Dame du Pré, Pont Audemer 27500, tel. 32 41 01 48. Typical seventeenth-century Norman half-timbered house. Choice of twelve bedrooms in the old house, or in a modern annexe recently opened. You must dine in the restaurant, if you intend to stay. Rooms at low to medium rates. Restaurant good but rather expensive.

Hotel le Pilori (LdF), 38 Place Victor Hugo, tel. 32 41 01 80. Centrally situated in a pleasant square, nine rooms at very low rates. Good regional cooking at low/medium prices.

Belle Île-sur-Risle, 112 Rte de Rouen, tel. 32 56 96 22. Lovely mansion in a 100-year-old park with splendid trees on an island in the Risle. Sixteen elegantly furnished rooms (those on the second floor have fine views), and a first-class restaurant which offers a mix of traditional and original dishes. Half-board is obligatory in season. Boats, tennis, swimming pool, sauna. Both rooms and restaurant rather expensive.

Honfleur and the Côte Fleurie

Honfleur

The direct route to Honfleur from Pont Audemer is by the N175 to St Maclou, and then the D180, but a much more attractive, if slightly slower, route is to join the D312 at Toutainville, just outside Pont Audemer. The D312 follows the valley of the Risle and then turns along the estuary of the Seine towards Honfleur, with several good viewpoints across the river mouth to Le Havre (see map, p. 106).

Honfleur, situated between hillsides and the river, is a small town with a long history. In medieval times it was already an important port; in the sixteenth century during the age of exploration it was a major point of departure for the great navigators who sailed west and south into the Atlantic; then, until the end of the eighteenth century, an important commercial port trading with the New World, and a base for corsairs. Today it has a small fishing fleet, a little diversified industry, and is a tourist destination.

The heart of Honfleur today is the Old Harbour (Vieux Bassin) which was completed in 1684, in the reign of Louis XIV, to handle the trade between France and its settlements on the American continent. Today it is a forest of masts of ocean-going yachts, and the fishing boats use a newer dock to the east created 100 years ago. It remains to be seen whether Honfleur's undoubted charm will survive the opening of a huge bridge across the estuary, at present under construction and due to be completed this year. The considerable population of Le Havre, at present 70 km away by road, will then be within a few minutes' drive.

What to see
The old harbour

Honfleur is one of those places where the whole is rather better than any of the parts. The old harbour is still surrounded by its cobbled quays backed by picturesque houses. Those on the St Catherine Quay are all tall and narrow. They all have slate roofs, but the façades in white, brown, rose and black are all different. Facing them on the other side of the old harbour, on the St Étienne Quay, there are more solid-looking two-storey bourgeois houses with mansarded roofs.

There are no imposing public buildings in Honfleur and it is a classic

134

example of how purely functional and organic growth can sometimes produce a town far more pleasing to the eye than the most careful and professional planning.

The Lieutenance

Near the entrance to the old harbour, beside the lock which is opened at high tide, there is a building called the Lieutenance. This is all that is left of the residence of the King's Lieutenant, who was the commander of the port in the eighteenth century. A tablet has been placed on its wall commemorating the sailing of Samuel de Champlain in 1608 from Honfleur to Canada, where he founded Quebec. The first 4,000 settlers in French Canada were almost all from Normandy.

It was the old harbour, with its picturesque houses and the Lieutenance, which made Honfleur so popular with artists from the early nineteenth century onwards. The painter Eugène Boudin was born here in 1824, the son of a river pilot. In his teens he worked as a hand on the boats which plied the Seine to Rouen. As an artist he was a master of seascapes with wonderfully painted skies. Other artists appreciated his skills, but he was an old man before he received public recognition. As a boy of fifteen Claude Monet worked with Boudin, who became the focus of a group of artists that painted regularly in the Honfleur area.

Musée Eugène Boudin

The museum has a good collection of the Honfleur school and other nineteenth-century artists, including Isabey, Boudin, Courbet, Jongkind, Monet etc, and a room devoted to more modern painters, including Dufy, Marquet and Villon. Open a.m./p.m. in season, afternoons only October to mid-March. Closed Tuesday and public holidays, and January and February.

St Catherine's Church

This unusual church and its separate steeple were built entirely in wood at the end of the fifteenth century. Though wooden churches are not unusual in parts of Scandinavia, especially Norway, they are rare in France. This one was built by Honfleur's shipbuilders, so it is not surprising that the interior of the church resembles the framework of a wooden ship, upside down. The church has some sixteenth-century carved wooden panels which show a group of very musical angels playing seventeen different instruments. There is also a fine eighteenth-century organ.

The entrance ticket for the Eugène Boudin Museum is also good for admission to the steeple of St Catherine's church, which houses a small exhibition of sacred objects. Open a.m./p.m. Palm Sunday to September. Closed Tuesday, and 1 May and 14 July.

Rue Haute

Any walk around Honfleur should include this charming old street with its many seventeenth- and eighteenth-century half-timbered houses, and flower-filled courtyards and patios. It gets its name from the bank of shingle created by the high tides, and on which it was built. In those days the street was occupied by fishermen and shipowners who, on the east side, had direct access to the shore from the backs of their houses. The estuary has since silted up and the sea has withdrawn hundreds of metres. The port of Honfleur is kept open by constant dredging.

Côte de Grace

For the energetic, it is a steep but pleasant climb up to the plateau of the Côte de Grace, from which there are lovely views across the sea and the estuary of the Seine. The seventeenth-century chapel of **Notre Dame de Grace** is a place of pilgrimage for mariners. The chapel on the left of the transept is dedicated to all those Canadians of Norman origin who left from Honfleur over the years for a pioneer life in eastern Canada.

Where to stay

Honfleur is popular and knows it, and for the most part prices are above average for what you get.

Hostellerie Lechat, 3 Place St Catherine, Honfleur, 14600 Calvados, tel. 31 89 23 85. Near the old harbour, and next to the steeple of St Catherine's church. Typically Norman atmosphere. Twenty-two rooms, most with bath etc, at medium rates up. Good restaurant offering some unusual dishes, medium plus prices. Restaurant closed Wednesday, and Thursday lunch.

Hôtel La Tour, 3 Quai de La Tour, tel. 31 89 21 22. Good value modern hotel with forty-eight well-fitted rooms all with bath etc, at prices a little above medium. No restaurant.

Mercure, Rue Vases, tel. 31 89 50 50. One of the modern chain of middle-market hotels, with fifty-six comfortable rooms at medium plus prices. No restaurant.

Ferme St Siméon et Son Manoir, Rte Adolphe Marais, tel. 31 89 23 61. The old Ferme St Siméon beloved of the mid-nineteenth-century artists, on a hill overlooking the estuary, has developed into a luxurious and expensive property of several buildings in a pleasant park. Rooms are in the Manoir, in fact three buildings, with the best rooms in the one called Le Pressoir. It has been altered lately and now has fewer rooms (twenty-two) and more apartments (sixteen). The restaurant is in the original seventeenth-century farmhouse. Tennis and a covered swimming pool. Everything here is of rare quality, including the breakfasts. But prices of rooms and meals in this luxurious hotel of the Relais et Châteaux group are rather more than expensive.

Auberge de la Source (LdF), Barneville-la-Bertran, 14600 Honfleur, tel. 31 89 25 02. Small hotel in a village in charming wooded countryside, only 6 km from Honfleur and 10 km from Trouville and Deauville, and so a good base for exploring this stretch of coast. The hotel has a nice garden and trout pond. Fourteen rooms, all with own bath etc, at medium rates. Good restaurant, menus a shade expensive, but half-board, which they like you to take, is reasonable. Closed Wednesday (except July and August) and from 15 November to 15 February.

Hôtel Ferme de la Grande Cour, Côte de Grace, Equamauville, tel. 31 89 04 69. More of an old manor house than a farm, in very pleasant surroundings 1 km or so up the hill from Honfleur, with fifteen rooms at low to medium rates. Good, simple meals, plenty of seafood at medium prices. Residents are expected to take half-board.

Where to eat

L'Ancrage, 12 Rue Monpensier, Honfleur tel. 31 89 00 70. Attractive restaurant by the old harbour, with terrace. Good food at medium plus prices, faithful local clientele. Closed Wednesday.

L'Absinthe, 10 Quai de la Quarantaine, tel. 31 89 39 00. Very good restaurant specialising in seafood, overlooking the 'new' harbour. Sympathetic surroundings, whether in the beamed dining room or on the lively terrace. Medium plus prices. Closed Monday evening.

Au P'tit Mareyeur, 4 Rue Haute, tel. 31 98 84 23. Intimate little restaurant in a very old house completely Norman in style, at the old harbour end of the Rue Haute. Good-value menu at a medium plus price. Closed Thursday, and Friday lunch.

The above is just a selection. There is a wide choice of cafés and restaurants at all levels in Honfleur.

Deauville-sur-Mer

From Honfleur, the coast road, the D513, leads via the Côte de Grace to the several well-known resorts of this stretch of the Normandy coast (see map, p. 153). The road, which is narrow in places, has some blind bends and is very crowded in summer, should be driven with care.

Trouville-sur-Mer

A bit tatty round the edges, especially as you drive down into it by this coast road, Trouville is, once in it, a fairly large resort. Established in the mid-nineteenth-century, it is crowded and lively in summer, a place which generates its own sympathetic and easy-going atmosphere. It has a good beach, and an important yacht marina, and there are still some fishermen whose boats are left high and dry on the bed of the River Touques at low tide. It has a large nineteenth-century casino, some nightlife, and a deck-board promenade, like Deauville, called Les Planches – the planks.

Separated from its neighbour, Trouville, only by the narrow River Touques, Deauville has a completely different character and history. When Trouville was already a popular resort, Deauville was just a mud-flat. It may well have been the first place in the world to have been planned and built from the start as a holiday resort. The idea was that of Dr Oliffe, the doctor at the British Embassy in Paris and friend of the Duc de Morny, who got together a group of speculators to finance the project. This was not too difficult for the Duc, since he was what they politely call in France the 'uterine brother' of the Emperor Louis Napoleon. In other words, he was the illegitimate son of the Emperor's mother, Hortense de Beauharnais, queen of Holland, who was herself the daughter of Napoleon I's Josephine by her first husband, the

Vicomte de Beauharnais. When Hortense separated from her husband Louis Bonaparte (younger brother of Napoleon I), she had an affair with the Vicomte Flahaut and gave birth to a son who became the Duc de Morny. So he had rich friends in, as they say, high places, and the money flowed in.

From the beginning Deauville was meant to be a resort for the rich and fashionable people of Paris. The death of the Duc de Morny in 1865 slowed up the development, but the railway from Paris had reached Deauville two years earlier and this ensured its future. In 1912 Deauville was relaunched by Eugène Cornuche, a former waiter, who had become director of the casino in Trouville and crossed the Touques to launch a new casino in Deauville. His idea was that Deauville should turn its back on the sea, and the centres of fashionable activity were the casino, the race course, and the golf course. He also thought of the 'Planches' – the board walk – the promenade where each evening in summer inhabitants of the smart suburbs of Paris would stroll and meet other inhabitants of the smart suburbs of Paris, and observe what they were wearing and, more especially, who they were with. Cornuche's idea was so closely followed that it was considered in bad taste actually to go on the beach, to such an extent that one Paris wit wrote, 'At Deauville there is also the sea'.

Things have changed slightly. A marina with many hundreds of deep-water moorings has been gained from the sea, and there are important yachting and power-boat competitions in summer. But horse-racing remains more important than boating, and the summer season includes polo and the sales of yearling thoroughbreds, and culminates with the Grand Prix de Deauville at the end of August. The really smart people only go to Deauville for this meeting, but the resort is animated, exhibitionist and entertaining all through summer. If you like that sort of thing, you will certainly enjoy a visit.

Deauville was from the beginning an artificial conception, and there remains a sense of strain and artificiality about it. Its *habitués* feel obliged to be seen, to wear the latest fashions, to visit whatever bars and restaurants are 'in' this year, and in as much as it is not a place to relax in, it is the antithesis of the normal holiday resort.

What to see Apart from a scattering of Victorian villas in various exotic styles which can be contrasted with some very modern architecture, there is nothing of historical interest in either resort. The **Musée Montebello** in Trouville is housed in a highly decorated brick-and-stone villa of the 1870s, which is a sight in itself. It contains a collection of the works of those artists, including Boudin, Isabey, Mozin, Van Dongen, Chapuis and Dufy, whose paintings helped to make the Normandy coast known to Parisians.

Where to stay **Normandy Hotel**, 38 Rue Jean Mermoz, 14800 Deauville, tel. 31 98 66 22. If you are rich enough and want to stay where, as I was once told, 'everybody who is anybody' stays in Deauville, this is the place.

Comfortable turn-of-the-century charm, 285 rooms (and twenty-seven apartments) at top rates, leaving medium prices at the post. Restaurants offer good food, but are likely to be remembered as financial rather than gastronomic experiences.

Hôtel Le Trophée, 81 Rue de Général Leclerc, tel. 31 88 45 86. Cheerful modern, well-equipped rooms, and a very good restaurant. Rooms and meals medium plus.

Golf Hotel, tel. 31 88 19 01. On the heights 3 km behind Deauville among the greens and fairways of an 18- and a 9-hole golf course, 169 charming rooms at top rates. Hotel restaurant **La Pommeraie** is on the low side of expensive.

Hôtel Campanile, Rte de Deauville, St Arnoult, tel. 31 87 54 54. Close to the golf course, this hotel in the well-known modern chain does not put up its prices to Deauville levels, and is probably the best value in the area. Fifty-eight rooms at low medium rates, and a good restaurant including the usual help yourself buffet, at medium prices.

Hôtel Carmen (LdF), 24 Rue Carnot, 14360 Trouville, tel. 31 88 35 43. Quiet hotel with fourteen rooms at low to medium prices, and a good traditional restaurant with menus at medium prices. Half-board obligatory in season. Closed Monday evening and Tuesday.

Le Clos St Gatien (LdF), St Gatien-des-Bois 14130, tel. 31 65 16 08. In a typical timbered Norman country house a few km inland from Deauville and Trouville and 9 km from Honfleur by D579 and D74. Well-equipped hotel (eg indoor and outdoor swimming pools) with fifty-four rooms at from low medium rates upwards. Good regional restaurant, medium prices. Open all year.

Manoir de Roncheville, Roncheville, St Martin-aux-Chartrains 14130, tel. 31 65 14 14. For those who like a high degree of comfort at a reasonable price and away from the madding crowd, this elegant manor house in grounds beside the River Touques has eight bedrooms at high medium rates, and a restaurant which offers refined and tasty country cooking at medium plus prices. 10 km inland from Deauville by the N177 and D58.

The above is just a selection among the forty or so hotels of all levels in Deauville, Trouville and surroundings, a few of which insist on holiday bookings.

Where to eat

Ciro's, Promenade des Planches, Deauville, tel. 31 88 18 10. This is THE place to eat and be seen. Animated atmosphere, plenty to look at, and good cuisine. Expensive.

Le Spinaker, 52 Rue Mirabeau, tel. 31 88 24 40. Serious Norman cuisine (Michelin star) with menus well above medium prices. Closed Wednesday.

Le Yearling, 38 Avenue Hocquart-de-Turbot, tel. 31 88 33 37. Pleasant restaurant with menus at prices a little above medium.

Le Bistro Gourmet, 70 Rue Gambetta, tel. 31 88 82 52. Unpretentious but tasty cuisine at medium prices up.

Restaurant du Port, 142 Blvd F-Moureaux, Trouville 14360, tel. 31 88 15 83. Near the fish market. Good, sound meals.

Les Vapeurs, 160 Blvd F-Moureaux, tel. 31 88 15 24. Trouville's most popular restaurant for more than fifty years, this brasserie is always packed. All à la carte but not too expensive. Also has fourteen rooms with bath etc, at medium rates.

Along the Côte Fleurie

The resorts of the Côte Fleurie are the holiday haunts, for the most part, of the Parisian well-to-do. The interesting thing about them is that each has a clearly defined character of its own, and attracts a different kind of bourgeois clientele. Trouville has the raciness of Deauville but, apart from its grandiose casino, none of its pretention.

Benerville and Blonville

Going west from Deauville on the coast road, you come to Benerville and Blonville which are just quieter extensions of Deauville, the sort of places where families rent a villa for the whole of the summer holidays from mid-July to the end of the first week in September, just before the *rentrée*, that great moment in the French year when the children return to school. They share, with Villers-sur-Mer, the same superb sandy beach that stretches all the way from Deauville.

Villers-sur-Mer

Villers-sur-Mer is a smart and lively resort, nicely situated on a wooded hillside beside the beach, with a fine mile-long promenade behind it, and surrounded by pretty countryside. It has many private villas, few hotels, but smart shops and good restaurants and cafés. The gently sloping beach is safe for children, and there are interesting walks in the area, along the beach to the cliffs known as the Vaches Noires, where the rocks are rich in fossils, and into the countryside.

Houlgate

Separated from Villers-sur-Mer by the 5 km of the Vaches Noires cliffs, Houlgate has its own magnificent sandy beach, and is also set in attractive countryside. Like Villers, it has many impressive private villas lining shady avenues, but its atmosphere is rather more friendly and relaxed. Its sea front is almost a museum of nineteenth-century seaside architecture. Adjacent are the **Vaches Noires cliffs**, where shrimping or hunting for fossils makes an interesting change from swimming and sunbathing.

Cabourg

Between the sea and the west bank of the River Dives, Cabourg has a very strong personality of its own. It used to call itself, and probably still does, 'the *plage* of the elite'. Even its layout is excessively formal: its nineteenth-century avenues – it was built in the 1860s – radiate fanwise from the casino in the middle of the promenade, and are linked to each by other avenues in a semi-circle. It was already fashionable with the top level of Paris society when **Marcel Proust** was taken there by his mother in 1881 at the age of ten.

They stayed at the Grand Hotel. Proust returned there in 1890 and every season from 1907–1914, while he was working on the early books of *À la Recherche du Temps Perdu* (*Remembrance of Things Past*). The association did much to reinforce the snobbish image of Cabourg, and its long promenade with its lawns and flowerbeds is named after the writer. Even today it remains a reserved sort of place, and it is easy to imagine the impeccably bred but rather stuffy *habitués* of the Grand Hotel in the past giving a haughty sniff of disdain at the mention of the more racy Deauville.

Having said that, it is fair to add that Cabourg also has all the normal attractions of a smart resort, including a wide sandy beach equipped with all the latest club facilities, where children of all ages can be left in the safe hands of qualified physical training instructors who will keep them occupied for hours with games and exercises, while parents relax.

Dives-sur-Mer

On the opposite bank of the river from Cabourg, Dives-sur-Mer is no longer *sur mer*, as the river silted up long ago and the major part of the town is well inland. It was here that William, Duke of Normandy, assembled his fleet of ships to transport 12,000 soldiers on his expedition to conquer England. He sailed first to St Valéry-en-Somme to take more troops on board, and then crossed the Channel and landed at Pevensey.

Today, Dives is an industrial town with no pretensions to being a tourist resort. Nevertheless, almost the only things of any historical interest on the Côte Fleurie are to be found in Dives.

What to see

The present massive building of the **Church of Notre Dame** was erected in the fourteenth and fifteenth centuries to replace the eleventh-century church that William the Conqueror knew. Above the main doorway, on the inside, is a list of names of the knights who accompanied Duke William, and some of the names have survived and become well-known in modern Britain. But, like the Roll of Battle Abbey, the list is based on Victorian scholarship rather than any contemporary Norman record, and is not complete or necessarily accurate.

Dives has a 500-year-old **market hall**, a splendid structure of oak pillars and rafters with a tiled roof, which is still in use.

At the **William the Conqueror Artisan Centre** the shops of craftsmen and antique dealers are attractively arranged around the courtyard of a sixteenth-century coaching inn, which was called the Auberge Guillaume le Conquérant and survived until after the Second World War. It was in poor condition and was renovated as this craftsmen's village.

Where to stay

Auberge des Frais Ombrages (LdF), 38 Ave de la Brigade-Piron,14640 Villers-sur-Mer, tel. 31 87 40 38. Good, comfortable hotel with fifteen rooms at low to medium rates and a restaurant strong on regional dishes at medium prices. Closed mid-February to April.

Hôtel 1900 (LdF), 17 Rue des Bains, Houlgate 14510, tel. 31 91 07 77. Pleasant modern hotel with nineteen rooms, some with sea views, at low to medium rates. Good regional cooking. Closed Monday evening and Tuesday.

Hôtel Santa Cecilia, Ave des Alliés, Houlgate, tel. 31 28 71 71. Twelve rooms at medium rates. No restaurant.

Pullman Grand Hotel, Promenade Marcel Proust, Cabourg 14390, tel. 31 91 01 79. What the French call a 'palace' hotel, with splendid marble hall and seventy luxurious rooms at from medium plus to expensive rates. Same beach and sea views as Marcel Proust enjoyed. Serious and reliable restaurant **Le Balbec**, offering both regional and *haute cuisine* at medium plus prices. Good value for the standards offered.

Hôtel de Paris, 39 Ave de la Mer, Cabourg, tel. 31 91 31 34. Modern rooms (twenty-four) with own baths etc, at low to medium rates. No restaurant.

Auberge de l'Oie qui Fume (LdF), 18 Ave de la Brêche-Buhot, Cabourg, tel. 31 91 27 79. This oddly named inn (The Goose who Smokes) is in other respects a straightforward *Logis de France*, with meals and rooms at a little less than average prices. Closed Sunday evening and Monday, and October to April.

Le Moulin du Pré, Bavent 14860, tel. 31 78 83 68. South-east of Cabourg 7 km by the D513 and the D95A, Route de Gonneville en Auge. Worth the finding for those who appreciate first-class, original cooking, this restaurant in a restored mill also has ten small but charming rooms (five with bath). Meals are expensive, rooms cheap. Closed Sunday night and Monday, and October.

Where to eat

La Bonne Auberge, 1 Rue Maréchal Leclerc, Villers-sur-Mer, tel. 31 87 04 64. Comfortable restaurant furnished in Norman style, with classic cuisine at medium plus prices. The inn also has a number of very comfortable rooms, again at high medium rates. Closed October to March.

Guillaume le Conquérant, 2 Rue Hastings, Dives-sur-Mer, tel. 31 91 07 26. Good restaurant with medium prices, in the stables of the sixteenth-century coaching inn mentioned above, part of the artisan's village.

Pays d'Auge

Inland from the resorts of the Côte Fleurie is the Pays d'Auge, a picture-book Norman countryside of apple orchards, cows in the meadow, and half-timbered farmhouses, the land of cider, fresh cream, rich butter, calvados, and cream cheeses in all shapes and subtleties of flavour.

Though there is nothing spectacular in the Pays d'Auge, there are several places worth seeing, and the scenery is unfailingly charming, especially in late spring when the apple trees are in full bloom. In addition, if you enjoy Norman cuisine, there are plenty of wayside inns and restaurants where you can sample it at its best and most traditional.

Lisieux

In the heart of the region, and its most important town, Lisieux is today a business and industrial centre with religious overtones, as it is an important place of pilgrimage associated with St Thérèse of the Infant Jesus. Lisieux is a crossroads of major routes and is subject to serious traffic jams, especially at weekends.

St Thérèse was born in 1873, as Thérèse Martin, in Alençon in southern Normandy, but it is Lisieux that has made an industry out of her. She lived in Lisieux from the age of four, and spent the last nine years of her life in the Carmelite convent of Lisieux, where she died of tuberculosis aged twenty-four. She became famous for her book *The Story of a Soul*, in which she states her simple belief that all the pain and miseries of life are worthwhile if endured as an offering to God. She was canonised in 1925.

What to see

Between 1929 and 1954 a **basilica** was built in St Thérèse's honour, with a design roughly based on the Sacré Coeur in Paris but considerably larger, the crypt alone having room for 3,000 pilgrims. The building is far from beautiful, and has been described as a 'monstrous concrete mushroom'. The interior is over-decorated and garish, the exterior is grandiloquent, and altogether it is difficult to imagine anything further removed from the simplicity of St Thérèse herself. In summer a miniature train painted in virginal white and decorated with flags carries tourists around the town from her former home to the basilica. Personally, I find this commercialised Walt Disney approach to such a subject sickening, and I doubt that it does much for the image of Lisieux.

Lisieux was very badly damaged during the Second World War, and lost most of what was an attractive old quarter. **St Peter's Church**, however, survived. It was built between the eleventh and thirteenth centuries and was a cathedral until the end of the eighteenth. It has a fine façade, with three portals flanked by two towers. The interior is harmonious and majestic, pure twelfth-century Gothic.

Where to stay

There is a wide choice of modest hotels in Lisieux. It will save trouble if you choose one which has its own parking facilities.

Garden's Hotel, Rte N13, Lisieux 14100, tel. 31 61 17 17. Comfortable modern hotel on the edge of Lisieux on the RN13, the Paris road. No parking problems. Sixty-nine rooms at medium rates. Heated pool. Good restaurant, medium-price menus.

Hôtel La Coupe d'Or (LdF), 49 rue Pont Mortain, tel. 31 31 16

84. Near the town centre, limited lock-up parking. Eighteen rooms at low to medium rates. Restaurant offering regional dishes at low medium prices.

Where to eat

Restaurant Le France, 5 Rue au Char, tel. 31 62 03 37. Near the town hall. Unpretentious, but very good value at low medium prices.

Auberge du Pecheur, 2 bis, Rue de Verdun, tel. 31 31 16 85. Near the station. Good, sound meals, nothing fancy, almost like home cooking. Range of menus at medium prices and upwards. Closed Tuesday and Wednesday.

Excursions from Lisieux

Though Lisieux itself may be of limited interest to most tourists, it is a good centre for those who want to explore the Pays d'Auge.

Cambremer

This village 15 km west of Lisieux via the N13, is famous for its cider and calvados. The **Route du Cidre** is signposted to a number of surrounding villages which have the right to label their cider *Cru de Cambremer*, if it is judged good enough. Farms on the route sell their products direct to visitors, and some have guest rooms, or *Camping à la Ferme*.

Beuvron-en-Auge

A prettily restored village with old Norman houses, covered market, craftsmen's shops. It can be reached by a pleasant drive across country from Cambremer by the D85 to Clermont-en-Auge. It is on the *Route du Cidre*.

Coquainvilliers

This small village on the D48 north of Lisieux has a well-known distillery, the **Moulin de la Foulonnerie**, which is open to the public and where the various stages of the distillation of calvados from cider are explained, and the stills and ageing rooms can be seen. Audio-visual aids. Open every day April to September.

St Germain-de-Livet

About 6 km south of Lisieux by the D579 and the D268A, with a delightful **château** which is one of the finest examples of the use of glazed tiles of different colours with brick to make a chequerboard façade, flanked by an earlier fifteenth-century wing which is stone and half-timbered. The château is built around an arcaded courtyard and the interior is well worth visiting, with a Louis XVI salon in one of the towers. Open for accompanied visits a.m./p.m. 1 Feb to September, and mid-October to mid-December. Closed Tuesday.

Crevecoeur-en-Auge

Seventeen km west of Lisieux by the N13, this **château** is situated picturesquely among trees and there is an extremely interesting group of buildings on the site, including the ruins of an original eleventh- and twelfth-century stone castle surrounded by a moat, a fifteenth-century farm, a sixteenth-century barn, a twelfth-century chapel, and one of the finest pigeon-cotes in Normandy, which had room for 1,500 birds. The whole ensemble was restored in 1972, and the fifteenth-century château itself is now a museum of Norman architecture, and, surprisingly, also of oil-industry techniques.

Livarot and Vimoutiers

Cheese lovers may like to continue south from St Germain de Livet and return north via the D64 , a pretty drive through the valley of the Touques, much of it beside the river. The village of Livarot has some attractive old houses and a **Conservatoire des Techniques Traditionelles Fromagères** open for guided visits, where the various stages in the manufacture of the pungent cheese which takes its name from the village are explained. (Since 1988 the museum side of the Conservatoire has been transferred to St Pierre-sur-Dives, 16 km west.) The Conservatoire also deals with Camembert and Pont l'Éveque cheeses. Visitors can taste and buy cheeses, and there is a café with reasonable fixed-price menus. Open for visits all day from 1 April to 31 October. The rest of the year it is open a.m./p.m. Wednesday to Sunday only.

Vimoutiers   Tourists who happen to be tyrosemiophiles (cheese label collectors) may like to continue south to Vimoutiers (9km) where there is a **Museum of Camembert**, with cheese tasting and a collection of Camembert labels from as far afield as Chile. Unlike many well-known French cheeses, Camembert was never protected by any kind of trade mark, so anyone could make their own version and call it Camembert. Open daily from April to 31 October, except Monday morning.

Vimoutiers is a pleasant town, almost entirely new. On 14 June 1944, an air raid destroyed 90 per cent of the former town and killed 200 civilians in a few minutes. The town was rebuilt with spacious streets and a huge main square, in the centre of which is a statue of Marie Harel, who made Camembert cheese famous. It is a copy donated by an American cheese importer: the original had its head blown off in the air raid.

St Pierre-sur-Dives   Sixteen km west of Livarot by the D4, this is another cheesy town, where many of the boxes used to pack Camembert are made; there is also a cheese museum. The little market town was severely damaged in 1944, but some nice old houses survived, as well as the impressive **abbey church**.

The village also has a remarkable **covered market**, like that at Dives-sur-Mer, but the original was almost completely destroyed in 1944 and this is a copy of the one built in the thirteenth century by the monks. In the wonderful joinery of the pillars, beams and rafters, there are no screws or nails, but nearly 300,000 chestnut pegs instead.

Where to stay   **Hôtel du Vivier** (LdF), Place de la Mairie, Livarot 14140, tel. 31 63 50 29. Typical small Norman inn with ten rooms at low rates, and a very good-value restaurant, also cheap. Closed for two weeks from end September into October. Restaurant closed Sunday evening and Monday.

Hôtel de France (LdF), 152 Grande rue, Orbec 14290, Calvados, tel. 31 32 74 02. *Logis de France* based on an old coaching inn, with twenty-five rooms at low rates up. The better rooms (eleven) are in a modern annexe. Good restaurant with menus starting at low prices.

Where to eat   **Le Pavé d'Auge**, Beuvron-en-Auge 14430, tel. 31 79 26 71. Good restaurant with refined cuisine and menus at high medium prices. Closed Monday evening and Tuesday.

Au Caneton, 32 Grande Rue, Orbec 14290, Calvados, tel. 31 32 73 32. Good, serious restaurant in a fine seventeenth-century house. Menus, starting at high medium, offer value for money. Closed Monday evening, and Tuesday.

Caen and the D-Day Beaches

Caen

For those visitors who come to France by the Portsmouth–Caen ferry, which docks at Ouistreham 12 km to the north, the city of Caen is unavoidable. The cultural, commercial and industrial capital of Lower Normandy, and the *préfecture* of the department of Calvados, it has a population of about 200,000, including its suburbs.

Caen was the first major objective of the invasion forces after the Normandy landings in the Second World War. From 6 June to 20 July 1944 it was bombarded and burned incessantly. Three-quarters of the city was destroyed, and another 10 per cent badly damaged. Almost all its lovely Renaissance mansions and streets of old houses were lost. The centre of the city was rebuilt on a rather grand scale, with wide tree-lined avenues and spacious squares. Those old historic buildings which could be repaired were intelligently restored, and many of the new buildings were put up in the lovely cream-coloured Caen stone, which in olden times was exported to England for use in important buildings, including the Tower of London and Canterbury Cathedral. Following its rebuilding, Caen experienced an industrial boom and almost doubled in size, but at present it is suffering a recession and considerable unemployment.

What to see
Caen
Memorial

This is easily reached by the ring road without going into Caen itself, and is signposted at several points. It is, in fact, a **Museum for Peace**, which by a mixture of techniques and exhibits, from uniforms to tanks, by photographs, diagrams, documents, recordings, television films and wide-screen cinema, tells the story of the build-up of Nazism, the Second World War, the D-Day landings and the Battle of Normandy, the work of the French Resistance, and the final victory. It is all very well done, sometimes very noisy, but successfully creating the magnitude and horror of the events, including the bombing of London, the evacuation of the children, and the terrible slaughter on the beaches of Normandy.

It is so laid out that everyone is obliged to follow the same route through the museum, with minor variations according to choice,

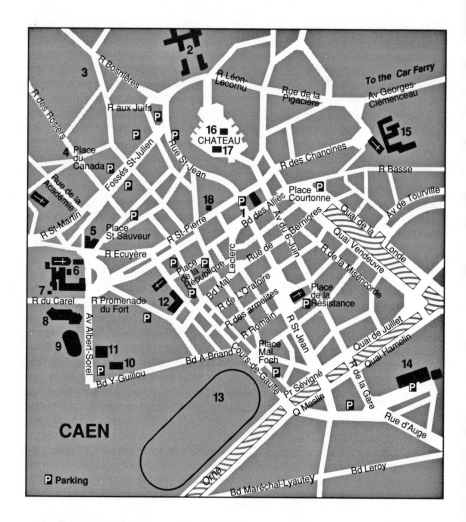

CAEN

1 Tourist Information	**10** Piscine
2 Université	**11** Centre de Congress
3 Jardin des Plantes	**12** Préfecture
4 Calvados Tourist Office	**13** Prairie Hippodrome
5 Palais de Justice	**14** Gare SNCF (Railway Station)
6 Abbaye aux Hommes	**15** Abbaye aux Dames
7 Hôtel de Ville	**16** Musée des Beaux Arts
8 Conservatoire	**17** Musée de Normandie
9 Stade Helitas	**18** Musée de la Poste

finishing in the wide-screen cinema which shows, in succession, a film of the D-Day landings, made at the time and showing the action on the different beaches; then a film of the Battle of Normandy, following the landings, with the wholesale destruction of towns and villages as the armies rolled remorselessly on. The final film is called *Hope* (*Espérance*), and though its intentions are good it is a long way the least successful of the three.

The Memorial does not close at lunchtime, and there is a self-service cafeteria where you can get lunch at a reasonable price.

The Château

The great fortress built by William the Conqueror in the eleventh century, and enlarged in the twelfth, thirteenth, fourteenth and fifteenth, was still in use as an army barracks early this century. It was very heavily damaged in 1944, and not much remains today apart from the great ramparts, but the rubble of destroyed buildings was cleared away from the base of the walls and replaced by grassy slopes, so that the impressive site of the castle is well defined. The modern Museum of Fine Arts has been established within the walls, as has the Museum of Normandy, once the Governor's house.

If you park near the University, it is only a short walk through the castle grounds to the ramparts.

Museum of Fine Arts

The comprehensive collection includes works from fifteenth-century Italian and Flemish masters right through to modern French painters. Veronese, Poussin, Rubens, Tintoretto, Courbet, Corot, Géricault, Monet and Bonnard are among the great artists represented, and there is a fine collection of engravings by Dürer, Rembrandt and Callot. There is also a good collection of early Limoges enamels, and fine French porcelain. Open a.m./p.m. in summer, afternoons only in winter. Closed on Tuesday.

Museum of Normandy

The history of Normandy from prehistory to modern times is illustrated in this museum in three sections, the first up to the coming of the Normans, the second describing their settlement and the development of agriculture, showing the implements used, and the third devoted to local crafts and industries over the ages, with the methods and tools used, as well as examples of traditional furniture and utensils used in Norman homes. Same hours of opening as the Museum of Fine Arts.

Église St Pierre

This church was started in the thirteenth, continued in the fourteenth and fifteenth, and finished in the sixteenth century. Gifts from the rich merchants of Caen enabled it to be richly decorated. Its 78 m spire, originally erected in 1308, was considered to be the finest in Normandy, but it fell during the battle of Normandy and crushed most of the nave. Both the spire and all the vaulting of the nave have been carefully restored to what they were, as has the beautiful Renaissance façade, opposite the château.

In the nearby Rue St Pierre, at numbers 52 and 54, are two of the sixteenth-century half-timbered houses still left in Caen. Number 52 houses a **Museum of Postal History and Communication** of considerable interest to serious philatelists and students of communication techniques. Open a.m./p.m. in summer, closed Tuesdays, and afternoons only in winter, closed Sunday and Monday.

Église St Sauveur   Further down the Rue St Pierre, on the right on the corner of the Rue Froide, is the extraordinary church of St Sauveur, also called Notre Dame de Froide-Rue, which distinguishes it from St Sauveur du Marché, in the Place St Sauveur. It has a double apse backing on to the street, the one on the left Flamboyant Gothic, the one on the right Renaissance. The duality is repeated in the interior, where there are two naves side by side; the one next to the street is fifteenth century, the original one fourteenth century.

It was the nuns attached to this church who cared for Beau Brummell, who died in Caen after a long exile in 1840. This famous English dandy had been a friend of the Prince Regent, but Brummell quarrelled with his royal patron, and shortly after is said to have asked Lord Alvaney, who was with the Regent, 'Who's your fat friend?', a remark which did little to repair their differences. Brummell fell on hard times and in 1826 he fled to France to avoid his creditors. In 1830 he was given the sinecure of British Consul in Caen, but after two years was made redundant. He lived on in poverty, sick and mad, sending out invitations to non-existent parties to which no one came.

Hôtel d'Escoville   This Renaissance mansion, built between 1533–38, now houses the tourist office, and is just across the street from St Pierre. The façade is rather severe, but the interior courtyard is harmonious and has some fine sculpted decoration.

Abbaye aux Hommes   Caen was William the Conqueror's administrative centre for Normandy and his favourite place of residence. He started the castle and he built Caen's two famous abbeys, the Abbaye aux Hommes and the Abbaye aux Dames. He was, in fact, an enthusiastic builder and was responsible for twenty-three abbeys and monasteries, but these two were wrung from him by circumstance. William had ignored the rules of the church by marrying his cousin, Matilda. The Archbishop of Rouen retaliated by excommunicating them both for marrying within forbidden limits. William was furious. He sacked the archbishop, and everyone else he thought was against him in the matter.

His victims included Lanfranc, then prior of the Abbey of Bec Hellouin, who was ordered to quit the monastery. Lanfranc did so, riding an old lame horse, all that his brother monks could spare. He had not journeyed far from his beloved monastery when, by chance, he met William. The duke received him with anger and threats, but Lanfranc parried the anger with a jest. 'I am obeying your orders as well as I can,' he said 'and I will obey them more quickly if you give me a better horse.'

He held the duke in conversation for an hour, and succeeded in persuading him that there was no point in defying the Pope. William had no intention of undoing his marriage, but was anxious to be reconciled with Rome. Realising that Lanfranc was no ordinary man, he charged him with the mission of reconciliation. Lanfranc, an Italian from Pavia, obtained a dispensation from the Pope for both duke and duchess on condition that they should make an important and permanent service to the Church.

William greeted the solution with enthusiasm and started the two abbeys in Caen. They were built on the grand scale and William supervised the work himself, spending great sums of money obtained in booty from his conquest of England. William dedicated the abbey to St Étienne (St Stephen) and made Lanfranc its first abbot, but he was not there long before being made Archbishop of Canterbury.

The conventual buildings of the abbey were rebuilt in the eighteenth century but the solid Romanesque abbey church remains, essentially the same as when it was built to Lanfranc's own plans. Tradition has it that as long as the church of St Étienne stands undamaged then the English throne too will remain intact. The inhabitants of Caen showed considerable faith both in this tradition and the durability of the English throne during the terrible bombardment of Caen in 1944. Hundreds of them sheltered in the massive old church and their faith was rewarded – in spite of dreadful destruction all round, St Étienne was almost untouched, and no one inside it was hurt.

The conventual buildings are now occupied by the town hall, but a part of them is open to the public and worth visiting. The guided visit takes about an hour and includes the refectory, a magnificent room panelled in carved wood, the former chapter house, now used for marriages, which also has the original wood carvings, the oval parlour, and the early eighteenth-century cloister. Open a.m./p.m. Guided visits start on the hour. Closed Saturday and Sunday. The entry is in the Esplanade Jean Marie Louvel.

Abbaye aux Dames   The Abbaye aux Dames was founded in 1062 by William's wife, Matilda. Its church is Romanesque, apart from a thirteenth-century chapel in the transept, but it is smaller, lighter, more feminine than St Étienne, with elaborate capitals instead of simple ones, a light arcade instead of a deep triforium, and a more general elegance all round.

The abbey buildings were reconstructed in 1704 by the architect who also restored the conventual buildings of the Abbaye aux Hommes. The buildings, which were badly damaged in 1944, have been well restored and since 1985 have been occupied by the offices of the *Conseil Régional de Basse Normandie*. They are open to the public every afternoon.

Where to stay   **Hôtel Moderne**, 116 Blvd Maréchal Leclerc, Caen 14300, tel. 31 86 04 23. Well situated in the centre of town near St Peter's Church and the castle. Private parking. Forty rooms, with good bathrooms, at medium rates upwards. No restaurant.

Hôtel Le Dauphin (LdF), 29 Rue Gemare, tel. 31 86 22 26. In a quiet situation but in the town centre not far from the castle. Twenty-two rooms either soundproofed or overlooking the garden at the rear, at medium rates. Good classical restaurant from medium prices up.

Climat de France, Ave de Montgomery, Quartier de la Folie Couvrechef, tel. 31 44 36 36. Off the *périphérique nord, sortie* Creully, D22. One of this modern chain with pleasant, functional rooms, with bath, and good value restaurant. Prices low medium for both rooms and meals.

Where to eat

La Bourride, 15–17 Rue du Vaugueux, tel. 31 93 50 76. In the pedestrian area near the château, this restaurant is one of the finest in Normandy (two Michelin stars); chef Michel Bruneau is a dynamo of skills and enthusiasm. At its cheapest, a meal here costs less than half what it would in a second-rate restaurant in London's West End – that is, expensive by French standards. Nice dining room in seventeenth-century house, and welcome and service first rate.

La Poêle d'Or, 7 Rue Laplace, off the Rue St Jean, near the river, tel. 31 85 39 86. Typical bistro with good meals at low medium prices. Closed Saturday and Sunday, and last fortnight of July.

Le Boeuf Ferré, 10 Rue du Croisier, tel. 31 85 36 40. Not far from the Abbaye aux Hommes. Generous helpings at medium prices, cuisine with a Gascon flavour. Advisable to book. Closed Saturday lunch and Sunday, and last fortnight of July.

Daniel Tuboeuf, 8 Rue Buquet, tel. 31 43 64 48. Another very good restaurant (Michelin star) in the Norman tradition, with menus from medium plus prices. Closed Sunday and Monday, and August.

The above is just a selection of the many restaurants in Caen. As well as brasseries and bistros there are many pizzerias, Chinese (Vietnamese) and North African restaurants, several of them in the Rue du Vaugueux. They are not much cheaper than sound, middle-of-the-road French restaurants.

Around Caen
Ouistreham/ Riva Bella

Probably few of the tourists arriving at Ouistreham, where the Portsmouth/Caen cross-Channel ferry actually docks, realise that they are next to a genuine resort with a marina for more than 600 yachts and one of the finest and biggest sand beaches anywhere on the Channel. Riva Bella, which is the seafront and resort area of Ouistreham, was flattened on 6 June 1944 when the 4th Anglo-French Commando landed here and attacked the German positions. It was rebuilt with wide avenues flanked by summer villas. The **No. 4 Commando Museum** is open every day from June to September, and at weekends only from Palm Sunday to the end of May. Ouistreham has a good example of a fortified church, half-Romanesque, half-Gothic, with a remarkable façade, tower and twelfth-century capitals (opposite the post office in the town centre).

The D-Day beaches

The biggest military operation in the history of the world, the Allied invasion of Normandy, began on the 6 June 1944. The forces used for this first day's assault alone were massive: 185,000 men and 20,000 vehicles, carried in 4,200 landing craft escorted by 1,200 warships, including seven battleships and twenty-three cruisers. In addition there were more than 20,000 airborne troops, carried in 1,087 aircraft and gliders, and a further 10,000 aircraft supported the landings with heavy bombardment and strafing of German defence positions.

The landings were made on five different Normandy beaches, which were named, from east to west, Sword, Juno, Gold, Omaha and Utah. They started at dawn and at the end of the day there were more than 156,000 Allied troops on Norman soil. At the cost of 2,500 dead, a foothold had been secured. In the days that followed more troops and vehicles poured across the Channel, their landing facilitated by the Mulberry harbours, assembled from huge concrete caissons – some of them weighed over 6,000 tons each – which had been painstakingly towed across the Channel at six knots by a huge fleet of tugs. The footholds became bridgeheads, the bridgeheads began to link up.

German resistance was fierce. The first Allied objective was Caen, and they got to within 5 km of it on the first day, but the battle went on for six weeks until 20 July, when what was left of it was finally captured. Bayeux, on the other hand, only 26 km west of Caen, was captured by the British 50th Northumberland Division on the first day and survived the Battle of Normandy practically unscathed. Bayeux was the luckiest town in northern Normandy, while the unluckiest village was Tilly-sur-Seulles, only 11 km south of Bayeux, which was captured, lost, and recaptured twenty-three times. By mid-August the Battle of Normandy had been won.

For tourists who want to see something of the D-Day beaches, Ouistreham is the logical place to begin. Sword beach runs from Riva Bella west to Langrune. In fact, the first invasion landing was not on 6 June, but the night before, when troops of the 5th Parachute Brigade made an airborne landing at the village of Bénouville, half-way between Caen and Ouistreham, and captured the bridges across the River Orne and the Caen–Ouistreham canal. Ranville, nearby on the other side of the canal, was captured by airborne troops of the Lancashire Fusiliers. In Bénouville there is a **6th Airborne Division Museum**, which is open daily from 22 March to 15 October.

The next beach west is Juno, from St Aubin to Graye-sur-Mer, and then comes Gold beach, from Ver-sur-Mer to Port en Bessin. At the centre of Gold beach was the town of Arromanches, and its capture was vital to the success of the invasion, because it was here that one of the artificial Mulberry harbours was to be set up. By a brilliantly fought

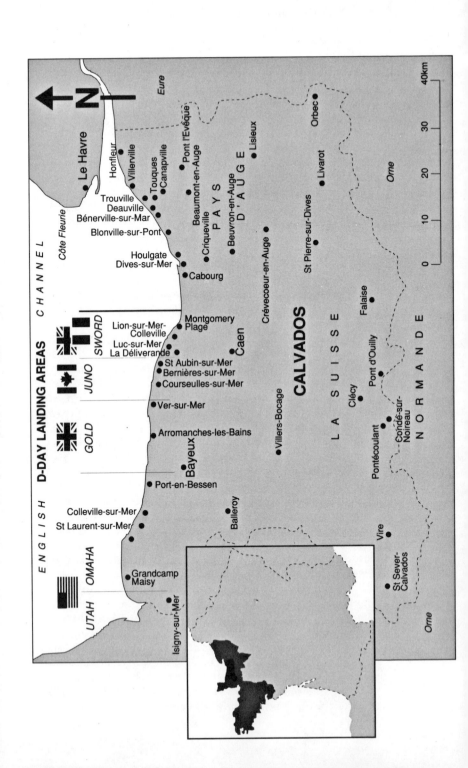

flanking movement, the 50th Northumberland Division had captured Arromanches by the afternoon of D-Day. The Mulberry harbour was started on 7 June and took a week to complete. It provided 12 km of sheltered moorings with water deep enough for the biggest ships, and enabled 9,000 tons of supplies to be landed every day to support the invading forces. In 100 days two-and-a-half million men, 500,000 vehicles and four million tons of supplies were landed.

What to see
Musée du Débarquement (Invasion Museum)

This is the best of several museums along the coast devoted to the Normandy landings. Situated beside the beach at Arromanches-les-Bains, so that you can look out of the window and see the actual scene where the events described took place, the museum is very well planned. The exhibits include plans, dioramas, models, arms and equipment, and films taken by Royal Naval photographers at the time of the landings.

Where to stay

Hôtel Le Normandie-Le Chalut (LdF), 71 Ave Michel Cabieu, Ouistreham 14150, tel. 31 97 19 57. Within 500 m of the ferry port, this is a pleasant hotel with twenty-three rooms at low medium rates. Sound restaurant with good regional cooking and wide choice of menus from medium plus prices. Good place to get your first taste of true Norman gastronomy. Wise to book well ahead in high season.

Delta Hotel, 37 Rue des Dunes, Ouistreham, tel. 31 96 20 20. New hotel (1990) with fifty-two soundproofed rooms all with bathroom *en suite*, at medium rates. Convenient for ferry. Good restaurant using local and seasonal products. Prices medium.

Hôtel de la Broche d'Argent (Univers) (LdF), Place du Général de Gaulle, Ouistreham, tel. 31 97 12 16. Near ferry, forty-four rooms, including annexe, at low to medium rates. Popular restaurant at medium prices.

Where to eat

Ferme St Hubert, Colville-Montgomery, 4 km south-west of Ouistreham by the D35, tel. 31 96 35 41. Like a private country house, dining room with beamed ceiling, tiled floor, huge fireplace. Tasty and generous Norman cuisine, good value, from medium prices.

Courseulles-sur-Mer

A charming little seaside resort near the mouth of the Seulles with sands for bathing, rocks for shrimping, a little fishing port, a yacht marina, and oyster beds for which it is well known. Canadian and some British troops came ashore here on D-Day – it was at the west end of Juno beach. Winston Churchill visited the west beach on 12 June 1944, De Gaulle on the 14th, and King George VI on the 16th. A Sherman tank stands in the main square as a reminder of those days, but the **local museum**, on the Arromanches road, concerns sea shells and oyster farming, not war. You can also visit the oyster parks. No need to take a tranquilliser first.

What to see

It's an attractive drive of a few km down the D170 to the old village of Fontaine-Henry and its unusual **château**. Built by the great family of d'Harcourt in the fifteenth and sixteenth centuries on the ruins of a much older fortress, the château is remarkable for the height and steepness of the roof of the main tower. The interior is completely furnished and contains some fine paintings, sculptures and a superb early sixteenth-century staircase. The château is open to the public p.m. June to 15 September, closed Tuesday and Friday.

Where to stay **Hôtel La Belle Aurore** (LdF), 32 Rue du Mi-Foch, 14470 Courseulles-sur-Mer, tel. 31 37 46 23. Small hotel overlooking the yacht marina. Seven simple rooms, at low medium rates, and serious cuisine at low medium prices. Hotel closed mid-January to mid-February.

Hôtel La Cremaillère-Le Gytan (LdF), Blvd de la Plage, tel. 31 37 46 73. Forty rooms from low to medium rates, the quietest and most comfortable are in the garden annexe. Good restaurant from medium prices.

Arromanches-les-Bains Apart from the interest of its excellent Invasion Museum, Arromanches is a typical French seaside resort, popular for family holidays, with a sandy bathing beach, and offshore rocks for crabbing and shrimping. The remains of the famous Mulberry harbour, still called Port Winston in the town, can be seen from the promenade.

Where to stay **Hôtel de la Marine** (LdF), Quai du Canada, Arromanches 14117, tel. 31 22 34 19. Thirty rooms from low to medium rates. Sound regional cuisine at medium prices. Closed mid-November to mid-February.

Bayeux

There was a Gallic settlement here for hundreds of years before the Romans came, and it is probably one of the longest-inhabited places in Normandy. It was always and still is essentially a market town for the produce of the fertile lands which surround it. Tradition has it that the Norman language continued to be spoken here long after it had been replaced by French in the rest of Normandy.

What to see **La Cathédrale de Notre Dame** is one of the finest Gothic cathedrals in France. It is one of many examples where a Christian church succeeded a Gallo-Roman temple on the same site. The first stone cathedral was built during the time of Odo, who was a half-brother of William the Conqueror, and bishop of Bayeux from 1049 to 1097. But this Romanesque cathedral was badly damaged by fire in 1156. All that remains from that period are the lower parts of the nave, and the bulk of the great towers of the façade, which have had buttresses and Gothic spires added since, and the crypt. The rest, including the lovely choir, is early Gothic.

The chapter house is early thirteenth-century, with a fifteenth-century glazed tiled floor with the representation of a labyrinth in the centre. It is thought that these labyrinths, which in the fifteenth and sixteenth centuries became popular in churches and gardens (mazes), are linked to pagan rites involving serpentine dances (still surviving in some parts of Scandinavia), and that in the medieval Christian church they were meant to symbolise the difficulties of the 'road to Jerusalem'.

The **Bayeux Tapestry** is a unique work of art, the world's first strip cartoon. It is often called the Tapestry of Queen Mathilde, though it is not a tapestry and had nothing to do with William the Conqueror's wife, Matilda.

Those visitors who do not know what to expect may well be surprised by the form it takes. It really is a strip, about 70 m long and only 50 cm high. It consists of a succession of scenes embroidered in wool in a limited range of colours on linen. It is roughly divided into fifty-eight scenes, meant to explain the events leading up to and the reasons for William the Conqueror's invasion and conquest of England. Only the last nine of the scenes refer to the actual Battle of Hastings. In the main scenes the adversaries are fairly consistently distinguished: the English have long hair and moustaches, the Normans are clean shaven and have short hair. (It is interesting to note that even today most Normans are clean shaven, as distinct, for example, from the Bretons, many of whom have beards.) The story is told in the wide central strip between two narrow bands, which show a succession of animals, like heraldic symbols, and everyday scenes of Norman life, like ploughing and sowing, and some fairly explicit rustic lust.

It seems likely that the work was commissioned by Odo, the bishop of Bayeux, and carried out in England by nuns already well known for their skill in embroidery, and it took about ten years to complete.

The Bayeux Tapestry is in a seventeenth-century building now called the **Centre Guillaume le Conquérant**, in the Rue Nesmond, near the cathedral. It is open all day, every day mid-May to mid-September, and a.m./p.m. for the rest of the year. The admission ticket is also good for the **Musée Baron Gérard**, adjacent to the cathedral, in the former Bishop's Palace. On the ground floor this houses fine collections of Bayeux pottery and lace, and on the first floor a varied collection of paintings and lithographs, including some by famous artists such as Utrillo and Van Dongen.

Where to stay   **Hôtel le Lion d'Or**, 71 Rue St Jean, Bayeux 14400, tel. 31 92 06 90. A part seventeenth-century coaching inn, in the pedestrian area of the city centre. Twenty-eight rooms at high medium rates around a flowery courtyard. Good restaurant (Michelin star) with traditional Norman cuisine from medium prices up.

Hôtel Argouges, 21 Rue St Patrice, tel. 31 92 88 86. Charming hotel in an eighteenth-century house near the city centre, with a pleasant garden. Twenty-three quiet, elegant rooms, all with own bath etc. Rates from low/medium.

Hôtel le Luxembourg (LdF), 25 Rue Bouchers, tel. 31 92 00 04. Once a coaching inn, damaged by fire a few years ago and completely renovated. Twenty-two spacious and well-furnished rooms, with good bathrooms, upper medium rates. Good restaurant, in a fine Louis XIII room with coffered ceiling, offers classical Norman cuisine from medium prices up.

Hôtel Campanile, at the angle of the ring road (Blvd du Maréchal Leclerc) and the road to St Lo, tel. 31 21 40 40. Forty-seven rooms at low medium rates, and the usual reliable restaurant with help-yourself buffet.

Hôtel Brunville, 9 Rue Genas-Duhomme, tel. 31 21 18 00. A good modern hotel next to the Luxembourg. Private parking. Thirty-eight well-equipped, sound-proofed rooms, all with bath etc, at low medium rates. Good restaurant, low medium prices.

Where to eat

Taverne des Ducs, 41 Rue St Patrice, tel. 31 92 09 88. This typical brasserie, not far from the Hôtel Argouges, might be anywhere in France. Meals until midnight, with menus at medium prices as well as more elaborate meals.

Excursion from Bayeux
Château de Balleroy

This attractive seventeenth-century château lies 15 km south-west of Bayeux off the D572, the road to St Lo. It was built in 1626 by the famous architect Mansart for Jean de Choisy, counsellor of King Louis XIII. It has a remarkable formal French garden designed by Le Nôtre, and is now owned by Malcolm Forbes, a multi-millionaire American magazine publisher and record-breaking balloonist. In the former stables of the château he has installed a unique museum, the only one in the world devoted entirely to ballooning and the history of balloons from the Montgolfier brothers to modern times. Every year in June international balloonists meet for a weekend of flying and socialising at the Château de Balleroy.

The château and the museum are open to the public a.m./p.m. every day except Wednesday.

The Normandy countryside

In addition to its variety of coastal resorts, historic towns and the picturesque valley of the Seine, there is another Normandy, well away from the sea, with its own delightful, scenic countryside, old villages, châteaux and manor houses. In central and southern Normandy visitors can explore and make their own discoveries, but there are some areas and towns worth recommending on their own account.

The Suisse Normande

This oddly named area bears no resemblance to Switzerland. But with its gentle hills, its hidden valleys with silver streams, its woods, occasional rocky outcrops and grassy slopes covered with gorse and broom in spring, it is both scenically beautiful and a wonderful setting for outdoor activities of all kinds. The GR221 and GR36 link the main centres and there are other good walks from most of the villages. There are several horse-riding centres, a canoe-kayak base at Thury-Harcourt on the Orne, rock climbing at Clécy, and possibilities for angling. Information on the availability of these and other sporting activities is available in the local tourist offices.

The Suisse Normande lies about 40 km south of Caen, and the most direct route is by the D562 to Thury-Harcourt, but a more scenic route is by the D212 which, for the latter half of the way, overlooks the valley of the Orne. A tour of the region can be made from Thury-Harcourt to Putanges, via Clécy, Condé-sur-Noireau, Pont d'Ouilly and Putanges.

Where to stay   **Hôtel Relais de la Poste**, Ave du 30 juin, Thury-Harcourt 14220, tel. 31 79 72 12. This old coaching inn has eleven rooms at low to medium rates, and a restaurant among the best in Lower Normandy, with a particularly good wine list. Menus from medium prices up. Closed January/February.

Auberge du Pont de Brie (LdF), Goupillières, 14210 Evrecy, tel. 31 79 37 84. Eight km north of Thury-Harcourt by the D212, this is a pleasant, tranquil inn with eight rooms at low to medium rates, and a good restaurant at medium prices up.

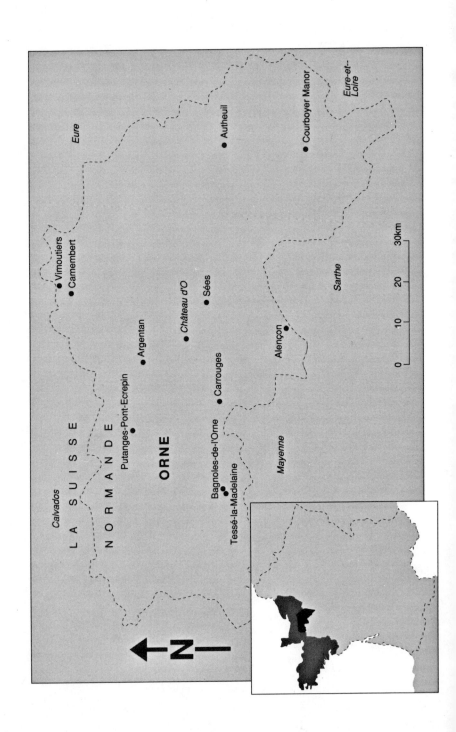

Camp site: Vallée du Traspy. A four-star municipal camp site to the east of the town, beside a stream, and near a recreational lake. Eighty-seven places.

Clécy

Very much a holiday centre for the whole of Suisse Normande, and rather swamped by visitors in the high season, but still a nice little town, on a particularly attractive stretch of river. There are pleasant riverside cafés where you can eat outdoors, and Clécy has facilities for fishing, canoeing, rock climbing, hang-gliding, and horse riding, as well as good walks and an 18-hole golf course.

What to see

Model railway enthusiasts and children will enjoy the model railway at the **Musée du Chemin de Fer Miniature**, which covers more than 300 sq m and where the trains run through a scaled-down countryside including houses, factories, castles and farms. All, including the trains, are illuminated at dusk. Open a.m./p.m. from Easter to the end of September. Sunday afternoon only during the rest of the year.

Croix de la Faverie is three-quarters of an hour's walk, there and back, to a little pine wood on a hill with characteristic views over the Suisse Normande, across the river to the escarpment called Les Rochers du Parc. Can also be reached by car, partly by unmade-up road.

The Château de Pontécoulant is accessible from Clécy by the D133A to St Pierre la Vieille and then south down the D166 about 12 km, or from the small town of **Condé-sur-Noireau** by the D166, about 8 km. Like so many other places in this area, Condé-sur-Noireau was completely destroyed in 1944 and was rebuilt in traditional style. It was the birthplace of the French Antarctic explorer, Dumont d'Urville, who discovered Adelie Land in 1840 and named it after his wife. The Château de Pontécoulant is a sixteenth- and eighteenth-century building, now a **departmental museum** with a good collection of Renaissance, Louis XV and Empire and Indo-Chinese furniture, as well as arms and paintings. Open a.m./p.m. June to September. Closed Tuesday.

Pont d'Ouilly is another pleasantly sited village at the confluence of the Orne and the Noireau and, like Clécy, an excellent centre for outdoor activity holidays. It is about 5 km by the D301 to the Rocher d'Oetre, a splendid viewpoint over the wild gorges of the Rouvre, a tributary of the Orne. There is a café at the site.

Where to stay

Hôtel le Moulin du Vey, Clécy 14570, tel. 31 69 71 08. A former flour-mill converted to a comfortable hotel in a flowery garden beside the river. Nicely furnished rooms, a little overpriced at high medium. Sound restaurant, medium plus prices. **Le Manoir du Placy** at 400m and **Le Relais de Surosne**, a creeper-covered mansion about 3 km away, are used as annexes to the hotel.

Hôtel le Site Normand (LdF), Rue des Chatelets, Clécy, tel. 31 69 71 05. Old-established, family-run hotel with fourteen rooms at low to medium rates. Good regional restaurant, meals excellent value at medium prices.

Auberge St Christophe, Pont d'Ouilly 14690, tel. 31 69 81 23. Creeper-covered roadside inn, only seven rooms but all with sanitation and air conditioning, and those on the garden side are quiet. Low medium rates. A good choice of menus from medium prices upwards. Closed part of October and February, restaurant closed Sunday evening and Monday.

Hôtel du Lion Verd (LdF), Place de l'Hôtel de Ville, Putanges-Pont-Écrepin 61210, tel. 33 35 01 86. Riverside terrace, twenty rooms from low rates to medium. Sound restaurant with menus at low medium prices. Closed 24 December to end January.

Where to eat   **Auberge du Chalet de Cantepie**, Clécy, half a km outside the village, tel. 31 69 71 10. Classical cuisine with menus from medium prices upwards. Good value. Closed Sunday evening and December.

Hôtel du Commerce, Pont d'Ouilly, tel. 31 69 80 16. Spacious and rather austere-looking dining room, but a good-value restaurant with a wide choice of menus from low prices up. Closed Sunday evening and Monday except July/August. The hotel also has some simple but adequate rooms at below average rates.

Falaise   In August 1944 the Battle of Normandy was almost over, but the German forces were still resisting fiercely in the Falaise area, and as the Allied forces tried to close the 'Falaise gap' in a pincer movement and encircle the German army, the town of Falaise was pounded to dust and rubble. When the Canadian forces entered the town on 17 August, they were unable to find where the roads had been, and had to bulldoze a new road straight through the middle.

But Falaise was rebuilt, and is today a prosperous market town more interesting in its historical associations with England than for any particular feature. In the centre of the town hall square, Place Guillaume le Conquérant, there is a suitably war-like statue of William, Duke of Normandy, King of England, a reminder that this was the birthplace of William the Conqueror. The statue dates from the middle of the nineteenth century.

What to see   The **château**, dominating the town from its rocky height, is imposing and looks a fitting birthplace for the Conqueror, but is, whatever the guide may tell you, a successor to the castle where William was born. The oldest parts of the present castle date from more than 100 years after his birth, and the whole building has been repeatedly restored and rebuilt. Floodlit on summer nights it looks very impressive. Open all day from May to September, but not worth the visit if you are pressed for time.

Beside the River Ante, at the foot of the rock crowned by the castle keep, a carved stone plaque flanked by little turrets, **La Fontaine d'Arlette**, illustrates the legend of Arlette, the tanner's daughter, who, as she knelt by the river with her skirts up doing some washing, was spotted by the seventeen-year-old Robert, later Duke Robert the Magnificent. This 'memorial' was put there in 1957, and whether it tells a true story is anybody's guess, as there are several versions of the legend. The part most likely to be true is that, when Robert had told his father that he fancied the tanner's daughter, and word had passed via the tanner to Arlette, she refused to meet him secretly but put on her best clothes and rode openly into the castle. Considering the great difference in their situations, her action required character, courage and pride, which all seem right for the girl who was to become the mother of the Conqueror, and who insisted on staying in the castle to look after her baby.

Where to stay   **Hôtel de Normandie**, 4 Rue Amiral Courbet, Falaise 14700, tel. 31 90 18 26. A well-run family hotel with twenty-seven rooms at low rates (only nine with bath etc). Good, traditional restaurant, generous helpings, low prices. Closed Friday evening, Saturday lunch, Sunday evening, Monday lunch.

Château du Tertre, St Martin de Mieux 14700, tel. 31 90 01 04. Three km south-west of Falaise and owned by an English businessman, Roger Vickery, this is a delightful eighteenth-century residence with nine charming bedrooms and two apartments at from high medium rates. Pierre Gay, a chef trained in three of the finest restaurants of France, provides superb and original menus, justifiably rather expensive. Closed Sunday evening and Monday, and February.

Where to eat   **L'Attaché**, N158 Falaise, on the northern side of Falaise, Rte de Caen (N158), tel. 31 90 05 38. A simple, straightforward restaurant of the kind that builds the French reputation for first-class meals at medium prices. Closed Wednesday and second fortnight of July.

Hôtel de la Poste, 38 Rue Georges Clemenceau. Ivy-covered building on the main road by the turning to Bagnoles-de-l'Orne. Pleasant dining room, serious cuisine with menus at low medium prices up. Very good value. Closed Sunday evening and Monday. Also has nineteen rooms (twelve with sanitation) but a main-road situation likely to be noisy in summer.

La Fine Fourchette, 52 Rue Georges Clemenceau, tel. 31 90 08 59. Classical cuisine with some emphasis on fish and shellfish. Good range of menus from low medium prices. Closed Tuesday evening and Wednesday except July/August.

Bagnoles-de-l'Orne

About 50 km south of the Suisse Normande, via the D962 to Flers, then the D18 to La Ferte Macé, then the D916, is the old-established spa of Bagnoles de l'Orne. There is no need to stop *en route*. Flers and

La Ferte Macé are both small industrial towns: nobody has much to say in their favour, and I am not the exception.

History

But Bagnoles-de-l'Orne is a different matter. The seventh most popular spa in France, it was probably known to the Romans, but is said to have been rediscovered by a local lord, Hugues de Tessé. The story says he had a favourite horse which had become old and sick but which he could not bring himself to destroy. Instead he let it loose in the forest. A month later it came back to him, capering about like a colt. He followed it into the forest, where it bathed in some hot springs. Seigneur de Tessé followed suit, and felt very much the better for it.

This story is what may be called a spa chestnut. It crops up in several places. I have heard it as far away as Auvergne, where a poor old dog too arthritic to move was abandoned by his master, a shepherd, and returned a few weeks later scampering about like a puppy. Anyway, Hugues de Tessé told all his friends and soon men and women were flocking to the springs. Someone, the monks probably, put it about that the bathing only did you good if you were naked, and this did nothing to reduce the popularity of the spot. In the nineteenth century, however, it was decided to have one radioactive bath for men and a separate one for women. Today the Thermal Establishment has all the latest modern equipment, and uses the water of the Grand Source which flows at 50,000 litres an hour at 25° C. Its curative qualities are due not to mineral content, but to its strong radioactivity.

Bagnoles today

Bagnoles today is a modern town, though with many turn-of-the-century hotel buildings, a certain amount of style, and quite a strong atmosphere of being a place apart, which is common to many spas. This rather strange feeling is due to the fact that almost all spas are built in places where if it had not been for the mineral springs, no one would ever have thought of building a town. Bagnoles, for example, is centred round a rather forbidding gorge deep in the heart of a forest.

Like most spas, Bagnoles has developed a full range of leisure activities, including horse riding, tennis with open and covered courts, forest walks, a 9-hole golf course, heated outdoor swimming pool, boating and trout fishing. There is a stylish casino beside the lake which, in addition to the gaming rooms, has a ballroom with live orchestra in season, a disco and a theatre.

The season in Bagnoles lasts from the beginning of May to the end of October. In summer the population, with visitors, reaches 15,000. In winter it is 800.

Where to stay

Bagnoles and its sister commune Tessé-la-Madeleine have well over forty hotels between them, so you 'pay your money and you take your choice'.

Hôtel Le Capricorne, Allée Monjoie, Bagnoles-de-l'Orne 61140, tel. 33 37 96 99. A modern hotel well situated between the forest and the lake, near the casino. Twenty-one rooms with bath etc at medium rates. Restaurant for dinner only, also medium priced. Open April to mid-October.

Le Manoir de Lys, Rte de Juvigny, 3 km outside the town by the Domfront road, tel. 33 37 80 69. This is a charming small Norman manor surrounded by flowers and shady trees, in a lovely setting at the edge of the forest. Ten rooms with bath etc at medium rates upwards. The patron, Frank Quinton, is the chef, and the cuisine is first class. High medium prices, and half-board obligatory in season. Closed January February.

Hôtel Nouvel (LdF), 8 Ave Albert Christophe, Tessé-la-Madeleine, Bagnoles-de-l'Orne 61140, tel. 33 37 81 22. Imposing old hotel, completely renovated. Thirty bedrooms, all with bath etc at low to medium rates. Large garden. Restaurant prices low/medium.

Hôtel Beaumont, 28 Blvd Lemeunier-Rallière, tel. 33 37 83 02. Creeper-covered hotel with thirty-eight rooms in pleasant grounds with a very good restaurant. Room rates start low, and menu prices from low medium with house wine included. Closed mid-November to mid-March.

Where to eat

Café de Paris, Ave R-Cousin, tel. 33 37 81 76. Pleasant restaurant next to the casino, with a view over the lake. Good fish dishes, and desserts with ice cream. Medium-price menus and upwards. Closed Monday except July/August.

Excursion from Bagnoles
What to see

The D908 runs through typical southern Normandy countryside, heavily wooded with small fields, to the village of **Carrouges**, where the headquarters of the Normandy Maine Regional Park is situated.

Originally a fourteenth-century fortress – only the battlemented keep remains from that period – the **Château de Carrouges** was acquired in 1450 by the Le Veneur de Tillières family, whose political adroitness kept them in important positions through all changes of government from monarchy to republic to empire and back again, for hundreds of years. One was a cardinal, another was ambassador to England and helped to negotiate the marriage of Henrietta Maria, sister of Louis XIII of France, to Charles I of England. As they prospered, the family transformed the old fortress over the years into a very elegant residence. It was acquired by the state in 1936, and has since been restored and kept in immaculate condition. Admission to the large park, which has splendid trees and flowerbeds, is free and it is worth taking a walk through it to admire the different views of the exterior of the castle. The interior is open to the public and is both impressive and interesting. The rooms still have their seventeenth- and eighteenth-century furniture, and good paintings, and the kitchens have a fine collection of period copper and other utensils.

The **Maison du Parc** is in one of the château's dependent buildings, a former chapterhouse. The **Parc Naturel Régional de Normandie-Maine** covers 234,000 hectares, and Carrouges is on the edge of the **Forêt d'Écouves**, just a part of the Parc, but at 14,000 hectares one of the largest forests in France. It is rich in birds and game, and offers very interesting walks. It is also hilly, and includes the Signal d'Écouves, at 417 m the highest point in the west of France. Full information on walks and leisure activities in the Forêt d'Écouves and the Parc are available at the Maison du Parc. In summer there are exhibitions of craftsmanship past and present, and concerts on summer evenings. The château is open to the public a.m./p.m. all year round. Closed Tuesday except from mid-June to the end of August, and on public holidays.

Alençon

Though Alençon is a good centre for exploring this scenic corner of Normandy, lying between the Forêt d'Écouves and the Forêt de Perseigne, another hilly and picturesque forest of mixed oak, beech and fir, the town itself is of limited interest to the visitor. It is a prosperous market town, and the Saturday markets in and around the cathedral square are colourful and interesting. Housewives may like to know that Alençon is a headquarters of the Moulinex company.

St Thérèse of Lisieux was born Thérèse Martin in Alençon, where her mother was a lacemaker. The house, in the Rue St Blaise, and the room where she was born, can be visited.

What to see
Church of
Notre Dame

The building was started during the Hundred Years' War, when Alençon was occupied by the English. It is mainly Flamboyant Gothic, with a particularly fine three-gabled porch richly embellished with sculptures. The rest of the exterior is something of a hotchpotch, as it was partly rebuilt after a fire in the eighteenth century in a style which clashes with the older parts. It is dominated by a square tower with a domed roof in slate, a tower which can charitably be called squat, and uncharitably ugly. There is some fine early sixteenth-century stained glass in the nave.

Musée des
Beaux Arts et
de la Dentelle
(Lace and Fine
Arts Museum)

Alençon has long been famous for producing some of the world's finest lace. The manufacture dwindled away during the nineteenth century to one-tenth of what it had been, but the tradition and techniques are maintained today. Some of the finest examples of Alençon lace, together with those from other parts of Europe, are exhibited in this Musée des Beaux Arts. There is also a large collection of French, Dutch and Flemish paintings. Open every day a.m./p.m., except Monday.

Where to
stay

Hôtel Le Grand Cerf, 21 Rue St Blaise, Alençon 61000, tel. 33 26 00 51. Good hotel in a nineteenth-century building with vast bedrooms, comfortably furnished. Thirty-three rooms (twenty-four with bath etc) from low rates up. Sound restaurant, medium price menus.

Hôtel Urbis, 13 Place Poulet Malassis, tel. 33 26 55 55. Near the town centre in the oddly named 'square of the badly seated chicken', this is one of the modern Ibis chain, called Urbis when in a town rather than on the outskirts. Usual dependable comfort. Fifty-two rooms at low medium rates. No restaurant.

Where to eat

Au Jardin Gourmand, 14 Rue de Sarthe, tel. 33 32 22 56. Near St Leonard's church. Small restaurant, classic cuisine with a good range of menus at medium prices. Closed Sunday evening and Monday.

L'Inattendu, 21 Rue Sarthe, tel. 33 26 51 69. Creative cuisine and pleasant service. Menus from medium prices up. Closed Saturday lunch and Sunday, and first two weeks of August.

Sées

It is a pleasant drive from Carrouges to Sées by the road called the Route des Trois Forêts, which does indeed pass through three forests, the one in the middle mainly pine, the others oak and beech.

Sées itself is a once-upon-a-time town, which seems pretty dull and lifeless today. But it has a cathedral, and so must have been important in the past.

What to see

The fourteenth-century **Notre Dame Cathedral** has twin spires, which can be seen from various viewpoints for 10 km around, and it looks particularly good when floodlit. But at close quarters the exterior is less impressive: the façade is spoilt by huge buttresses added in the sixteenth century to prop it up. The interior is impressive in its soaring simplicity: its proportions have a mathematical beauty, but apart from magnificent fourteenth- and fifteenth-century stained-glass windows in the transept, choir and deambulatory (restored), it is remarkably plain.

Where to eat

L'Île de Sées at Macé, 5 km from Sées by the Argentan road and D303. Good country restaurant with menus from medium prices up. Also has sixteen rooms at medium rates. Restaurant closed Sunday evening and Monday.

Excursion from Sées (or Macé)

Eight km north-west of Sées by N158 and surrounded by a wide moat on which swans glide, the romantic **Château d'O**, towered and turreted like a fairytale castle, is one of the loveliest in France. The château itself is a harmonious mixture of periods, the earliest fifteenth-century Gothic, and there are two fine examples of Renaissance dovecotes (complete with doves), a chapel, an orangery and a farm. It is all surrounded by a delightful park.

O is the name of a family well known in Normandy since the eleventh century. François d'O, who spent a great deal of money improving the château, was a favourite of the homosexual and transvestite Henri III, and was a disastrous Superintendent of Finances under his successor Henry IV until he was replaced by Sully, who soon put things right.

Though the façades are original, most of the interior was reconstructed during the eighteenth century. Several rooms, including a grand salon with eighteenth-century murals, are open to the public, as well as the entrance hall and kitchens. Open p.m., except Tuesday, and closed February.

Where to eat   **La Ferme d'O**, tel. 33 35 35 27, is a restaurant installed in the former stables. Good regional cooking with menus from medium up. Closed Tuesday lunch.

Cherbourg to Mont St Michel

Cherbourg

Unlike Dieppe, Cherbourg is not a place to which it is easy to become attached, but it has an unusual history. It is strategically placed in the Channel but exposed to the elements, and originally it had no real harbour. It was a ship's captain who thought of the the idea of making a protective jetty by sinking a long line of huge wooden cones filled with stone, but the work, started in 1776, took many years as the sea repeatedly broke it down. Napoleon I liked the idea and planned to make Cherbourg a naval base, and so the work went on, but he was long dead before it was completed in 1853. The new port was opened by Napoleon III, and in 1869 the first transatlantic ship used it. When a new deep-water channel was dredged in 1933, Cherbourg enjoyed a short heyday when the great liners such as the *Normandie*, the *Île de France*, the *Queen Mary*, and the *Queen Elizabeth* docked there, carrying the rich and the famous between Europe and the United States.

Then, at the end of the Second World War, Cherbourg had another period of key importance as a supply port for the Allied armies fighting the Battle of Normandy. Pluto, the underwater pipeline which pumped oil for the armies from the Isle of Wight, was installed in 1944 and terminated at Cherbourg. The Germans had mined the harbour and sunk ships in it to prevent its use, but Royal Navy frogmen cleared it in record time and the oil line was in use by 12 August 1944, and the port dealt with an enormous amount of traffic.

Cherbourg today

Nowadays Cherbourg is of lesser importance. Most of its transatlantic terminal has been demolished, but it is still a French naval base, building and operating submarines; its regular traffic is from the cross-Channel ferries, and in summer there are boats to Guernsey. There are the usual good shops for tourists and some acceptable restaurants, but it is not really a holiday destination, though there are points of interest.

What to see

Musée Thomas Henry (Museum of Fine Arts)

Situated in the Centre Culturel, Rue Vastel, the collection of paintings in this museum is not large, but the quality is first class, including Italitan primitives, works by Poussin, Jordaens, Teniers,

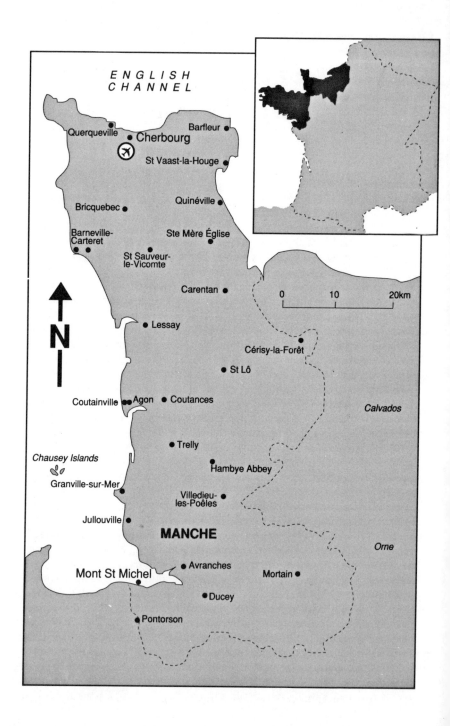

ENGLISH
CHANNEL

Querqueville • Cherbourg
Barfleur •
St Vaast-la-Houge •

Quinéville •

Bricquebec •

Barneville-
Carteret •

Ste Mère Église •

St Sauveur-
le-Vicomte •

Carentan •

0   10   20km

• Lessay

Cérisy-la-Forêt •

• St Lô

Coutainville •• Agon • Coutances

Calvados

• Trelly

Chausey Islands

Hambye Abbey •

Granville-sur-Mer •

Villedieu-
les-Poêles •

Jullouville •

MANCHE

Orne

Mont St Michel
• Avranches
Mortain •

• Ducey

• Pontorson

Murillo, Chardin and Greuze, and a collection of thirty paintings by the much underestimated and now unfashionable Millet. Born a peasant a few miles west of Cherbourg in the village of Gruchy, where his house still stands, Millet had a remarkable natural gift for drawing, which he developed with years of study in Paris, and then became one of the Barbizon group of painters. He painted what he knew best, the life of the peasants, and was the first artist to paint them seriously – previously they had been treated as jolly, boozy yokels, as by Brueghel. Open a.m./p.m. every day except Tuesday.

Where to stay

Hôtel Mercure, Gare Maritime, Cherbourg 50100, tel. 33 44 01 11. Modern chain hotel overlooking the marina and handy for the ferry terminal. Eighty-four rooms from medium rates. Restaurant with menus from medium prices.

Hôtel la Régence (LdF), 42 Quai de Caligny, tel. 33 43 05 16. Fifteen rooms at medium rates, and restaurant with menus from medium prices.

Hôtel Campanile, La Glacerie 50470, tel. 33 43 43 43. A short way inland from the town by the N13, and just off this main road to Caen and Paris. Another one of a modern chain which has nearly 300 hotels in France. Forty-three rooms at medium rates and a sound restaurant with menus at medium prices.

Where to eat

Le St Jours, 59 Rue au Blé, tel. 33 53 67 64. Refined cuisine by Patrick St Jours, and all menus always available. Prices from medium up. Closed Sunday.

Around Cherbourg

The countryside around Cherbourg is wild, particularly to the west with outcrops of rock and few trees, and those twisted by the wind. The coast itself is rugged and at the headland called the Nez de Jobourg it becomes grandiose. Between this granite monster and the lower Cap de la Hague to the north there is a great sweep of sand, the Bay of Ecalgrain. Offshore is the island of Alderney, and the stretch of water in between, dreaded by shipping, is the notorious Alderney Race, where the tides can flow at eight knots. At Goury near the point of the Cap is a famous lifeboat station whose men have saved hundreds of sailors from ships wrecked in these waters.

Next to the church at Querqueville, a few kms west of Cherbourg, is the small trefoil-shaped **St Germain chapel**, not of any great beauty but interesting because, dating from the sixth to eighth centuries, it is perhaps the oldest Christian shrine in western France.

Further south from Cherbourg the countryside becomes rather less bare, and some of the smaller roads are banked like Devon lanes and in spring are a mass of primroses, violets and foxgloves. The fields become more fertile as you move south; early vegetables are grown in the coastal strips. The scenery is rustic and unspoiled rather than picturesque.

Bricquebec

A pleasant little red granite town built around the ruins of a fourteenth-century **castle**, Bricquebec has a large market square with

171

hotels and cafés. An entrance gateway leads into an inner courtyard of the castle, which has retained its ramparts and has an impressive ten-sided keep nearly 25 m high. Part of the charm of the place is that houses have been fitted into the castle walls, and one of them is a comfortable hotel.

Where to stay   **Auberge du Vieux Châteaux** (LdF), 4 Cours du Château, Bricquebec 50260, tel. 33 52 24 49. Attractive hotel in the ramparts next to the keep. Queen Victoria stayed here in 1857 after visiting Cherbourg on the occasion of the opening of the railway from Caen. She had bedroom No 2. Don't worry: it and the rest of the hotel have been modernised since. Rooms vary in size and price from low rates up, but most have their own sanitation etc, and none are expensive. Restaurant has a good range of menus from low medium prices.

The West Coast

Barneville-Carteret   The west coast of the Cotentin peninsula has some long stretches of fine sandy beaches, many of them, like the Bay of Ecalgrain, deserted even in the height of summer, but there are also some good, old-established family resorts. The first of them, 16 km south-west of Bricquebec, is Barneville-Carteret. Though now one commune, the town really consists of three agglomerations – Carteret, Barneville and Barneville-Plage – and between them they have all that a summer holiday resort requires. Carteret has a granite cape with cliffs, rocks and small sandy coves, and from the cliff-top you can look straight across to Jersey, silhouetted by the sunset. There is a small port and fishing boats sell their catch on the quay, and in summer there are boat trips to Jersey. Carteret is separated from Barneville by what is called a *havre*, a wide estuary partially closed by a long sand bar running in a north–south direction. There are several of them on this coast, and they occur where three conditions exist: a low sandy coast, a small but fast-flowing river, and an offshore current with a constant direction. The result is a splendid sandy beach, Barneville Plage, almost enclosing at high tide a huge stretch of water – eighty hectares – ideal for all water sports. At low tide there are sandy mud flats with channels. Bathing from the beaches is safe, in water warmed by the Gulf Stream.

What to see   The **Église St Germain**, Barneville, is a good example of a late eleventh-century Romanesque church, with a fifteenth-century tower. The nave is remarkable for the fine decoration of its arches and capitals.

Where to stay   **Hôtel de la Marine**, 11 Rue de Paris, Carteret 50270, tel. 33 53 83 31. Not the most beautiful hotel to look at, but some of its thirty-one comfortable bedrooms at high medium rates have sea views, and the restaurant offers high standards (Michelin star) at medium plus prices. Closed Sunday evening.

Hôtel Les Isles (LdF), 9 Blvd Maritime, Barneville-Plage, tel. 33 04 90 76. By the beach, and some of the thirty-four rooms have sea views. Low to medium room rates. Nice little garden. Good restaurant with views of the sea and a choice of menus at medium prices.

Port Bail

At the southern end of the 5 km-long beach of Barneville, this is another little port situated on a *havre*, this time at the mouth of the Ollonde. With less modern development than Barneville, it is an attractive place at high tide, less appealing when the mud flats are exposed. It is used by yachtsmen, particularly from the Channel Islands, and there is a motor launch service to Jersey in the summer.

The coast road, the D650, runs south about 1.5 km inland and at fairly regular intervals there are side turnings to the right which lead to undeveloped and deserted sandy beaches, often without even a name. There are also one or two places of interest.

What to see

Those interested in church architecture may like to stop at **Lessay** to visit the remarkable Romanesque abbey church, almost completely destroyed in 1944 but painstakingly rebuilt from the rubble just as it was before. Everything but the dust was used.

Coutances

Reached from Lessay direct by the D2, Coutances is impressively sited on a hill. It is a pleasant town, not too much damaged in 1944 and still with several of its original streets, and crowned by its cathedral, an architectural jewel.

What to see

Notre Dame Cathedral is one of the most majestic cathedrals in Normandy, indeed in all France. It is thirteenth-century Gothic and was built on the foundations of an earlier Romanesque church burned to the ground in 1218. What remained of the Romanesque towers of the façade was enclosed in stonework in the Gothic style, and any heaviness that might have resulted was dispelled by the addition of soaring spires, rising to 78 m and flanked by sets of elegant turrets. Between the two towers the western façade is a *tour de force* of the Gothic style, setting off a splendid window above the porch. The lantern tower over the transept is another Gothic masterpiece combining strength, soaring elegance and refinement of detail. The chevet is a blend of Romanesque shapes and vertical lines of purely Gothic inspiration, and it is well worth walking round to the lawns at the back of the cathedral to get a good view of the chevet and the lantern tower behind it. The interior is as majestic and graceful as the exterior. There is some splendid stained glass, some in the transept dating from the thirteenth and fourteenth centuries. Altogether it is a lovely cathedral which will impress the layman and delight the more knowledgeable with its richness of variety and detail. Good *Son et Lumière* shows during the summer season.

Église St Pierre is another beautiful church, fifteenth and sixteenth century with a very fine Renaissance lantern tower.

Coutances has a shady and beautifully kept **jardin public**, with flowerbeds arranged in formal patterns. From July to 15 September, the gardens are illuminated at night.

Where to stay   **Hôtel Cositel** (LdF), Rte de Coutainville, 50200 Coutances, tel. 33 07 51 64. Comfortable modern hotel about 1 km from the centre. Fifty-four rooms at low medium rates. Restaurant with medium-price menus.

Hôtel Le Parvis, Place de la Cathédrale, tel. 33 45 13 55. Simple but pleasant hotel in the cathedral close. Twelve rooms from low to medium rates with a sound restaurant, good value meals.

Hôtel La Verte Campagne, Trelly, 50660 Quettreville-sur-Sienne, tel. 33 47 65 33. About 12 km south of Coutances by the D971, signposted from Trelly and the hamlet of Chevalier. An eighteenth-century farmhouse, restored and renovated and converted to an attractive *auberge*. Seven bedrooms (five with bath), from low to medium rates. Walls covered in climbing roses, pleasant garden and deep in the heart of the *bocage*. Very good restaurant, menus from high medium prices. Essential to book ahead in high summer. Closed Sunday evening and Monday.

Agon-Coutainville
An old-established resort, but it has kept up with the times and is now one of the most popular places on this coast, with something for everybody. The resort is 10 km from Coutances, and has the tidal estuary of the Sienne, another *havre*, behind it to the south east, and the sea in front, with 8 km of fine sand beach. As everywhere else on this coast, it can be breezy on the beach, but you can find your own dune for shelter. At high tide bathing is safe, and at low tide the sea goes back for 1 km or so, but the exposed beach is a paradise for shrimpers, crabbers and shell hunters. The resort has terrace cafés and restaurants, a casino, racecourse, tennis courts and facilities for water sports of all kinds.

Where to stay   **Hôtel Hardy**, Place du 28 Juillet, 50230 Coutainville, tel. 33 47 04 11. Sixteen rooms, some small though comfortable, all with bath etc, at medium rates. Essential to book well in advance.

Excursions from Coutances
Abbaye de Hambye
The picturesque ruins of this ancient abbey are not easy to find. The D7 from Coutances takes you 14 km south to the village of Lengronne, where you turn left on to the D13 which 8 km further on reaches Hambye, but you won't find the ruins there. You must carry on another km to the crossroads at Le Bourg, where you turn right on to the D51, which meanders down the valley of the Sienne. After about 2 km the road divides into three. Keep to the left, the D258, and almost immediately a track leads down towards the river and the ruins, reached through a monumental gateway.

The abbey was founded in 1145, but the monks were driven out at the time of the Revolution, and in 1810 the buildings were sold for use as a source of building stones.

The imposing abbey church is open to the sky, but its pillars still stand firmly against the erosion of time and weather. The choir has five radiating chapels with round pillars supporting narrow Gothic arches. Above the crossing of the transept two storeys of the tower remain, with paired windows on each side, lighting the choir. The former refectory has some pieces of antique furniture, and the walls are hung with seventeenth-century tapestries from Rouen. Open a.m./p.m., closed Tuesday. The conventual buildings are open for guided visits in the summer season, closed the rest of the year.

Villedieu-les-
Poêles

Reached from Hambye by the D51 or direct from Coutances by the D7 and the D33, this lively town – whose name means 'God's town of the Frying Pans' – has two claims to fame. The first is that it was here that the first headquarters of the Knights of St John of Jerusalem were founded in the twelfth century by Henri I Beauclerc, the son of William the Conqueror. It was the Knights who gave it the name of God's Town. In the sixteenth century they became the Sovereign Order of Malta. The association with the Order of Malta was broken at the time of the French Revolution, but every four years there is a great procession, called the Grand Sacre, held for the existing Knights. It takes place on the third Sunday after Whitsun (the next occasion will be June 1995).

The town's second claim to fame is that for hundreds of years it has been the chief centre in France for the manufacture of copper utensils of all kinds. The Knights of Malta allowed freedom from taxes to artisans who set up workshops. They began with the making of copper objects for churches, then the great milk churns for farms throughout Normandy, and then pots and pans and other kitchen utensils. With the arrival of tourism, the genuine craftsmanship has been almost entirely swamped by a huge production of overpriced near-rubbish. If you want something shiny, in dubious taste and more or less useless, this is a good place to get it. If you want something of quality, you will have to hunt for it, and it will not be cheap.

Villedieu has some interesting things in it, but it is a town which too often shows the ugly face of tourism, where the visitor is too often regarded as a potential victim to whom the least must be offered for the biggest possible return.

What to see

Founded by the Knights of St John, the **Bell Foundry**, Rue du Pont Chignon, still makes bells for churches, ships and public buildings the world over. If you are lucky you may see the casting, which takes places about once a fortnight. Open every day a.m./p.m. Closed Sunday and Monday 15 September to 1 June.

At **Atelier du Cuivre**, 54 Rue Général-Huard, you can see a fifteen-minute video on the history and development of copper working, followed by a tour of the workshop where each of the different techniques is demonstrated. Open every day a.m./p.m. Closed Sunday and Monday 17 September to end May. The **Maison de l'Étain** at 15 Rue Général-Huard is similar but is concerned with pewter, instead of copper. Same opening hours as the copper workshop. One ticket gives admission to both.

Where to stay

Auberge de l'Abbaye, Hambye 50650, tel. 33 61 42 19. Close to the entrance to the abbey, not in the actual village, this is a little country inn *par excellence*. Only seven bedrooms, but clean and comfortable, and low to medium rates. Restaurant where you get fresh country produce delightfully cooked, at medium prices. Book at weekends. Closed Sunday evening and Monday.

Hôtel St Pierre et St Michel (LdF), 12 Place de la République, Villedieu-les-Poêles 50800, tel. 33 61 00 11. Typical small, provincial hotel. Twenty-three rooms at low to medium rates. Rather noisy situation, so ask for a room away from the street. Good restaurant, low medium prices.

Le Fruitier (LdF), Rue Général de Gaulle, tel. 33 51 14 24. Also in a potentially noisy corner situation, but in other respects very good value. Forty-eight rooms at low rates. Good restaurant offering regional cuisine from low to medium prices.

Where to eat

Les Chevaliers, Rue d'Estouteville, Hambye 50650, tel. 33 90 43 09. Straightforward country restaurant of high standards and medium prices. Advisable to book a table. Also has six clean but simple rooms at low rates.

Restaurant de l'Abbaye, tel. 33 61 42 21. Like the Auberge (see above), it is near the abbey. Charming country cottage restaurant, very Norman, lots of cream, and everything absolutely fresh. The omelettes come straight from the chickens to your plate with only the briefest pause in between! Good charcoal grills. All à la carte at medium prices. Also has a few pretty but simple rooms, inexpensive.

Granville-sur-Mer

This is much the biggest of the seaside resorts on the west coast of the Cotentin, and it is also something of a surprise after the long series of flat beaches and sand dunes. Granville consists of an upper and lower town. The upper town is built on a rugged, high-sided spur of granite jutting out into the sea for more than 1 km. This is the original Granville, founded by the English in 1439 as a fortified base from which to capture Mont St Michel, the last stronghold in Normandy not in their hands. They were not successful, and instead the knights of Mont St Michel recaptured Granville three years later.

The lower town is devoted to commerce, industry and tourism. Granville has a casino, good restaurants, and plenty of leisure facilities. Its beach, however, is a minor attraction. It is sandy but narrow, exposed to the wind, and virtually disappears at high tide. But Granville has the interest of being a real port with some commercial activity, and has one of the most important fishing fleets in Normandy. There is also a marina with moorings for more than a 1,000 yachts. There are huge sandy beaches within easy reach both north and south of the town, at Donville and St Pair.

What to see

Haute-Ville (the Upper Town) is the old fortified town, still surrounded by its ramparts, which is entered via the Grande Porte, accessible by a drawbridge. It is possible to walk round the Haute-Ville on the ramparts and to reach viewpoints at either end, the Pointe du Roc and the Place de l'Isthme. In summer there are boat services to Jersey and Guernsey, and launch trips to the much closer Chausey Islands.

Where to stay

Hôtel Les Bains, 19 Rue Georges Clemenceau, Granville-sur-Mer 50400, tel. 33 50 17 31. Modernised hotel overlooking the sea. Forty-four soundproofed rooms, almost all with bath etc, at high medium rates. Good restaurant, menus at medium prices.

Hôtel le Hérel, Port de Hérel, tel. 33 90 48 08. Modern hotel overlooking the port and the sea. Good chain hotel standards both in rooms (low medium rates) and restaurants (low to medium prices). Closed Sunday evening and Monday.

Hôtel Normandie Chaumière (LdF), 20 Rue Paul Poirier, tel. 33 50 01 71. A small hotel in a busy part of town. Seven rooms at low rates. Good traditional restaurant, medium prices. Closed Sunday evening and Monday.

Where to eat

La Citadelle, 10 Rue Cambern, Haute-Ville, tel. 33 50 34 10. A serious restaurant with good-value menus starting at medium prices. Closed for lunch except Sunday in high season, and Monday.

Le Phare, 11 Rue Port, tel. 33 50 12 94. Near the harbour. Not the most enticing décor, but the restaurant has a view of the harbour. Choice of menus at medium prices up. Closed Tuesday evening and Wednesday in high season.

Jullouville

Not a place which appears much in guide books, since it lacks anything of historical, religious or architectural interest, but Jullouville has a number of things in its favour as a family holiday resort. Only 6 km south of Granville it has, with its neighbour Carolles further south, a milder local climate in which mimosa and palm trees flourish. Until a few years ago it was a rather up-market resort with comfortable villas scattered in the pine forest which backs the magnificent sandy beach, kept spotless by dawn cleaning patrols. At low tide there are sand flats rich in marine life in one part of the beach. Mussels and edible crabs are easy to find, and a bagful of cockles can be raked in half an hour. All the usual seaside activities are available, including sailing and other water sports, plus tennis, etc. But in the past ten years Jullouville and its immediate neighbour Edenville have become increasingly popular. All the plus factors are still there but the atmosphere has become less relaxed, a bit brash, with rather too many garish amusement arcades, bars and cafés for some tastes.

Carolles

Carolles, the neighbouring village, is a small, old-fashioned resort of a different character on a rocky headland with a sheltered sandy beach at the foot of the cliffs, and the bigger beaches within easy reach.

Where to stay   There are flats and villas to rent, many close to the beach. Details from the *Syndicat d'Iniative*, 5610 Jullouville.

Hôtel Equinoxe, 28 Ave de la Libération, Jullouville 50610. Modest hotel with thirteen rooms at low to medium rates. Closed mid-November to mid-March.

To Mont St Michel

Jullouville is the last real seaside resort on this coast. From this point southwards the road keeps fairly close to the coast and at some points there are views across the Bay of Mont St Michel. The next places, Carolles and St Jean-le-Thomas, have sandy beaches but at high tide the water is so shallow that bathing is impossible except for the tiniest tots. At low tide the water recedes across miles of treacherous mudflats.

Further on, from the Bec d'Andaine near the village of Genets, there are more views of Mont St Michel. It was from this point in the Middle Ages that pilgrims crossed the flats 'in peril of the sea' to the abbey.

Avranches   Situated on the direct route from Cherbourg to the south, and also on the direct route from the north east of France to Brittany, Avranches is a commercial, industrial and crossroads town which can in no way be considered a resort, but its position makes it a useful stopover town. Traffic problems are frequent in the height of summer.

What to see   The **museum** is housed in the former Bishop's Palace, originally dating from the fifteenth century. It was often used as a prison in the past, and has not been much modified since. The most interesting of its exhibits are in a restored vaulted room. It contains relics of St Thomas à Becket and a rare collection of early illuminated manuscripts from the library of the Abbey of Mont St Michel, plus finely bound books of the sixteenth, seventeenth and eighteenth centuries: a treat for book-lovers. Open from April to mid-November, closed Tuesday.

The former cathedral was pulled down in 1799, because it was in danger of falling down. All that remains is a broken stone, **La Plateforme**, enclosed by chains, which marks the spot where Henry II of England knelt before the Papal representatives and did penance for the murder of Thomas à Becket, killed by over-zealous knights who took his rhetorical question 'Is there no one to rid me of this insolent priest?' as a command. The stone is in the Square Becket in front of the *préfecture*. Mont St Michel can be seen from the terrace.

Église St Gervais is a nineteenth-century church of little interest except that it has an important treasure, which includes what is said to be the skull of St Aubert, nicely mounted in an ornate case. St Aubert founded the first church on Mont St Michel, then called Mont Tombe, but he did it only after St Michael had appeared to him in three successive dreams, telling him to build the church there. The third time he was so annoyed that his instructions had been ignored that he made his point clear by tapping St Aubert on the head, but he overdid it rather, making a hole in his skull. Not everyone believes this story – but there is the skull in St Gervais with the hole neatly displayed.

It was from Avranches on 1 August 1944 that General 'Blood and Guts' Patton led the newly formed American 3rd Army in a tremendous thrust across France which took them as far as Belgium. There is a fine **memorial to General Patton** in the square named after him, which contains trees from different American states planted in soil brought from America.

Where to stay   **Hôtel La Croix d'Or**, 83 Rue de la Constitution, 50300 Avranches, tel. 33 58 04 88. All the charm of a former post-house of stage-coach days, combined with modern comfort. Thirty rooms (twenty-five with bath) from low to high medium rates. Restaurant with menus from medium prices. Closed from mid-November to mid-March.

Hôtel Les Abrincates, 37 Blvd du Luxembourg, tel. 33 58 66 64. Frankly modern hotel with comfortable, well-equipped rooms, all with bath etc, at low medium rates. Restaurant with good choice of menus from low medium prices.

Hôtel du Jardin des Plantes (LdF), 10 Place Carnot, tel. 33 58 03 68. Nineteen rooms at low rates. Sound restaurant, menus at medium prices up.

Mont St Michel

Right on the western boundary of Normandy, separated from Brittany only by the narrow river Couesnon, Mont St Michel is visited by more than one-and-a-half million tourists every year. Whatever the weather, the sight of it from the coast roads around the bay is impressive. It can be lovely at sunrise and sunset, and when reflected in the still waters of a calm high tide. In bright moonlight, or wreathed in sea mist so that it seems to float above the ground, it appears enchanted. From a distance it is undeniably a beautiful sight and, except for those visitors genuinely interested in its remarkable architecture, it is a moot point as to whether it improves on closer acquaintance.

History   Geologically, Mont St Michel is an isolated granite rock in the shape of a broad-based cone. In Roman times and for some hundreds of years after, it was surrounded by forest and protected from the sea by a low bank of sand and shingle. In the year AD 709 the sea broke through the protective bank, flooding the forest for good. It became a swamp, the trees died and rotted away, and what had been a forest became a vast mudflat, over which the tide rushes twice a day at considerable speed. At low tide the water retreats 11 km from the

Mont, and if you are there at the right time it is worth watching it race in again.

At about the same time as the sea swamped the forest, Aubert, despite the hole in his head, followed St Michael's instructions and built the first church on the top of the rock. In 966, Richard I, Duke of Normandy, established an abbey and thirty Benedictine monks from Jumièges settled on the rock. In 1020 a new abbey church was started. It took a long time to build, because the top of the rock cone was only about 10 m square, and only the crossing of the church was actually founded on the rock; the crypts and important substructures had to be built before the rest could be put on top. That church in the Romanesque style was completed in 1080, and part of the nave and the square of the transept remain from those days.

The abbey had a rough time, being repeatedly struck by lightning, damaged in battle and destroyed by fire, but after each disaster it rose again – rebuilt, restored, extended. After being partly destroyed by Bretons, who set it on fire in 1204, the abbey was rebuilt with the help of a donation from King Philippe Auguste. It was at this time, between 1205 and 1228, that the most intricate and beautiful part of the abbey, called Le Merveille, was built on the north side.

In the fourteenth century, during the Hundred Years' War, Mont St Michel became a fortress, and it was then that the ramparts and the whole system of fortifications as the visitor sees them today were built. The original choir collapsed in the late fifteenth century and was rebuilt in the Flamboyant Gothic style. Further alterations were carried out in the eighteenth century, and in 1897 the last refinement of a belfry and spire were added. The heavy-handed and over-elaborate restorers of the nineteenth century have often been justly criticised, but this was one instance where they got it absolutely right. Today Mont St Michel without its elegant belfry and spire would seem crippled.

At the French Revolution the few monks remaining were evicted and the buildings subsequently became a prison, one, incidentally, from which only one man ever escaped.

Tourism

Today tourists have replaced pilgrims, and shoddy commerce has replaced religious faith. It is a long climb to the top of the rock and on a hot day in summer it can be a penance. There may be thousands of other tourists pushing their way up or down the single street – 6,000 is the limit allowed at any one time and it is often reached. Restaurant and *crêperie* prices are exorbitant and the goods in the souvenir shops are for the most part third rate.

What to see
The
Fortifications

Visitors who do not wish to tour the abbey can walk half-way round the rock by way of the ramparts, stopping at the North Tower to watch the incoming tide, if the hour is right, and then visit the abbey gardens from which the western side of the rock and the chapel dedicated to the founder, St Aubert, can be seen. The return, downhill, can be made either by the ramparts, or the Chemin de Ronde, or the main street, the Grande Rue.

The Abbey To see the abbey church and buildings it is obligatory to join a guided tour. The ticket office is at the top of a steep staircase with ninety granite steps, and the tour starts from the west platform. From Easter to September some of the tours are in English, and the times are available from the Tourist Information Office, in the Corps de Garde de Bourgeois, at the entrance to the Mount. The abbey is labyrinthine and the tour, which takes an hour, is based on the logic of getting people through it quickly and effectively, and does not tackle one level or one period at a time, so visitors who are not fluent in French are strongly advised to take the English tour.

The highlights are the abbey church itself, and that part of the abbey buildings on the north side called Le Merveille. It was built early in the thirteenth century, and includes the Salle des Chevaliers (the Knights' Hall), the Salle des Hôtes (the Guests' Chamber), and above them the refectory and the lovely cloister. All these are masterpieces of Gothic style and craftsmanship. The great rooms lower down – the crypts, the monk's workshop, the old Carolingian church, St Stephen's chapel – are heavier and more sombre and, taken with the refinement of the rooms above, the whole shows the wonderful combination of determination, artistic skill and constructive, almost engineering, genius which over hundreds of years created this remarkable building, described by Guy de Maupassant as 'this granite jewel'.

There are three Benedictine monks and three nuns in residence in the abbey, and a public Mass is held every day. From mid-June to the end of September the abbey is open at night for a tour of twenty rooms accompanied by music. This presentation, called *Les Imaginaires du Mont St Michel*, is from 10 p.m. to midnight (last admissions) until the end of August, and then from 9 p.m. to 11 p.m. until the end of September.

There are other things on the Mount open to the public – museums, exhibitions, etc – but they are essentially tourist traps of little interest.

Bay of Mont This is to be looked at, not explored on foot. There are fatal
St Michel accidents every year among people who ignore this advice. Sudden sea mists can develop in which people quickly lose their sense of direction, and flounder about in water of uneven depth. There are ever-changing pockets of quicksands, especially near the edges of the freshwater streams which cross the flats.

Where to **Hôtel St Pierre** (LdF), Grande Rue, 50116 Le Mont St Michel,
stay tel. 33 60 14 34. A fifteenth-century house with twenty-one modernised bedrooms, some with views over the bay, at high medium rates. Busy brasserie-type restaurant, reliably good cuisine. Menus are good value at from low medium prices up.

Hôtel Les Terrasses Poulard, Grande Rue, tel. 33 60 14 09. Newish building with attractive bedrooms, some on the small side, with views over the town or the sea. Large dining room with landward views of the bay. Seafood specialities. Rooms and menus for the most part medium plus, somewhat overpriced. Guests must take half-board in high season.

Hôtel du Guesclin (LdF), in the town, tel. 33 60 14 10. Straight-forward hotel run by a pioneer of the *Logis de France* organisation. Thirteen rooms at low to medium plus rates. Good value meals at low/ medium prices. Closed 15 October to 15 March, and Tuesday evening and Wednesday out of season.

Hôtel de la Digue, near the land end of the Causeway, on the D976 2 km from the Mount, tel. 33 60 14 02. Rather nice modern building with thirty-five bedrooms at low/medium rates and restaurant at medium prices, both having views across the bay to Mont St Michel. Closed from November to March.

Mercure Mont St Michel, on the approach road, tel. 33 60 14 18. One of the modern chain of large hotels. One hundred comfortable rooms at medium rates. Good restaurant at medium prices.

Auberge de la Selune (LdF), 2 Rue St Germain, 50220 Ducey, tel. 33 48 53 62. About 20 km east of Mont St Michel, well away from the summer scramble. Comfortable hotel with a garden to the banks of the Selune. Twenty-three rooms with bath at low medium rates. The patron, M Girres, is a first-class chef, and the menus from medium prices are good value. Closed February.

Hôtel Manoir de la Roche Torin, Courtils, 50220 Ducey, tel. 33 70 96 55. About 12 km from Mont St Michel, this is a small country-house hotel with twelve bedrooms at high medium rates. Near the edge of the bay, down a lane off the D75, it offers comfort and calm, not easily found in this area in the high season. Good restaurant from medium plus prices. Closed 15 November to 15 March.

NB After Paris, Mont St Michel is easily the most visited tourist destination in France, and apart from those listed there are many other hotels in the villages in the Mont St Michel region. The roads are very busy in the summer and noisy at night. It is important to book in advance and insist on a quiet room.

Where to eat

Preferably somewhere else, if you like value for money. But if you want to eat on Mont St Michel itself, the best bets are the restaurants of the hotels mentioned or **Mère Poulard**. It is now over sixty years since Annette Poulard died, and there can be very few people left able to compare the omelettes served there today with the ones which she cooked and which made the restaurant famous. (Part of her secret was added egg white and a lot of beating.) Another speciality is *agneau pré salé* – roast lamb from the salt meadows around the edge of the bay. The cuisine is good and reliable, without being distinguished, and you pay for the name. Menus from well above average upwards. There is a hotel side, also expensive.

Leaving the Mont St Michel area heading west, you arrive at once in a new region where the people have their own language and customs, and where the houses, villages and countryside have a new look: what is, in fact, though it has been part of France for hundreds of years, a different country – the old province of Brittany.

BRITTANY

St Malo

After the nine-hour Channel crossing from Portsmouth, the approach to St Malo in the light of the dawn with the cliffs of the bays, the headlands and the islands all touched with rose and gold, is a landfall to match any in Europe. If it is impressive and welcoming even after this short spell at sea, imagine what it must have been to the crews of the cod-fishing boats returning after months in the cold and hostile waters off Newfoundland. Today St Malo no longer depends entirely on the sea, on fishing and the 'legitimate' piracy of the corsairs as it did in the past, but it is still an important fishing port and one of the few that continue to send cod-fishing boats to the Grand Banks off Newfoundland.

Since 1967 St Malo has been joined together with St Servan, Paramé and Rothéneuf to form the one big town of St Malo, and this fusion has brought added prosperity. St Malo itself, with cross-Channel traffic carrying 700,000 passengers and increasing commercial traffic as well as the fishing fleet, is one of the few French ports in expansion. Paramé, with its huge beach of golden sand, and Rothéneuf, with its cliffs and sandy coves, are very popular tourist resorts. St Malo itself, situated on granite headlands at the estuary of the Rance, is an excellent family holiday resort. It is picturesque and has its own sheltered sandy beaches and tourist attactions of all kinds. There is a casino, dozens of bars, restaurants and terrace cafés. It is also an important yachting centre, with its own large marina: the famous transatlantic solo race to the West Indies, the *Route du Rhum*, starts here.

There is always plenty to do and see in St Malo, whatever the weather, and it is a good centre for excursions. Cancale, Mont St Michel, Dinan, Dinard and the resorts of the Emerald Coast are all within an easy drive. It is a lively town all year round. As well as being a centre of commercial and industrial activities and tourism, it is a *sous-préfecture* of the department of Ille-et-Vilaine.

History   St Malo was founded in the sixth century by a saint from Wales of that name, probably the same man after whom the church of St

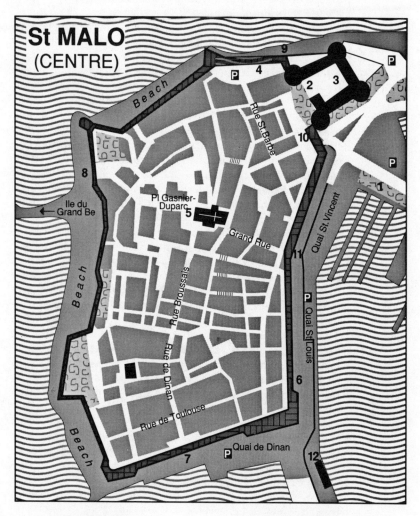

St MALO
(CENTRE)

Beach

Ile du Grand Be

Pl Gasnier-Duparc

Grand Rue

Rue St.Barbe

Rue Broussais

Rue de Dinan

Rue de Toulouse

Quai St.Vincent

Quai St.Louis

Quai de Dinan

Beach

1	Tourist Office	7	Porte de Dinan
2	Castle	8	Porte Champs Vauverts
3	St Malo Museum	9	Porte St Thomas
4	Aquarium	10	Porte St Vincent
5	St Vincent's Cathedral	11	Grande Porte
6	Porte St Louis	12	Ancienne Gare Maritime

 Ramparts   P Parking

Maclou in Rouen is named. The first community was on the mainland at what is now the suburb called St Servan, but Norman attacks forced the population to move to the offshore island, which could be more easily defended, and on which they built the town which is the old St Malo, eventually linked to the mainland by a causeway.

It became the seat of a bishopric, ended at the time of the French Revolution. Its importance grew from the time of Henri IV, and during the time of the Religious Wars, St Malo declared itself a republic and remained one for four years. Its sense of independence was made clear in its well-known motto, *Ni Français, ni Breton; Malouin suis* (Neither French nor Breton; I am Malouin). During the seventeenth and eighteenth centuries the activities of its daring privateers led to several clashes with the English. In 1944, although St Malo was cut off by the advance of American forces into Brittany the German garrison refused to surrender, and most of the walled town was battered into ruins before they did so.

A remarkable number of famous men were born in old St Malo, in a space no bigger than that of a small London park. They include the explorer Jacques Cartier (1494–1557) who explored the eastern coast of Canada and discovered the mouth of the St Lawrence river, and the heroic Porçon de la Bardinais who, given the job of protecting St Malo's merchant ships in the Mediterranean against the Barbary pirates, was instead captured by them. He was taken before the Bey of Algiers, who allowed him to return to France to negotiate a peace with Louis XIV on condition that if he failed, he would return to Algiers. His mission did fail and he went to his home in St Malo, put his affairs in order, said goodbye to his family, and kept his word by returning to Algiers, where he was tied across the mouth of a cannon and executed.

Other famous Malouins were the great corsairs, Duguay-Trouhin and Robert Surcouf, the great French writer François René de Chateaubriand; the explorer, Mahé de la Bourdonnais, who governed the French East Indies and colonised part of India; Broussais, a doctor who transformed the practice of medicine in the early nineteenth century; Gournay, a famous French economist; and the controversial religious writer, de Lammennais.

What to see
St Malo Intra
Muros

This is the name of the old city of St Malo within the walls (*intra muros*) and it is signposted as such. The great ramparts themselves were almost all that remained after the bombardment. Built to withstand the fury of Atlantic storms and tides which can rise as much as 15 m, the granite walls were not much damaged and the city inside them has been reconstructed scrupulously in its old style and the same, rather sombre granite. An idea of what was achieved can be obtained from photographs in the **Musée de la Ville** in the keep of the castle just inside the St Vincent gateway, the main entry to St Malo Intra Muros, on the right. The museum concentrates on the history of the town and the lives of its great men and sailors. Open a.m./p.m. every day. Closed Tuesday from October to May.

The Ramparts

It is possible to walk right round old St Malo on the ramparts, reached by a stone staircase to the right of the St Vincent gateway, behind the Hôtel de France et Chateaubriand. There are fine views over the islands and beaches, the estuary of the Rance across to Dinard, the Côte Émeraude and out to sea, and over the old town and the rest of St Malo.

Between Porte St Thomas and the Tour Bidouane, there are seaward views of the **Fort National** and the Île du Grand Bé. The Fort National was built by Vauban, the great French military architect, in 1689 on the orders of Louis XIV and was originally called Fort Royal. It became the Fort National at the time of the Revolution. The fort can be reached on foot (twenty minutes there and back) from the beach at low tide, and is open to the public for guided visits from May to October.

Île du Grand Bé

This can also be reached on foot at low tide, after descending to the beach near the Tour Bidouane. It takes about three-quarters of an hour there and back, and the walk should not be started when the tide is coming in. The writer Chateaubriand is buried on the island in a tomb facing the open sea: he wished, he said, to be alone in death, as he had been in life. There are splendid views from the island in all directions, particularly of the Emerald Coast, and the estuary of the Rance.

Cathédrale St Vincent

The cathedral was badly damaged in 1944, losing its spire and the south transept, but it has been meticulously reconstructed. It is said to be on the site of the sixth-century monastery founded by St Malo and the present building, started in the twelfth century, was altered and restored several times up to the nineteenth century, before the thirty years of rebuilding which took place from 1944. It has some beautiful modern stained glass by Jean le Moal and Bernard Allain in the choir, and in the sides of the nave by Max Ingrand. The tombs of the explorer Jacques Cartier, and the famous corsair Duguay-Trouhin are in a chapel on the north side of the choir.

Place Chateaubriand

Just inside the St Vincent gateway is the space known as the Place Chateaubriand, with the château, which contains the town hall as well as the **Musée de la Ville**, on one side and a number of large café terraces opposite. It is a pleasant spot for a coffee or a drink after walking round, or for a meal, particularly at night, when the château is floodlit.

St Servan

This suburb of St Malo, close to the Intra Muros, has two points of interest. First is the **Corniche d'Aleth**, a cliff path around a small peninsula which gives wonderful views across the estuary of the Rance to Dinard and the Emerald Coast. It starts from the Place St Pierre, where there is a car park. Nearby is the **Tour Solidor**, a fourteenth-century tower, restored in the seventeenth, which contains a museum that will interest everyone keen on boats and sailing. Called the **Musée**

International du Long-Cours Cap Hornier, it is devoted to sailing ships and mariners who rounded Cape Horn between the sixteenth and twentieth centuries. There are many early nautical instruments, ship's logs and models of clippers, windjammers and smaller ships, including the *Victoria*, the first ship to complete a voyage around the world, with Magellan's expedition, which started in 1519.

Paramé The suburb immediately to the east of St Malo Intra Muros is reached by the Chemin de Sillon. Paramé has two km of fine sands, backed the whole length by an impressive promenade. It was founded as a resort more than a hundred years ago and was for a time exclusive and fashionable. When he was Prince of Wales, Edward VII had a villa built here in Moghul Indian style, with domes and turrets. Today it is just a popular resort, with no sights other than its varied mix of modern and period seaside architecture.

Rothéneuf A few km further east, Rothéneuf is another popular resort, officially part of St Malo, but different in character from Paramé. It is situated on a *havre*, like those on the west coast of the Cotentin, at high tide a wide and picturesque bay, which is left exposed as sandy mudflats at low tide. There are cliffs and sandy coves round the corner facing the open sea. Rothéneuf is known for its *rochers sculptés* (sculpted rocks), nearly 300 heads and figures carved in the granite rocks. They are the work of a local priest, Abbé Foure, who from 1870 spent twenty-five years making his mark on the world.

Manoir de Limoëlou Situated in the Rue David Macdonald Stewart, Rothéneuf, this is the home of the explorer, Jacques Cartier, who discovered the St Lawrence river and explored eastern Canada in the early sixteenth century. The fifteenth- and sixteenth-century house, extended in the nineteenth century, had remained a farm since Cartier's day and had become run down, but it has now been restored and furnished in the style of that period. The visit includes an audiovisual presentation of the explorer's voyages to Canada.

What to do St Malo is not only a good centre for land excursions, it is a great place for those who are good sailors and like relatively short sea trips. Dinard, Cap Fréhel, the valley of the Rance and Dinan, the island of Cézembre which has a south-facing sandy beach, the Chausey Islands and the Channel Islands are among places with regular boat services or launch trips in summer.

Where to stay The majority of hotels in St Malo do not have restaurants and those that do strongly prefer you to eat in them. In summer half-board is obligatory in some.

Hôtel Central, 6 Grande Rue, Intra Muros, 35400 St Malo, tel. 99 40 87 70. Well-run, comfortable hotel in the middle of the old town. Forty-six bedrooms, rather small but comfortable, prices for rooms and meals medium plus. Restaurant closed Sunday evening and Monday out of season.

Hôtel de la Cité, 26 Rue St Barbe, Intra Muros, tel. 99 56 66 52.

Near the château and just inside the ramparts. Parking space. Completely renovated old building. Forty-one comfortable bedrooms, prices medium plus. No restaurant.

Hôtel La Porte St Pierre (LdF), 2 Place Guet, Intra Muros, tel. 99 40 91 27. Very nice old hotel, run by the same family for more than fifty years. Thoroughly modernised and with a very good value restaurant with a covered terrace. Twenty-seven bedrooms, prices medium. Menus from low prices upwards.

Hôtel Les Thermes, 100 Blvd Hebert, Paramé, 35400 St Malo, tel. 99 56 02 56. A former 'grand hotel', now completely modernised to high standards of comfort, next to the beach. 182 bedrooms at prices from medium to rather expensive. Good classical restaurant (**Le Cap Horn**) with menus from medium plus to expensive.

Hôtel Le Valmarin, 7 Rue Jean XX, St Servan, 35400 St Malo, tel. 99 81 94 76. Small hotel in an eighteenth-century mansion with garden. Quiet situation, but not far from the main routes south and west into Brittany. Twelve spacious, well-furnished bedrooms all with own bath etc, prices medium plus. No restaurant. Closed in winter except 20 December to 7 January.

Manoir de la Grassinais (LdF), 12 Rue Grassinais, tel. 99 81 33 00. Three km south of the centre by Ave Général de Gaulle, this is an attractive hotel around a courtyard. Twenty-nine modern bedrooms, functional and quiet. Prices medium. Restaurant with excellent cuisine, menus very good value at medium prices.

The above is only a selection of the fifty or so hotels in St Malo, which include some modern chain hotels such as Mercure, just outside the Intra Muros, and Mascotte, near the Paramé beach.

Where to eat

Many restaurants, though not all, offer menus at reduced prices for children – this usually means under eight years old.

Les Écluses, Gare Maritime de la Bourse, tel. 99 56 81 00. Attractively situated restaurant, near where the boats leave for the Channel Islands, and with views of the ramparts and across the Rance to Dinard. Sound cuisine with menus a little above medium prices. Parking for fifty cars.

À L'Abordage, 5 Place de la Poissonerie, Intra Muros, between the château and the cathedral. Charming but serious restaurant. Welcoming, friendly service supervised by Madame, and the chef/patron gives generous helpings and maintains high standards of classical cuisine. Range of menus from low prices upwards. Closed on Monday, and from 15 November to 15 December, and one week in February.

Le Saint Placide, 6 Place du Poncel, St Servan, tel. 99 81 70 73. Good-quality, straightforward, solidly comfortable restaurant. Classic cuisine with some original touches. Prices from medium upwards. Closed Saturday lunch.

L'Atre, 7 Esplanade Cmdt Menguy, St Servan, tel. 99 81 68 39. Good standards all round. Covered terrace with views of the Tour

Solidor and across to Dinard. Prices medium. Closed Tuesday evening (out of season) and Wednesday.

Brasserie de l'Ouest, 4 Place Chateaubriand, Intra Muros. Conveniently situated, lively atmosphere, with orchestra in summer season.

Dinard and the Emerald Coast

A more beautiful coastline than that which lies west of the estuary of the Rance as far as Pléneuf-Val André does not exist anywhere in France, and it is difficult to imagine one anywhere in the world. It has everything that a coast can have in the way of variety. There are numerous offshore islands, some big, some small, some easily reached on foot at low tide, some almost out of sight in the sea haze. There are great headlands flanked by rose-red granite cliffs rising straight from the waves, while between them huge stretches of golden sand alternate with rocky coves with just a pocket handkerchief of sand. There are sheltered bays and river mouths crammed with boats of all shapes, sizes and colours, and all facing a sea which, in summer sun, really does sparkle in blue and emerald green.

Dinard

This resort is the finest of the Emerald Coast. Even the adolescent French, the most scornful of all critics, find it hard not to like it, and there's no denying that Dinard has a certain style and elegance. Founded by a rich American who built the first luxury villa there in the 1850s, Dinard soon became a resort popular with other Americans and well-to-do English families. Sumptuous villas were built surrounded by gardens in which palms, fig trees, oleanders, aloes and mimosa flourished in the mild climate, and were followed by Victorian and Edwardian hotels in the grand manner. Some of these older buildings remain, but Dinard has also moved with the times without losing any of its style and, perhaps because of its nautical associations – many of the most successful of St Malo's nineteenth-century master mariners retired to villas in Dinard or its neighbour St Lunaire – without ever becoming stuffy.

What to do   The resort has a splendid modern casino, golf course, a famous horse-riding centre where international competitions are held, a racecourse, a flying club, an indoor Olympic swimming pool with warmed sea water just behind the main beach, and facilities for a dozen other sports, including sea and freshwater fishing, martial arts and fencing. All the clubs welcome holiday visitors.

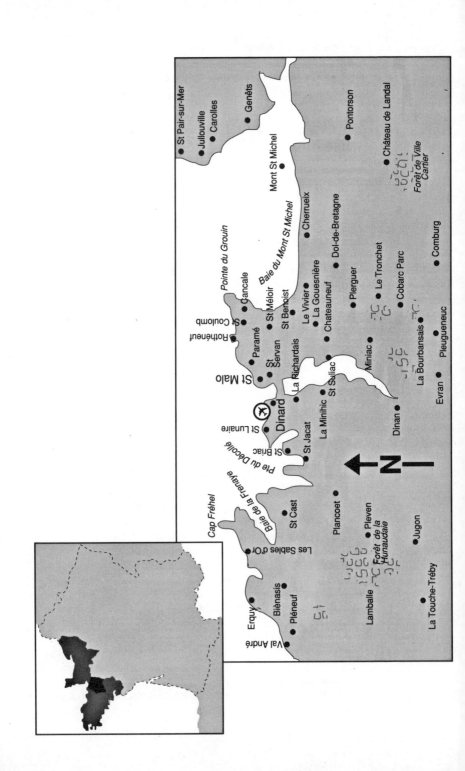

All this behind three of the finest sand beaches imaginable. The main beach is called the Grand Plage or the Plage de l'Écluse: golden sands, sheltered by headlands on either side and backed by the casino, luxury hotels, the Olympic pool and the Palais des Congrès, it is the lively heart of Dinard. The other two beaches, Plage de la Prieuré and the Plage de St Enogat, are just as sandy and picturesque, and equally animated. From the end of La Prieuré beach the Promenade du Clair de Lune, reserved for walkers, follows the water's edge. There is always something to do in Dinard, whatever the weather, and the Emerald Coast has one of the best sunshine records in France.

The attractions of St Malo are a short drive away on the other side of the Rance by the road which runs along the top of the Rance barrage, opened in 1967. The combination of the Atlantic and Channel tides and the flow of the river gives the Rance the highest tidal variations in Europe, and the barrage successfully harnesses this tidal power to produce electricity.

Where to stay

Le Grand Hôtel, 46 Ave Georges V, 35800 Dinard, tel. 99 88 26 26. An old-fashioned 'palace' hotel in appearance but with a completely modernised interior. Sixty-three bedrooms, most with sea view, all with bath. Good restaurant. Prices medium plus. Closed November to April.

Hôtel de la Plage, 3 Blvd Féart, tel. 99 46 14 87. In town but close to the main beach. Eighteen comfortable rooms, some with balconies. Good range of menus. Prices medium.

Hôtel Restaurant Altair (LdF), 18 Blvd Féart, tel. 99 46 13 58. Twenty-one bedrooms at cheap to medium prices. Half-board obligatory in season. First-class cuisine with good-value menus at medium prices. Closed Sunday dinner and Monday.

Hôtel Balmoral, 26 Rue Maréchal Leclerc, tel. 99 46 16 97. Calm, comfortable, traditional hotel not far from the Plage du Prieuré. Thirty-one bedrooms, all with bath etc, at low to medium prices.

Hôtel Climat de France, 14 Rue des Genêts, La Richardais, Dinard, tel. 99 46 69 55. One of this widespread modern chain, 2 km from Dinard close to the Barrage de la Rance, and so also convenient for St Malo. Good restaurant, medium prices for both rooms and meals. Useful overnight stop.

Where to eat

Brasserie de la Mer, 4 Blvd Wilson, 35800 Dinard, tel. 99 46 15 71. View of the Grand Plage. À la carte at a wide range of prices. Closed November to 14 April.

La Paix, 6 Place de la République. Small family restaurant in the heart of Dinard, specialising in seafood. Medium prices. Closed 16 November to 14 March.

La Vallée, 6 Avenue Georges V, tel. 99 46 94 00. Traditional restaurant overlooking the harbour where the fishing boats tie up. Menus from medium prices upwards. Closed from 15 November to 5 February.

Le Petit Robinson, 38 Rue de la Goujeonnais, 35780 La Richardais, tel. 99 46 14 82. Three km south-east of Dinard on the D114, but a popular restaurant. Traditional cuisine as well as plain grills of excellent quality. Also seven bedrooms, all with bath etc. Medium prices all round. Restaurant closed Sunday evening, and Monday except July–August.

Excursion from St Malo or Dinard: Dinan

Thirty km south of St Malo and twenty-three south of Dinard, Dinan is one of the loveliest and most interesting old towns in Brittany. It is in two parts, the old port at the riverside, now used only by the pleasure boats which offer trips on the river, and the main town on the cliff high above.

Despite the fact that there are several parking areas, just outside the ramparts, parking can be a problem in the high season. On the right sort of day it can be well worth making the trip up the Rance to Dinan by boat, as the river, sometimes like a lake and sometimes shut in between wooded cliffs, offers a remarkable variety of lovely scenery. A decision should be made in advance, after inquiries at the *Syndicat d'Initiative*, about how to return, as for reasons of time it may be advisable to return by bus or train. There is also the climb up to Dinan, and the walking in the old town – which is so interesting that it will take you further than you realise – to take into consideration..You will feel the need for a meal, or at least a prolonged and restful drink, before returning. (Boat trips on the Rance, even if you do not go as far as Dinan, are well worthwhile.)

What to see

Though there are one or two points of special interest which should not be missed, it is the ensemble of the old town with its many half-timbered houses, Renaissance and eighteenth-century mansions, Gothic churches, castle and ramparts, which is the real monument. It is a place to wander in and make your own discoveries among the narrow alleys, courtyards and cobbled streets lined with old mansions. Information from the Tourist Office in the Hôtel Keratry, a sixteenth-century mansion in the Rue de l'Horloge, is a great help (also guided tours in season).

St Sauveur

The building is partly twelfth-century Romanesque, but mostly fifteenth-century Flamboyant Gothic, and the difference is particularly noticeable in the interior where the right side of the nave is Romanesque and the left side, the choir and the transept are Flamboyant. In the left arm of the transept a cenotaph contains the heart of the great French soldier, Du Guesclin. Among his many exploits, Du

Guesclin defended Dinan against a siege by the English in 1357 and is said to have saved the town by challenging an English knight, Thomas of Canterbury, to single combat on a 'winner takes all' basis. If he won, the English would withdraw, if he lost he would surrender. Du Guesclin won, and the English kept the bargain and called off the siege. Du Guesclin also won a wife. A charming and cultured girl, Tiphaine Raguenel, daughter of a Breton viscount, whose skills included astrology, predicted his victory, and was so impressed by his bravery and skill that she persuaded him to marry her. The union between the rough, bloodthirsty and ugly aristocrat who eventually became Constable of France, and the gentle and clever Tiphaine was, by all accounts, remarkably happy.

The dome of the sixteenth-century tower was struck by lightning in the eighteenth century and was replaced by a wooden slate-covered spire. There is an impressive eighteenth-century altar, and there is a good fifteenth-century stained-glass window in the north aisle. Most of the rest of the stained glass is modern. The **Place St Sauveur** in front of the church is surrounded by fifteenth-century houses.

From the Place St Sauveur, with your back to the church, turn right, and then right again into the Rue Haute Voie, then left into the Rue Jerzual.

Rue Jerzual

This street is lined by well-restored, half-timbered and gabled houses of the sixteenth century, many with the ground-floor studios of potters, weavers, glass-blowers, cabinet-makers and sculptors. It leads to the fourteenth-century gate, and from there a road leads down to the old Gothic bridge. In the other direction the Rue Jerzual leads, by a left turn, to the **Place des Merciers**, a picturesque square with an old well and surrounded by more gabled houses.

Tour de l'Horloge

From the Place des Merciers, the Rue de l'Horloge leads to the Tour de l'Horloge. This tower contains the town clock, bought in 1498, and the great bell given by Duchess Anne of Brittany in 1507. It is a stiff climb to the top (158 steps), but once up there you have panoramic views over the town and its setting. Open July–August only, a.m./p.m.

The château

Late fourteenth century, this consists of a massive oval keep, called the Donjon de la Duchesse Anne, a gateway with two towers and the Tour de Coetquen. It is open from March to October, a.m./p.m., but is of limited interest and contains a museum of which the same can be said.

Though it cannot be called a holiday resort in any usual sense, Dinan is a place which, for those visitors with an interest in history and a sense of the past, is well worth a stay of one or two nights.

Where to stay

Hôtel Avaugour (LdF), 1 Place du Champ Clos, Dinan 22100, tel. 96 39 07 49. Comfortable hotel with a good reputation. In the town, but some of the twenty-seven rooms (all with bath etc) overlook the garden and the ramparts and are quiet. Prices medium. Traditional cuisine at medium plus prices.

Hôtel de France (LdF), 7 Place du 11-Novembre, tel. 96 39 22 56. Fourteen bedrooms, all with bath etc, at low to medium prices. Good restaurant with menus from medium prices upwards.

Hôtel Campanile, Route de Ploubalay, Dinan-Taden, tel. 64 62 46 46. Outside the old town. One of a pleasant modern chain which offers forty-nine functional rooms and a good restaurant at medium prices.

Where to eat

Chez La Mère Pourcel, 3 Place des Merciers, tel. 96 39 03 80. Old Dinan favourite in a fine medieval house. Jean Luc Danjou offers very good cuisine from medium prices to fairly expensive. Closed Sunday evening, and Monday except July/August.

Les Grandes Fosses, 2 Place du Général Leclerc, tel. 96 39 21 50. Superb cuisine based on fresh local produce with no lack of inspired touches. Very good value at medium prices. Last orders 9.30 p.m. Closed Thursday.

Excursion from Dinan
Château and Game Park La Bourbansais

The Château La Bourbansais is situated at Pleugueneuc, about 15 km south-east of Dinan by the D794 and N137 (35 km from St Malo or Dinard). This very attractive *château de plaisance* was built in 1583 by Jean de Breil, a member of the Breton Parliament, and has been in the hands of the same family ever since, never having been sold. There are magnificent gardens in the French style, as well as an eight-acre game park with animals and birds from all five continents, among them ostriches, flamingos, llamas, zebras, wolves, kangaroos and more. The château itself, on the site of a Roman villa, was rebuilt and extended during the seventeenth and eighteenth centuries. It is open to the public and some of the most important rooms can be visited. There is some fine eighteenth-century furniture, Aubusson tapestries, and a collection of porcelain. Open all day from June to August, p.m. only from October to March, a.m./p.m. at other times of the year.

Other resorts of the Emerald Coast (east to west)

St Lunaire

The next resort west from Dinard (5 km), St Lunaire is a reserved and stylish place with two magnificent sand beaches, which has been popular with English families for the past hundred years. The beaches are separated by a headland, the **Pointe du Décollé**, from which there are panoramic views east and west of the Emerald Coast.

St Briac

The excellent 18-hole golf course, usually known as the **Golf de Dinard**, is in fact at St Briac, just west of St Lunaire. St Briac is an attractive resort, rather more relaxed and less sophisticated than either Dinard or St Lunaire. It has several sheltered and sandy beaches and a yachting harbour, and the estuary of the Fremur and the bays around St Briac and the offshore islands make a fascinating cruising ground.

St Jacut-de-la-Mer

A fishing village and small resort with something of everything, especially for children. Situated on a peninsula with huge bays on either side, it has ten sandy beaches, boats for hire, rock pools to fish in, woods to scramble through, and children's beach clubs.

St Cast-le-Guildo

A larger and more straggly resort than St Lunaire, with a huge expanse of sand and a small fishing port specialising in shellfish. The main beach is enclosed by two headlands, both giving good coastal views, and there is a second huge beach, **Pen Guen**, backed by pine woods and sand dunes, to the east on the edge of the resort. Pen Guen itself is on a cliff in a pine forest dotted with comfortable villas. St Cast has a busy harbour full of pleasure boats of all kinds, as well as nearly 3 km of its own beach. There are good hotels and restaurants, and many comfortable villas for rent.

Les Sables d'Or Les Pins

This resort, in a situation of pine woods and sand dunes, with 2 km of lovely beach of fine golden sand, was created from scratch in the 1920s. It has a casino, and a 9-hole (18-tee) golf course. The beach here, like all those on this stretch of coast, is made yet more attractive by the wonderful scattering of islands off shore. From the resort a corniche road, the D36A, leads out to the point of **Cap Frehel**, with its 70 m granite cliffs plunging sheer to the sea. The cape is a bird sanctuary. From the top (145 steps) of the lighthouse on the western side the views in clear weather extend to Jersey to the north, Granville to the east, and Île de Bréhat to the west. On the eastern side of the cape, **Fort La Latte**, a picturesquely sited fortress built between the fourteenth and seventeenth centuries, is open for guided visits from June–September. It is reached from the mainland on foot across drawbridges.

Erquy

Another really good family resort with seven beaches (the one nearest the town is the least attractive), and an animated fishing port specialising in Coquilles St Jacques and other shellfish. Erquy is in a sheltered position where oleanders, fuschias, mimosa and camellias flourish. A lively, interesting and unsophisticated resort.

Le Val André

Another family favourite, an old-established resort which still has a period flavour about it, with a long promenade behind a great stretch of sandy beach. It cannot be said too often that the beaches of the Emerald Coast are far better than the vast majority of the beaches in the Mediterranean package tour resorts, more sand, more cliffs, more rock pools, more variety, and the water is warm and the bathing safe. There are good shops, restaurants and hotels, and a casino. The atmosphere is more friendly and relaxed than in St Cast.

This lovely stretch of coast is served by about 60 km of main roads which bring dozens of fine sand beaches within easy reach, none overcrowded and some little used, so that visitors can explore and find their own favourite place. All the resorts have an individual character and are within easy reach of others that are slightly different.

Where to stay

Hôtel le Vieux Moulin, 22750 St Jacut-de-la-Mer, tel. 96 27 71 02. Straightforward holiday hotel with twenty-nine rooms at rather below medium rates. Restaurant (dinner only), medium prices. Open Easter to September.

Hôtel Ar-Vro, 10 Blvd de la Plage, 22380 St Cast-le-Guildo, tel. 96 41 85 01. Roomy hotel in a wooded setting next to the beach, long popular with British families. Forty-seven bedrooms at slightly above medium rates. Restaurant with sea views and sound but uninspired cuisine, a bit overpriced.

Hôtel Les Arcades (LdF), 15 Rue Duc d'Aiguillon, St Cast-Le-Guildo, tel. 96 41 80 50. Near the beach in a quiet pedestrians-only street. Thirty-two bedrooms, all with bath etc, some with sea view. Good restaurant, wine included. Closed 3 November to 20 March.

Hôtel La Voile d'Or (LdF), Les Sables d'Or Les Pins, tel. 96 41 42 49. By the beach. Twenty-six roomy bedrooms, sea views, good value restaurant. Medium prices. Closed mid-November to mid-March.

Hôtel Le Brigantin, Place de l'Hôtel de Ville, 22430 Erquy, tel. 96 72 32 14. Nice hotel with pleasant, enterprising management. Spacious bedrooms, well equipped, and all with bath etc. Bistro-type restaurant in Breton style. Low to medium prices for both rooms and board.

Grand Hôtel du Val André, Rue Amiral Charner, 22370 Pleneuf-Val-André, tel. 96 72 20 56. Old-style hotel with modernised interior, well run, spacious, and with direct access to the beach. Thirty-nine bedrooms, restaurant with terrace facing the sea. Half-board obligatory in season. Prices medium, rooms and board. Closed 11 November to 19 March.

Hôtel de France et du Petit Prince (LdF), Pléneuf, tel. 96 72 22 52. About 2 km from the beach in the little town of Pléneuf, opposite the church. Forty-four bedrooms, some simple, but the best rooms and the good regional restaurant are well worth the low/medium prices. Closed November to April.

Where to eat

The majority of hotel restaurants are open to the public as well as to residents.

Restaurant Le Terrier, St Jacut-de-la-Mer, tel. 96 27 41 76. Charming little house in its own garden near the beach. The *patronne* does the shopping, and offers the best that she finds according to season and cooks it herself. Menus from below average (very good value) upwards. Closed Sunday evening.

Le Biniou, St Cast-le-Guildo, tel. 96 41 94 53. Dining rooms facing the sea at Pen Guen beach. Sound, if uninspired, cooking and pleasant surroundings. Menus at medium prices. Closed Tuesday except 15 June to 15 September, and 12 November to 20 March.

L'Escurial, Blvd de la Mer, Erquy, tel. 96 72 31 56. The dining room has views over the beach and the port, and Madame Bernard's culinary skills are mainly devoted to seafood. Medium prices upwards. Closed Tuesday evening and Wednesday, except July/August.

La Cotriade, 1 Quai Célestin Bougle, Port de Plégu, Le Val André, tel. 96 72 20 26. Bar downstairs, dining room upstairs with wonderful views across the whole of the Bay of St Brieuc. About the best on the Emerald Coast, if not the most comfortable. Prices fairly expensive. Closed Thursday, except July/August.

Au Biniou, 121 Rue Clémenceau, Le Val André, tel. 96 72 24 35. Pleasant restaurant specialising in seafood, good value at medium prices. Closed Thursday except July/August.

Picnic excursion

As a change from the coast, the short trip inland to the **Forêt de la Hunaudaie** is worthwhile. Reached via Plancoët from any of the resorts of the Emerald Coast, and then from Plancoët to the village of Pleven and the D28, the forest is a good area for picnics. Pleven itself is situated beside a long lake created by a barrage on the Arguenon river, and 2 km to the south are the vast and impressive moated ruins of the **fortress of Hunaudaie**. This twelfth- to fourteenth-century castle in a wooded setting has five sides and five great towers, and is a solemn reminder of the enormous difference in feudal times between the power and life of the lords and that of their subjects. In the fifteenth and sixteenth centuries the Lords of Hunaudaie were the terror of the region. No traveller passed through the forest untaxed, either in money or goods. In 1505 his men even stopped the great Duchess Anne, and took her to their lord. He made an exception in her case and offered her a banquet instead. According to old records the table was 'four times covered with thirty-six dishes of different meats, and finally a calf roasted whole was brought in by eight squires, standing on its legs with an orange in its mouth.'

The castle was made more livable in, in the seventeenth century by the creation of manorial living quarters within its walls, but was burned and partly pulled down at the Revolution. Open a.m./p.m. during July/August and on Sunday afternoons only from April to July and during September.

Where to eat

Chez Crouzil, 20 Les Quais, 22130 Plancoët, tel. 96 84 10 24. This charming restaurant was once a *Relais Routiers* and, not surprisingly, very popular with lorry drivers, but the chef-patron, Jean Pierre Crouzil, decided to set his sights higher. He redecorated and refurnished the restaurant, and offers ambitious cuisine based on the best produce of the region. Menus from medium plus upwards, and the lorry drivers pass by with a sigh of regret. Closed Sunday evening and Monday.

Château de Combourg

From Dinan by the D974, or St Malo by the N137 and D974, the château dates originally from the twelfth century, was enlarged in the fourteenth and fifteenth, and restored inside and out in the nineteenth.

In the eighteenth century the castle was bought by the father of the French writer, François René de Chateaubriand, who spent some years of his childhood there.

The castle is in a wooded setting on a rise overlooking a small lake. It is square with round battlemented towers at each corner, each with a conical roof. It still belongs to a member of the Chateaubriand family, the Comtesse de Durford. The inside is comfortably furnished and suggests little of the sinister place described by Chateaubriand in his writing, though it is still said to be haunted by a black cat bricked up in the walls 300 years ago and by the wooden leg of its owner, which taps along the corridors without even a ghostly body. Several rooms are open to the public, including the writer's bedroom in the Cat Tower, and there are many souvenirs of Chateaubriand in the castle. Accompanied visits, exterior a.m./p.m., interior p.m. only, April to October. Closed Tuesday.

Rennes and its Region

Rennes

Rennes is not an exciting town, and it is tempting to say that for tourists who have a limited holiday period at their disposal it is not worth the time devoted to a visit. However, it is the administrative capital of Brittany, and the *préfecture* of Ille et Vilaine. It has led the great commercial and industrial expansion of Brittany that has taken place since the Second World War, and in that time its population has doubled. It lies at the junction of the Ille and the Vilaine, both attractive rivers, but in Rennes they have been canalised and in places put underground. Its position, far from the centre of the province and almost on the border with Normandy, is due to its historic role in monitoring the schemes of the kings of France and defending the duchy against them.

In 1720 much of the town was burned down when a drunken carpenter knocked over an oil lamp and set fire to a pile of shavings. The narrow, medieval streets of largely wooden houses burned for six days. Rennes does not have a true old quarter but some of the streets north-east of the **Cathédrale St Pierre** survived the fire, and there are some old half-timbered and Renaissance houses here and there in these streets.

What to see
Palais de Justice

The finest building in the town is the early seventeenth-century Palais de Justice, originally the Parliament of Bretagne. The interior has a whole suite of beautifully decorated rooms, of which the most impressive is the magnificent Grande Chambre, the former parliamentary debating chamber. The walls are hung with ten Gobelin tapestries depicting the history of Brittany, which took twenty-four years to complete. Open for visits, but it still functions as the law courts, so the visit depends on the availability of the rooms.

Musées de Bretagne et des Beaux Arts

Both these museums are in the same building beside the canalised Vilaine, and one ticket gains admission to both. The Musée de Bretagne is worth a visit for anyone with the slightest interest in Brittany. It gives a complete history of the province from prehistoric times onwards, with documents and exhibits of all kinds interestingly arranged in a sequence of rooms. There are fine collections of Breton

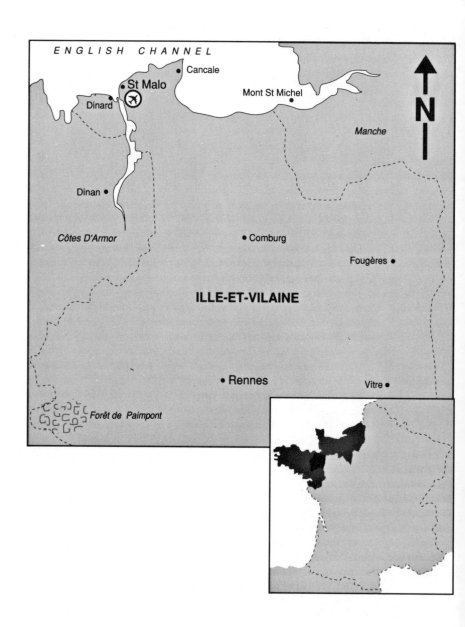

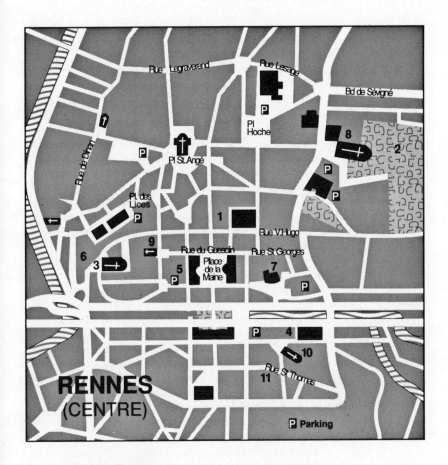

RENNES
(CENTRE)

P Parking

1 Law Courts
2 Thabor Gardens
3 St Peter Cathedral
4 Fine Arts Museum & Breton Museum
5 City Hall
6 Mordelaise Gate
7 St Germain's Church
8 Church of Our Lady (S .Melaine)
9 St Saviour's Church
10 All Saints Church
11 Cour des Carmes

furniture, porcelain and costumes, as well as sections on the fishing industry and musical instruments, and items from the Gallo-Roman and medieval periods.

The Musée des Beaux Arts has a representative collection of paintings from the fourteenth century to the twentieth, with some works by famous artists, including Georges de la Tour, Veronese, Jordaens, Chardin and Greuze, and two drawings by Leonardo da Vinci. More recent artists represented include Boudin, Gauguin, Sisley and Picasso. Open a.m./p.m. Closed Tuesday and public holidays.

Where to stay

Whatever else it may lack, Rennes has no shortage of good hotels and restaurants, though they rarely go together. As in several other of the larger towns in Brittany, hotels with restaurants are few and far between.

Hôtel Mercure-Altea, 1 Rue Capitaine Maignan, Parc du Colombier, 35000 Rennes, tel. 99 29 73 73. Large modern hotel (140 bedrooms) of good standard, not too far from the centre, south of the Vilaine. This one does have a restaurant and it is good. Prices for rooms and meals medium plus.

Garden Hotel, 3 Rue Duhamel, tel. 99 65 45 06. Close to the centre just south of the Vilaine, off the N157 (Quai Émile Zola), this hotel has twenty-four quiet, simple rooms at low/medium rates. No restaurant.

Hôtel Le Président, 27 Ave Jean Janvier, tel. 99 65 42 22. Straightforward but comfortable hotel (thirty-four bedrooms), in the road which leads from the Vilaine to the main railway station. No restaurant. Medium prices.

Hôtel Germinal, 9 Cours de la Vilaine, 35510 Cesson-Sévigné, tel. 99 83 11 01. Modern interior in a nineteenth-century mill on an island in the Vilaine, pleasant setting, nineteen pretty rooms, restaurant. Medium prices. Closed 1 to 21 August.

Where to eat

Rennes is distinguished by the quality and good value of its many restaurants. The following is a brief selection.

Le Galopin, 21 Ave Jean Janvier, 35000 Rennes, tel. 99 31 55 96. Next to the Hôtel Président. Brasserie style on three floors, offering traditional cuisine of a good standard. Medium prices. Open to midnight. Closed Sunday.

Ti-Koz, 3 Rue St Guillaume, behind the cathedral, tel. 99 79 33 89. Worth a visit as much for the wonderful old Breton setting in a half-timbered house – which may once have been an ancient chapel or, according to some, a family home of Tiphaine Raguenel, wife of Bertrand du Guesclin – as for the authentic Breton cuisine. Prices medium plus.

La Chope, 3 Rue La Chalotais, tel. 99 79 34 54. Lively brasserie on two floors, with cheap menus and à la carte dishes. Closed Sunday.

Le Piré, 18 Rue du Maréchal Joffre, tel. 99 79 31 41. Rather luxurious restaurant with dining room looking on to an interior garden courtyard. Cuisine of gourmet standards (Michelin star), though the cheapest menu is only medium price. Also has four vast, luxurious and expensive bedrooms.

Auberge de la Hublais, 28 Rue de Rennes, Cesson-Sévigné, tel. 99 83 11 06. Five km east of Rennes by the N157, this attractive rustic inn offers refined cooking from low prices upwards. Closed Sunday and Monday evening, and 17 to 30 August.

Fougères

History

Forty-seven km north-east of Rennes by the N12, throughout the Middle Ages Fougères was a frontier town with a formidable castle, one of the strongest in Europe, designed to protect Brittany from invaders. The town itself is on a hill and the castle is, unlike most, below its town and outside it, rather than in the centre and above it. This unusual position on a lower hill is due to the fact that in those days it was surrounded not only by a loop of the River Nançon, but by marshes which made it almost impregnable. Almost, but not quite: over the centuries it was fought over by English, French and Breton forces and was captured by, among others, Henry II of England and Du Guesclin.

After the Revolution, Fougères was a stronghold of the Chouans, the royalist counter-revolutionaries who tried to restore the monarchy. A force of several thousand guerrillas led by the seventeen-year-old Aimé Picquet du Boisguy succeeded in defying Republican armies for three years. When a truce was declared in 1796 he was interned, but escaped in 1799 and fought on until a final peace was arranged in 1800. The monarchy was restored in 1815 and du Boisguy died in 1839, loaded with honours by successive kings.

In the past Fougères was a textile town, making sheets from the thirteenth to the sixteenth centuries, and then sails for the French fleet. In the nineteenth century the town turned to making slippers and then shoes, and at the outbreak of the Second World War had 100 factories employing 10,000 people. This had fallen to 3,000 by 1975, and about a 1,000 today. The industry now specialises in top-quality shoes for women.

What to see
Château de Fougères

This great castle, covering more than two hectares, is an imposing example of medieval military architecture, with thirteen towers linked by battlemented curtain walls. It was built between the twelfth and the fifteenth centuries. The best of the castle can be seen from the exterior. Walk down from the old town, from the Place des Arbres, via the Rue des Vallées, the Rue des Tanneurs, the picturesque Place du Marchix, the Rue Nançon, left into the Rue Fos Keralix and left again into the Rue Bouteiller, and follow round the outside of the castle walls. In the interior of the castle there is a small shoe museum in the Tour Raoul, exhibiting shoes made in Fougères over the past 300 years.

St Sulpice Church

This is a rather elegant Flamboyant Gothic structure which took from the fifteenth to the eighteenth century to build. On the right of the south porch there is a sculpture of the fairy Melusine combing her hair, a reminder of the legendary links between the Lusignan family, lords of the town in the Middle Ages, and the enchantress (la Mère Lusigne).

Forêt de Fougères

Three km north-east of the town by the D177, the road to Flers, this is an unusually attractive and interesting forest, mostly of beech – more than 1,700 hectares of them. The forest is fairly open, dappled with sunlight in summer, and has small lakes, stretches of heath and several megalithic monuments, including two dolmens, and an alignment of boulders called the **Cordon of the Druids**. A good place for walks and picnics.

Where to stay

Hôtel des Voyageurs, 10 Place Gambetta, 35300 Fougères. Long-established hotel in an old building with completely modernised interior, and air-conditioned bedrooms with bath etc. Low to medium prices.

Hôtel Campanile, Route d'Emée, Fougères, tel. 99 94 54 00. Fifty modern bedrooms at medium rates. Sound restaurant.

Where to eat

Le Haute-Seve, 37 Blvd Jean Jaures, tel. 99 94 23 39. First-class cuisine in a comfortable restaurant, from medium prices upwards. Closed Sunday evening and Monday.

La Petite Auberge, La Templerie, 10 km east of Fougères by the N12, tel. 99 95 27 03. A country restaurant well worth a pause for lunch or dinner. Excellent cooking at prices well within reach, from medium upwards.

Vitre

Twenty-eight km east of Rennes by the N157, Chateaubourg and the D857, and set on a promontory dominating the valley of the Vilaine, Vitre is another frontier town whose job was the defence of Brittany against attacks from the east. It rivals Dinan as the Breton town which has best conserved its medieval aspect: it has whole streets of medieval houses, and its splendid fortress is far more impressive than Dinan's castle. The old town still has its ramparts to the north and east, those to the south and west having been lost or incorporated into buildings. The best views of Vitre are from the Fougères road as you come down towards the town, and from the road from Rennes.

History

The town grew up around the thirteenth-century castle, and prospered from the fifteenth to the eighteenth century on the manufacture of coarse cloth and other products from hemp. The Guild of Overseas

Merchants in the town exported their produce to England, Germany, Spain, Portugal and even America.

In the sixteenth century the castle became the property of the Rieux and then the Coligny families, both strongly Protestant, who played a leading part in the Religious Wars. The Duc de Mercoeur, leader of the Catholic League, besieged the city for five months in 1589, but was unable to take it. When Henri IV visited Vitre shortly afterwards, he said, 'If I were not king of France, I would be happy to be a merchant of Vitre.' But when the religious troubles broke out again after the revocation of the Edict of Nantes, there was an exodus of the hardworking Protestants, and the town's economy went into a long decline.

In the past twenty years Vitre has played a leading part in the astonishing revival of the Breton economy; it now has diversified industry including important shoe factories, and is a leading centre for the manufacture of dairy products.

What to see
The château

Originally eleventh century, the château, which occupies a triangular site, was completely rebuilt between the thirteenth and fifteenth centuries, and is a classic example of feudal military architecture. It has a great tower at each corner of the triangle, with smaller towers in between, and is entered across a drawbridge and between two battlemented towers. The town hall is within the walls, established in the former residential quarters. The largest of the towers, the Tour St Laurent, which was the castle keep, now contains a **Museum of Art and Archaeology**, the Tour de l'Argenterie has a **Museum of Natural History**, and the Tour de l'Oratoire has a chapel which contains a superb sixteenth-century triptych with thirty-two panels in Limoges enamel, depicting scenes from the Old Testament.

The old town

The picturesque streets of the old quarter are immediately opposite the entrance to the château. A simple tour follows the Rue Baudrairie, then to the right into the Rue d'Embas, then to the left along the Promenade St Yves (Tourist Office), then left and right into the Rue Poterie, and then by the Promenade du Val around the outside of the ramparts.

Château des Rochers-Sévigné

Six km south-east of Vitre by the D88, it was from this chateau that Madame de Sévigné wrote most of the letters which made her one of the great figures of French literature. She had married the Marquis de Sévigné who, after running through her fortune and deceiving her with countless other women, got himself killed in a duel over a courtesan. Left a widow at twenty-five with two young children, Madame de Sévigné was philosophical about it. She had loved her husband, she told a friend, but had never been able to respect him. As a widow she continued to live mostly at the château for reasons of economy. She had chances, but chose never to marry again. To one friend who wished to marry her and console her for her husband's behaviour, she said, 'I am less put out than you might suppose'. But she ensured that her daughter, Françoise, married well, to the Count of Grignan who was Lieutenant General of Provence for forty years. It was to Françoise, at her château of Grignan in Provence, that Madame de Sévigné wrote her letters, still in print today after 300 years.

The fifteenth-century château was renovated in the seventeenth. It is in private hands today, but the chapel built by Madame de Sévigné for her uncle, the Abbé Coulanges, in 1671 and her room in the north tower are open to the public. The room contains Madame de Sévigné's furniture and other souvenirs, including family portraits. Open a.m./p.m. from mid-February to mid-November for accompanied visits.

Where to stay **Hôtel Le Petit Billot**, 5 Place du Général Leclerc, 35500 Vitre, tel. 99 75 02 10. Typical small-town provincial hotel. Twenty-two bedrooms at low/medium rates. Good-value restaurant (separate management), prices medium. Closed Sunday out of season.

Hôtel Le Chêne Vert, Place Général de Gaulle, tel. 99 75 00 58. Simple hotel with a popular restaurant which offers varied and interesting cuisine. Both rooms and meals at low rates. Closed Saturday, Friday evening out of season, and last week of September to end October.

Hôtel Ar Milin, 30 Rue de Paris, 35220 Châteaubourg, tel. 99 00 30 91. At Châteaubourg, half-way between Rennes and Vitre, this is a country hotel in a converted mill in its own park. Peaceful and comfortable rooms, some with balconies overlooking the river; tennis, fishing, sauna, jacuzzi. Restaurant overlooking the park, beams and granite fireplace, reliable cuisine. Rooms at medium rates upwards; menus from medium to well above. Closed Saturday evening and Sunday November to February (restaurant), and 19 December to 7 January (hotel).

Where to eat **Le Pichet**, 17 Blvd de Laval, 35500 Vitre, tel. 99 75 24 09. Attractive little restaurant opening on to a pleasant garden. Good traditional cuisine with menus from medium price upwards. Closed Sunday evening and Monday.

La Taverne de l'Ecu, 12 Rue Baudrairie, tel. 99 75 11 09. Near the château, in the old town in a seventeenth-century house. Splendid old dining room with monumental fireplaces, one used for grills. Good-value menus at low to medium prices. Closed Sunday evening and Monday.

Paimpont – Forest of Legends

In the past inland Brittany was called Argoat, the country of the woods, to distinguish it from the coastal strip called Armor, the country of the sea. Little remains of the huge forest of Argoat and it is now broken up into smaller forests, mostly in the department of Ille-et-Vilaine. The largest of them is the Forêt de Paimpont, also called Brocéliande.

The Arthurian legend

The ancient myth-makers told stories of King Arthur and the Knights of the Round Table, and they set them both in Britain (Grande Bretagne) and in Brittany (Petit Bretagne). In Brittany this forest of Brocéliande was the centre of Arthurian legend. Arthur and his knights were said to have visited it in their quest for the Holy Grail, the chalice used by Christ at the Last Supper and in which his blood was collected at the Crucifixion, and which tradition said was brought to Brittany by Joseph of Arimathea.

The chief characters in the legends are Merlin, the magician, who was said to be the son of the Devil; a nun, who used his diabolical powers for good and was adviser to Uther Pendragon, Arthur's father, and afterwards to Arthur; the enchantress Morgan la Faye, who was Arthur's half-sister; and the fairy Viviane. Tradition has it that Viviane was born in the Château of Comper, which still stands, but that she later lived in a castle beneath the waters of a lake and was known as the Lady of the Lake.

One day Merlin met Viviane at the **Fountain of Barenton** in the forest and fell in love with her. Though he could read the future and knew what would happen to him, he taught her his magic spells, including how to keep someone in an invisible prison for eternity. Viviane is said to have lured him into a hollow tree and closed it round him, or alternatively to have put him inside a large stone beside the fountain.

Morgan-la-Faye's domain was the Val Sans Retour, in another part of the forest. In this 'Valley of No Return' Morgan trapped all those knights who had been unfaithful to their ladies. The knights imagined themselves surrounded by walls of fire through which they could not pass. There they stayed until Lancelot, who was pure in heart – because although he was having an affair with Guinevere, Arthur's queen, he was faithful to her – broke Morgan's spell and set them free. Irreverently, it can all be seen as an early medieval soap opera.

In the hot, dry summer of 1990, Morgan's Val Sans Retour really did go up in flames, together with 800 hectares of the rest of the forest. Since it includes heathland and fourteen lakes as well as woods, an important part of the woodland was destroyed. No trees were left around the Val Sans Retour, but the setting of the Fountain of Barenton, high in the forest, was left intact. Pure water comes from a spring walled in stone at the base of a great tree. Whether the tree or the stone slab encloses Merlin or not, no one knows, but the stone does have the reputation of working magic. For hundreds of years it was the custom to sprinkle water on the stone after drinking, and this was said to bring on a violent rainstorm. It is recorded that the parish priest of Concoret successfully ended a drought in this manner in 1833, and Baring Gould writing at the turn of this century says the practice still continued then. One authority claims that it was done as recently as 1925. What is undoubtedly true is that in parts of rural France certain parish priests have been credited with the power of rainmaking through prayer, usually in association with a local saint, never the Virgin.

Anyone interested in the Arthurian aspects of the forest could do worse than to call for a drink or a meal at the Auberge de la Table Ronde at Neant-sur-Yvel, where the patron, M Morice, is an expert on this subject. At least he will be able to indicate the way to the Fountain of Barenton, not that easy to find, and if you understand French, he can tell you a great deal more.

What to see
Paimpont

A large and pleasant village in the middle of the forest beside a small lake. It has a thirteenth-century abbey church, altered and renovated in the seventeenth. The interior contains fifteenth- and sixteenth-century statues of saints, some fine seventeenth-century woodcarving, and an ivory Christ made in the eighteenth century.

Where to stay

Auberge de la Table Ronde (LdF), Neant-sur-Yvel, 66430 Mauron, tel. 97 93 03 96. A country inn with ten bedrooms, all with bath etc. M Morice, the patron , is not only knowledgeable about the forest, but is a good host who supplies his restaurant from his own butcher's shop. Rooms and meals at low rates. Closed Sunday evening and Monday, except July/August.

Relais de Brocéliande, Paimpont 35380, tel. 99 07 81 07. Straightforward village hotel with rooms and meals at low/medium prices.

Manoir du Tertre, Le Tertre, Paimpont-Beignon, 35380 Plélan-le-Grand, tel. 99 07 81 02. Four km south from Paimpont towards Beignon by the D71. Well-furnished sixteenth-century manor set in its own grounds. Room rates medium plus, menu prices medium. Closed Tuesday. Hotel closed 23 January to 27 February and 1 to 7 October.

Where to eat

Any of the above or **Restaurant des Forges**, Les Forges de Paimpont, 35380 Plélan-le-Grand, tel. 99 06 81 07. Three km south of Paimpon through the forest by the D773. Pleasant, welcoming country restaurant with good food at low prices. Good house wine and cider.

St Brieuc and North to the Pink Granite Coast

St Brieuc and surrounds

St Brieuc itself would be best avoided by tourists, but there is no solution to the problem of how to do it. It is an important industrial town for northern Brittany and holiday visitors do not come high on its list of priorities, but those wishing to go north along the west coast of the Bay of St Brieuc or to the resorts of the Pink Granite Coast are obliged to cross St Brieuc, and the best way to do it is to keep to the N12 right through the town and to carry on until you can turn right on to the D786, which leads to several coastal resorts and to Paimpol.

Almost every turning to the right off this road leads to a village by the sea, most of them too small to be considered resorts, though they all have a beach or a sandy cove, and some a port.

Binic

Once a base for boats that went cod-fishing off Newfoundland, Binic still has the air of a fishing port. It is most attractively sited in a fold between lush woods and hills, and has views across the Bay of St Brieuc to Le Val André. Its harbour does not dry out, but the tide recedes so far from the beach that bathing is only practical at high tide.

Excursion
Zoo Moulin de Richard

The zoo is at Trégomeur and reached from Binic by the D4 towards Lantic, but turn left after 3 km on to the D47 to Trégomeur. The game park covers twelve hectares and has a good range of animals including lions and zebras, as well as smaller species and birds. A small train runs round the park.

St Quay-Portrieux

This once rather humdrum fishing port has become more of a resort, and has moved a little upmarket since its amenities were improved by the construction of a large marina. It now has quite a lot of character. Like Binic, it was once a winter base for boats of the Newfoundland cod-fishing fleet, and it still has a coastal fleet operating in the Bay of St Brieuc catching mackerel, sea bass, Coquilles St Jacques and other shellfish. It also has four sandy beaches, with beach clubs for children and sporting amenities, including tennis, table

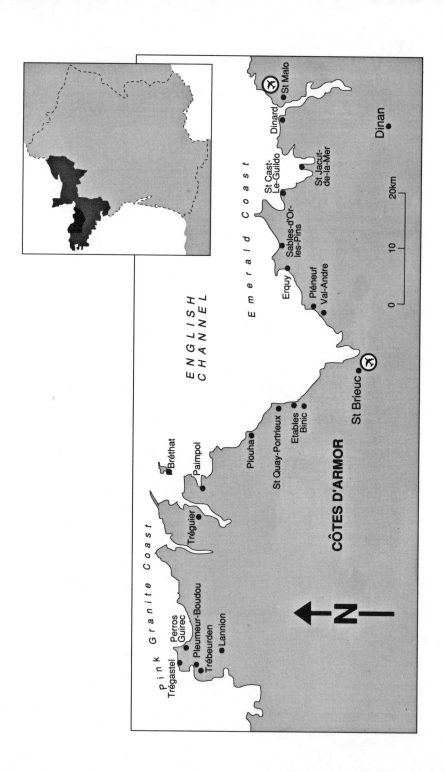

tennis, boules, etc. There are two more lovely beaches at **Étables-sur-Mer**, virtually part of the same resort although the centre of Étables is about a mile from the beach.

Walking
Walkers may like to know that the GR34 follows the coastline from Binic all round the Pink Granite Coast to Perros Guirec and beyond, and can be picked up in or near any of the coastal places mentioned in this section.

Plouha
The inland town of Plouha is interesting in that, coming west from St Malo, it is the first truly Breton town, where Breton rather than French is the language of the local people. During the war British agents and pilots shot down over France were taken by the Resistance to a safe house not far from Plouha, and from there to the beach now called Plage Bonaparte, where a fishing boat would take them out to a waiting ship of the Royal Navy. In this way, 135 of them were returned to London under the noses of German sentries.

The nicest of the the several beaches within easy motoring distance of Plouha is **Bréhec-en-Plouha**, a lovely little place, a cove of fine, soft sand with safe bathing, shielded by rocks and facing south, and a harbour for small craft and a few fishing boats. There is not a lot in the way of accommodation: some cottages to let, and a few cafés and *crêperies*.

What to see
La Chapelle de Kermaria-an-Isquit is 3.5 km north-west of Plouha by the D21, or 5 km south east of Bréhec-en-Plouha by the D54, at Kermaria. The church, originally built in thanks by a knight returning from a thirteenth-century crusade, was enlarged in the fifteenth and eighteenth centuries. It has been well restored. In the porch there are painted wooden statues of the Apostles, except for St Luke, which was stolen. The chief interest of the church is the painting of the Danse Macabre in the nave. This theme, in which skeletons alternate with the living whom they lead in a sinister dance of death, was popular in the fifteenth century. There is another famous example in the church of St Robert at La Chaise Dieu in Auvergne. In this Breton church, *l'Ankou*, Death, leads the pope, cardinals, kings, archbishops, farmers, peasants, tradesmen – people of all kinds – in this dance of death. Altogether there are forty-seven figures, each led by a skeleton, and this theme illustrating the impartiality of Death was often used by the Church to remind the faithful of their Christian duty, and that all, rich and poor, great and small, should be prepared always to appear before God.

Where to stay
Hôtel Gerbot d'Avoine (LdF), 2 Blvd du Littoral, St Quay-Portrieux, tel. 96 70 40 09. Twenty-six bedrooms, half of them with bath etc., low/medium rates. Regional menus at low/medium prices. Restaurant closed Sunday evening and Monday out of season.

Hôtel Ker Moor, 13 Rue Président Le Senecal, 22410 St Quay-Portrieux, tel. 96 70 52 22. In Breton, Ker Moor means 'the house by the sea', and the hotel is on the cliff above the beach (direct access).

213

Sound restaurant, half-board obligatory in season. Rooms and meals medium plus.

Château de Coatguelen, Pléhédel, 22290 Lanvollon, tel. 96 55 33 40. Just off the D7 about 8 km from Bréhec-en-Plouha. A Relais et Châteaux hotel in its own 100-hectare park, with sixteen beautiful rooms and a gourmet restaurant, 18-hole golf course, small fishing lake, tennis, swimming pool, and riding centre. Expensive.

Where to eat   Apart from those in hotels, good restaurants are rather scarce on this coast, but all the small resorts have their summer cafés and *crêperies*.

Mouton Blanc, 52 Quai République, St Quay-Portrieux. Simple restaurant. Regional food at medium prices.

Paimpol

This little town occupies a special place in the Breton mind. It is and has been for centuries a fishing port. Even in the seventeenth century its ships went every year to Newfoundland; from 1852 it also sent a fleet to fish in Icelandic waters, and continued to do so for eighty-three years. Each year they stayed away for six months, the whole of spring and summer, and not all the men who sailed came back. During the time that Paimpol sent a fleet to Icelandic waters, 100 ships and more than 2,000 fishermen were lost. This saga of the seas was told by the famous French author, Pierre Loti, in his book *Iceland Fisherman*, and he lived in Paimpol while he wrote it. The most famous Breton song, 'La Pampolaise', known as the 'Marseillaise' of Breton fishermen, refers to a fisherman's wife awaiting his return from Iceland.

But the industry which inspired Loti's book and 'La Pampolaise' is dead – the last two Iceland schooners sailed from Paimpol in 1935. But there is still a coastal fishing fleet, and a commercial port which has a small trade in sand and Scandinavian timber, and though it is not a resort and has no beach of its own, it is visited in summer by tourists.

Where to stay   **Hôtel de la Marne** (LdF), 30 Rue de la Marne, 22500 Paimpol, tel. 96 20 82 16. Twelve bedrooms at medium rates, and good regional cuisine with seafood specialities at medium prices upwards. Half-board obligatory in season. Closed Sunday evening and Monday.

Hôtel Repaire de Kerroch, 29 Quai Morand, tel. 96 20 50 13. Small hotel in an eighteenth-century mansion overlooking the yacht basin. Eleven pretty bedrooms, medium rates. Good cuisine with menus a little above medium prices. Closed Wednesday lunch.

Hôtel Le Barbu (LdF), Pointe de l'Arcouest, 22620 Ploubazlanec, tel. 96 55 86 98. Situated at sea's edge 6 km from Paimpol. Twenty bedrooms all with sea view, and garden with swimming pool. Rooms and meals at medium plus prices.

Relais Brenner, near Pont de Lézardrieux, 22500 Paimpol, tel. 96

20 11 05. Four km west of Paimpol by the D786, this attractive Relais et Châteaux hotel is set in lovely gardens above the banks of the Trieux river. Splendid views and sunsets. First-class cuisine; spacious, comfortable, well-furnished rooms with views of the park and the river. All a bit special but prices not exorbitant, from medium plus upwards. Closed mid-November to February.

Where to eat

La Vieille Tour, 13 Rue de l'Église, 22500 Paimpol, tel. 96 20 83 18. Very good cooking, generous helpings, charming surroundings, pleasant welcome. Medium plus. Closed Sunday evening and Wednesday.

Excursion from Paimpol

Pointe de l'Arcouest and the Île de Bréhat

Boats for the Île de Bréhat leave from the jetty at Pointe de l'Arcouest 6 km north of Paimpol. The road down to the jetty offers lovely views over the bay and the island. Bréhat, which is really two islands joined by a bridge built in the eighteenth century by Vauban, the military architect, enjoys a very mild climate, surrounded by sea warmed by the Gulf Stream. Cliffs and high land in the more savage northern island protect the sunny southern slopes. Mimosa, figs, oleander, palms and eucalyptus thrive there, and its country lanes are often bordered by honeysuckle. Bréhat is part of an archipelago, with something like a hundred smaller islands scattered in the sea around it, about a dozen of which have one or two houses occupied only in summer, mostly by rich Parisians.

Bréhat is more itself outside the high season. Only 1.5 km or so wide and 4 km long, it can be too crowded in summer, despite the fact that no cars are allowed on the island. At the height of the season there can be as many as 3,000 visitors on the island, ten times the normal population, and its beauty is rather swamped. But it *is* a beautiful place, with its flowers and grassy slopes, its pine trees and palms, the tiny coves of its ragged and indented coastline, and its family of rose and orange granite islands in a sea that varies from indigo to emerald.

Bréhat is at its best in June and September, when it is possible to explore on foot and find your own small beach or bathing place. Bicycles can be hired from Madame Dalibot in Port Clos, near where the boats arrive, from April to September, but the island is so small that most people will find walking no bother.

Where to stay

NB The two small hotels on Bréhat are normally fully booked in July and August, and it is advisable to book well ahead at any time in summer.

Hôtel Le Bellevue, Le Port-Clos, 22870 Île de Bréhat, tel. 96 20 00 05. Well modernised small hotel overlooking the port and the beach. Seventeen bedrooms, all with bath etc, at medium rates. Large restaurant caters for day visitors as well as hotel residents. Delicious fresh seafood, simply prepared. Medium plus prices.

Where to eat

Le Chardon Bleu, Le Bourg, tel. 96 20 00 08. Roomy restaurant in the village. Open all year.

Ti Jeannette, Route du Bourg, tel. 96 20 00 53. A *crêperie* with a terrace on the garden. Open April to October and on winter weekends. Picnic snacks can be bought all year round.

Tréguier

From Paimpol the D786 leads west across the River Trieux to one of Brittany's most interesting and attractive old towns, Tréguier, at the confluence of the Guindy and Jaudy rivers. Unlike most Breton towns, Tréguier is situated on a hill and down the slope to the port quarter beside the huge estuary of the rivers. Although it is some 15 km from the open sea, quite large coasters can use the port, and it is crowded with yachts and leisure craft of all shapes and sizes.

Tréguier was the home town of St Yves, the most popular of all Breton saints, who was born here in 1253. After studying law in Paris, he returned to Tréguier and became a priest, but also practised law. He was famous for his clarity and conciseness and because he took the cases of the poor, both to help them and to avoid taking rich business from his brother advocates. He became known as 'the poor man's lawyer', and was the precursor of 'legal aid'. He died in 1303 and was canonised in 1347, the only lawyer and the only Breton saint to achieve that eminence. Every year, on the third Sunday in May, there is a *pardon des pauvres*, when a procession of hundreds of pilgrims makes its way from the cathedral to the church at Minihy-Tréguier, where St Yves was born.

What to see
St Tudwal's Church

Tréguier was founded in the sixth century by St Tudwal, the son of a Welsh prince, who founded a monastery. In 855, the Breton king, Nominoë, created a bishopric, and Tréguier remained a cathedral city until the Revolution. The present church, the former cathedral, was started in 1339 and took 150 years to complete. It was built on the site of an earlier twelfth-century building, of which all that remains is the Hastings tower. The spire, 63 m tall, was added in the eighth century.

In the interior each pair of pillars in the nave is different, the aisles are flanked by richly decorated chapels, and there are fine rose windows in the chapels of the deambulatory. The forty-six choir stalls date from 1509 and were carved with remarkable realism by two local craftsmen. The tomb of St Yves is a late nineteenth-century copy of the monument originally provided by Duc Jean V of Brittany in the fifteenth century.

The cloister, built in 1450, with its courtyard full of hydrangeas and flanked on three sides by galleries with graceful Flamboyant Gothic arches, is most attractive.

Place du Martray

In the centre of the town, this old square has a number of half-timbered houses. The statue in the square is of Ernest Rénan, a distinguished writer and philosopher born in Tréguier who became a member of the French Academy, and whose *Life of Jesus* so outraged local Catholics that they demonstrated at the unveiling of the statue in 1903, and had to be kept in check by the army. There are more old houses in the streets north and south of the cathedral, Rue Colvestre, Rue Rénan, and in the Place Notre Dame de Colvezou.

Where to stay

Hôtel Kastell Dinec'h (LdF), Rte de Lannion, Tréguier 22220, tel. 96 92 49 39. About 2 km west of Tréguier via the D786, this is a small manor house with its own gardens and swimming pool. Fifteen charming bedrooms at medium plus rates. Closed January to 15 March.

Hôtel des Isles (LdF), Blvd de la Mer, Port Blanc, 22710 Penvenan, tel. 96 92 66 49. Port Blanc is about 12 km from Tréguier and has no beach, so hardly a resort but it is a tranquil and beautiful spot with great coastal scenery. Twenty-five bedrooms at low medium rates, and the restaurant is cheap but sound. Closed January to 25 February and 5 October to end December, except weekends.

Perros Guirec and Along the Coast

Perros Guirec

Like Dinard, which it equals in hotels and holiday accommodation, Perros Guirec is an old-established seaside resort, more international than Breton in flavour. In summer its population increases from 7,000 to more than 30,000, but the visitors do not destroy its rather sedate and respectable atmosphere. Those who know English West-Country resorts will find that it has much in common with places like St Ives or Ilfracombe, though it is rather more upmarket.

The town occupies a low, wooded promontory with a small port and yacht basin on the southern shore and two fine beaches on the northern coast. Both the beaches have good sands and safe bathing, and face an emerald sea studded with rocks and islands. Trestraou is the larger beach and is backed by cafés, restaurants, casino, swimming pool, and a Palais de Congrès. A cliff path, part of the GR34, links the two beaches and follows the coast to Ploumanach and beyond.

What to see

Not a lot in the sighseeing sense. The village church, **St Jacques**, is unusual in that it has two naves; the one on the west is Romanesque (twelfth century) with massive cylindrical pillars, and the one on the east is fourteenth-century Gothic. The southern porch is a good example of the Romanesque style. In the interior there is a twelfth-century font in granite.

A path leads from the Trestaou beach to a viewpoint with orientation table, just before you reach the Trestrignel beach. From the other end of the Trestaou beach, a footpath, here called the Sentier des Douaniers, follows the coast for 6 km with panoramic views to Ploumanach. About half-way is the small chapel of **Notre Dame de Clarté**, which is the object of an important *pardon* on 15 August.

A **Festival of Classical Music** is held in the Palais de Congrès in July and August.

Excursion from Perros Guirec
Les Sept Îles

The Seven Islands lie a few km off the Pink Granite Coast, and launches leave from Trestraou beach to make round trips of this archipelago which has been a bird sanctuary since 1912. The trip includes landing on the Île aux Moines, on which there was once a monastery, and a visit to its lighthouse. Landing is not permitted on any other of the islands, which have colonies of guillemots, Torda penguins, several kinds of seagull, kittiwakes, fulmars, cormorants and puffins. Baby puffins were introduced from the Faroe Islands in recent years to make up for numbers lost as a result of oil slicks. The island of Rouzic has a summer population of 6,000 pairs of gannets.

Ploumanach

It is worth walking at least some of the way to Ploumanach along the cliff path to see the Pink Granite Coast at first hand. The huge pink granite boulders, some as big as haystacks, eroded into all kinds of weird shapes by thousands of years of wind and weather, crop up everywhere, beside the path, behind the beaches, in the middle of fields or camp sites.

Ploumanach itself, about 5 km walk by the path or a short drive, is an enchanting place. A small, sandy bay liberally sprinkled with 'stage' rocks that break the beach up into warm, calm lagoons, it is a wonderful place for children, who can find their own rock and set up a pirate's camp or a headquarters for whoever is the latest strip-cartoon hero. A good part of Ploumanach's charm is its chaotic nature, which makes it a good deal less sedate than Perros Guirec. In the high season it suffers from its own popularity, becoming rather overcrowded and littered, but essentially it is a fascinating place.

Where to stay

Hôtel le Sphinx, 67 Chemin de la Messe, 22700 Perros Guirec, tel. 96 23 25 42. Old-fashioned villa hotel overlooking Trestrignel beach, with a garden sloping down towards it and a path to it through the rocks. Modernised interior with twenty spacious bedrooms. Good restaurant but half-board only. Prices medium plus. Closed 5 January to 15 February.

Hôtel le Trestraou, Blvd Joseph Le Bihan, tel. 96 23 24 05. Large old hotel nicely sited immediately behind the Trestraou beach. Fifty-seven rooms at medium rates. Restaurant for residents, half-board.

Hôtel Feux des Îles (LdF), 53 Blvd Clemenceau, tel. 96 23 22 94. Eighteen comfortable bedrooms at medium rates, and a good value restaurant, specialising in seafood, at medium prices upwards. Open every day in season.

Hôtel Les Rochers, Chemin de la Pointe, Ploumanach, 22700 Perros Guirec, tel. 96 91 44 49. Attractive small hotel facing a picturesque little port. Fifteen bedrooms at medium rates. Good restaurant, half-board obligatory in season. Closed October to March.

Camp Site Between Perros-Guirec and Ploumanach there is a very large and well-equipped camp site, **Le Ranolien**. In July and August, despite its size it is very crowded, and gets a bit tatty round the edges due to over-use.

Where to eat   **Le Parc**, Ploumanach, tel. 96 91 40 80. A small *Logis de France* hotel, well known for its good regional restaurant which offers a choice of menus at low/medium prices. Ten bedrooms with bath etc, at medium rates. Closed 25 September to 25 March.

Trégastel Plage   Although it is only about 5 km further and has all the same advantages – gigantic rose-coloured rocks in and around sandy coves and warm lagoons, and superb coastal scenery – Trégastel gets less overrun in summer. It is a good place for a holiday with smallish children. The harbour itself dries out at low tide, but there is a choice of beaches and lagoons within easy reach with plenty of safe exploring to do, particularly if you have a canoe or a rubber dinghy.

The road from Perros Guirec, the D788 via Ploumanach and Trégastel to Trébeurden, is known as the Corniche Bretonne. In addition to the resorts, it passes a number of large, undeveloped beaches which, though rarely deserted in summer, are less crowded.

What to see   The road also passes the **Telecommunications Centre of Pleumeur-Boudou**, unmistakable with its great white 'balloon', called the Radome. It is a balloon in fact as well as appearance, as its shape is maintained by slight air pressure. It was here that the first communications by satellite (Telstar) were made in 1962. The centre is open to the public, including children, for guided visits (one hour) which include film, demonstration of models, technical explanations, and a visit inside the Radome. Makes a change from castles and churches. Open the end of April to September, mornings until 11 a.m., and afternoons 2 p.m. to 4.45 p.m., every day except Saturday.

Trébeurden   This is a lively and sophisticated resort, popular with yachtsmen and amateur tunny fishermen as well as families. It is delightfully set among pines, with half-a-dozen beaches of fine yellow sand, a little port, and a scattering of offshore islands, at least one of which can be reached on foot at low tide. The largest beach, **Tresmeur**, is 1 km long.

Where to stay   **Hôtel Bellevue** (LdF), 20 Rue des Calculots, 22730 Trégastel Plage, tel. 96 23 88 18. Well-run hotel in a peaceful situation with garden (200 m from beach). Thirty rooms with bath etc, at medium rates. Good restaurant (closed Monday lunch), medium prices. Closed from 25 September to Easter.

Hôtel Mer et Plage, Plage de Coz-Pors, Trégastel, tel. 96 23 88 03. Beach hotel with twenty rooms at low to medium rates. Restaurant at medium prices. Closed November to February.

Hôtel Ti-Al-Lannec (LdF), Allée de Mezo Guen, 22560 Trébeurden, tel. 96 23 57 26. In a wooded setting on a cliff. Thirty spacious, comfortable rooms all with bath etc, and some have coastal views. Medium plus rates. Attractive dining room. Good cuisine and wine list, at prices from slightly above medium. Closed mid-November to mid-March.

Manoir de Lan Kerellec, Pointe de Kerellec, 22560 Trébeurden, tel. 96 23 50 09. A Relais et Châteaux hotel. Luxurious old manor with sixteen spacious rooms all with bath and sea views. Superb dining room built in the form of the hull of an upturned boat. First-class cuisine. All rather splendid, and justifiably expensive. Closed November to mid-March.

Golf Hôtel de St Samson, Ave de Jacques Ferronière, Pleumeur-Boudou, 22560 Trébeurden, tel. 96 23 87 34. Nice modern hotel beside a good 18-hole golf course only 4 km from the beaches. Driving range, putting green, tennis courts, swimming pool. Fifty-four rooms (all with bath) at medium rates upwards. Sound restaurant with menus at medium prices.

Where to eat **Le Beau Séjour**, Plage du Coz-Pors, Trégastel, tel. 96 23 88 02. Restaurant and terrace facing the sea. Good choice of menus at medium prices. Also a well-run hotel with fourteen rooms with bath etc. Medium rates. Closed 3 October to 18 March.

Glann Ar Mor, 12 Rue de Kerariou, Trébeurden, tel. 96 23 50 81. Modest in size and setting, but the cooking is talented and based on all the best local products, not exclusively fish. Medium prices. There are also eight cheap and simple bedrooms. Closed Wednesday outside high season.

Auberge La Vieille Église, Trégastel Bourg, tel. 96 23 88 31. A very good-value little restaurant specialising in local seafood. Prices low/medium. Advisable to book. Closed February and Sunday evening, and Monday out of season.

Lannion This old Breton town has become, like so many others, rather modern round the edges as a result of the increased prosperity of Brittany in the past decade or so. Though it is several km inland on the River Léguer, and cannot really be called a resort, it merits a mention for several reasons. It is not only within easy reach of all the beaches mentioned above from Perros Guirec on, it is also close to several other big beaches. Lannion is also an attractively sited town and has a number of hotels. In the high season when the resort hotels are packed, anyone touring the region may well find a room in Lannion, especially if you book a day ahead.

What to see Apart from its medieval houses, Lannion has the interesting **Brelevenez Church**, originally built by the Templars in the twelfth century, rebuilt in the fourteenth, and with a spire added in the fifteenth. The church can be reached by car, or on foot up a flight of 142 steps. There are good views over the town and the valley of the Léguer from beside the church.

Where to stay **Hôtel de Bretagne** (LdF), 32 Ave Général de Gaulle, 22300

Lannion, tel. 96 37 00 33. Simple hotel with twenty-eight rooms at low/ medium rates. Local cuisine with menus at less than usual prices. Restaurant closed Saturday, and Sunday evening.

Hôtel Climat de France, Rte de Perros Guirec (D788), tel. 96 40 70 18. Well-equipped modern chain hotel on the edge of town behind the Rallye hypermarket, but in a quiet situation and with some sporting amenities. Forty-seven comfortable rooms (with bath etc) at low/ medium rates. Good restaurant, medium prices.

Where to eat

Restaurant Ar Vro, Plouec'h, 5 km south-west by the D786, tel. 96 35 24 21. Nice setting with terrace facing the beach. Very good cuisine at medium prices upwards. Closed Sunday evening and Monday.

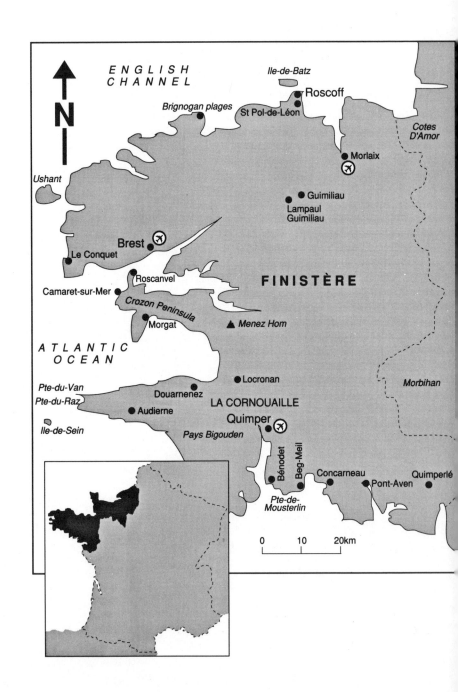

Northern Finistère

Finistère (the 'End of the Earth') is the remotest part of Brittany, and so the furthest from French influence. It has retained its customs, its attitudes, and the use of the Breton language more stubbornly than any other part of the province. Even within Finistère, different areas have traditionally been shut in on themselves, their people endogamous – that is, they marry within the tribe, so that in some small towns one person in every four or five will have the same surname. Another consequence is that, until very recently, the local dialects were so strong that people from different regions understood each other only with difficulty. While parts of Finistère are strongly religious in their own fashion, some sociological writers have referred to a 'pagan' population along parts of the northern coast – a rough, brutish people, wreckers and robbers of ships, ready with violence against the customs officers. There are still villages on the north coast in the Guisseny region proud of this old reputation.

The extreme west coast northwards from the Pointe de St Mathieu, with its 30 m granite cliffs, has been described as 'a coast of iron' and 'sinister and formidable', and so it can seem at times of equinoctial gales and winter storms. But it is also warmed by the Gulf Stream and has several wide, calm estuaries and fjords, called *abers* (as in Wales), that penetrate 6–7 km inland.

Morlaix

This is a town which is not only picturesque and interesting in itself, but also a good base for touring this northern part of Finistère, including the 'parish enclosures'. It is built at the junction of two rivers, the Keffleut and the Jarlot, and at the head of an estuary which opens out into the huge Bay of Morlaix. The rivers form a valley so deep that when the railway came to this part of Brittany in 1863 the only answer was to take it across the valley on a huge viaduct. This impressive piece of nineteenth-century engineering, nearly 60 m high and 300 m long, dominates and unites the town and makes it unforgettable without in any way spoiling it.

Morlaix was an important port in the past, and still has some limited commercial activity, but its quays are mostly lined with scores of private yachts. Most of the things worth seeing in Morlaix are near the centre, and although it is an uphill and downhill town it is worth a leisurely exploration on foot.

What to see
The Viaduct

The spectacular viaduct is built on two levels, the lower one of which is open to visitors on most days. Like most of Brittany, Morlaix has become more active in recent years, but there was a period earlier this century when it went into a decline and became a sleepy provincial town. One writer likened the trains crossing the viaduct to 'ships sailing over a drowned and silent city'.

The old town

From the back of the church descend the Rue Ange-de-Guernisac which is lined with old houses, some half-timbered, some slate-hung, with craftsmen's workshops at ground-floor level. At the Place des Viarmes turn right into the Rue Carnot and left into the Grande Rue. Most of the houses in this pedestrianised street date from the sixteenth and seventeenth centuries, and some have very fine façades decorated with statues. At Number 32 there are statues of St John the Baptist and St Philippe, and at second-floor level a very unusual statue of the birth of the Virgin Mary.

Maison de la Reine Anne

Brittany's famous Duchesse Anne, twice Queen of France, almost certainly had nothing to do with this house, but it is one of the last remaining examples of a style of Breton mansion called a *Maison à Lanterne*. The particular characteristic of these Renaissance houses is that they are built round an inner courtyard. They are usually of three or four storeys with galleries, reached by a spiral staircase in one corner, around the four sides leading to living quarters. Open for guided visits April to September, all day in July–August, a.m./p.m. at other times. Closed Sunday, and Monday in April, May and September.

Where to stay

Hôtel Europe, 1 Rue d'Aiguillon, 29210 Morlaix, tel. 98 62 11 99. Fifty-eight comfortable bedrooms. Good restaurant, with both dining room (l'Europe) medium plus prices, and brasserie somewhat cheaper. Room rates low /medium.

Hotel Le Shako (LdF), Rte de Lannion, tel. 98 88 08 44. Twenty bedrooms at low /medium rates, and good regional restaurant at low prices. Closed Sunday.

Where to eat

Marée Bleue, 3 Rampe St, Melaine, tel. 98 63 24 21. Modestly priced restaurant conveniently near the town centre. Closed Monday.

Bistrot Boeuf, 7 Place des Viarmes, tel. 98 88 61 18. Pleasant bistro for simple meals at reasonable prices. Stays open late. Same proprietor as Hôtel Europe. Closed Sunday, Monday lunch.

Parish enclosures

Morlaix is a good base from which to visit the best of the *enclos paroissiaux*, at St Thégonnec, Guimiliau and Lampaul-Guimiliau. There are a number of others, but they differ only in arrangement and in having simpler details. The parish enclosure consists essentially of a large walled 'churchyard' which, in addition to a small cemetry, often completely paved, includes the church and its forecourt, an ornate calvary, and an ossuary or charnel house. The whole is usually entered through an elaborate gateway in the form of an Arch of Triumph, symbolising the entry of the good into heaven. The ossuaries exist because in the past the local cemeteries were so small that at intervals the tombs had to be emptied to make room for new burials. The bones and skulls removed were placed in the ossuary, the skulls with the name of the dead painted on each in black. The ossuaries were, and sometimes still are, used as funerary chapels.

The remarkable calvaries consist of a monument crowned by the figure of Christ with, at lower levels, scenes from his life, such as the Nativity, the Three Wise Men, the Kiss of Judas, Pilate washing his hands, and so on. At Guimiliau, the most elaborate of the calvaries, there are 200 figures carved in granite. The carving was done by village masons, rough and simple but expressive, with no pretensions to art other than to tell a story. The village priest used them for teaching, standing on a platform and pointing out the characters in each episode with a stick as he explained what had happened. Some of the calvaries were erected at the end of the sixteenth century in the hope of warding off the Black Death which was then spreading across France, others in gratitude when it was over.

St Thégonnec　　St Thégonnec lies just south of the N12 about 9 km from the centre of Morlaix. It and the neighbouring village of Guimiliau, 6 km south-west, have the best enclosures, because for centuries they have been bitter rivals and every time one village made an improvement the other would try to cap it. Even today the two villages turn their backs on each other, and there is no way of getting from one to the other except with your own transport. St Thégonnec is famous for its calvary (1610), and has an ossuary (now a funerary chapel) completed in 1682. It is open to the public from Easter to the end of September, and has a carved and painted oak Entombment (1702). In the church itself there is an impressive and intricately carved pulpit, which some consider a Breton masterpiece and others feel is overdone.

Guimiliau　　At Guimiliau the funerary chapel is less impressive than that at St Thégonnec, but the calvary is earlier and better than that of its rival. An irreligious friend of mine described parish enclosures as 'about as exciting as a pile of wet sandbags', but though some people may share his opinion, there are certainly those who differ. Personally, I found the churches themselves more interesting. That at Guimiliau, with its slightly wonky columns, a splendid baptistery with spiral wooden pillars supporting an ornately carved baldaquin, a pulpit carved with panels representing the cardinal virtues, three finely carved retables, and a choir with a late sixteenth-century stained-glass window, is full of interest. It has two naves, five side chapels and a wood-panelled ceiling.

Four km further west, the village of Lampaul-Guimiliau has another good example of an *enclos paroissial,* and another church with an interior full of interesting details. The nave is crossed by a rood-beam carrying a crucifixion flanked by wooden statues of the Virgin Mary and St John, and each face of the beam is carved with religious scenes. All the carvings are painted. Beams of this kind, called *poutres de gloire,* were used in small churches to separate, symbolically, the choir from the rest of the interior. There are also six seventeenth-century altar-pieces carved in realistic style, a baptismal font with polychrome cover, seventeenth-century choir stalls, and unusual banner cupboards.

Where to stay

Hôtel de l'Enclos (LdF), Lampaul-Guimiliau, tel: 98 68 77 08. Pleasant hotel popular with anglers. Thirty-six rooms at low/medium rates, and a good regional restaurant also very reasonably priced. Open every day in season.

Where to eat

Auberge de St Thégonnec, 6 Place de la Mairie, 29223 St Thégonnec. Hard to fault this restaurant: stylish setting, good food, generous helpings, efficient service, good wines, from medium prices upwards. The inn also has a few rooms, two with bath, at low rates. Closed Monday lunch in season.

St Pol de Léon and Roscoff

From Morlaix to St Pol de Léon is only 18 km by the D58, and the port of Roscoff is just 6 km further. The countryside around these two towns is fertile and may interest market gardeners, as it is given over to the cultivation of artichokes, onions and early vegetables of all kinds,

St Pol de Léon

What to see

but it is of little scenic interest to most tourists. St Pol de Léon is a rather sedate market town but it has two churches worth visiting.

The **Church of St Pol** looks like and is a former cathedral. The present building was erected in the thirteenth and fourteenth centuries on foundations from a hundred years earlier. The nave and its side aisles, the façade and the towers were built first, and the side chapels, choir and apse were added in the fifteenth and sixteenth centuries. The little door under the right-hand tower was reserved for lepers. The building has some interesting details but is chiefly remarkable for its grace and harmony both inside and out. There is some good sixteenth-century stained glass on the right-hand side, and a large fifteenth-century rose window in the transept. The carved choir stalls are sixteenth century.

Once the meeting place of the town council, the mainly fifteenth-century **Kreisker Chapel** is now the college chapel. It is famous for its impressive steeple, 77 m high, 1 m less than that of St Pierre de Caen, on which it was modelled, though some judges consider that the Kreisker, built in local granite, is finer than its model. The chapel has a fifteenth-century Flamboyant Gothic porch on the north side. The western façade has some good fifteenth-century stained-glass windows. In the chapel south of the choir there is a seventeenth-century carved oak reredos. The chapel is open to the public mid-June to mid-September a.m./p.m. If you have the necessary puff, 170 steps lead up the tower to galleries which give a superb view of the Bay of Morlaix and the coast.

Roscoff

Roscoff is a small, quiet town whose granite houses have their backs to the wind, for it is built on the point of a flat peninsula and the climate, though pleasantly warm all year round, can be 'bracing'. It is respectable enough today but quite ready to admit that for hundreds of years the main occupations of its inhabitants were smuggling and piracy. The men of Roscoff were considered fearless and godless by the more conventional inhabitants of inland towns and villages, but when their illegitimate occupations were policed out of existence they turned their strength and determination to the cultivation of the land, and no land is better cultivated than the endless fields of vegetables around Roscoff. Dug, turned, manured, weeded, drained for generations now, they are impeccable.

Brittany Ferries

It is 160 years or so since the first shipload of onions left Roscoff for southern England, and about seventy years since the first 'Johnny Onions' came ashore at Portsmouth with his bicycle and his strings of onions (there is even a street called Rues des Johnies in Roscoff). In the 1960s, Alexis Gourvennec, the young head of a farmer's co-operative, led agitation for the building of a deep-water port for Roscoff, and when it was constructed the farmers started their own shipping line, Brittany Ferries, in 1972. The idea sprang from tradition as well as the desire for more trade. Brittany had had trade and cultural links with England, Wales and Ireland for more than a thousand years but these were brought to an end by French government policy after the union of Brittany with France in 1532, and Gourvennec wanted to revive these links.

After a dodgy start, Brittany Ferries has been a great success and has contributed more than any other single enterprise to the revival of the regional economy. These days Roscoff has more than a string of onions to its bow. It has France's most important **Oceanographic and Marine Biology Laboratory**, attached to the University of Paris, it is an important centre of medical research specialising in seawater cures, and in addition to the ferry terminal at Bloscon it has a fishing port specialising in lobster and crayfish, and a yacht marina with sailing schools. As a seaside resort it is a quiet, usually uncrowded place with a selection of beaches, some of fine sand, some of shingle, good hotels and restaurants, and plenty of good sightseeing destinations near by.

What to see

The **Church of Notre Dame de Kroaz-Batz** is a sixteenth-century Flamboyant Gothic church with a remarkable Renaissance spire. The exterior walls and the tower are decorated with carved ships and cannons, reminders of Roscoff's maritime history. The fine alabaster carvings in the north aisle are fifteenth-century English work.

There are some sixteenth- and seventeenth-century granite houses around the Place Lacaze-Duthiers just north of the church, and in the Rue Amiral-Reveillère. Number 25, called **Mary Stuart's House**, has an elegant façade and an interesting courtyard. The name recalls the fact that in 1548 Mary Stuart, later Mary Queen of Scots but then a little girl not quite six years old, landed at Roscoff on her way to be betrothed to the Dauphin of France. Two hundred years later, Bonnie Prince Charlie came ashore here after his flight from Culloden.

As part of the Oceanography Institute, the **Charles Perez Aquarium** is concerned exclusively with the marine life off the coasts of Brittany and in the Channel, and although there are no exotic rainbow fish or monsters of the deep, there are a good many po-faced and apparently serious-minded species which will interest students and specialists. Open a.m./p.m. from June to September, and p.m. only in March, April, May and October.

Where to stay **Hôtel Gulf Stream**, Rue Marquise de Kergariou, Roscoff, tel. 98 69 73 19. Peaceful modern hotel by the beach. Thirty-two comfortable rooms at rates on the high side of medium. Sound restaurant with good wine list. Menus medium plus prices. Closed October to mid-March.

Hôtel Le Brittany, Blvd St Barbe, tel. 96 69 70 78. Small hotel with twenty-five well-furnished bedrooms, at medium rates upwards. The restaurant, **Le Yachtman**, has good views of the old port and the Île de Batz. Sound menus starting at medium prices. Closed Monday lunch and 15 November to 15 March.

Hôtel Bellevue (LdF), Rue Jeanne d'Arc, tel. 98 61 23 38. On the seafront, with dining room with panoramic views. Twenty rooms at medium rates. Sound regional restaurant, medium prices upwards. Closed 11 November to 20 March.

Where to eat **L'Auberge des Druides**, Rte du Car Ferry, tel. 98 69 70 44. Pleasant candle-lit restaurant in a Breton cottage between the car ferry port at Bloscon and Roscoff itself. Moderate prices.

Les Chardons Bleus (LdF), 4 Rue Amiral de Reveillère, tel. 98 69 72 03. Good regional restaurant with menus at low/medium prices. Also ten rooms at medium rates. Closed Thursday except July/August.

Château Kerjean This impressive château is easily reached from Roscoff and St Pol de Léon via the D788. After about 13 km on this road you come to the village of Berven, and then after a further 2 km to the hamlet and crossroads at Mengleuz. Turn left here to St Vouglay on the D30, from which a road leads to the château. As you approach it seems to be a castle, a fortress, surrounded by walls 6 m thick and a deep moat, but as you move into the courtyard you are faced with a rather gracious Renaissance *château de plaisance*. The courtyard has a nice well, protected by a dome supported by pillars.

The château has belonged to the State since 1911 and all but one wing has been restored. The interior has an exhibition of antique Breton furniture, including sideboards and examples of the typically Breton *lit-clos*. The tour of Kerjean also includes the vast kitchen with two monumental fireplaces, and the considerably less impressive sink, from which water drained out into the vegetable garden (a system still used in luxury holiday hotels in the tropics). On the other side of the courtyard there is an interesting old chapel with a wooden vaulted roof in the form of the upturned hull of a ship.

One of the early owners of the château, René Barbier, had a beautiful wife, Françoise, and somewhat riskily used to boast about her love and faithfulness. A group of four knights became rather bored with this line of talk and vowed to seduce her and send her ring, a brooch and a lock of her hair to her husband. According to the story Françoise outwitted them, locking them up in a room to await her husband's return, and got them to do a bit of weaving to pass the time. Not every seventeenth-century husband would have believed this story, but apparently the Seigneur Barbier did, so all was well.

The château, which also has temporary exhibitions in the high season, is open all day every day July–August, a.m./p.m. June and September, except Tuesday, and p.m. only (not Tuesday) in April, May and October. In July–August there are *son et lumière* shows every Friday evening.

Wild Finistère

Westward to Brest

The D10 west from Roscoff to Plouescat and on to Goulven passes a number of bays with magnificent-looking beaches of fine white sand. As a rule, they are deserted because at high tide the water is too shallow for bathing and at low tide there isn't any.

Goulven

The village of Goulven, for example, has one of these bays where the sea goes out 5 km at low tide, leaving hard, dry sand behind. No swimming, but the almost permanent wind and the huge sands make *Land-yachting* this bay probably the most important of several land-yachting centres on this coast. The local club has over 100 members.

Ornithology

The shores of the Bay of Goulven are also very popular with several species of wading birds and ducks, varying according to the time of year. An ornithological club with headquarters in the Cultural Centre at Lesneven, a few km inland, arranges outings. Goulven also has a fine late Gothic church with several interesting features, including statues of the apostles in the Renaissance porch.

Brignogan Plages

This village is now a small resort, but it had the reputation not all that long ago – shared with its neighbours, Kerlouan and Guiscenny – of being a village of ship wreckers and robbers. Brignogan was converted to a tourist resort in 1934. It has a sailing school, a horse-riding establishment and beaches. Most of the holiday accommodation is some way from the beaches which, although of gritty sand, have the advantage of being well sheltered by rocks and dunes.

Nearby is the country of the *abers*, the narrow sea-lochs which reach well inland. The main road, the D10, crosses the first of them, the **Aber Wrac'h**, which is pretty, particularly at high tide, but at low tide it is the same story, at least anywhere near the mouth, with the water reduced to a trickle between mudflats.

The road, now called the D28, continues south from Lannilis, and crosses the **Aber Bénoit**, before turning west and running through wild and empty country to Ploudalmezeau. From here it is only a few km to **Portsall**, a small port with a couple of beaches and a bay, where on 16 March 1978 the *Amoco Cadiz* was wrecked, and spilled 300,000 tons of oil. On the opposite side of the bay from Portsall is the ruined **castle of Trémazan**. This thirteenth-century castle between the villages of Kersaint and Trémazan still has its four-storey keep, its ramparts overgrown with ivy, brambles and broom, and battlemented walls. It is a romantic ruin, abandoned to rough weather and the years, to seabirds and crows. At the end of the nineteenth century a madman lived in the ruins for twenty years, consoling himself with the thought that though he did not have much of a house he was, at least, Napoleon.

Le Conquet

The first place on this extreme western coast which could make a good holiday base is also the last, Le Conquet. It is a little fishing port, specialising in crab and lobster, with a good deep harbour. It also has a small beach, but across the inlet and on the other side of the low, rocky Kermovan peninsula there is a lovely beach of fine white sand 1.5 km long, the **Anse des Blancs-Sablons**.

History

Le Conquet is a very old settlement and was a prosperous trading port 1,000 years ago, sufficiently rich to be several times raided by the Normans, and later, in the thirteenth, fourteenth and sixteenth centuries by the English. But all that remains of this colourful past is one fifteenth-century house, **La Maison des Anglais** (1 Rue Aristide Briand). In 1558 an English attack left only eight houses undamaged, all belonging to English subjects, so there is not much to see in Le Conquet, but it is a genuine little place, picturesque and charming. The church was rebuilt in the nineteenth century, but retains a sixteenth-century stained-glass window of the Passion in the choir, and some fifteenth-century sculptures in the porch.

Where to stay and eat

Hôtel Restaurant de la Pointe St Barbe, 29217 Le Conquet, tel. 98 89 00 26. Modern building on the rocks immediately above the sea. Forty-nine attractive bedrooms, many with sea views. The new dining room also has panoramic views. Talented chef. Both rooms and meals at a wide range of prices from low/medium to medium plus. Closed mid-November to mid-December.

Ushant (Ouessant)

This interesting island (7 km by 4 km), which is 30 km north-west of Le Conquet, is reached by a daily boat service from Brest which calls at Le Conquet at 9.30 a.m. The return service leaves the island at 5 p.m. Cars can be transported if reservations are made in advance and if they stay on the island for at least a month. There are extra services on Friday and Saturday. Except in the most settled weather, the excursion should be taken only by those who know they are good sailors. The waters around Ushant are among the most dangerous in the world, and countless ships have been wrecked there. Although the average temperature in January and February is the highest in France, terrible gales rage in winter and the seas are savage. Even in summer the currents around the island reach 16 km an hour, and summer fogs are common.

Traditions

The island is extraordinary in several ways. It is probably the only place in Europe where it is traditionally the girl who proposes marriage to the man she loves. This is because for centuries, and even today, the young men of the island worked away from it, in the navy, the merchant navy or on deep-sea fishing boats, and later on offshore oil platforms or in Brest. All the responsibility on the island was the woman's. She grew the vegetables, looked after the sheep, made the decisions. If an agreement was reached between the lovers, she would go during his absence to live in the house of his parents to demonstrate to his mother that she could run a house.

That is only one of the odd things about the people of Ushant. In the fifteenth century a colony of Italians settled there and brown hair, brown eyes, a sallow complexion and a sing-song accent are said to be typical of the true people of Ushant. More, the women traditionally wore the same square, flat coiffe, as the women of Siena, Italy, used to do.

The people are historically very independent and do not take kindly to being told what to do. When Louis XV appointed a governor in 1711, he was stoned as soon as he set foot on the island.

Economy

Nothing grows on the island but grass, which becomes impregnated with salt from the wind-driven spray. This enables the people to raise a high quality lamb, like those bred on the saltings of the Bay of Mont St Michel. But on Ushant they have to be provided with stone-wall shelters from the wind and in February, the most violent month, they are roped together in twos to stop them being blown away. In the past, because there were no trees, all the household furniture was made from wood saved from shipwrecks. It was then painted blue to invoke the protection of the Virgin Mary.

The population of the island is decreasing. The men still go away to work, but tourism has improved the island's economy. The women no longer have to cultivate their own potatoes, and they can import their furniture.

Ushant is an island to walk about on and explore. The boat lands at a new harbour in the Baie du Stiff. From June to September the boats are met by buses. Otherwise the island's only town, **Lampaul**, is 4 km walk away on the other side of the island, but bicycles can be hired.

What to see

In the little hamlet of **Niou Uhella** a short distance outside Lampaul towards the Creach lighthouse, two houses have been established by the Parc Régional Naturel d'Armorique as a small museum of life and traditions on Ushant, the **Écomusée de Niou Uhella**. One of them has its original furniture intact, all made from wood from shipwrecks. The other houses a collections of tools, costumes and so on relating to life on the island. Open for guided visits a.m./p.m. July to September, and p.m. only Easter to June.

The **Creach Lighthouse**, together with the Eddystone light, marks the entrance to the Channel. The 500-million candlepower light with a range of 200 km is said to be one of the most powerful in the world. In the old engine room a museum has recently been installed which illustrates the history of lighthouses from earliest times to the present day. Open all day June to September; p.m. only, except Monday, for the rest of the year.

When a sailor from Ushant was reported lost at sea, his family and friends gathered and prayed for a night around a small wax cross, as big as a man's hand, which symbolised the man himself and was placed on a table before them. At the time of the burial service, the wax cross was placed in a reliquary, and later transferred with great solemnity to a mausolem, where it joined the crosses of all those others lost at sea. The wax cross is called a *proella*, a word that means 'homecoming'. The custom continued until recent years, and the crosses can be seen at **Lampaul Cemetery**.

Where to stay and eat

Hôtel Restaurant Le Fromveur, Lampaul, tel. 98 48 81 30. Seventeen bedrooms. Closed 31 December to 15 March.

Hôtel Restaurant L'Océan, Lampaul, tel. 98 48 80 03. Fourteen bedrooms, eleven with sea views. Open all year.

Hôtel Restaurant Roch Ar Mor, Lampaul, tel. 98 48 80 19. Only five rooms but with sea views. Large restaurant, terrace. Closed December to March.

Brest

The D789 from Le Conquet leads directly to Brest, 24 km away. My advice is not to take it. Brest is an industrial town and France's chief naval base, and it is no more a holiday resort than Chatham or Plymouth. It is also a city of more than a quarter of a million inhabitants. If you come from Le Conquet and want to go further south in Brittany, you will have to cross the whole of it from east to west before you reach the bridge across the Elorn. It is not likely to be a pleasure. There is a lot to be said for taking the D67 instead which, via St Renan, Gouesnon, Guipavas and Le Relecq-Kerhuon bypasses Brest altogether and brings you to the same bridge in forty comfortable km rather than thirty that will seem much longer.

Brest has some good hotels and restaurants but a high percentage of them are closed for part of the summer, some for all of it. From the tourist point of view there is very little of any interest in Brest, apart from a good aquarium called **Océanopolis**, near the marina. If you happen to be keen on bagpipes, the Bretons, who play the pipes, hold a three-day festival of bagpipe music in August in Brest.

Though Brest lacks interest, and is also the wettest place in France, it does have a magnificent position on one of the finest natural harbours in the world, the **Rade de Brest**. This huge roadstead of 150 sq km of deep water is reached from the open sea by a channel more than 5 km long and almost 2 km wide, and the harbour itself has an irregular coastline and some islands. It is best seen from the southern side, from Spanish Point on the Crozon Peninsula, and is a wonderful sight on a sunny day, when the traffic may include battleships putting out to sea, or submarines cruising sedately on the surface back to home base.

The Crozon Peninsula

The Albert Louppe bridge, 1 km long and more than 40 m above the water, crosses the Elorn river 2 km east of Brest carrying the N165 to Quimper and southern Brittany. After 30 km there is a sortie to the right to the small town of Le Faou and the D971, the road to the Crozon peninsula.

Economy

In the past the people of this remote peninsula lived from farming and fishing, but over the last twenty-five years the number of farms has been halved, and almost all the farmers left are near retirement age. Fishing is also in decline. The port of Camaret was once famous for its locally caught lobsters and crayfish, but the few fishing boats left have to go as far as the west coast of Africa to catch them. In the past few years many new holiday homes have been built on this scenic peninsula, tourist hotels have risen up, and facilities for leisure activities of all kinds have been installed. Tourism is filling the economic gaps, and today the peninsula is popular with people who like quiet family holidays with plenty of outdoor activity.

From Le Faou the D971, a corniche road, follows the estuary of the Faou river to the Téréneze bridge across the River Aulne.

What to see
Landevennec

This village, picturesquely sited on its own small peninsula at the mouth of the Aulne, has a Benedictine abbey, completed in 1958, next to the ruins of the old abbey founded by St Guenole in the fifth century. The new abbey has a shop which sells books and souvenirs made by the monks. The ruins of the old abbey are open a.m./p.m. on weekdays, and signs indicate its different parts. Near the village in a corner of the Aulne estuary is a 'cemetery' of old warships.

Menez Hom

The D60 from Landevennec crosses the D791 to Argol village, where it makes a sharp left turn and follows a scenic route, with the Aulne valley on the left and the isolated hill of Menez Hom on the right. Bear to the right on the D47 to St Marie du Menez Hom on the D887, where you turn right and a long km brings you to the D83, on the right, which climbs the hill to a parking area near the top, from which it is an easy five-minute stroll to the summit of this last outpost of the Black Mountains. On a fine day the views from the top are marvellous in all directions, and the whole of the wild Crozon peninsula, roughly shaped like a huge crucifix fallen forward into the sea, is at your feet.

Crozon-Morgat

As you come back down from Menez Hom, turn right again on the D887 which quickly brings you to Crozon, the main village and crossroads of the peninsula, and only 1 km from Morgat, to the south. Morgat is an attractive and stylish small resort, which has a harbour with room for the reduced fishing fleet and more than 600 yachts. It also has a lovely sweep of golden sands, facing south and framed on one side by a pine-clad promontory and on the other by a rocky spur. Just round the promontory are some large sea caves with multicoloured rocks, to which there are frequent boat trips every day in summer: the 45-minute trip is popular and it is advisable to book in advance in high season. Morgat has facilities for horse-riding, tennis, sea and river fishing, and all water sports.

Where to stay
Hôtel Le Julia, 43 Rue de Treflez, 29160 Crozon-Morgat, tel. 98 27 05 89. Modern hotel, twenty-two bedrooms at low to medium rates. Regional restaurant also at low/medium prices. Closed mid-November to mid-February.

Hôtel de la Ville d'Ys, Port de Morgat, 29160 Crozon-Morgat, tel. 98 27 06 49. Forty-two bedrooms at medium rates, and reasonably priced restaurant. Open Easter to September.

Camaret
From Crozon the D8 leads to the old fishing port of Camaret, 10 km away. There is an attractive harbour, still active with a few fishing boats and more pleasure yachts, which is protected by a natural jetty called the Sillon. On the other side of the jetty there is the **Plage de Correjou**, a sand and shingle beach. About half-way between Camaret and Crozon is the **Anse de Dinan**, a bay with a very fine sandy beach. The coastal scenery all round, a mixture of rocks and sandy bays, is impressive, but visitors intending to bathe should ask local advice as there are dangerous currents in some places.

From Camaret a scenic road, the D355, makes the tour of the northern arm of the **Roscanvel peninsular**. At the extremity, if you can park, which may not be that easy in high summer, it is worth leaving the car and walking the few metres to **Spanish Point**, where you get the best possible view of the Rade de Brest. The road continues down the other side of the arm to Roscanvel, overlooking the atomic submarine base at Île Longue, and on to Crozon.

Just to the west of Camaret are the **Alignements de Lagatjar**, an arrangement of 143 prehistoric menhirs in white quartzite, which at some time in the distant past were levelled by an earthquake. In 1928 the Ministry of Fine Arts had them raised and put back in position. Unless you are an expert, it is easy to run out of enthusiasm for large lumps of stone. About 1 km further south, the southern arm of the peninsular ends at the **Pointe de Penhir**, 70 m above the waves and with spectacular views of the wild rocks immediately below, called the Tas-de-Pois (Heap of Peas), to headlands and bays in almost every direction, and out to sea to the archipelago of islands, large and small, with Ouessant in the distance.

Where to stay
Hôtel de France (LdF), 19 Quai Toudouze, 29570 Camaret, tel. 98 27 93 06. Overlooking the port, with twenty-one bedrooms, and better than average cuisine. Prices from low to medium plus for both rooms and meals. Open April to October.

Douarnenez

From the Crozon peninsula the coast swings round in an arc forming the huge Bay of Douarnenez, and then out to the west along another large peninsula. The town of Douarnenez itself is a rather grim, hardworking fishing port. There are two main points of interest for the tourist: the port area, Rosmeur, where there is always some activity among the boats of the still important fishing fleet, and a daily *criée*, the market where fish is auctioned on the quays, and the interesting Musée de la Mer (Museum of the Sea). Douarnenez is an important centre for canning sardines, pilchards, and other fish and a lot of the catch goes to these factories. Some also goes directly to the fish restaurants around the port, so this is a good place for an excellent seafood meal.

The village of **St Anne-la-Palud** holds one of the biggest *pardons* in Brittany on the last Sunday in August or the first in September. It is an interesting event, but one of those in which the religious content is almost lost in a commercial, fairground atmosphere. It attracts tens of thousands of visitors.

What to see
Musée de la Mer

Those interested in boats will find this unusual museum in the Port Rhu area of Douarnenez, across the town from Port Rosmeur, well worth a visit. Partly in a disused nineteenth-century cannery and partly in the harbour, it has a first-class collection of fishing boats, yachts and ferries of all kinds, both French and foreign. There is also a workshop demonstrating the construction and repair of fishing boats, and a collection of primitive boats made in horse-hide, sealskin and other unusual materials, and including coracles of various kinds from Ireland, Scotland and Wales. Open all day June to September inclusive, and a.m./p.m. for the rest of the year.

Boat trips

There are many boat trips available from the port around the Bay of Douarnenez, including a return trip to Morgat (4½ hours). The bay can be rough.

Where to stay

Hôtel de La Plage, St Anne-la-Palud, 29127 Plonevez-Porzay, tel. 98 92 50 12. A Relais and Châteaux hotel, the best on this stretch of coast, and one of the best in Finistère. Modern, but alone on a wild and deserted beach. With heated swimming pool, tennis and sauna. Twenty-six spacious rooms, all with bath etc, with views of countryside or sea. First-class restaurant (Michelin star). Rooms from medium plus to expensive. Menus expensive. Open April to October.

Where to eat

Le Tristan, 26 bis Rue de Rosmeur, Port de Douarnenez, tel. 98 92 20 17. Serious restaurant specialising in fish and shellfish, all fresh, nothing frozen used. The dining room has a view of the port. Menus medium prices upwards.

Le Pourquoi Pas?, Quai du Port Rhu, Douarnenez, tel. 98 92 76 13. Cheerful restaurant/pub atmosphere, some outside tables. Good seafood meals at medium plus prices.

Locronan | Situated in a hilly and wooded situation inland, 10 km east of Douarnenez, Locronan is a town that tourism has brought back from the dead. It was once a very prosperous place which for centuries made the sails for the wooden ships of the French navy and other sailing vessels. It was a town of weavers, but during the nineteenth century, with the coming of steamships, the industry died, and it became a depressed town with only 700 inhabitants and twenty-five sailcloth makers left, many of its fine old houses in disrepair. But at the beginning of this century Locronan had a far-sighted mayor, Charles Danielou, who organised the restoration of the old buildings, banned demolitions, and even arranged for parts of old buildings which were being taken down in Quimper to be brought to Locronan for use in repairs. Today, its central square is surrounded with impressive sixteenth- and seventeenth-century Renaissance houses, granite built and well maintained, and there are more of them in adjacent streets.

What to see | *Loc* comes from the Latin *locus*, a place, and in Breton it usually means a holy place. Ronan was an Irish saint who founded a monastery here in the fifth century.

The spacious **Église St Ronan** dominates the main square. It was built in the Flamboyant style in the early part of the fifteenth century, and has not been altered since. The **Penity chapel**, which communicates with the church by an archway, contains a monument to St Ronan sculpted about 1430.

The charming sixteenth-century chapel of **Notre Dame de Bonne Nouvelle** is reached via the Rue Moal, which has some old houses and leads downhill from the central square. The stained-glass windows of the chapel are modern.

The popularity of Locronan has brought many craftsmen to the town. At the **Maison des Artisans**, in the main square, the weaving tradition is maintained, and the work of woodcarvers and other craftsmen is also exhibited. The **Atelier St Ronan** is a similar workshop, where the weavers specialise in table linen, and there is a saleroom. In the other direction, at the start of the road to Châteaulin, there is a large glass showroom, and a workshop where two glassblowers can often be seen at work. The number and variety of craftsmen make Locronan a better place than most to look for a worthwhile souvenir.

Every six years Locronan has an important religious procession which follows the limits of the land held by the former monastery, a sort of 'beating the bounds'. But the walk – the full distance is 11 km – always follows the sun, from east to west, and stops at certain 'sacred' stones, so it seems that it may have a pre-Christian, Druidical origin. The occasion is described not as a *pardon*, but as a *tromenie* (in Breton, *tro-minihy*), a 'tour of the monastery'. The next **Grand Tromenie** is in 1995. There is a Petit Tromenie, with a much shorter route, every year on the second Sunday in July.

Where to stay | **Hôtel Bois de Nevet**, Rte du Bois de Nevet, Locronan, 29136

Plogonnec, tel. 98 91 70 67. Modern hotel in a peaceful situation in the wooded countryside about 1 km outside the village. Thirty-three functional bedrooms, all with bath etc, at low medium rates. Restaurant prices medium.

Hôtel du Prieuré (LdF), 11 Rue du Prieuré, tel. 98 91 70 89. Twelve rooms at low medium rates. Good restaurant with menus at low/medium prices. Closed October, and Monday out of season.

Manoir de Moellien, 29127 Plonevez-Porzay, tel. 98 92 50 40. A seventeenth-century granite manor house tucked away in a pine forest. Dining room and lounge in the main house, ten ground-floor bedrooms with bath etc in a single-storey annexe. All comfortably furnished in Breton style. Room rates medium. Excellent but rather expensive restaurant. Closed January to March.

La Cornouaille

The region south and west of Douarnenez is known as La Cornouaille, although it is administratively part of Finistère. For the most part it is a gentler region than the more rugged and exposed northern stretches of Finistère, but it is varied and packed with points of interest and has a number of attractive resorts. It already has a touch of the south about it, though in the extreme west it still possesses a wild and rugged coast.

Audierne and the Pointe du Raz

Audierne, 22 km south-west of Douarnenez by the D765, is a busy fishing port attractively sited at the foot of a wooded slope at the estuary of the River Goyen. Audierne still has a general-purpose fleet mainly occupied with short-range and commercial fishing. There are thirty large stone ponds in which the catch of crabs and lobsters are kept alive for sale. On the edge of the town are extensive beaches of fine sand.

Île de Sein There is a daily boat service from Audierne (St Evette) to this strange offshore island. Despite the fact that it is so low-lying that the sea washes over it completely from time to time – twice in the past hundred years – and that nothing except grass grows there, the island has been inhabited from time immemorial. It was the last stronghold of the Druids, long after the rest of Brittany had been Christianised. The Romans spoke of a Druid Temple there with nine virgin priestesses. The people did not become Christians until the seventeenth century, when they were converted by Jesuit fathers. It is said that almost every stone of the church they built was carried to the site on the heads of the women.

Until they were converted they had lived by wrecking and robbing ships, as well as fishing, but in the eighteenth century they became famous for their fearless skill in rescuing the crews of wrecked vessels, and the island is still an important lifeboat station. During the Second World War the island became famous when every man there left to answer General de Gaulle's appeal to join him in England and fight for freedom.

The boat trip takes 1 hour 10 minutes, and when you arrive there is a limited amount to see. The harbour is safe and is used by private yachts, but the surrounding seas are dangerous and one reef, partly submerged, extends almost 20 km beyond the point of the island. It

239

took fourteen years of effort to build a lighthouse on one of the furthest of these rocks. It was eventually completed in 1881.

About 500 people live on the island. The solid, granite houses of the village have no real streets between them, just alleys about 1 m wide to economise on space and protect against the wind, and wide enough, they say, to roll a barrel. There is a small hotel, the **Hôtel Ar-men** (tel. 98 70 90 77).

Pointe du Raz

This is commonly considered to be the Land's End of France, and like Land's End it is a very popular tourist destination and heavily commercialised. In fact the Pointe de Corsen, Pointe St Mathieu and Pointe de Kermovan, further north on the Finistère coast, are all further west than the Pointe du Raz, but they are less spectacular. The Pointe du Raz, sharply stabbing the ocean in defiance and with its string of offshore, wave-battered rocks with the Vieille lighthouse on the last of them, is a more convincing Land's End.

Those who prefer rather less commercialism in beauty spots may like to make the very short drive to the **Pointe du Van**, on the other side of the Baie des Trépassés (Bay of the Dead), which is equally wild and spectacular, and has equally splendid views of the coast, the sea and the islands in all directions, and has so far been spared the souvenir stalls. Do not venture on the cliff paths here, or in any other part of this wild coast, unless you have non-slip shoes and a sound head for heights, and even then prudence is advised.

It used to be thought that the **Bay of the Dead** got its name from the number of bodies of shipwrecked sailors that were washed up there, but research has shown that the set of the offshore currents makes this unlikely. It is suggested instead that the name recalls an ancient Druid custom of putting the dead to sea in a last voyage to the 'happy isles' across the then unknown ocean. I can only comment that to most modern Bretons this would seem to be a waste of a good boat, unless, of course, the Druids used only old and leaky boats beyond repair.

Where to stay

Hôtel Le Goyen, Sur le Port, 29113 Audierne, tel. 98 70 08 88. Very good, comfortable hotel with twenty-nine rooms, most overlooking the port, and a restaurant (Michelin star) where the meals are a gastronomic experience: 'natural' oysters of unmatched flavour from around the Île de Sein, and delicious lobsters and crayfish. Even the potatoes, grown locally on land enriched with kelp, have a special flavour. Rooms at medium plus rates. Restaurant expensive, but sound value. Closed from mid-November to mid-December.

Hôtel Au Roi Gradlon (LdF), 3 Blvd Manu-Brusq, tel. 98 70 04 51. Modern hotel immediately beside the beach, with twenty rooms, all with bath etc, and restaurant with sea views. Medium prices all round. Closed January/February.

Hôtel de la Baie des Trépassés (LdF), 29113 Plogoff, tel. 98 70 61 34. Right next to the beach, a modern functional hotel with twenty-seven bedrooms at low/medium rates. Restaurant at medium prices, half-board obligatory in season. Closed January/February.

Quimper

The word *kemper* in Breton means the confluence of two rivers, and the city of Quimper (pronounced Camp-Air) lies at the junction of the Steir and the Odet. Towns which are not flat are often built on seven hills – nobody ever heard of a town built on four hills, or six, or eight. Seven is the magic number, and Quimper is no exception. The most noticeable of its hills, Mont Frugy, looks down on the centre of the town and the River Odet, and was attractively wooded until the hurricane of 1987 tore down most of its trees.

History and legend

With its two rivers, their bridges decorated with geraniums, its chestnut trees, scattering of old houses and cobbled streets, and its lovely cathedral, Quimper is a pleasant town. It is said to be the oldest city in Brittany, having been founded by King Gradlon in the fifth century, after his own city of Ys had been engulfed by the sea as a punishment for the insatiable debauchery of his daughter, Dahut, who was enslaved by the Devil. But there are several versions of the legend, all more far-fetched than usual, and all that is agreed in Quimper is that the city was founded by a king called Gradlon, and that he made St Corentin its first bishop. Whatever else he did, St Corentin contributed nothing to the incredible variety of Breton fish and seafood recipes. He lived all his life, so the tale goes, on the same fish. He ate half each day, and put the other half back in its pond, where it grew again ready for the next day's meal.

Roman remains have been found in the Locmaria quarter of Quimper, and the 'events' which gave birth to these extraordinary legends took place more than 100 years after Constantine the Great, by the Edict of Milan in AD 313, had freed the Christians from the prisons and the mines, in other words at a time when accurate historical records were being kept in southern Europe. So, though the records were lost or never made, and the folk memory became impossibly embroidered, it is likely that there is a grain of truth somewhere in these legends.

Parking in Quimper, even out of season, requires a good deal of patience, but it is worth taking your time because there is a lot to see in the town itself, and it makes an excellent centre for touring much of southern Brittany.

What to see
St Corentin's Cathedral

The route to the centre of Quimper is not always obvious to the stranger, and the lovely twin spires of the cathedral are a useful landmark. Keep them in sight and, in spite of one-way streets, you will get there in the end. The cathedral, the finest Gothic cathedral in

Brittany, was nearly 300 years in building, between 1239 and 1515, and was restored in the nineteenth century, when the two spires were added. The interior is curious in that the nave is at a slight angle: the masons took it to one side in order to avoid building on unstable ground. As it is, the floor of the choir developed a noticeable slope over the centuries, and has recently been stabilised. The cathedral has a remarkable set of fifteenth-century stained-glass windows, mostly in the higher part of the nave and the transept. There are also in the various chapels a number of fifteenth-century tombs of distinguished people of the past.

Outside, between the two towers, there is an equestrian statue representing King Gradlon. Until the eighteenth century the king was fêted on 26 July every year. As part of the celebrations, a man climbed up to the statue and mounted the horse behind the king. He put a napkin round the king's neck and offered him a glass of wine, which he then drank himself on the king's behalf. He then wiped the statue's lips and threw the glass down into the square. If one of the spectators managed to catch the glass before it broke, he was rewarded with 100 gold crowns. It is said that, to protect their finances, the town council made sure that the glass used had recognisable scratches on it.

The old quarter Quimper is a good town to wander in. Part of the River Steir just before the confluence with the Odet has been canalised and covered over, and this area is now a pedestrian precinct. The area in front of the cathedral has some old, half-timbered houses, particularly in the Place Terre-au-Duc and the Rue St Mathieu. Near the cathedral, in the Rue du Guéodet, is the interesting Maison des Caryatides, where the façade has statues of men and women in sixteenth-century costume at ground-floor level.

There is often a story behind a street name. The **Rue René Madec**, which runs from the bank of the Odet to the Place Terre-au-Duc, is named after one of the most unusual Frenchmen of the eighteenth century. René Madec was born in 1738 in a house still standing in the Place Terre au Duc. He went to sea as a cabin-boy in a ship of the French East India Company. He deserted in Pondicherry, switched from being a sailor to a soldier, then a mercenary. He then entered the service of the senior Vizir of the Mogul Empire, and rose to become Lieutenant-General of that empire, leading campaigns against the British in India. His activities earned him a colossal fortune, and when he returned to France he was honoured by the king, and bought himself a castle and a town house in Quimper, Number 5 in the street of his name. He died at forty-six after a fall from his horse.

While you are in this area the covered market is worth a visit. The original one burned down in 1979 and was replaced by this successful and impressive building which has a view of the cathedral spires through the roof. The ground floor has a mouth-watering display of regional produce. The Tourist Office is on the first floor, where there is also an excellent restaurant.

Musée des Beaux Arts

This is housed in part of the town hall on the north side of the Place Laennec, just north of the cathedral. It has a better-than-average provincial collection with Italian, Flemish and French works from the sixteenth century onwards, as well as a fine collection of nineteenth- and twentieth-century drawings, including works by Cocteau, Picasso and the author Max Jacob, who was also a talented artist and was born in Quimper. Open a.m./p.m. every day except Tuesday and public holidays.

Pottery factories

Glazed earthenware has been made in the Locmaria area of Quimper since the late seventeenth century. Quimper pottery was especially popular in the United States and the Henriot-HB factory was bought by a group of American importers. The factory, Rte de Bénodet, is open for a tour of the workshops and also has a museum of the best examples of Quimper ware. Open Monday to Friday a.m./p.m., closed for lunch 11.30 a.m. to 1.30 p.m. If you do not want to go to the workshops, there is a shop in the Place St Corentin. The workshops of the much smaller Keraluc factory, Rue de la Tromenie, can also be visited a.m./p.m. Monday to Friday.

Église Notre Dame de Locmaria

Beside the Odet and next to the potteries is a rather nice Roman-esque church, originally eleventh century, when it was part of a Benedictine abbey, but changed in the fifteenth century, and restored in the nineteenth. The nave has Romanesque arches on cruciform pillars, and there is a rood-beam at the entrance to the transept, carrying a figure of Christ in a red robe.

River Odet

The people of Quimper like to describe the Odet as the loveliest river in France. It is a bold claim, but the trip by boat from Quimper to Bénodet is worth an hour and a quarter of anybody's time. The boats leave from Corniguel, Quimper's port on the southern edge of the town, which is a big surprise if you have only seen the narrow Odet in the town centre. Just beyond Locmaria, the river begins to open out until it is more than 1 km across. There is plenty of room beside the quays for coastal trading vessels. After becoming more like a lake than a river, the Odet closes in again and winds its way through the gorges of **Le Vire Court**. The whole trip is full of variety, and passes several villages, churches and châteaux. One of them, near Quimper, the **Château de Kerbenes**, belonged to Alexandre Masse, a Quimper clothing manufacturer who first thought of putting four holes instead of two in buttons, which helped him make a fortune. On arrival you could cross the bridge to the pretty harbour of **St Marine**, and have a drink or a coffee and watch people messing about in boats before returning to Quimper by bus or boat.

Where to stay

Hôtel La Tour d'Auvergne (LdF), Rue des Réguaires, 29000 Quimper, tel. 98 95 08 70. Old-style hotel, well-modernised, within 200 m of the cathedral and with its own lock-up parking. Forty-two bedrooms with bath etc, at medium rates upwards. Good restaurant, rather expensive. Restaurant closed Saturday lunch except in high season.

Hôtel Ibis, Rue Gustave Eiffel (Zone Industriel de l'Hippodrome), tel. 98 90 53 80. On the eastern edge of town near the Route de Brest, this is one of the modern chain. Seventy-two comfortable rooms at medium rates. Simple restaurant at low/ medium prices.

Hôtel Griffon, 131 Route de Bénodet, tel. 98 90 33 33. About 3 km from the centre, near the Rallye hypermarket. Comfortable modern hotel, with covered and heated swimming pool. Forty-eight bedrooms, all with bath etc, at medium rates. Good restaurant at medium prices. Closed Sunday lunch.

Where to eat

L'Ambroisie, 49 rue Elie Fréron, tel. 98 95 00 02. Small, classical restaurant with menus from medium prices upwards. Closed Monday evening.

L'Astragale, 4 Rue Aristide Briand, tel. 98 90 53 85. Popular restaurant in a lively part of town. Menus at low prices.

La Jonquière, Les Halles, tel. 98 95 30 05. In the market, so the chef here does not have far to go for his fresh regional produce. Good food at reasonable prices.

Bénodet

There is absolutely nothing wrong with Bénodet except that it suffers in the high season from its own popularity. It has three beaches of golden sand backed by pine trees, a *port de plaisance* for hundreds of yachts, and the wide estuary and the open sea on which to sail them, a casino and a Palais de Congrès (more humbly in English a Conference Centre), lively cafés, good restaurants, and Quimper and its cultural sights are only half an hour's drive away. Altogether it is difficult to imagine a nicer small resort than Bénodet, but the beaches, which are equipped for all forms of water sport and for children's activities, do get crowded in July and August.

In Brittany, as in most of the west of France, final consonants are pronounced, so this resort is 'Bénoday' to the French, but 'Bénodett' to the locals.

What to see

There are really no 'sights' in Bénodet, unless you count the **Église St Thomas**, originally a twelfth-century chapel dedicated to Thomas à Becket. It was enlarged in the fourteenth century, and virtually rebuilt in the nineteenth.

If you are anywhere near Bénodet on 15 August, do not miss the firework display. I mention it here because this is a particularly spectacular one, but in principle, wherever you are in France on 15 August, or 14 July, even in country towns far inland, there is almost certain to be a firework display really worth seeing.

Where to stay

Hôtel Gwel-Kaer, Ave de la Plage, 29118 Bénodet, tel. 98 57 04 38. Modern holiday hotel with a bar and terrace with direct access to the beach. Twenty-four rooms, all with bath, and some with balconies overlooking the sea. From low medium rates upwards. Sound cuisine at medium prices upwards. Half-board obligatory in season. Closed December/January.

Hôtel le Minaret (LdF), Corniche de l'Estuaire, tel. 98 57 03 13. If you want something different this is it, a 1920s villa in Moorish style, with gardens said to be inspired by those of the Alhambra. Sufficiently authentic for the Pasha of Marrakech, who once stayed here. Twenty rooms all with bath etc, some of them very spacious, at medium rates. Restaurant also reasonably priced, but half-board is obligatory in season.

Hôtel des Bains de Mer (LdF), 11 Rue de Kerguelen, tel. 98 57 03 41. Thirty-two rooms at medium rates, and sound regional cuisine with menus at low/medium prices. Closed mid-November to mid-March.

Where to eat **Restaurant du Centre**, 56 Ave de la Plage, tel. 98 57 00 38. Straightforward cuisine with emphasis on seafood; *crêperie* section in July–August. Closed Saturday out of season.

Hôtel Restaurant de la Poste, Rue Église, tel. 98 57 01 09. Sound restaurant in the centre with menus at low/medium prices. Also nineteen simple rooms at low to medium rates.

Ferme du Letty, 2 km south-east of Bénodet, tel. 98 57 01 27. A place for gourmets or the special occasion. Fine old Breton farmhouse among the saltings of the estuary, where Jean Marie Guilbault, one of Brittany's finest chefs, produces meals which are masterpieces of originality and skill. Prices from medium plus upwards, but worth it. Closed October to February.

Pont l'Abbé and Pays de Bigouden

Eleven km west of Bénodet by the D44, Pont l'Abbé is in itself an unexciting little town in a wooded and watery position, but it is interesting in that it is the capital of the Pays de Bigouden, a region inhabited by a mysterious and individual people. Strictly speaking, the word *bigouden* refers to the special *coiffe*, the lace headdress shaped like a funnel, about 30 cm high, with pendant ribbons but no brim. The *bigouden* is kept stiff by heavy starching, or by a cylinder of cardboard inside it, and is worn over the hair piled up in a tight bun. It is seen regularly at local *pardons*, and about 100 older women in the area still wear it daily, although it takes half an hour to prepare and put on.

The *bigouden*, which comes from the Breton word *beg*, which means a point (in the plural *bigou*), is so called because it used to be made in two pieces, front and back, each of which came to a point. It has given its name to the people and the region. The people are considered almost as a separate tribe by other Bretons. They are physically distinctive, both men and women being bigger than the usual Breton; they are also very dark, and often have almond-shaped eyes, as if they were of some Asiatic race. Some scholars have said that this is a result of the constant screwing up of the features induced by wearing the tall *coiffe*, but the *coiffe* only began to get taller at the beginning of this century, and 100 years is not nearly long enough to make a physical change in the features; in any case many of the men have a similar set of the eyes, and they wear round, flat hats. Doctors have noticed certain other physical differences, including a more frequent tendency to dislocation of the hip.

The Bigouden people are considered more enterprising, more socially ambitious than other Bretons: as schoolteachers they strive to become headmaster, in the army they want their stripes. This social awareness is shown in other ways. You can still buy postcards of Bigouden men in their traditional dress, a round black hat and a dark jacket richly embroidered with red, green or gold thread. The embroidery was done by a guild of men with their own set of rules. They knew the local hierarchy and the precise social position of everyone in the community, and they embroidered each suit, usually first made for a wedding, with the precise amount of embroidery indicating the social status of the owner. The last members of this guild stopped working in the 1950s and the traditional embroidery is now done by women.

The craftsmen of Bigouden work in different ways from those in the rest of Brittany, using their own traditional tools. If the Bigoudens were originally an immigrant tribe, as many scholars believe, where they came from remains a mystery.

Isolated among the dunes a few km north of Pointe de la Torche is a small chapel, **Notre Dame de Tronoen**, with beside it what is believed to be the oldest calvary in Brittany. It dates from between 1450 and 1470 and has been eroded by centuries of wind and weather, but many of the figures and groups are still impressive. The chapel is believed to be built on a site which in pre-Christian times was devoted to the worship of Venus, as many little figurines of the goddess have been found there.

Where to eat **Restaurant le Chandelier**, 16 Rue de la Marine, Le Guilvinec, tel. 98 58 91 00. Serious restaurant with menus at medium prices upwards.

Hôtel du Port, 53 Ave du Port, Le Guilvinec, tel. 98 58 10 10. Restaurant with strong emphasis on seafood. Menus at medium prices upwards. Also has forty rooms at medium rates. Open all year.

There is a fish auction on the quay most afternoons at Le Guilvinec, one of Brittany's most important fishing ports, and you can expect dinner menus based on unbeatably fresh fish in the local restaurants.

Loctudy Unlike those already mentioned, Loctudy is a fishing port of some importance which is also an attractive holiday resort. It is situated at the entrance to the estuary of the Pont l'Abbé river, on the west bank 6 km south of Pont l'Abbé, and it has several good sandy beaches sheltered from winds. Île Tudy is not an island but a narrow peninsula opposite Loctudy, almost closing the entry to the Pont l'Abbé river. It is the best part of 20 km by road from its twin resort, but in summer a regular ferry crosses the narrow channel between them. Île Tudy has 4 km of sandy beach stretching all the way to St Marine, opposite Bénodet.

What to see

Loctudy Church dates from the early twelfth century and is one of the best Romanesque churches in Brittany. The façade and steeple were added in the eighteenth century, but the interior remains pure Romanesque in style, both in the nave and the choir, which has a deambulatory with radiating chapels. Both the capitals and the bases of the columns are sculpted with interesting details.

Where to stay and eat

Hôtel Tudy, 29750 Loctudy, tel. 98 87 42 99. Pleasant small hotel, with nine bedrooms at low medium rates. No restaurant. Open all year.

Hôtel Moderne (LdF), 29980 Île Tudy, tel. 98 56 43 34. Nineteen rooms at low rates. Regional restaurant menus at medium prices. Closed October to March.

Hôtel des Dunes (LdF), 29980 Île Tudy, tel. 98 56 43 55. Twelve rooms at low to medium rates and sound regional restaurant with menus at medium prices. Closed mid-September to April.

Along the coast

Beg-Meil

Continuing east from Bénodet, the next real holiday resort is Beg-Meil, long popular with British visitors. It is an attractive place, with a little port with a cobbled quay, and a whole selection of beaches of fine sand backed by dunes and a wood of pines and cypresses. Those that know the resort but have not seen it for a few years will find that the trees were noticeably thinned out by the hurricane of 1987, though some remain. Altogether, with its sheltered beaches, several of them cove-like with a few rocks here and there for variety, its dunes and trees, its sub-tropical vegetation and the beautiful blue of the sea, Beg-Meil is a delightful place for a quiet holiday. For those who want something less developed, there is a sandy beach with rocks and rock pools at one end at the **Pointe de Mousterlin**, about 4 km west of Beg-Meil. There is also a roomy hotel, a few fishing boats, but little else. Mousterlin is reached by the D134, turning to the right off the D44 about 4 km out of Bénodet.

Where to stay

Hôtel de la Pointe de Mousterlin, 29170 Fouesnant, tel. 98 56 04 12. Modern hotel within a few metres of a vast beach. Fifty-two bedrooms at medium rates. Good traditional restaurant at medium prices upwards. Closed October to mid-April.

Hôtel Thalamot (LdF), Le Chemin Creux, Pointe de Beg-Meil,

29170 Fouesnant, tel. 98 94 97 38. Pleasant hotel surrounded by flowers and greenery, but near the beaches and the port. Thirty-five rooms at medium rates. Restaurant (terrace or interior) with range of menus at medium prices, house wine included. Closed mid-October to mid-April.

Hôtel de Bretagne, Beg-Meil, tel. 98 94 98 04. Twenty-eight rooms at medium rates. Sound restaurant with medium-price menus. Closed October to March.

Concarneau

Anyone on holiday in Cornouaille within an hour's drive of Concarneau should make the visit. It is a well worthwhile excursion, but whether it is a suitable place for a holiday is more debatable. It does have beaches, but they are town beaches and so lack freshness and compare unfavourably with the great majority of the others on this southern coast of Cornouaille. Though it is not uninterested in tourism, and makes an effort to be a resort, Concarneau cannot really disguise the fact that it is a serious and important fishing port, the second most important of France, which sends its boats far and wide. As well as coastal and intermediate distance fishing fleets, it has an important deep-sea fleet whose boats bring back frozen cargoes, mostly tunny, from the Atlantic and Indian Oceans. Concarneau also has hotels and a wide choice of good restaurants. Guess what they serve.

What to see

La Ville Close is Concarneau's big tourist attraction, a rocky island in the harbour where the town began more than 1,000 years ago, because it was easily defended. It is now connected to the quay by bridge. The little town has only half a dozen streets, and is completely surrounded by ramparts which were rebuilt at the end of the the seventeenth century by the great French military architect, Vauban. It is possible to walk round the Ville Close on the ramparts (admission fee): it is only 350 m by 100 m, and there are good views of the town and the fishing ports. The streets are given over almost entirely to souvenir shops, art galleries and the like, and this is one place where you are very likely to see women in local costume and *coiffe* who sell lace and embroidery to tourists.

The **Musée de la Pêche** is an interesting exhibition of boats and equipment, illustrating the development of commercial fishing techniques over the past 100 years or so. The museum was once a sardine cannery and some of the smaller boats are shown in a vast hall, others are afloat in the harbour. You can visit a trawler which was still in service ten years ago, and get a good idea of the tough life of the fishermen. The museum, which is just inside the Ville Close, is open from 9.30 a.m. to 8.30 p.m. every day July/August, and a.m./p.m. at other periods.

Concarneau is one of the best places to see a traditional fish auction, *la criée*, where shopkeepers, hoteliers, restaurateurs and so on bid against each other for the day's catch. It always takes place at 7 a.m.

and 10 a.m. in the sheds on the quays in Concarneau on the first four days of the week.

Where to stay

Hôtel des Sables Blancs (LdF), Plage des Sables Blancs, 29110 Concarneau, tel. 96 97 02 78. About 1 km from the port but right by the best beach. Forty-eight rooms, most with bath etc, at low to medium rates. Quiet situation, with terrace and garden. Very good restaurant, low to medium plus prices. Closed 15 October to March.

Where to eat

Le Galion, 15 Rue St Guénole, Ville Close, tel. 98 97 30 16. In an old granite house at the far end of the Ville Close. Comfortable beamed dining room with some good paintings. First-class cuisine (Michelin star), at medium plus prices. Advisable to book a table. Though Le Galion is primarily a restaurant, it does have five good bedrooms with bath. Closed mid-January to March.

La Coquille, 1 Quai du Moros, tel. 98 97 08 52. You get the sea in your plate here. It is right by the quays and the chef buys his fish at the *criée*. Dining room and terrace. Medium plus prices.

Chez Armande, 18 bis Ave de Docteur-Nicolas, facing the yacht basin, tel. 98 97 00 76. Everything traditional here, from the Breton-style decor, to the classic cuisine with the emphasis on seafood. Closed Wednesday.

Auberge de Kerandon, Rte de Quimper, tel. 98 97 08 79. Old manor house with splendid dining room, and garden terrace, in a country setting on the edge of Concarneau. Medium prices but good value. Closed Monday.

Towards Pont Aven

From Concarneau the D783 leads via Trégunc to Pont Aven, a distance of 14 km. Those who like beaches, however, may like to turn off just beyond Trégunc for Néves and **Raguenès Plage**. When I first saw it more than twenty years ago, this was one of the loveliest and wildest of Breton beaches, great stretches of sand in either direction broken here and there by a few rocks, and an island off shore. There are now two or three good camp sites set well back from the beach, and a couple of small hotels, but the space still well exceeds the development. In those days **Port Manech**, a few km to the east, was an exclusive, upmarket little resort. It has been developed slightly since, and has some holiday houses and two camp sites, but it remains attractive, beautifully situated, with a wooded hillside looking down on a bay at the mouth of the Aven, with a port and a perfect beach.

Pont Aven is a place whose particular charm somehow escapes me. It is agreeable enough, but not more so than a score of other villages at the head of Breton estuaries. It owes its reputation to Paul Gauguin. The great artist lived there briefly between 1887 and 1889, but he did not like the local people and they didn't like him, and as he was not famous at the time they made no special effort to disguise the fact. But Pont Aven was already known to artists, Gauguin's presence attracted more, and soon there was a Pont Aven 'school'. None of its artists approached Gauguin in stature, though Maurice Denis and Paul

Sérusier, among others, made a reputation. In 1889 Gauguin felt that Pont Aven was too crowded, and 100 years later many would agree with him. He moved, with Sérusier and other friends, to Le Pouldu, about 25 km further east along the coast, and it was here that Gauguin made his longest stay in Brittany, was happiest, and produced most work.

What to see The **Musée de Pont Aven** is not much more than a public gallery which holds temporary exhibitions each year of painters associated with Brittany, rarely distinguished, not often of the Pont Aven 'school', and you are not likely to see a Gauguin there. It does have an audiovisual presentation relating to the Pont Aven 'school'. Open a.m./p.m. April to December.

The sixteenth-century Tremalo Chapel stands on the wooded hillside a short distance outside Pont Aven. Its chief interest is that it still contains a seventeenth-century wooden polychrome statue of Christ, which served as a model for Gauguin's painting *The Yellow Christ*.

The **Maison de Marie Henry** is in Le Pouldu, not Pont Aven, but is mentioned here in case some art lovers want to follow in Gauguin's footsteps in Brittany. This is not the actual inn where Gauguin and his friends lived, but a faithful reproduction in a neighbouring identical house, using period furniture and copies of paintings made with the help of photographs of the originals.

Where to stay **Hôtel Chez Pierre** (LdF), Rues des Îles, 29920 Raguenès Plage, 11 km from Pont Aven, tel. 98 06 81 06. Thirty-five rooms at low to medium rates, and better than average restaurant with menus at medium prices. Closed October to April.

Hôtel des Ajoncs d'Or (LdF), 29120 Pont Aven, tel: 98 06 02 06. Twenty-one rooms at medium prices. Sound restaurant, also moderately priced.

Hôtel Ar-Men, Route du Port, Le Pouldu, 29121 Clohars-Carnoët, tel. 98 39 90 44. Traditional family hotel. Thirty-eight rooms with bath etc. Rates medium to medium plus. Good restaurant with menus at medium prices upwards.

Where to eat In general not recommended in restaurants in Pont Aven, unless you do not mind paying over the top for what you get. Or for a change, you could try the **Tahiti**, 21 Rue de la Belle Angèle, Rte de Bannalec, tel. 98 06 15 93. Chinese cooking in Tahitian style.

Quimperlé This is a placid country town, picturesque and full of charm. It stands, like Quimper, at the confluence (*kemper*) of two rivers, in this case the Elle and the Isole, which join to become the Laïta, which flows into the sea at Le Pouldu. It has a lower town between the two rivers, and an upper town on the hill across the Isole. Wherever one looks – at the flower-lined quays, the shady squares, the old bridges, or the venerable houses on the wooded hillside – the view is pleasant. The rivers are reckoned to be good for both salmon and trout fishing, and just south of the town is the oak and beech forest of Carnoët, which has a number of signposted paths for walkers, including GR342, and horse-riders.

What to see   Built in the twelfth century as a copy of the Church of the Holy Sepulchre in Jerusalem, from plans brought back by Crusaders, the **Church of St Croix** consists of a rotunda with an entry porch, an apse on either side and a larger one at the back, so that the whole forms a Greek cross. The church was heavily damaged in 1862, when its seventeenth-century steeple collapsed. Most of it had to be rebuilt, but the large Romanesque apse and the eleventh-century crypt were not damaged and these are the most interesting parts of the church. In the Rue Brémond-Ars, north of St Croix, and the Rue Dom Morice, a turning off it, there are some old half-timbered and corbelled houses.

It is a pleasant 15 km drive from Quimperlé, via the Carnoët forest, by the D49 to the sea and beaches at Le Pouldu.

Where to stay   **Hôtel de l'Hermitage**, Manoir de Keroch, Rte du Pouldu, 29130 Quimperlé, tel. 98 96 04 66. Tucked away in lovely countryside about 2 km south of the town by the D49. Twenty-four rooms in cottages and pavilions in the grounds of an old manor. Medium rates. Heated swimming pool. Good restaurant.

Where to eat   **Le Bistro de la Tour**, 2 Rue Dom Morice, 29130 Quimperlé, tel. 98 39 29 58. Charming restaurant in the lower town near St Croix church. Good wines. Pleasant service, medium prices, house wine included. Closed Monday, and Sunday evening except in high season.

Relais du Roch, Rte du Pouldu, 29300 Quimperlé, 2 km by the D49, tel. 98 96 12 97. Pleasant restaurant where chef Michel Lenormand offers excellent cuisine with original touches, at medium prices upwards. Closed Monday, and Sunday evening out of season.

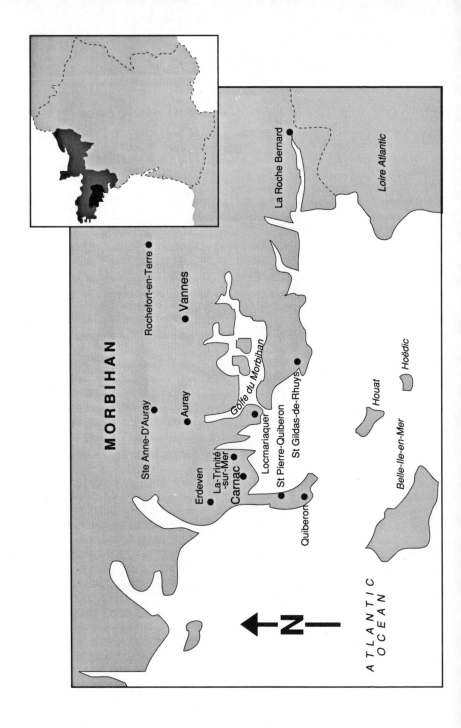

Morbihan

The River Laita at Quimperlé marks the boundary between Finistère and the department of Morbihan. In Breton *mor*, as in *armor*, is the word for sea, and *bihan* means 'little', and this little sea is the huge, land-locked Gulf of Morbihan with its countless inlets and islands, a geographical feature unique in France. But Morbihan is also the land *par excellence* of prehistory, of dolmens, menhirs, and megaliths of all kinds, and at Carnac these great stones lie close to magnificent beaches. The department also has the unusual Quiberon peninsula, and offshore islands which include the beautiful Belle-Île-en-Mer.

Lorient and Auray

Lorient
This important naval base and fishing port is the largest town in Morbihan, but is of no interest to the average tourist. It was founded in the late seventeenth century as a base for the newly formed Compagnie des Indes (The French East India Company), which thrived for more than 100 years but eventually failed. The State took over the installations and Napoleon fortified Lorient as a naval base. In the Second World War, the Germans used it as a submarine base, and as a result it was virtually bombed out of existence and had to be completely rebuilt after the war.

Auray
The natural 'capital' of the region of the megaliths, Auray is an attractive, old-fashioned place situated at the head of a sea-loch, formed by a river called the Loch. Though the town has no major sights, it is worth exploring as it has interesting old streets, particularly across the bridge in the St Goustan suburb, with restored medieval houses, and there is a promenade beside the Loch with good views over the port, now given over almost entirely to yachts and cabin cruisers.

Auray is only 6 km from the village of **Ste Anne d'Auray**, where in 1623 an illiterate Breton peasant, Yves Nicolazic, said that St Anne, the mother of the Virgin, had appeared to him and directed him to a spot where there had once been a chapel dedicated to her. She told him, with some precision, that 'the chapel was destroyed 924 years and six months ago, and I desire that it should be rebuilt'. Yves told the clerics of his vision, and they thought him mad. But St Anne reappeared to him on 7 March 1625 and told him to dig in a certain spot. He did as he was told in the presence of witnesses, and unearthed a statue of St Anne dated 701. The bishop gave permission for the chapel to be built, and Ste Anne d'Auray has been a place of pilgrimage ever since. In 1866 the seventeenth-century chapel was replaced by a basilica, reckoned by experts to be a notably unsuccessful and messy piece of architecture. In front of the basilica there is a war memorial erected in 1932 to the memory of the 250,000 Breton soldiers and sailors who lost their lives in the First World War, the highest ratio – one in fourteen of the population – of any region involved in that war.

If you are not a pilgrim, Ste Anne d'Auray seems a rather dreary little town, but it comes to life on 26 July, when one of the most important *pardons* in Brittany is held there and usually attracts about 25,000 people.

Auray itself has a good choice of hotels and is a good base from which to explore the coastal areas of Morbihan.

Where to stay   **Hôtel Le Branhoc**, Rte du Bono, tel. 97 56 41 55. One and a half km from the town centre on the road to Bono, the D101. Modern hotel in a calm situation, twenty-eight rooms with bath etc, at medium rates. No restaurant.

L'Auberge (LdF), 56 Rue Vannes, Ste Anne d'Auray 6 km, tel. 97 57 61 55. Delightful little Breton inn with six bedrooms at low/medium rates, and a good restaurant offering menus from low to medium plus prices. Closed Tuesday evening and Wednesday.

La Croix Blanche (LdF), Rue de Vannes, Ste Anne d'Auray, tel. 97 57 64 44. Twenty-three rooms at from low to medium rates, and a sound regional restaurant, low to medium plus prices.

Where to eat   **L'Abbaye**, 19 Place St Sauveur, St Goustan, tel. 97 24 10 85. A seventeenth-century house in the old quarter, St Goustan, across the river. Dining room with old Breton furniture and traditional Breton cuisine. Menus at medium prices. Closed Sunday evening and also Monday.

La Closerie de Kerdrain, 20 Rue L. Billet, tel. 97 56 61 27. A first-class restaurant where Fernand Corfmat offers the best of Breton cuisine at prices – from medium to medium plus – which are very good value. Nice welcome and atmosphere. Closed Monday evening and Tuesday out of season.

The Quiberon peninsula

The peninsula was once an island but is now joined to the mainland by an isthmus which, at its narrowest near the Forêt de Penthièvre, is barely 50 m wide – just room for the road and a sand beach on either side. The peninsula is a Jekyll-and-Hyde sort of place. The isthmus is sandy but the part which was an island is granite: its west coast, rocky and exposed to the Atlantic winds, is known as the Wild Coast, and bathing from its beaches is extremely dangerous. Currents make it impossible even for strong swimmers to regain the shore once they have gone too far, and there are numerous drownings. The eastern coast, facing the Bay of Quiberon, is all sweetness and light and relative safety, with a succession of sheltered, cove-like sandy beaches.

Quiberon

Quiberon itself is a well-developed resort long popular with British holiday-makers, with a wide choice of holiday hotels and restaurants. It stretches from side to side of the peninsula, with the small fishing quarter, **Port Maria**, well-known for its sardines, in the west, and **Port Haliguen**, with a yacht marina, in the east. Quiberon, in the middle, has a lovely arc of south-facing sandy beach, and two or three smaller ones. It has some of the best hotels in Brittany, and a famous Thalassotherapy Institute with sea-water treatment of motoring and sporting injuries. There are tennis courts, gardens, well-organised beach clubs for children, café terraces, and all the fun of the fair, without the shoddiness.

The east coast also has the smaller resort of **St Pierre-Quiberon**, which has two good sandy beaches, and a headland, Beg Rohu, where the **National Sailing School** is based.

There are good walks all round the western and southern coasts of the peninsula, and Port Maria is the departure point for boat trips to the islands of Houat and Hoëdic, and Brittany's largest and loveliest island, Belle-Île-en-Mer.

Where to stay

Sofitel Thalassa, Pointe de Goulvars, 56170 Quiberon, tel. 97 50 20 00. Modern and luxurious but rather lacking in charm. Connected by a corridor to the Thalassotherapy Institute, and there are two sections to the hotel, normal and 'dietetic' for those wanting a 'cure'. Despite the fact that some of its rooms are small and that the cuisine falls short of its pretentions, this is probably the most expensive hotel in Brittany. Closed January.

Hôtel Ker Noyal, Rue St Clément, Chemin des Dunes, tel. 97 50 06 41. Close to the beach, with 100 comfortable, spacious rooms, at upper medium plus rates. Excellent service and welcome. Expensive restaurant of a high standard. Closed November to February.

Hôtel Le Bellevue, Rue de Tiviec, tel. 97 50 16 28. Well-run modern hotel with thirty-nine spacious rooms, with balconies or terraces directly overlooking the beach, rates medium plus. Garden and heated pool. Restaurant from medium plus prices upwards, half-board obligatory in season. Closed early November to March.

Hôtel Europa, Port Haliguen, tel. 97 50 25 00. Modern hotel facing the sea. Fifty-three rooms, all with bath, at medium rates upwards. Also a dozen studios with kitchenettes, let by the week. Restaurant with menus at medium prices. Closed mid-November to March.

Auberge du Petit Matelot (LdF), Plage de Penthièvre, 56510 St Pierre-Quiberon, tel: 97 52 31 21. Near the beach on the safe side of the peninsula, with twenty-five rooms at low to medium rates and better-than-average regional restaurant. Menus at medium prices. Closed November to 15 March.

Where to eat

La Goursen, 10 Quai de l'Ocean, Port Maria, Quiberon, tel. 97 50 07 94. Lively bistro restaurant specialising in seafood. Menus from medium prices up are good value. Closed Tuesday, and Wednesday lunch.

Les Pêcheurs, Port Maria, tel. 97 30 48 32. Fisherman-style décor, and traditional Breton fish recipes. Meals also served on the terrace. Medium prices. Closed Sunday evening and Monday out of season, and 15 November to 15 December.

Le Relax, 27 Blvd Castero, Plage de Kermorvan, tel. 97 50 12 84. Remarkably good-value meals, at low to medium prices, in this rotunda restaurant with views of the Bay of Quiberon. Closed Monday and January.

Excursions from Quiberon: Belle-Île-en-Mer

This is the largest and most attractive of all the islands off the Brittany coast. It lies 15 km out to sea, south of Quiberon, and there is an all-year-round daily service, augmented in the summer season, to the island. Other summer services operate from La Trinité-sur-Mer and Port Navalo (Morbihan), and Pornichet, La Turballe and Le Croisic (Loire Atlantique). It is popular with rich and well-known people who want to get away from it all, and as a result most of its hotels and restaurants tend to be rather expensive.

The island is a tableland rising to about 60 m above sea-level, and its character is almost a repetition of that of the Quiberon peninsula. Its west coast, facing the Atlantic, is savage and storm-tossed; its southern coast has some sheltered beaches, and the east coast is almost cosy, broken up by valleys coming down from the higher land and ending in sandy coves. Some of the upland is moorland, covered in heather and gorse, some is cultivated, and the valleys are fertile. The scenery is varied, and in places beautiful. The island is 18 km long and from 5 to 10 km wide, much too big to be seen completely in a there-and-back quick visit. It has more than 160 km of roads, four little towns, including the capital, Le Palais, and dozens of hamlets. Its variety is best seen by exploring it in a small car or by bicycle. Both can be hired in Le Palais, or cars can be brought across on the boat from Port Maria, but this is more expensive and reservation has to be made well in advance.

History

At the end of the nineteenth century the island had 10,000 inhabitants; this has fallen to 4,500 today. They live by fishing (there is a fish cannery on the island), farming and tourism. In 1658 the island was purchased from the then owner, the Baron de Retz, by Nicholas Fouquet, Finance Minister to Louis XIV, who wished to make it a safe retreat and had it fortified. But Fouquet, who paid 1.3 million pounds (*livres*) for the island, never set foot on it, because during the same period he had built himself the most magnificent château in France, Vaux le Vicomte, and made the mistake of inviting the young king to the incredibly lavish 'house-warming'. Louis was both outraged and green with envy at this display of magnificence and unlimited ambition on the part of a subject. He reacted by going off and commissioning an even more splendid palace – Versailles – which turned out to be nothing like as successful a building as Vaux le Vicomte, and plotting Fouquet's downfall. In 1661 d'Artagnan and his musketeers arrested Fouquet in Nantes. He had done a great deal for the development of French trade, but he was charged with embezzlement and sent to prison for life. Fouquet's wife, the Marquise Madeleine de Castille, was allowed to keep Belle-Île until 1704, when the king bought it from her. He made it a duty-free zone and base for the French East India Company. After several unsuccessful attempts in the seventeenth century, it was eventually captured by English forces under Admiral Keppel and General Hodgson in 1761, and two years later it was exchanged for Minorca.

The citadel prison at Le Palais, which was not closed until 1961, was long considered a safe place to keep revolutionaries, and its inmates have included Karl Marx, the son of Toussaint l'Ouverture of Haiti, and Ben Bella of Algeria.

The beauty of the island has made it popular with painters, musicians and actors. Courbet painted there in 1847, Claude Monet spent two months working there in 1886, and the famous actress, Sarah Bernhardt, converted an old fort into a holiday home. Several French film stars have kept homes on the island for use when 'resting', and it remains a wonderful place for a quiet holiday and 'recharging the batteries'.

What to see   The little capital of the island, **Le Palais**, has more than half the inhabitants and is dominated by the fortress, planned and started by Vauban in the seventeenth century but not finished until nearly 200 years later, under the Second Empire. The **Citadel**, now abandoned, is open to the public a.m./p.m. March to October.

Sauzon is a picturesque village-port on the tidal estuary of the miniature River Sauzon, a creek really.

Four km across on the other side of the island from Sauzon, the **Grotte de l'Apothicairerie** is a large and impressive cave, floored with white sand, which gets its name from the fact that it was used by cormorants who ranged their nests on ledges round the sides of the cave, like the jars on the shelves of an old-time apothecary's shop. The steps which lead down to the cave are slippery.

Grand Phare is an important lighthouse near the south coast. Its light has a maximum range of 120 km, one of the most powerful in Europe. It is 46 m high, and there are splendid views over the island from the platform. Open for guided visits (15 minutes) from 1 July to mid-September.

The two beauty spots of **Port Goulphar** and **Port Coton** are on the coast within a few minutes' walk of each other and of the lighthouse. Port Goulphar is on a pretty inlet and has good hotels.

At the south-east end of the island, furthest from Le Palais, **Locmaria** village is interesting in that its people live from the land, not the sea. Many tourists never get this far and it remains a peaceful place, although it has several good beaches within easy reach including **Les Grands Sables**, the largest on the island. There are others at Port Maria, Port Blanc, and Port Andro.

Houat and Hoëdic These two small islands are also reached by regular boat service from Quiberon, one hour to Houat, half an hour longer to Hoëdic. Out of season it may not be possible to return on the same day.

Houat This is a granite island about 5 km long by 1.3 km wide, and has a population of nearly 400, almost all in the island's one village. There are many beaches in small coves between the cliffs, and one lovely beach more than 1 km long on the north coast facing Hoëdic.

Hoëdic This is a smaller island, 2.5 km by 1 km, also granite, with a population of 126, but it is one of the few places in Brittany where the number of fishing boats has increased in recent years. On both islands the men catch lobsters and other shellfish commercially, but the people also depend heavily on tourism. Like Houat, Hoëdic also has numerous beaches between the cliffs.

Each island has a simple hotel, and both are popular with yachtsmen. The islands have tracks rather than roads and the only mode of transport is Shank's pony. Although the islands are supposed to be part of the commune of Belle-Île, they in fact govern themselves and make their own decisions.

Where to stay **Hôtel Castel Clara**, Bangor, 56360 Belle-Île-en-Mer, tel. 97 31 84 21. A Relais et Châteaux hotel in a lovely position overlooking the sea and Port Goulphar. Thirty-three comfortable rooms, all with bath, and ten apartments. Rates expensive. A very good restaurant, also frankly expensive. Must be one of the few places outside Paris where the bar is open all night. Closed mid-November to mid-February.

Hôtel Le Cardinal, Pointe du Cardinal, Sauzon, 56360 Le Palais, tel. 97 31 61 60. Modern hotel, not much character, but beautifully situated. Seventy-six small, comfortable rooms with balconies and coastal views. Rates moderately expensive. Sound restaurant. Closed October to March.

Hôtel le Bretagne, Quai Macé, Le Palais. Traditional hotel facing the port. Most rooms with bath etc. Reasonably priced restaurant.

Hôtel le Phare (LdF), Sauzon, tel. 97 31 60 36. Fifteen rooms at low medium rates. Restaurant offers menus at medium prices upwards. Closed Sunday evening and Monday, and February.

Where to eat **Le Goeland**, 3 Quai Vauban, Le Palais, tel. 97 31 81 26. Restaurant-cum-pub with views over the port. À la carte only, medium plus prices. Closed Monday out of season.

Le Contre Quai, Sauzon, tel. 97 31 60 60. Restaurant in a charming house near the port, good menu plus à la carte, prices medium plus. Closed Monday lunch and Tuesday, and November to February.

Carnac

Megaliths

French towns and even villages have a passion for calling themselves the capital of this or that, usually something grown or treated there, which could be anything from artichokes to kidney disease. The claims are often dubious or contested, but Carnac is certainly the world's capital of 'big stones': that is, megaliths.

Carnac has the most elaborate stone avenues in the world; nearby at Locmariaquer is the largest menhir in the world; the Île aux Moines just off the coast has the most extraordinary cromlech in the world, and on the island of Gavrinis there is a tumulus with a dolmen whose walls have been engraved with designs by men of the New Stone Age.

The first interesting thing about all these megaliths is that thousands of years ago they were put where they are in meaningful patterns. The second interesting thing is that nobody has succeeded in discovering just what the meaning of the various alignments is: plenty of supposition, plenty of theories, but no concise explanation – which is just as well for the inhabitants of Carnac, who are well aware that an unsolved mystery is a bigger tourist attraction than a concise explanation. Another interesting question without a positive answer is, how did people who had no sources of power and had not even invented the wheel get these great stones, some of which weighed over 300 tons, just precisely where they wanted them? The largest of the menhirs, called the Men-ar-Groac'h (Fairy Stone) at Locmariaquer, was 22 m high and weighed 342 tons in a single piece of granite, rather taller and heavier than five Challenger tanks piled on top of each other. It was struck by lightning in the eighteenth century and fell, and lies in four pieces on the ground. It was only one of several thousand, yet when an Italian engineer called Domenico Fontana succeeded in the sixteenth century in raising upright an Egyptian obelisk which had lain on the ground in Rome since the days of Caligula, he employed between 800 and 900 men and seventy horses. It took him a year and cost a fortune – yet the obelisk weighed less than the Fairy Stone.

What to see
The stones

The chief alignments of stones are those of **Menec**, which has 1,099 stones in eleven rows and ends in a cromlech of seventy more stones; **Kermario**, which has 1,029 stones in ten lines; and **Kerlescan**, which has 555 in thirteen lines. There are also numerous dolmens, and a number of tumuli. The one thing that most experts are agreed on is that the stones and dolmens were being erected in the late Neolithic age, between 2000 and 1000 BC. The much more ingenious Pyramids and the elaborate Minoan palace at Knossos were built during approximately the same period, and the last megalith may have been erected only a few hundred years before the Chinese built their Great Wall, so although the arrangement of the big stones is the work of intelligent people, they were far from sophisticated.

What there is to be seen today is neither attractive nor authentic. Some stones fell down and were broken up and used for building. More were knocked down, because in the nineteenth century it was believed that gold and precious objects were buried beneath them, similar things having been found in dolmen burial chambers. Farmers moved others out of their way when cultivating. When the Historical Monuments Commission was formed in France towards the end of the nineteenth century, efforts began to put things right. Some fallen stones were re-erected, but not always the right way up.

The interest is in the puzzle, and tourists who are not archaeologists and who do not have an expert with them to explain things are likely to be disappointed.

Musée de Prehistoire

Anyone who does feel interested in the story of the megaliths should visit the Museum of Prehistory (properly called the Musée James Miln–Le Rouzic). James Miln was a wealthy Scot who made the excavation of the Carnac area his hobby, and Le Rouzic was a local boy who worked with him, and then continued the work after Miln's death, and in a more professional manner. The museum expounds clearly the history of the area and most of the speculations concerning the origin of the stones, from prehistory, through Roman times to the present day, and includes all sorts of things relevant to menhirs, including the Asterix and Obelix cartoons. There was an eighteenth-century theory that the stones had been erected by Romans camped on the site, to act as windbreaks for their tents! It has also been suggested that in the Second World War American GIs thought the Germans had put them there as tank traps. Open a.m./p.m., and closed Tuesday, except July/August, and on public holidays.

Carnac Plage

The resort which has developed beside Carnac's splendid sandy beaches is now considerably larger than the village of Carnac itself, and it is possible to have a very good holiday in Carnac-Plage without ever 'doing' the megaliths, though you cannot avoid seeing them.

Carnac has six beaches, all good. Two of the best are the smaller ones, **Ty-Bihan** and **Men-Du**. The **Grand Plage** is more than 1 km long and has a small yacht basin at one end, with ramps where yachts and dinghies can be floated into the water. Apart from all the usual water sports, there are facilities for parasailing, golf, horse-riding, tennis and children's beach clubs. There is also an up-to-the-minute **Thalassotherapy Centre** with all the latest forms of sea-water treatments, as well as a heated sea-water swimming pool.

Excursions from Carnac

If Carnac can be called the capital of megaliths, Locmariaquer is the capital of dolmens. The huge, broken menhir, the Fairy Stone, and

Locmariaquer

the most important of the dolmens, called **La Table des Marchands** (The Merchants' Table), are both fenced off and closed for lunch from 12.30 p.m. to 2.30 p.m. Some dolmens are exposed and some covered by a tumulus. The Merchants' Table has been re-covered with earth to protect it, but a passage leads into it and you can stand beneath the huge slab of granite which forms the roof. Linear designs etched in the stone are said to represent ploughing. Two other dolmens, **Mané-Lud**, at the entrance to the village among a group of houses, and **Mané-Rethual**, in the middle of the village, have etched or 'sculpted' support stones in the interior. Mané-Rethual has a long tunnel, an *allée couverte*, with walls and roof composed of stone slabs, leading to the large central chamber.

Alignements de Kerzeho

About 5 km north-west of Carnac by the D781, near the village of **Erdeven**, there are 1,129 stones in these alignments which are more than 2 km long. Erdeven has two immense beaches, **Kerhilio** and **Kerminihy** (naturist), backed by sand dunes which provide the only shelter from the almost permanent breeze.

Where to stay

Hôtel Le Diana, 21 Blvd de la Plage, 56340 Carnac, tel. 97 52 05 38. Thirty-one bedrooms with a high degree of comfort, rates expensive. Heated swimming pool and exercise room. Facing the beach. Fairly expensive restaurant, and half-board obligatory in season. Closed October to Easter.

Hôtel Lann-Roz (LdF), 36 Rue de la Poste, tel. 97 52 10 48. Fourteen rooms, all with bath, at medium rates. Good restaurant slightly above medium prices. Closed 2 January to 2 February.

Hôtel Les Ajoncs d'Or (LdF), Kerbachique, Route de Plouharnel, tel. 97 52 32 02. Nineteen bedrooms at medium rates. Regional cuisine above average standards, medium prices upwards. Closed November to February.

Vannes and the Gulf of Morbihan

Vannes gets its name from the Veneti, a maritime Celtic tribe who led the resistance against the Romans. They were defeated in a naval battle in 56 BC, which took place just off the Rhuys peninsula. Julius Caesar did not take part but is said to have stood on top of a tumulus at Tumiac to watch the battle. His forces were led by Brutus, who twelve years later took part in Caesar's assassination.

Vannes has always been one of the most important towns in Brittany. It was the capital of the first Duke of Brittany, Nominoë, who defeated the Franks and made Brittany independent in the ninth century, and set the boundaries of the province, which are much the same today. At different times in later periods it was used as a capital by other dukes, and it was in Vannes in 1532 that King François I made official the union of France and Brittany.

Vannes today

Today Vannes is an attractive and interesting town on a semi-circle of low hills, linked to the Gulf by a long canalised port which comes right into the town and is lined on both sides by neatly parked ocean-going yachts. At the end of the port is the Place Gambetta, backed by a graceful nineteenth-century crescent, with the St Vincent Gate, one of the four remaining gates of the town, in the centre. The Place is lively, with café terraces and restaurants. On the hill behind the Place Gambetta is the most convincing old quarter of any size of any town in Brittany, its narrow streets of half-timbered and encorbelled houses huddled round its cathedral. The ground floors of many of these old houses now form boutiques, antique shops and other luxury establishments. At night, brilliantly lit and contrasting with the dark alleys, they seem like a succession of Aladdin's caves. It makes strolling through the old quarter at night a completely different, though equally interesting, experience from seeing it in the daytime.

Vannes is one of those pleasant towns where the overall effect is more impressive than any single thing that contributes to it. It is also the most convenient base from which to explore the fascinating Gulf of Morbihan.

What to see
The ramparts

Vannes still has most of its thirteenth-century ramparts, renovated in the seventeenth century. From the Place Gambetta take the road on your left (as you face the port), and then keep left into the Rue Decker. This leads past beautifully maintained gardens in the formal French style, beneath the ramparts. Beside the little stream in the gardens are some unusual seventeenth-century wash-houses, where only a few years ago some of the townswomen still did their laundry. The largest of the towers in the ramparts, La Tour du Connetable, dates from the middle of the sixteenth century, and its roof was restored in the seventeenth.

The old quarter

A leaflet with comments in English on the most interesting buildings in the old streets and a suggested route through them can be picked up from the Tourist Office near the Place Gambetta and the port. It barely mentions the cathedral, **St Pierre**, a macédoine of stone which took 600 years to complete, with repeated alterations and renovations, and contains something of everything and nothing of any great distinction. In the narrow streets around the cathedral there are a considerable number of fifteenth- to seventeenth-century houses, most of them now well restored.

La Cohue

This is the most important of the sights in the old town, a remarkably ancient building opposite the forecourt of the cathedral. It served originally as a market; part of the building dates from the eleventh century, and even its great portals are thirteenth century, but most of it is fourteenth and sixteenth. It is a two-storey building, and the upper floor was used in the past by the Parliament of Brittany and by the Law Courts. It now houses the **Musée des Beaux Arts**, which contains a collection of paintings by Breton artists of the past 200 years and folk art in the form of polychrome wood sculptures. A second museum is devoted to the Gulf of Morbihan, its geological formation, history, way of life, oyster farms, fishing techniques and the special boats used there. The museums are open a.m./p.m., but closed Tuesday and Sunday outside the summer season.

Aquarium
Océanographique

On the quay near the exit of the yacht basin, this modern aquarium has more than 1,000 fish from different seas all over the world. Their natural environments have been recreated in more than fifty glass tanks: warm water and corals for tropical fish; rocks and ice-cold water for northern species; waterfalls and simulated streams for freshwater species – even a pool full of sharks.

**Excursions
from Vannes**
By water

The **Gulf of Morbihan** is approximately 25 km by 15 km and contains hundreds of islands. Its variety is inexhaustible: at different times of the day, at different states of the tide, in different weather and from different positions, it offers new aspects and vistas. In all but the most violent weather it provides safe conditions and endless variety for the small boat sailor, the only difficulty being the strong currents in the narrow passage to the open sea. Numerous boat trips around the Gulf are available from Vannes.

The **Île aux Moines** is the largest island in the Gulf, and has the highest population, about 550. It is a tranquil island where palm trees, mimosa, camelias, oranges and lemons flourish, and Breton poets have made the girls of the island famous for their beauty. The island has a picturesque village, two dolmens, and several viewpoints.

The **Île de Gavrinis** is some way by boat from Vannes, and can be reached more conveniently by car to Larmor-Baden, about 14 km, and then a short boat trip to the island. The island contains the most interesting of all the megalithic monuments of this region, a dolmen considered by experts to be the finest in the world. The tumulus containing the dolmen is 8 m high and about 100 m round, and a tunnel 14 m long, supported by twenty-nine slabs of granite, leads to a burial chamber roofed with a single slab 4 m by 3 m. Almost all the stones of the tunnel, the roof of the burial chamber, and part of its walls are decorated with mysterious engraved designs, among which snakes, fish bones, leaves of bracken, an axe and a human figure have been recognised, as well as circles and spirals.

By road

The chief points of interest on the large **Rhuys Peninsula** which encloses the Gulf of Morbihan in the south are the Château de Suscinio, St Gildas de Rhuys, and the tumulus of Tumiac. Take the N165 (Nantes road) from Vannes and turn left on to the D780 after a few km.

The **Château de Suscinio** is an unusual-looking château built in the thirteenth to fifteenth centuries in an exposed position so close to the sea that its moats used to be filled by the tides. It is partly ruined, but is in the process of being restored steadily, though very slowly. There is a staircase (131 steps) to the top of the North Tower, from which there is a good view over the Gulf and the peninsula. Open a.m./ p.m. from April to September, except Wednesday morning.

Abelard, a teacher and philosopher in twelfth-century Paris, fell desperately in love with Héloise, a respectable bourgeoise twenty-two years his junior. They had a child and married, but the scandal was too much for the uncle of Héloise, a canon, and he had her shut up in a convent. Abelard, whose reputation as a scholar extended all over France, became a monk. Duke Conan IV of Brittany appointed him abbot of the monastery of **St Gildas-de-Rhuys**, where the monks had become rowdy and undisciplined. The monks met Abelard's efforts to restore order with scorn and threatened to strangle him if he interfered. In his passionate love letters to Héloise, Abelard also described his miserable existence and the dangers to his life. In fact the monks did try to poison him, and Abelard was obliged to escape secretly.

The former abbey church has some twelfth-century parts in the choir and the transept, but was mostly rebuilt in the sixteenth and seventeenth centuries.

On the northern side of the peninsula, the little port of **Le Logeo** encapsulates all the charm of the Gulf and will remind those who have seen one of a typical Cornish creek.

On the way to the head of the peninsula at Arzon and Port Navalo, about five minutes' walk off the main road, 2.5 km before Arzon, is the **Tumulus of Tumiac**. The tumulus is about 20 m high and 200 m in circumference, and it was from the top of this mound that Julius Caesar is said to have watched the naval battle against the Venetes. The Romans were losing when the wind dropped, leaving the sailing ships of the Venetes helpless and enabling the Roman galleys, propelled by oars, to counter-attack and win. Today the view encompasses peaceful yachts and wide views over the Gulf and the ocean – but no galleys.

Where to stay

Hôtel Le Roof, Presqu'île de Conleau, 56000 Vannes, tel. 97 63 47 47. Forty-one bedrooms, medium rates upwards, characterised by modern comfort rather than country charm. Well sited overlooking the Gulf of Morbihan, about 5 km south of the town. Sound restaurant with menus at medium plus prices.

Hôtel La Marebaudière, 4 Rue Aristide Briand, tel. 97 47 34 29. Spacious hotel in a calm situation close to the town centre. Forty soundproof rooms at medium rates. No restaurant.

Hôtel Mascotte, Ave Jean Monnet, tel. 97 47 59 60. Modern hotel within walking distance of the old quarter. Good parking facilities. Sixty-five comfortable rooms with good bathrooms. Restaurant sound, prices medium.

Hôtel Image St Anne (LdF), 8 Place de la Libération, tel. 97 63

27 36. Well-run hotel conveniently situated not far from the town centre. Thirty bedrooms, twenty-six with bath etc, at medium rates, and a good restaurant with menus from low medium prices.

Where to eat

Le Richemont, Place de la Gare, Vannes, tel. 97 42 61 41. Superb cuisine in which chef Régis Mahé brings a touch of the warm south to Brittany. Menus from medium prices upwards, but all great value for money. Closed Sunday evening and Monday; also 18 February to 4 March, and November.

La Marée Bleue, 8 Place BirHakeim, immediately behind Hôtel La Marebaudière (see p. 264), tel. 97 47 24 29. Good restaurant with menus from low medium prices, house wine included.

La Capitainerie, Rue du Port, tel. 97 47 54 50. Good little restaurant conveniently placed adjacent to the car park beside the port. Specialises in fish and shellfish, at low medium prices.

Château de Josselin

As a change from beaches and watery scenes, it is a pleasant cross-country drive to this imposing sixteenth-century château, and the old town around it.

Leave Vannes by the N166, the main road to Ploermel and Rennes. Beyond Elven the N166 crosses the **Landes de Lanvaux**, a mixture of moorland and forests which was once one of the wildest stretches of country in Brittany. During the past 100 years it has been reduced by cultivated areas, but is still relatively unspoilt and thinly inhabited. It is good walking country, and the GR38 runs the length of it from Rochefort-en-Terre to Baud. About 30 km north of Elven, at Le Roc St André, turn left on to the D4 for Josselin, 16 km.

History

One of the most common photographs seen of Brittany is that of the Château of Josselin with its towers and façade reflected in the calm waters of the Oust. It is not only one of the finest castles in Brittany, it stands at the very heart of its history. There has been a castle on the site for a thousand years, but it was destroyed, rebuilt and renovated on several occasions. The river façade is fourteenth century, and was built by Olivier de Clisson (1336–1407), a professional soldier. De Clisson's early life was tragic and dominated by the War of Succession in which two cousins, Jean de Montfort and Charles de Blois, fought for the duchy for twenty-five years. De Clisson's father at first was on the side of de Blois, but changed sides, and was captured and executed by the French king, who supported de Blois. King Philip sent the decapitated head to Nantes, where it was displayed on a pike at the city gates. Olivier de Clisson, then eight years old, was taken by his mother to stand before his father's head and swear vengeance. She then sent him to safety in England, and at the head of an army of 400 men, she attacked in succession seven castles belonging to supporters of Charles de Blois and massacred the garrison in each of them.

With this background it is not surprising that de Clisson became a remarkable soldier. In 1364 he fought in the terrible battle of Auray on the side of the Montforts, supported by English troops under Sir John

Chandos, against the army of Charles de Blois, supported by French troops led by du Guesclin. Charles de Blois was killed, du Guesclin captured. De Clisson lost an eye in the fight. The de Montforts had won, and one of the least-known and bloodiest wars of France was over. De Clisson had no quarrel with the new king of France, Charles V, and fought in his army and rose to become Constable of France. He bought the Château of Josselin in 1370. He had married Marguerite de Rohan, and when he died in 1407 Josselin passed into the hands of the Rohans, who still own it today. The present duke is an unpretentious man who takes seriously his job as mayor of the community.

The interior façade, facing the park, is a splendid piece of late Gothic work of the early sixteenth century, decorated with some of the finest carving in granite to be found in Brittany. The Rohans abandoned this castle in the eighteenth century and after the Revolution it became dilapidated, but it was completely renovated in the latter part of the nineteenth century. Some of the ground-floor rooms are open to the public and include portraits and souvenirs of the Rohan family, and among the furniture is the table on which the Edict of Nantes was signed in 1598. The château is open for accompanied visits a.m./p.m. in July/August, and p.m. only outside these months from Easter to September. Closed 8 and 9 September.

Musée de Poupées   There are more than 500 dolls in this collection put together by the Rohan family over a long period. Now housed in a museum created from the former stables of the castle, the collection contains dolls from the seventeenth to the twentieth century, from all over France and several other countries, and in authentic costumes of great diversity. Open a.m./p.m. every day June to September, and p.m. Wednesday, Saturday and Sunday October to mid-November, and March to May.

Notre Dame du Roncier (Our Lady of the Bramble Hedge)   The first chapel on this site was built about AD 800, when a peasant clearing some brambles from his land found a wooden statue of the Virgin beneath them. The statue was burned during the Revolution, but the church remains a place of pilgrimage and an important *pardon* is held annually on 8 September. The present building was started in the twelfth century and has been several times altered and restored; most of it today is in the Flamboyant Gothic style. In the interior, in a chapel on the right-hand side, is the fifteenth-century marble mausoleum of Olivier de Clisson and his wife.

Josselin is only about 30 km from the Paimpont Forest (Brocéliande) and its Arthurian associations.

La Baule and its Region

En route to La Baule

On this anti-clockwise tour of Brittany the last important region for the holiday visitor is that around the big resort of La Baule, which lies about 60 km south-east of Vannes. The quickest route is by the N165 to La Roche Bernard and then the D774 south to Guérande and La Baule. But the first part of this drive is main road motoring of little interest, and if you are not in a hurry a good alternative is to drive from Vannes to Questembert and then Rochefort-en-Terre, before turning south on to the D774 for the 24 km to La Roche Bernard.

Rochefort-en-Terre   Though it has no major sights, this village, in a picturesque situation on a promontory between deep valleys, is an attractive place with a nucleus of fifteenth- to seventeenth-century houses in the centre, around the Places des Halles, the Grande Rue, and the Place des Puits.

The château   The castle was built in the thirteenth and fourteenth centuries to replace a more primitive fort, and has been rebuilt three times. It was bought early this century by an American, Alfred Partidge Trafford Klots, who restored it by using authentic seventeenth-century bits from other properties in the area. Every year from 1911 he gave the villagers geranium plants and organised a competition with an award for the house best decorated with flowers. So Rochefort-en-Terre was, in fact, the first *village fleuri* in France, and has continued to attract tourists ever since.

The castle was bought in 1978 by the department of Morbihan, who have installed a regional museum, which includes *coiffes*, traditional tools and household objects. The château is open for guided visits a.m./p.m. June to September, and Saturday, Sunday and public holidays at other times of the year.

Where to eat   **Le Lion d'Or**, rue du Pelican, Rochefort-en-Terre, tel. 97 43 32 80. Well-furnished old Breton house offering good, classic cuisine at medium prices. Closed Monday out of season.

La Roche Bernard   On the banks of the Vilaine, which is almost but not quite the departmental boundary, La Roche Bernard is the last village in Morbihan. It is not a place of any great interest, but has a suspension

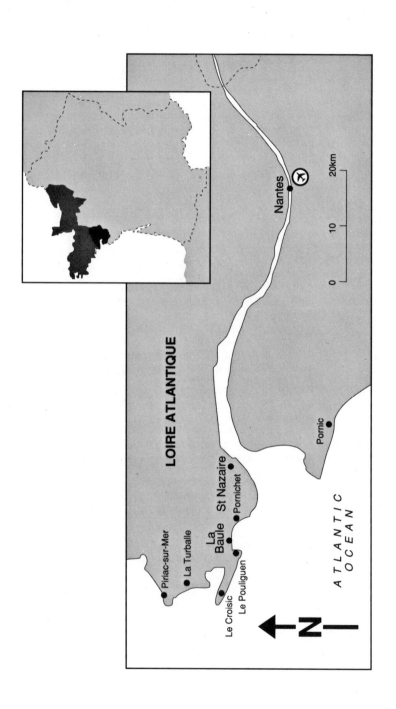

bridge with a road surface 50 m above the water. By a hairpin bend as you take the road out of La Roche Bernard for La Baule, there is a belvedere reached by a flight of steps which gives a good view of the Vilaine in both directions. On the other side of the road from this viewpoint, there is an old quarter of narrow alleys linked by stone staircases, with some sixteenth- and seventeenth-century houses. But the real interest in La Roche Bernard is for those feeling hungry.

Where to eat and stay

Auberge Bretonne, 2 Place du Guesclin, La Roche Bernard, tel. 99 90 60 28. In a renovated seventeenth-century house at the top of the village is one of the finest restaurants in Brittany: delicious food beautifully prepared, and backed up by the sort of wine list that true wine lovers could spend the afternoon reading. Medium plus prices up, but still remarkable value for money. The inn also has eleven comfortable bedrooms from medium rates up. Half-board is obligatory. Closed Thursday, and Friday lunch, and mid-November to mid-December.

Auberge des Deux Magots (LdF), 1–3 Place du Bouffay. Fifteen tastefully furnished bedrooms, at medium rates. Restaurant with cooking in the best Breton tradition, medium prices. Closed Sunday evening and Monday out of season, and mid-December to mid-January.

Towards La Baule

The direct route to La Baule from La Roche Bernard is by the D774, but a more interesting route is to follow the main road only as far as Herbignac and there to turn off down the left fork, the D47, to St Lyphard.

This south-eastern corner of Brittany is a region with a split personality. Its coastline, with its bays, beaches and fishing ports, resembles that of much of Brittany, but inland there is a curious region unlike any other in the province. This area, known as the **Grande Brière**, is a vast, almost roadless peat marsh covering thousands of hectares. For hundreds of years it has been the common property of the inhabitants of the fourteen parishes around its edge, an arrangement unique in Europe. They share the cutting of the peat, the reeds for thatch, the osiers for basket-making, the fishing for eels, pike and other fish, and the hunting and wild fowling. Traditionally, the women of the region make the orange-flower wreaths worn with bridal dresses. Once made from cloth dipped in wax, they are now plastic, and are exported all over Europe. La Grande Brière is at the heart of the **Parc Régional de Brière**, which includes an ornithological reserve.

What to see

The village church at **St Lyphard** has a belvedere in the steeple (135 steps) which gives panoramic views over the whole marsh, with its lakes, interconnecting canals and villages, as well as to the estuary of the Loire to the south, of the Vilaine to the north-west, and the walled town of Guérande and its salt-pans.

Another reason for choosing this route instead of the direct one is the unique hamlet of **Kerhinet**, with its thatched cottages which the Parc

Régional has restored as a monument of Breton rustic architecture. Cars have to be left outside the village, which is explored on foot. A 'museum' shows a house and the lifestyle as it was in past: beaten earth floors, simple furniture, one room for cows, another for pigs, an annexe with the tools for peat-cutting and basket-making, and so on. The village is a conservation area.

Where to stay　　**Auberge de Kerhinet**, Kerhinet, 44410 St Lyphard, tel. 40 61 91 46. A long, low, stone-built thatched cottage, altogether delightful. Seven bedrooms, all with bath etc, at low medium rates. The restaurant, while it is one of THE places to eat frogs' legs or eels fresh from the marsh, has a wide variety of other dishes, at low medium prices.

La Baule

This important and stylish resort consists of three communes, Le Pouliguen in the west, La Baule in the centre, and Pornichet in the east, which together form one agglomeration around a gently curving bay 10 km across, protected by headlands on either side.

In the mid-nineteenth century a forest of pines was planted on the dunes to fix them in position. In 1879 the railway, running only 2 km behind the coast, was extended from St Nazaire to Le Croisic on the Guérande peninsula. Property developers were not slow to see the possibilities. The first streets of La Baule were laid out, the first villas built, and it soon became fashionable. By the 1920s La Baule was an international resort for what in those days was called 'society', now the 'jet set'. It has been further developed since the Second World War.

Today, La Baule is a modern seaside resort par excellence. It claims to have the finest beach in Europe, and there is not much doubt that it is certainly the best of the developed beaches: 8 km of broad, uninterrupted, clean golden sands. It has every conceivable amenity of a modern resort: palace hotels, casinos, café terraces, night clubs, discos, dozens of restaurants, beautiful parks and gardens, futuristic apartment blocks, racecourse, golf course, eighty tennis courts and all other sporting amenities, and a magnificent four-lane boulevard-cum-promenade behind the whole length of the beach, the western end reserved for pedestrians.

La Baule has been said to be the Deauville of Brittany, and on the whole it is a fair comparison. Like Deauville, La Baule is smart, and it is 'horsey'. It not only has a racecourse and three riding establishments, but is also a centre of international show-jumping events. Like Deauville, La Baule is an artificially created seaside resort with no history and no industry. It is, perhaps, rather more a family resort than Deauville and, like all such one-purpose summer places, the whole caboodle drops dead at the end of every summer, when the children return to school.

It gives a few autumnal twitches here and there, but two-thirds of the hotels and many of the restaurants are closed throughout the winter.

Pornichet Now a continuation of La Baule, at the eastern end of the great sweep of beach, Pornichet was already becoming a fashionable little resort popular with the literary world of Paris in the 1860s, before La Baule was built. It has a tiny fishing port, and a yacht marina built out from the beach.

Le Pouliguen This is a much older place than either Pornichet or La Baule, having been a fishing port since the sixteenth century. It still has many of its narrow, winding streets and old houses. It is separated from La Baule only by a narrow, tidal canal which allows sea-water to flood into the salt-pans behind the town. There is a yacht basin at the mouth of the canal, and a sheltered, sandy beach.

Where to stay La Baule is in general an expensive place, and the best of its hotels are among the most expensive in France outside Paris. Apart from the grand hotels there are about forty others to choose from, rated three stars or less. Listed here is one in each class.

Castel Marie-Louise, 1 Ave Andrieu, 44500 La Baule, tel. 40 60 20 60. Near the beach but in its own peaceful grounds. A Relais et Châteaux hotel. Twenty-nine spacious bedrooms. Restaurant provides buffet lunches in summer, superb cuisine at dinner. Rooms and meals very expensive.

Hôtel Christina, 26 Blvd Hennecart, tel. 40 60 22 44. Modern holiday hotel close to the beach. Thirty-six pleasant, functional rooms, all with bath etc, at medium plus rates. Good restaurant, but half-board is obligatory in season. Hotel open all year, restaurant closed October to Easter.

Hôtel La Palmeraie, 7 Allée des Cormorans, tel. 40 60 24 41. Modest hotel in a calm situation among the pines, but close to the beach. Garden and terrace, and twenty-three rooms with bath etc, at medium rates. Medium prices in restaurant. Closed October to Easter.

Hôtel Beau Rivage (LdF), 11 Rue Jules Bénoist, 44510 Le Pouliguen, tel. 40 42 31 61. Beside the beach of Le Pouliguen. Fifty-four rooms, all with bath, etc, at medium rates. Restaurant prices medium upwards. Closed October to Easter.

Hôtel Les Océanides (LdF), 4 Blvd des Océanides, 44380 Pornichet, tel. 40 61 33 25. Fourteen simple but comfortable rooms at low medium rates, some with bath, and a reliable restaurant, moderately priced. Open all year.

Where to eat **La Marcanderie**, 5 Ave d'Agen, La Baule, tel. 40 24 03 12. Mouth-watering meals in this charming and pleasant restaurant, where cuisine and wines are first class. Menus at medium prices up, but good value for money. Closed Sunday evening, and Monday out of season.

Henri, 161 Ave de Lattre de Tassigny, tel. 40 60 23 65. Not just a holiday restaurant; this one is open all year and is a favourite with local

businessmen. Sound, classical cuisine and comfortable, modern surroundings. Prices not much above average.

Le Rallye, 22 Rue du Croisic, Le Pouliguen, tel. 40 42 30 71.
Simple, unpretentious restaurant where you eat well at prices becoming harder to find in holiday areas. Good welcome and service, and
good value for money. Closed Monday.

Excursions from La Baule

The marshy land and mudflats immediately to the north and north-
west of La Baule have been converted over the centuries into a
chequerboard of salt-pans. There are few things less stimulating to the
imagination than oyster farms at low tide, but first on what must be a
fairly short list come salt-pans. However, south of the salt pans and
immediately west of Le Pouliguen is the narrow granite peninsula of
Le Croisic, with the ocean to the south and the enclosed bay called the
Grand Traict to the north.

Le Croisic

La Baule is a world of its own, but in the old fishing port of Le
Croisic, only 10 km to the west, you are back in a recognisable Brittany.
The town (population 4,400) lies mostly on the sheltered north side of
the peninsula. It still has some fishing boats but, like many Breton
villages which had their origins in the sea and fishing, Le Croisic now
caters mostly for tourists and yachtsmen.

It is a pleasant and interesting little place, its quays lined with
seventeenth-century houses, and there are more old houses, both
granite and half-timbered in the narrow streets around the church,
Notre Dame de Pitié. A picturésque road runs along the southern coast
which, from the Pointe de Croisic back to Le Pouliguen, is known as
the Côte Sauvage. But there are sandy beaches in coves between the
rough granite rocks. The beach for Le Croisic is at **Port Lin** on the
south side of the peninsula, about 800 m from the town centre, and
there are holiday hotels by the beach.

Batz-sur-Mer

Sandwiched between the salt pans and the sea, about half-way
between Le Croisic and Le Pouliguen, Batz-sur-Mer has several sandy
beaches within reach. It has an interesting old church, **St Guénolé**,
rebuilt in the fifteenth and sixteenth centuries and with a 60 m steeple
added in the late seventeenth. Those strong on their legs may like to
climb the 182 steps up the tower to get panoramic views across to the
Rhuys peninsula, the estuary of the Loire, Belle-Île and the island of
Noirmoutier, not forgetting the salt pans immediately below and the
bay of La Baule.

Where to stay

Grand Hôtel l'Ocean and **Hôtel Les Vikings**, Port Lin, 44490
Le Croisic, tel. 40 62 90 03. By the Port Lin beach, with fine views.
Thirty-eight rooms all with bath etc, at medium rates up. Particularly
good restaurant, à la carte only, rather expensive. Both open all year.

Where to eat

Le Bretagne, 11 Quai Petite Chambre, Le Croisic, tel. 40 23 00 51.
Cheerful and pleasant restaurant with excellent cuisine at medium
prices upwards. Good value for money. Closed Sunday evening and
Monday.

Guérande

There could hardly be a stronger contrast than that between swish, modern La Baule and this completely walled old town which still has a medieval air, only 6 km to the north. The ramparts, built in the fifteenth century, have six towers and surround the town without a break, apart from the four ancient gateways. Part of the moat below the walls was filled in in the eighteenth century, but there is still water in the northern and western sections. A few hundred years ago Guérande was a prosperous sea port but its access to the sea gradually silted up, and it became a sleepy inland town. In the mid-nineteenth century, Honoré de Balzac described it as a 'magnificent jewel of feudal times, with no other reason for its existence than that it has never been demolished'. Guérande snoozed on for another 100 years until, in the past decade, tourism has brought some stirrings of life.

What to see

The present **St Aubin's church** was built in the twelfth and thirteenth centuries, reconstructed and altered in the fourteenth and fifteenth, and heavily restored in the nineteenth. The west front has a good example of a fifteenth-century exterior pulpit, reached by a door opening from the interior and with a canopy. The most interesting points of the interior are the historiated capitals to the Romanesque columns in the nave, and a superb eighteenth-century stained-glass window showing the Assumption of the Virgin. The church is open for accompanied visits July/August. Organ concerts are given on Friday evening at 9.30 p.m. (admission 45 fr).

The fortified structure of **Porte St Michel** is the most impressive of the four gateways and was used as a residence by the governors in the fifteenth century. Today it houses a folk museum showing aspects of life in the town in the past: typical furniture, pottery and everyday household objects and tools of the region, and a collection of costumes. Open Easter to September.

From Guérande the D99 leads nort-west to the fishing port of **La Turballe**. Unlike other Breton ports, La Turballe was created in the early nineteenth century by building long stone jetties out from the beach, and became the most important sardine fishing port in Brittany. It is now divided in two, with a yacht marina to the south and the fishing port to the north. Between them is a stone pier with the building for the *criée*, the fish auction. South of La Turballe, stretching towards Le Croisic, are 8 km of sandy beaches, parts of which are popular with nudists.

From La Turballe the road continues, with some good coastal viewpoints, to a fishing port of a completely different kind. **Piriac-sur-Mer** is a very old settlement, believed to have been a headquarters of early Breton kings in the sixth century. It was one of the first deep-sea cod-fishing ports, and this activity kept it prosperous until the seventeenth century. It still has its narrow, winding streets around the church, and in the church square facing the port itself there are some fine seventeenth- and eighteenth-century houses.

There are several beaches, with both sand and rocks. Altogether Piriac is a picturesque and attractive place, and it is a sufficient advertisement for its charm that tourists have been visiting it for well over 100 years. Among its 'regulars' in the nineteenth century were Gustave Flaubert, Alphonse Daudet and Émile Zola, as well as many painters.

Where to stay

Hôtel Les Remparts, 15 Blvd du Nord, 44350 Guérande, tel. 40 24 90 69. Small modern hotel, eight rooms all with bath etc, at low medium rates. Restaurant reasonably priced, half-board obligatory in season.

Hôtel La Poste, 26 Rue de la Plage, 44420 Piriac-sur-Mer, tel. 40 23 50 90. Close to the beach. Fifteen simple bedrooms (thirteen with bath etc), at low to medium rates. Sound restaurant at medium prices. Closed November to Easter.

On the Loire

St Nazaire

I once knew a man whose idea of a good holiday was touring underground railway systems, and there may be someone somewhere for whom looking at submarine bases is the perfect relaxation. It would be a reason for visiting St Nazaire, where the ex-submarine *Espadon*, built in 1957 and the first French submarine to navigate beneath the ice of the Antarctic, is open to the public, but the visit must be reserved in advance (tel. 40 66 82 16). The port was used by the Germans as a submarine base during the Second World War and was destroyed by Allied bombing. It was rebuilt in a grim and monotonous style, and is an uninspired place today, although one in three of the population is less than twenty years old.

Dr Samuel Johnson said that the best view in Scotland was that of the high road to England. For the tourist, the best view from St Nazaire is without doubt that of the magnificent bridge, more than 3 km long and 130 m above the water, which links the two banks of the estuary of the Loire, between St Nazaire and Mindin on the south side. This wonderful piece of engineering is a boon to all tourists travelling from the western Channel ports to south-west France. The main road to it actually by-passes the city altogether, so there is no delay.

It is still, of course, possible to cross the river at Nantes, which may seem a more direct route on the map. In practice it is not and my advice is, don't try it. Even well out of season it can be a frustrating waste of time, and in the heat and height of summer it is only for those who actually enjoy driving their cars at less than walking pace for an hour or two.

Nantes

Nantes was a city of major importance in the history of Brittany. Today it is a city of major commercial importance in the region of the

What to see

Pays de la Loire. It is not a city of any importance for the tourist *en route* for somewhere else whose time is limited, and it is best avoided. Nantes was the capital of the duchy of Brittany during several periods of the Middle Ages. The **Château des Ducs** was built at the end of the fifteenth century by Duke François II and finished by his daughter 'the good Duchess Anne', twice queen of France. The château, a combination of fortress, with massively thick walls surrounded by a wide moat, and palace, with the ducal living quarters in the inner court, impressed King Henri IV when he visited it at the end of the sixteenth century and signed the Edict of Nantes there.

Today the château contains three museums. The **Musée des Arts Decoratifs** has a surprisingly modern collection (of the past twenty years) of the work of textile and tapestry artists from several countries. The **Musée d'Art Populaire Régionale** has fine collections of *coiffes* (lace headdresses) and Breton costumes, as well as furniture, pottery and other local crafts. The **Musée des Salorges**, also called the Musée Marin, has exhibits concerning all aspects of the maritime life of Nantes from the seventeenth century onwards, including whaling and the trade in slaves and sugar on which the prosperity of Nantes was built in the nineteenth century. The château is open to the public a.m./p.m., closed on Tuesday and public holidays.

Where to stay

There are well over 100 hotels in the Nantes agglomeration and few of those in the centre have a restaurant.

L'Hôtel, 6 Place de la Duchesse Anne, 44000 Nantes, tel. 40 29 30 31. Well-run, pleasant hotel. Thirty-one attractive bedrooms, some overlooking the Château des Ducs, some the gardens. No restaurant. Room rates medium.

Hôtel Amiral, 26 Rue Scribe, tel. 40 69 20 21. Nice new hotel in a pedestrianised street in the town centre, behind the theatre, Place Graslin, but about 1 km from the Château des Ducs. Forty-nine comfortable, well-decorated rooms, with double glazing, at low medium rates. No restaurant, good breakfasts.

Where to eat

Several of the better restaurants in Nantes are closed in July and/or August, itself a comment on the tourist attractions of the city. Most of those which are not are expensive for what they offer.

La Cigale, 4 Place Graslin, tel. 40 69 76 41. Brasserie restaurant in the *Belle Époque* style. Medium prices à la carte. Cheap for children. Open all year.

L'Antarctic, 21 Rue Scribe, tel. 40 73 81 01. Good newish restaurant behind the theatre and near the Hotel Amiral. Open to midnight.

Le Pont Levis, 1 Rue du Château, tel. 40 35 10 20. Kept by a former butcher and good on meat dishes. Moderate prices, and value for money.

South of the Loire Estuary

South of the Loire, there is another strip of coast which has been developed as a holiday area. The best part, from the Pointe de St Gildas south-east to Pornic, has recently been given the name the **Jade Coast**. It is the most southerly of all the areas mentioned in this book, something like 320 km south of Cherbourg, and has a good sunshine record.

Pornic

This is the nicest of the small resorts on the Jade Coast. It is one of the many places in Brittany which was a market town and fishing port long before it went in for tourism. It has several beaches, the best of which is Noevillard, next to a deep-water yacht marina with berths for 800 boats. There are views from the beaches across to the large island of Noirmoutier.

The old fishing port is still used as such, though on a much smaller scale than in the past, and it is also used by yachts. In summer there are twice-daily services from the jetty to Noirmoutier (one hour), and at some states of the tide the boat leaves from Noevillard. The château at the entrance to the port was built in the fourteenth century and restored in the nineteenth. It belonged originally to Gilles de Rais (or Retz – the surrounding countryside is still called the Pays de Retz) who had a distinguished career as a soldier fighting for Joan of Arc, but after her death went in for unsavoury practices such as black magic, infanticide and wife murder. He was burned at the stake in Nantes, and is remembered as the original Bluebeard. The château is not open to the public.

St Marie is a 'bourgeois' suburb of Pornic with big, old-fashioned villas in shady gardens and small, cove-like beaches.

Where to stay

Alliance Hotel, Plage de la Source, Pornic, tel. 40 82 21 21. This very well-equipped hotel beside the beach was for a time recently a Holiday Inn, and includes a swimming pool, tennis and facilities for the disabled. Ninety bedrooms, with bath etc, at medium plus rates. Restaurant also in the medium plus price range.

Hôtel Les Sablons (LdF), 13 Rue des Sablons, St Marie-sur-Mer, 44210 Pornic. Simple but comfortable hotel, all thirty bedrooms with bath etc, room rates medium. Good restaurant, from medium prices. Tennis. Restaurant closed Sunday evening and Monday out of season.

Where to eat

Beau Rivage, Plage de la Birochère, Pornic, tel. 40 82 03 08. Pleasant restaurant in which the cuisine reaches consistently high standards. Good-value menus from medium prices. Closed Monday evening and Tuesday out of season, and January.

Rulers and Governments of France

The Capet Dynasty

HUGUES CAPET, believed to have been born about 938, was elected king of the French in 987. The election was not unanimous. The rulers of Flanders, Aquitaine and Toulouse voted against him. The dynasty he founded lasted more than 300 years. He married Adelaide of Aquitaine (1), and Constance de Provence (2). Died 996.

ROBERT II (The Pious). It is not known when he was born, but he was the son of Hugues Capet and succeeded him in 996. He married Rozala of Flanders. Died in 1031

HENRI I, probably born about 1008, came to the throne in 1031, married Anne of Kiev. He was the son of Robert II and died in 1060.

PHILIPPE I, born 1052, came to the throne in 1060, married Bertha of Holland. He died in 1108. Relationship to predecessor, son.

LOUIS VI (The Fat) born 1081 and came to the throne in 1108. Married Lucienne de Rochefort (1), Adelaide de Savoie (2). Died 1137. Relationship to predecessor, son.

LOUIS VII (The Young), born 1119. Came to the throne 1137. He married Eleanor of Aquitaine (1), Adele de Champagne (2). Died in 1180. Relationship to predecessor, son.

PHILIPPE II (Philippe-Auguste) born 1165. Came to the throne 1180. Married Ingeborg of Denmark, and then Agnes de Meranie. Died in 1223. Relationship to predecessor, son.

LOUIS VIII (The Lion), born 1187, came to the throne 1223, married Blanche de Castile. Died in 1226. Relationship to predecessor, son.

LOUIS IX (St Louis), born 1215, came to the throne 1226, married Marguerite de Provence. Blanche de Castile was Regent during his minority. He died in 1270. Relationship to predecessor, son.

PHILIPPE III (The Bold), born 1245, came to the throne in 1270. He married Isabela de Aragon. Died 1285. Relationship to predecessor, son.

PHILIPPE IV (The Handsome) born 1268, came to the throne 1285, married Jeanne de Navarre. He died in 1314. Relationship to predecessor, son.

LOUIS X (The Battler), born 1289, came to the throne in 1314, married Marguerite de Bourgogne. Died 1316. Relationship to predecessor, son.

JEAN I born in 1316, came to the throne in 1316, and died in 1316.

PHILIPPE V (The Tall) born in 1291, came to the throne in 1316, married Jeanne de Bourgogne. Died in 1322. He was the uncle of Jean I.

CHARLES IV (The Handsome) born 1294, came to the throne in 1322. Married Blanche de Bourgogne (1), and Marie de Luxembourg (2). Died in 1328. Relationship to predecessor, brother.

The Valois Dynasty

PHILIPPE VI (Philippe de Valois) born 1293, came to the throne in 1328. Married Jeanne de Bourgogne (The Lame). Died in 1350. He was the nephew of Philippe IV, and so was only distantly related to Charles IV, his predecessor.

JEAN II (The Courageous) born 1319, came to the throne in 1350. Married Bonne de Luxembourg. Died 1364. Son of Philippe VI.

CHARLES V (The Wise) born 1337, came to the throne in 1364. Married Jeanne de Bourbon. Died 1380. Relationship to predecessor, son.

CHARLES VI (The Mad), born 1368, came to the throne in 1380. Married Isabeau of Bavaria. Died 1422. Relationship to predecessor, son.

CHARLES VII born 1403, came to the throne 1422. Married Marie d'Anjou. Died 1461. Relationship to predecessor, son.

LOUIS XI born 1423, came to the throne in 1461. Married Charlotte de Savoie. Died 1483. Relationship to predecessor, son.

CHARLES VIII born 1470, came to the throne 1483. Married Anne of Brittany. Died 1498. Relationship to predecessor, son.

The Valois-Orléans Dynasty

LOUIS XII (The Father of the People) born 1462, came to the throne 1498. Married Jeanne de France (1), Anne of Brittany (2) and Mary of England (3). Died in 1515. He was descended from the first son of Louis d'Orléans, the brother of Charles VI, so was only distantly related to his precedessor.

The Orléans-Angoulême Dynasty

FRANÇOIS I born 1494, came to the throne 1515. Married Claude de France. Died in 1547. His relationship to his predecessor was remote, as he was descended from the third son of Charles d'Orléans, another brother of Charles VI.

HENRI II born 1519, came to the throne 1547. Married Catherine de Médici. Died 1559. Relationship to predecessor, son.

FRANÇOIS II born 1544, came to throne 1559, married Mary Queen of Scots. Died 1560. Relationship to predecessor, son. Catherine de Médici ruled as Regent.

CHARLES IX born 1550, came to the throne 1560. Married Elizabeth of Austria. Died in 1574. Relationship to his predecessor, brother. During his minority Catherine de Médici was Regent.

HENRI III born 1551, came to the throne in 1574. Married Louise de Vaudemont. Assassinated 1589. Relationship to predecessor, brother.

The Bourbon Dynasty

HENRI IV (Henri III of Navarre) born 1553, came to throne 1589. Married Marguerite de Valois (1), and Marie de Médici (2). Assassinated in 1610. He was only remotely related to his predecessor, being descended from the sixth son of Louis IX.

LOUIS XIII born 1601, came to the throne in 1619. Married Anne of Austria. Died 1643. Relationship to predecessor, son.

LOUIS XIV (The Sun King) born 1638, came to the throne in 1643. Married the Infanta Marie-Thérèse. Died in 1715. Relationship to predecessor, son. During his minority France was, in effect, ruled by Cardinal Mazarin. When he died in 1660, Louis began his fifty-five years of personal rule.

LOUIS XV born 1710, came to the throne 1715. Married Marie Leczinska. Died 1774. Relationship to predecessor, great-grandson.

LOUIS XVI born 1754, came to the throne 1774. Married Marie-Antoinette of Austria. Died 1793, on the guillotine.

The First Republic

Set up in 1792 by the leaders of the French Revolution.

The First Empire

Napoleon Bonaparte became Emperor of the French in 1804. He had been born in Corsica in 1769. After his defeat by Wellington at Waterloo, he was exiled to St Helena where he died of cancer in 1821.

Restoration of the Monarchy – the Bourbon Dynasty

LOUIS XVIII born 1755, came to the throne 1815. Married Marie-Josephine de Savoie. Died 1824. He was the brother of Louis XVI.

CHARLES X born 1757, came to the throne 1824. Married Marie-Thérèse de Savoie. Deposed after the July Revolution 1830, when he fled to England. Died 1836. Relationship to predecessor, brother.

The Bourbon-Orléans Dynasty

LOUIS-PHILIPPE, born 1773. Came to the throne 1830. Proclaimed king in 1830. Married Maria Amelia of the Two Sicilies. Died 1850. His relationship to his predecessor was remote. He was descended from Philippe d'Orléans, brother of Louis XIV.

The Second Republic

1848–52. Elected President, Prince Louis Napoleon.

The Second Empire

NAPOLEON III (Louis Napoleon) born 1808, became Emperor in 1852. Married Eugenia de Montijo. Died 1873.

The Third Republic

September 1870 to July 1940.

The Fourth Republic

November 1945 to May 1958.

The Fifth Republic

September 1958–

Useful Reading

Brittany

Bretagne et Bretons, Jeanne Laurent (Arthaud, Paris).
La Bretagne, J. Markale (Sun, Paris: collection *Voir en France*).
Brittany, Henry Myhill.
The Horse of Pride, P.-J. Helias (Yale University Press).
La Légende de la Mort, Anatole Le Braz (Jean Lafitte, 1982).
France in the 1980s, John Ardagh (Pelican). Interesting section on Brittany.
Memoirs d'outre-tombe, Chateaubriand (*Livre de Poche* series).
Iceland Fisherman, Pierre Loti.

Normandy

Return to Normandy, Vivien Rowe.
The Norman Achievement 1050–1100, David C. Douglas (Eyre & Spottiswoode).
Overlord, Max Hastings (Michael Joseph). The Normandy landings.
The Cathedrals of Normandy, J. Perkins.
The Normans in European History, C. J. Haskins.
Normandie, B. Hucher (Sun, Paris: collection *Voir en France*).

Index